R,Λ L

||| || | ||||||||||| ||| | |||| |||
D1284265

THE FEDERAL REPUBLIC OF

**Sponsored by the Conference Group on
German Politics**

THE FEDERAL REPUBLIC OF GERMANY AT FORTY

EDITED BY
PETER H. MERKL

NEW YORK UNIVERSITY PRESS
New York and London

Library of Congress Cataloging-in-Publication Data
The Federal Republic of Germany at forty/edited by Peter H. Merkl.
P. cm.
Bibliography: p.
Includes index.
ISBN 0–8147–5445–7 (alk. paper)—ISBN 0–8147–5446–5
(pbk.: alk. paper)
1. Germany (West)—Politics and government. I. Merkl, Peter H.
DD258.75.F43 1989
943—dc20

New York University Press books are printed on acid-free paper,
and their binding materials are chosen for strength and durability.

Book design by Ken Venezio

p 10 9 8 7 6 5 4 3 2 1
c 10 9 8 7 6 5 4 3 2 1

CONTENTS

CONTRIBUTORS

GERARD BRAUNTHAL teaches at the University of Massachusetts at Amherst and is the author of articles and books on West German domestic politics, such as *Socialist Labor and Politics in Weimar Germany: The General Federation of German Trade Unions* (1978) and *West German Social Democrats, 1969–1982: Profile of a Party in Power* (1983).

WILLIAM M. CHANDLER teaches at McMaster University, Ontario, and is the author of several books on Canadian politics and parties public policy, and federalism, and on German politics, most recently of *Federalism and the Role of the State* (with F. Bakvis).

RUSSELL J. DALTON, Florida State University, focuses his research on political change in the Federal Republic and other European democracies; his recent books include *Politics in West Germany* (1989), *Citizen Politics in Western Democracies* (1988), and *Germany Transformed* (1981).

WERNER J. FELD, University of Colorado at Colorado Springs, has published a number of books and articles. His most recent books are *Arms Control and the Atlantic Community* and *International Organizations* (2d ed.).

LILY GARDNER FELDMAN, Tufts University is Peace Fellow at the United States Institute of Peace. She is author of *West Germany and Israel: A Special Relationship.*

ARTHUR B. GUNLICKS, University of Richmond, Virginia, is the author of *Local Government in the German Federal System* (1986) and the contributing editor of *Local Government Reform and Reorganization: An International Perspective* (1981). He is also the author of numerous articles on West German local government, federalism, and political parties.

M. DONALD HANCOCK, Vanderbilt University, is the author of various books and articles on Sweden, Germany, and comparative public policy, including *West Germany: The Politics of Democratic Corporatism* (1989).

ARNOLD J. HEIDENHEIMER, Washington University, wrote books on comparative public policy, party finance, corruption and other subjects, including *The Governments of Germany* (4th ed. with Donald Kommers). His first book on the FRG was *Adenauer and the CDU* (1960).

JUTTA A. HELM, Western Illinois University, has written on protest, participation, and workplace democracy in West Germany. She currently is working on a study of the British and West German coal industries.

MICHAEL G. HUELSHOFF, University of Oregon, has worked on energy policy and is the author of "International Dimensions of Adjustment Strategies: Linking Corporatism to International Regime Theory," and "The Political Economy of the SPD" in the 1980s.

EMIL J. KIRCHNER teaches at the University of Essex and is the author of books and articles on the European Community and European liberal parties; including *Liberal Parties in Western Europe* (1989).

GERALD R. KLEINFELD, Arizona State University, has been founder of the German Studies Association, Editor of *German Studies Review*, and Director of Consortium for Atlantic Studies, author of articles on the German question and German-American relations.

DONALD P. KOMMERS teaches at Notre Dame University and is the author of books and articles on the West German Federal Constitutional Court and on German politics; including *Judicial Politics in West Germany* and, with A. J. Heidenheimer, *The Governments of Germany.*

ANDREI S. MARKOVITS, Boston University and Center for European Studies, Harvard University, has published extensively on social democracy and labor politics in the Federal Republic. His *Politics of the West German Trade Unions: Strategies of Class and Interest Representation in Growth and Crisis* (1986) was also published in Spanish. He is currently concluding a study (with Philip Gorski) entitled *The West German Left: Red, Green and Beyond.*

PETER H. MERKL teaches at the University of California, Santa Barbara, and is the author of books and articles on German politics, comparative parties, and most recently *Political Violence and Terror: Motifs and Motivations* (1986), and *When Parties Fail . . .* (with Kay Lawson) (1988).

RICHARD L. MERRITT, University of Illinois at Urbana-Champaign, focuses his research on international political communication, especially using quantitative approaches. His recent books on Germany include *Living with the Wall* (1985) and *Berlin Between Two Worlds* (1986).

JOYCE M. MUSHABEN teaches at the University of Missouri-St. Louis. Her recent publications have focused on youth and peace movements in both Germanies, Green politics, and "German identity," including a book in progress, *The Post-Postwar Generations: Changing Attitudes Towards the National Question and Changing Perceptions of the Atlantic Alliance in the FRG.*

WILLIAM E. PATERSON is Reader in German Politics at Warwick University and cofounder and former Chairman of the British Association for the Study of German Politics. He is the author of *The SPD and European Integration* (1974), coeditor with Alastair H. Thomas of *The Future of Social Democracy* (1986), with S. Bulmer of *The Federal Republic of Germany and the European Community* (1987), and with W. Grant and C. Whitston, *Government and the Chemical Industry: A Comparative Study of Britain and West Germany* (1988).

ANN L. PHILLIPS, Ford Foundation Fellow at the American Institute for Contemporary German Studies, is a specialist on Soviet-GDR relations, author of *Soviet Policy Toward East Germany Reconsidered: The Postwar Decade* (1987) and a forthcoming monograph on the SED-SPD Dialogue, among others.

GORDON SMITH, London School of Economics, has written extensively on West German and European politics including *Democracy in Western Germany* (3d ed. 1986) and *Politics in Western Europe* (5th ed. 1989). He also coedits the journal *West European Politics*.

CHRISTIAN SØE teaches at California State University, Long Beach. He has written extensively on the FDP and German political liberalism. He is the editor of the annually revised anthology, *Comparative Politics*, and is director of the Pacific Workshop on German Affairs.

JAMES CLYDE SPERLING, University of Akron, recently completed his dissertation, "*Three-Way Stretch: The Federal Republic of Germany in the Atlantic Economy, 1969–1976*" (University of California, Santa Barbara), and has reviewed literature for the *American Political Science Review* and *Journal of Politics*.

INTRODUCTION: FORTY YEARS AND SEVEN GENERATIONS

Peter H. Merkl

At first glance forty years for the Federal Republic may not seem a venerable age. In the twentieth century, however, the most dramatic changes have happened in ever-shorter time spans. Consider for example how the role of the United States in the world and its internal life changed from 1898 to 1938: From the days of the Spanish-American war when we were hovering timidly at the edge of an entirely new role as a world power—through the upheavals of the First World War which left us the prosperous heir apparent of British economic power in the world—to the nadir of the Great Depression and the rise of the New Deal. Or the forty-year span, say, since 1944 when the wartime alliance of Britain, the United States, and the Soviet Union against Germany and its Axis friends had gloriously turned the tide and confronted the lion in his continental den. The end of World War II left America, at least for a while, in a position of global hegemony. The next decades put this country on a veritable rollercoaster ride of changing policies toward defeated Germany and, more important, the Soviet Union. With the latter we soon went from wartime alliance to cold war confrontation, and after a respite of détente back to the cold war rhetoric of 1984. With Germany the ride followed contrapuntal lines. The vengeful mood of the Morgenthau Plan and the beginnings of denazification and democratic reeducation soon changed to lenience and, increasingly, a supportive partnership with a West German state arose from the ashes of World War II. The trajectory of U.S.-German relations climbed to such heights as permitting West Germany to participate in the Marshall Plan, underwriting its new currency and, eventually, supporting rearmament and the absorption of the new German armed forces into NATO. The partnership reached its highest point in the age of Konrad Adenauer, the first chancellor (1949–1963) of the Federal Republic (FRG) and a remarkable European statesman who managed, under American tutelage, to rehabilitate at least West Germany in the eyes of the world from the deep disgrace and hostility of the Nazi years. Adenauer dissolved a heritage of German nationalism into the larger communities of Franco-German reconciliation, the European Community, and the Atlantic partnership. The fourteen years of Adenauer's rule were about the same length as the lifetime of the fateful Weimar Republic (1919–1933), Germany's first try at democracy, and yet the period was long enough to witness the beginnings of a relative decline in the warmth of the U.S.-German relationship. The American superpower had accomplished containment of Soviet expansion by consolidating Western Europe, including the Federal Republic, and turned to other global preoccupations and economic problems at home and abroad. Ten years later, after the debacle of America's intervention in Vietnam, observers on both sides of the Atlantic began to notice the passing of a generation which, in the United States and in Europe, had brought about and maintained its close collaboration against the Soviet challenge to the war-ravaged continent. "Successor generations" on both sides of the Atlantic, they feared, no longer fully shared the convictions and experiences of the postwar years. The botched gesture of President Reagan's visit to the Bitburg military cemetery in 1985 was, among other things, meant to salve symbolically the wounds of this growing estrangement.

LIFE CYCLES AND TWENTIETH-CENTURY HISTORY

As we contemplate the forty years of the Federal Republic (1949–1989), we should not overlook the cataclysmic changes in the German history of the preceding forty years, 1909–1949, either, since some of the significance of the peaceful and relatively settled life of West Germany lies precisely in its avoidance of the extremism and nationalism of the past. The average duration of a human life, whether it is that of a political leader or of an average German, is much longer than the fourteen years of Weimar or the twelve years of the Third Reich. More important still, as individual lives link eras of contemporary German history, their individual life cycles often tend to replicate in adulthood, or in the mature years of a statesman, what the individuals may have learned in their formative years— say, between the ages of fifteen and twenty-five. Transmitted by this life cycle replication, the historical experiences of one era thus may pattern the responses of leaders and masses in a later period.[1] The leaders, furthermore, may pass on the formative experiences of their own youth decades later to those growing up then.

1909 was the last year in office of Chancellor Bernhard von Bülow (1900–1909) who, more than any other figure before Adolf Hitler, embodied the German imperialistic obsession with his slogans of a German "place in the sun" and a major role in "world politics." He was born in 1849 and grew up in the heady days of Otto von Bismarck's wars of national unification (1864–1871) which kindled his lifelong nationalist enthusiasm and may have persuaded him to view himself as a second Bismarck who would lead his nation into the glorious role of a world power, promoting German naval expansion to compete with Britain on the high seas and rivaling the colonial empires of his day. Von Bülow's successors, von Bethmann-Hollweg, Georg Michaelis, Kaiser Wilhelm II himself, and most of the important German generals of the disastrous bid for world power in World War I were born within ten years of von Bülow and shared the formative experience of growing up in the enthusiastic days of the foundation of the German nation-state.

By way of contrast, World War I and the decade prior to its outbreak were the formative period of most of the leaders of the Third Reich who evidently absorbed both its Pan German and *völkisch* obsessions and, as soldiers in the war, the desperate determination of many to fight on to the bitter end, unwilling to seek a peace of reconciliation or to concede defeat. World War II and the goal of the racial empire of a German master race was their way of winning at last what they could not win twenty years earlier. Other members of the World War I generation, of course, reacted to the experience with pacifism and a desire for international understanding. But, in the meantime, the mass of average Germans who had been in the First World War had been voters and joined movements and parties throughout the Weimar years which perpetuated the wartime nationalism throughout the Weimar Republic and eventually helped the Nazis into power. The soldiers of World War II, on the other hand, were of later generations, born mostly between 1902 and 1928 and growing up politically in the turbulent confrontations of the republic or the orchestrated patriotism of the Third Reich.

Political Generations of Post-1945 Leaders

Because of the way individual lives overlap these historical periods (see table I.1), an account of the major post–World War II generations has to begin with people born long before 1945, both at the level of the masses of Germans and of their postwar leaders. Konrad Adenauer (born 1876) was atypical in that he really belonged to the generation that until 1930 produced most Weimar chancellors and, in fact, he came close to becoming a chancellor himself during those days. A few post-1945 German leaders such as Ernst Reuter, Kurt Schumacher, Carlo Schmid, Ludwig Erhard, and Walter Ulbricht were of the World War I generation, which is not to say that they absorbed quite the same message as the leaders of the Third Reich. Nevertheless, the wounds received in that great patriotic struggle may explain, for example, the nationalistic undertones in Schumacher's socialist rhetoric as well as Erhard's frequent appeals to "the German people," a phrase not heard for nearly twenty years after 1945. Other postwar leaders such as Willy Brandt, Kurt Georg Kiesinger, Gerhard Schröder, Franz Josef Strauss, and Erich Honecker were born in the first post–World War I generation (1902–1915) that grew up amidst the political confrontations of Weimar. Of this generation, many joined militant groups ranging from the communist Red Front to the bourgeois youth leagues of the Right and the Nazi storm troopers.

A more recent set of West German leaders, such as Helmut Schmidt, Hans-Dietrich Genscher, Wolfgang Mischnick, Egon Bahr, Hans-Jochen Vogel, Rainer Barzel, Gustav Heinemann, Friedrich Zimmermann, Annemarie Renger, Liselotte Funke, Katharina Focke, Hildegard Hamm-Brücher, Horst Ehmke, Alfred Dregger, and Gerhard Stoltenberg are of the World War II generation (born especially 1916–1928, but also earlier)[2] and very likely shared the experience

Table I.1
German Political Generations in the Twentieth Century

1. *World War I leaders: born* 1845—1860, *formed* 1860–1885 (during national unification).
   Weimar Republic leaders: born 1865–1880, *formed* 1880–1905 (peace time); *Post-1945 leaders:* Adenauer (born 1876), Heuss (1884).

2. *World War I "Front Generation":*
   (a) *Masses born* 1890–1901, *formed* 1905–1926 (during imperialistic adventures and war), served in war, suffered deprivations during and after war; *voted* 1919–1933 and *supported the Third Reich* 1933–1945.
   (b) *Most Nazi leaders* were born of this generation (Hitler 1889).
   (c) *Some post-World War II leaders* also (Erhard, Schumacher, Ulbricht).

3. *Post-World War I Generation: born* 1902–1915, *formed* 1917–1940 (during civil disturbances, inflation, depression, Third Reich at peace)
   (a) *They joined Nazi storm troopers, Communist fighters, other paramilitaries and other parties; supported Third Reich.*
   (b) *Some postwar leaders:* Brandt, Strauss, Honecker.

4. *World War II Generation:*
   (a) *Masses born* 1916–1928, *formed* 1931–1953 in the Third Reich and WW II, and in immediate postwar ruins (or in POW camps).
   (b) *Produced some West German leaders of the last ten years:* Helmut Schmidt, Genscher, Lambsdorff, Vogel, Richard von Weizsäcker.

5. *First Postwar Generation: born* 1928–1940, *formed* 1943–1965 (during reconstruction from ruins to prosperity); *Voted since* 1948, supporting democracy, Western alliance, restitution to Jews.
   (a) A generation of nonjoiners, "Count-me-out."
   (b) *Produced recent leaders:* Helmut Kohl, Johannes Rau, and Hans Apel.

6. *Second Postwar Generation: born* 1941–1959, *formed* 1956–1984 (during age of reforms, also television, civic education).
   (a) A highly "critical" and rebellious generation, politicized, and mobilized in student revolt, citizen initiatives, Jusos, and neo-Nazi NPD.
   (b) Produced leaders of Greens, feminists, peace movement.

7. *Third Postwar Generation: born* 1960–1970, *formed* 1975–1995 (during oil crises, economic slowdown, structural unemployment).
   (a) Today's environmentalist Greens, feminists, peace movement, and other new social movements.

of the final verdict on the German pursuit of world power and its catastrophic aftermath. So, of course, did most of the German masses in 1945. When we look at some of the early post-1945 surveys in Western occupation zones and in the first years of the Federal Republic and notice that, in the early fifties, as many as 12–15 percent of the people still expressed Nazi views and a nostalgia for the prewar Third Reich, we have to remember their generational composition. In 1950, more than two-thirds of the West German population and three-fourths of the voters belonged to the World War II and earlier generations who had once given the Nazi regime enthusiastic majorities even if many of them had become disillusioned after 1943. Millions of Nazis had to be resocialized and absorbed among the voters—many of the less important ex-Nazis even regained civil service positions and pension rights under Article 131 of the Basic Law—or at least were persuaded not to band together against the democratic regime in Bonn. To have the Federal Republican python swallow the huge ex-Nazi pig without noticeable indigestion was one of the greatest achievements of Chancellor Adenauer's powerful political machine. Without this the FRG might long ago have succumbed to the same fate as the Weimar Republic.

The First Postwar Generation

The first postwar generation (born between 1929 and 1940) came to political maturity in the twenty years after the war and its formative experiences ranged from the earliest postwar phase amid ruins and masses of hungry, downtrodden people to the years of successful rebuilding and the "economic miracle." Politically, its members grew up in the middle of an intense withdrawal from political engagement (other than voting) in the "count-me-out" (Ohne-mich) generation that was mostly interested in the pursuit of private happiness, careers, and prosperity. They were glad that the date of their birth had spared them involvement with the Nazis and their antagonists, the Gnade der späten Geburt (the unearned grace of having been born too late—or, there but for the grace of God . . .), as Chancellor Helmut Kohl was to put it in a much-resented phrase on the occasion of a recent state visit to Israel. Kohl indeed is of this first postwar generation and represents its viscerally pro-American and pro-Israeli attitudes as well as a tender regard for the social and political institutions and processes of the conservative democracy built up in those years.

Those who, like Kohl, later rose to become political leaders of the Federal Republic, of course, did not stay away from political engagement like most of the Ohne-mich generation. From a sense of personal obligation they sought political responsibility at lower levels while their elders wrote their fears of plebiscitarian democracy into the Basic Law and built up the anti-communist and West-integrated Federal Republic. Other leaders of this generation have been Johannes Rau, the 1987 SPD candidate for chancellor, Peter Glotz (SPD), Theodor Waigel (CSU), Norbert Blüm, Kurt Biedenkopf, Heinz Riesenhuber (all three CDU), Hans (Johnny) Klein (CSU), Martin Bangemann, and Gerhart Baum (both FDP). There were fewer women leaders in this generational group and, in fact, this generation only slowly made its way into positions of power. For instance, in the eighth German *Bundestag* in 1976, the year Kohl for the first time became the CDU/CSU candidate for chancellor, deputies of this generation were still outnumbered 4:5 by the World War II generation. It takes time, of course, for a person to attain a position in the political elite. West German politics is not hospitable to *Wunderkinder* and even Kohl's political career is considered unusually fast: He joined the CDU at age 27, was CDU state chairman in Rhineland Palatinate at 36, minister president (governor) at 39, national CDU chair at 43, and chancellor at 52, after winning his first nomination for the position at age 46.

AN UPSURGE IN POLITICAL PARTICIPATION

In the meantime, the second and third postwar generations have entered the political fray with telling results. The second generation can be said to have started with the birth cohorts of 1941—such cut-off points are likely to be rather arbitrary and, as long as they are not connected to preexisting limits such as the draft age for a major war, should be taken with a grain of salt—and to end in the latter half of the fifties. This would give it formative periods ranging from about the end of the chief period of the great economic buildup through the age of reforms of the 1960s and early seventies to the impact of the energy crisis (1959–1979), a period that also witnessed the accelerating effects of civics education and television on all young Germans. Whatever may have been the precise causes, this is a highly mobilized, critical, and politically rebellious generation and it rose to challenge every shibboleth of the preceding generations, beginning with their avoidance of political engagement. The paralyzing shock of the war, the disclosure of the Nazi crimes, and the impact of defeat and devastation had worn off and the formative years found these birth cohorts in a prosperous society under a politically respectable regime. By 1970, in any case, the population share of the World War II and older generations had dropped to no more than a third of the West German populace, reducing still further the weight of the tarnished past.

The surge of political participation from the mid-sixties on could take on one sacred cow of "the system" after another without the fear of anarchy and communist takeover that had made the preceding generation so uptight and anxious to cling to Western protection. In the face of the resistance of their elders and the conservative parties, the rebellious young particularly singled out five shibboleths of their elders and mounted their critical attacks in ever-changing versions of these same points. They challenged the assumptions that:

1. West German society and politics were really democratic. Instead, the generational rebels pointed out the remaining authoritarianism of German schools, universities, and the average family. They also criticized the oligarchic procedures of the major parties, proposing instead democratization *at the base*. In the seventies they similarly challenged local government and the planning bureaucracy with countless citizen initiatives against environmental deterioration and public construction projects.
2. Only capitalism and the free market can assure individual happiness and freedom. Instead, they evinced considerable interest in socialism—although less in the Soviet or Eastern European communist version which they found intolerably repressive and bureaucratic. The personal freedoms of women, juveniles, gays,

and minorities have been a persistent theme of their "new individualism."

3. Communism is a monster and the security of the Federal Republic from the Soviet Union requires extraordinary measures and constant vigilance. Instead, the young rebels were quite ready to cooperate with the long-ostracized domestic Communist party and groups and insisted that the Federal Republic reassess its relations with the East and perhaps even recognize the Oder-Neisse border and the German Democratic Republic.

4. All democratic and foreign policy wisdom comes from the United States. The American civil rights movement and the mobilization of their American coevals against the war in Vietnam confirmed the critical attitude of the second postwar generation towards U.S. foreign policy in the world and, in particular, toward the third world nations. It would be an exaggeration to call this a wave of anti-Americanism but it combined readily with anticapitalism and a new identification with developing, ex-colonial nations. For the young rebels, it was the end of the German love affair with the United States which had long blinded West Germans to our race problems, flaws in American democracy, and the seamy side of superpower politics.

5. Israel can do no wrong and because of the holocaust, Germans should refrain from any criticism of it no matter what the Israeli government or people may do, especially following the 1967 war. Again, this was no wave of left-wing anti-Semitism. The critical generation, in fact, excoriated its own elders for the horrors of the past and exposed some of the hypocritical conspiracies that had permitted some prominent ex-Nazis to escape punishment and ostracism. But in place of the unquestioning philo-Semitism of the first postwar generation, this generation insisted on weighing the past moral debts of the World War II and earlier generations against their new sense of moral obligation toward third world nations, including the Palestinians and other Arab nations.

To the leaders of the Federal Republic, both Christian and Social Democrats, this was a stunning reversal of long-accepted political attitudes. It was nowhere more obvious than in the hostility of the student movement to the Springer empire of newspapers which had always been the epitome of the anticommunist, unquestioningly pro-American and philo-Semitic, and to the constitutional consensus of the West German political elites. There were even undertones of nineteenth-century German idealism, romanticism, and nationalism which have since become more pronounced throughout West German culture. What made the great change difficult to ignore in the long run, moreover, was the enormous upsurge in participation, the mobilization of the long-silent, obsequious German Ohne-mich masses who began to assert themselves against their by and large well-meaning leaders in never-ending waves, beginning with the demonstrations of the extra-parliamentary opposition (APO) to the emergency legislation of the sixties, the student revolt, and the Young Socialists (*Jusos*) and Young Democrats (of the FDP). The citizen initiatives alone involved larger numbers than all the members of the FRG parties from right to left. The women's movement aimed at raising the consciousness of the majority of Germans of the seventies, and the Greens and other new social movements of the eighties sought to mobilize similar numbers against nuclear power, nuclear weapons, and environmental pollution. The most virulent and extreme of these manifestations, to be sure, may have become counterproductive, raising their own antagonists and soon being forgotten. But the overall effect of more than two decades of massive protests has been the creation of a vibrant and energetic democratic culture which no longer tolerates unquestioningly the tutelage of political elites however well-meaning they may be.

The second postwar generation, of course, also generated a set of political leaders although it may still be too early to tell which of them will stand out in the end. Among them are many of the prominent figures of the movements and upheavals of the last twenty years, such as Erhard Eppler and Volker Hauff, Karsten Voigt and Wolfgang Roth, Björn Engholm and Oskar Lafontaine of the SPD, and also a number of rising women leaders such as Heide Simonis, Anke Fuchs, and Ingrid Matthäus-Maier, who was originally with the FDP. Still with that party are Irmgard Adam-Schwaetzer, Helmut Haussman, and Jürgen Möllemann. The women who lead the Greens have tried to avoid the spotlight because of the pronounced disdain of that party for personality cults and elitism but such names as

Jutta Ditfurth and Petra Kelly will undoubtedly play prominent roles in the future. The CDU's Rita Süssmuth rounds out the strong female contingent of this generation's political leaders. Their male equivalent in the CDU/CSU is still hard to pinpoint except perhaps for Volker Rühe and Horst Teltsckik but there are, of course, a number of promising Green leaders such as Otto Schily and Joschka Fischer.

The Third Generation and the Limits to Growth

If the second postwar generation ended its period of formative experiences with the energy crises of the seventies, there was already a third postwar generation waiting, born between about 1959 and 1970—and perhaps there is a fourth generation (born since 1970) growing up or still in school today—and having its formative experiences in the seventies and eighties, that is under the impact of the "limits to growth," growing youth unemployment, the great battles of the women's movement to legalize abortion and raise women's consciousness of other issues, struggles against nuclear plants and other environmental concerns and, last but not least, the campaign against the deployment of new nuclear missiles in the Federal Republic. This third generation gathered under some of the leaders from the second postwar generation in large organizations such as the Greens, the women's and peace movements, and other new social movements, and in local actions such as the antinuclear campaigns of Brokdorf or Wackersdorf, or the squatters' riots of Berlin. In the eighties many of them voted for the Greens rather than the SPD—militant feminists even tried to launch a women's party because they felt that they could not trust any of the established parties—although they often could agree more readily on what they wished to oppose or reject than on a positive program and a realistic approach towards its enactment.

The highly emotional battles of the seventies left even the militants exhausted and cynical. Being tarred with the terrorist brush by the resurgent conservative opposition and by public hysteria over the actions of the Baader-Meinhof and similar groups also silenced many and lowered the expectations of the "system-changers" and reformers. Except for recognizing limits to economic growth, values had not really changed much since the late 1960s and neither had the protest leaders. But the climate of long-range economic stagnation, structural unemployment, and youthful hopelessness, underlined by government cutbacks in education grants (*Bafög*) made for a very different mood among the young. There also occurred considerable depolitization, especially after the fall of Helmut Schmidt when the Kohl government began to call for a "return to *Leistung*" (achievement) and hard work among old and young alike, rather than political agitation or "waiting for government handouts." Large parts of youth did respond by turning conservative, though more in the sense of passive acceptance of the worsening situation rather than of ideological activism. Those not fortunate enough to be given a chance in the new *Leistungsgesellschaft* became bitter or responded with aimless pursuits—such as living hedonistically from day to day with "no future" in sight—or by participating in violent confrontations with the police, for example over the construction of nuclear plants or airport runways, or in street battles against the eviction of youthful squatters from empty apartment houses slated for destruction.

The third generation is still too young to single out future German political leaders in its midst. Delimiting generational groups, in any case, is a rather arbitrary exercise when we are talking about people still in their twenties. It becomes much clearer at a distance in time when differences in outlook and behavior become more obvious. By 1993 the World War II and older generations will have shrunk to less than a fifth (17.1 percent) of the total and to about one-fifth of those eligible to vote. These are the only surviving Germans we can seriously hold responsible for the Third Reich, the war, and the holocaust—and many of them may either have opposed the Nazi government, have been painfully denazified, or have seriously repented their loyalty to an infamous regime. Then there is the first postwar or Kohl generation and the second postwar generation, which together form almost two-fifths of the total population and half of the current voters. They express some guilt feelings and support restitution for the crimes of the earlier generations of Germans even though they were indeed "born too late" to have been involved in those misdeeds whatever opinions they may have on the questions of today. Finally, there will be (in 1993) the next generation(s) of Germans who despite the declining birthrate will already number more than two-fifths of the total population and nearly one-third of the eligible voters. Even they express some guilt feelings and existential uncertainties today although they were not even born until more than a decade after World War II and grew up under the safety shield of NATO and in a well-heeled welfare state that gives them economic security.

We could also look at these generational divisions in 1993 from the perspective of the second and third postwar generations vis à vis the founders of the Federal Republic (including the large silent majority, of that day) who built a rather authoritarian democracy with safeguards against expressions of the popular will.[3] The younger generations, by 1993, will constitute two-thirds of the population and more than half (56.2 percent) of its eligible voters. This should certainly give them enough weight to dominate the politics of the country. In 1970, when they were already raising the rafters of the republic—the rebellious young were only a minority of their age cohorts but an active one—this generation only constituted 12 percent of eligible voters (above the voting age of twenty) even though their share of the population was already two-fifths.

THE PLAN FOR THIS BOOK

If this is the progression of political movements and generations of the forty years of the Federal Republic from 1949 to 1989, what might be the best way to explain the trends and portents of German society and politics? We obviously require broad, sweeping interpretations rather than detailed research. There is already so much narrow research that one can hardly see the forest for the trees. We also need to look beyond any one moment, period, or partial picture of this moving panorama to concentrate on the larger trends and issues that can be charted throughout the forty years. And it may often be necessary to look at the past record of a given trend and to speculate about its likely future. We have also taken care to assemble well-established experts of German contemporary affairs, and, to assure objectivity, we selected only non-German scholars so that our perspectives would not be distorted by observers writing *pro domo* or from a partisan point of view.

The logical point to begin are the trends in the political values and attitudes that have occurred over the generations of the Federal Republic. Foremost among the salient topics is the question of the changing sense of German identity as it has manifested itself in the recent revival of the debate on "the German question" (see the essay by the historian Gerald Kleinfeld). The uncertain identity of West Germans has had to separate itself also from its nurturant godfather, the United States, as Andrei Markovits perceptively points out. A state-of the-art survey of the changing social consciousness (by Russell Dalton) is next. And, since one in every two Germans is a woman, the extraordinary evolution of the role of women over four decades and more called for critical analysis (by Joyce Mushaben). Sets of social values, or a culture, always tend to build institutions that both reflect them and influence the inculcation of the values of the next generations. Hence, social values are not always easy to separate from the structures they create and are often better treated together, as Richard Merritt has done with Protestantism in Berlin and divided Germany.

Narrowing the focus to political values, we turn to the "rules of the game" of West German politics. Donald Kommers puts the West German constitution into the crucible of critical assessment in the light of forty years of experience. Michael Huelshoff explores the patterns of West German corporatism, and Donald Hancock adds to this a portrait of the "ambivalent insider," the trade unions who have joined the system without entirely giving up their mental reservations. The complex situation is illuminated brilliantly by Jutta Helm who dissects the value-laden subject of the transformation of the Ruhr Valley at a confluence of attitudes of social partnership, industrial decay, and environmental conscience. Then Arnold Heidenheimer, who was practically "present at the creation" of the Federal Republic and has written so much about it, reflects on the legacies of Adenauer's "chancellor democracy," one of the most effective political machines ever in operation. The *sine qua non* of Adenauer's edifice was his clever harnessing of campaign finance sources, a subject Arthur Gunlicks explores systematically from the beginning to the end of the period in question. The emerging party system—the party state that dominates West German politics—is sketched expertly by Gordon Smith. The trends of the party system naturally require also detailed accounts of each of the major partisan forces of the politics of the Federal Republic today: the Social Democrats (Gerald Braunthal), the Christian Democrats (William Chandler), the Free Democrats (Christian Soe), and the Greens (William Paterson), in their significance and evolution over the forty years.

The forty-year-old political system, inevitably, needs to be understood also in its international context which for a state in the midst of European nation-states is an indispensable corrective to any assumption of untrammeled domestic evolution. While some young Germans wish it were located in Switzerland instead, the Federal Republic, over these forty years, has always been in the middle of East-West confrontations, to some extent still a client state of the United States, and deeply involved in NATO and in the European Community. There has also been a special relationship between the FRG and Israel which is here described in detail by Lily Feldman. The role of NATO (Werner Feld), the European Community (Emil Kirchner), and the intersecting pulls of the United States and the international economy on the Federal Republic (James Sperling) define the West German position in the Western alliance. But on the other hand, there is the vast communist empire, the Soviet Union and its satellites, which were an object of great fear in the days of Adenauer. From the late 1960s, West Germans began to strive for a modus vivendi with the East, and Willy Brandt's Ostpolitik of the early seventies opened doors of trade and military détente that seemed to beat the swords of the cold war into plough shares of peaceful coexistence. But the opening to the East did not entirely escape serious criticism even though relations with the East have historically been enormously attractive to the Germans. By today, a firm bipartisan consensus supports Ostpolitik and yet, progressive Social Democrats have been seriously weighing a "second phase" of Ostpolitik (see the essay by Ann Phillips) that would push on into a future of close East-West cooperation. All of these essays were written especially for this book and with an eye to significant links from the past to the present and future.

NOTES

1. While this replication of a generational historical experience happens soon and often continuously in the life of an average person, with political leaders there may be a lag of as much as 20–30 years until the person attains high office.
2. In World War II few escaped service of one sort or another. Also since the range of birth cohorts indicated here is rather large, the formative experiences are not as clearly determined as they would be if we distinguished between those drafted into World War II at a mature or a more impressionable age, as well as between those in the war while German arms were still spectacularly triumphant and those who directly experienced the defeats of 1943–1945.
3. The fear of popular majorities led to the avoidance of the initiative and referendum, and the choice for an oligarchic "party state" with a parliamentary executive, the chancellor, protected by special safeguards, rather than a plebiscitarian president. The founders ranged over the various prewar and war generations, while the first postwar generation later defended their work against the critical young rebels.

I
VALUES AND THE GERMAN IDENTITY

1

THE GERMAN QUESTION, YESTERDAY AND TOMORROW

Gerald R. Kleinfeld

We are no longer in a postwar world. The very mention of the word "postwar" can even conjure up some confusion. "Post" which war? World War II has been over so long, and the twenty-first century is nearly upon us. In what sense can this still be called a postwar world? The defeat of Nazi Germany carried the two great flanking powers, the United States and the Soviet Union, into the heart of Europe, from which they have not yet withdrawn. Bismarck's Reich, expanded by Hitler, crumbled and was divided. The United Kingdom, France, and the United States of America received occupation zones in the west and the south. The easternmost segments of Germany were made parts of Poland and the U.S.S.R. A Soviet zone of occupation was carved out of the central part of what had been Germany, but which now was "east" Germany. Austria was de-annexed and made independent again. Fleeing from the incorporation of their homes into the Soviet Union and Poland, millions of Germans packed what they could carry and settled in the west. A smaller, divided, Germany emerged. The eastern provinces, less virtually all of their inhabitants, were populated by citizens of the Soviet Union and Poland, and quickly lost their German character. The remainder of the former Reich was occupied, and divided into five segments: four occupation zones and the former capital, Berlin, which was itself divided into four sectors.

This division was not intended to be permanent, and mayoral elections were even subsequently held in Berlin for the entire city. But, the Allied powers could not agree on the nature of a single postwar German state, on what was to be done with Germany.

Negotiations held over years produced no result, while temporary decisions had to be made in order to permit life to go on in each of the occupation zones. The temporary decisions, in turn, produced new realities. Failing to agree on what should be done, the conquerors stayed on and two separate German polities emerged. As time passed, the war receded into more distant memory. Was the postwar division to be permanent? The German question, whether and how to put Germany together in one piece, is one of the last remnants of the postwar era that takes on ever more significance as a new Europe emerges and the flanking powers are threatened by their own overcommitments.

It is tempting to suggest that the German question is solely a result of the postwar disagreements among the Allied powers, but this is not the case. The German question is a historical issue, arising out of a number of factors, and its resolution must take all of them into account.[1] In the center of Europe, the Germans achieved unity late. Their geography worked against them. Lacking natural frontiers, Germans also border nine different countries, more than any other people in the world. Their history is one of a centuries-old failure to create a nation-state. The Holy Roman Empire never became one, and finally disintegrated at the beginning of the nineteenth century. It was replaced by a congeries of thirty-nine separate states and principalities joined in a confederation more designed to prevent German unity than to embody it. In 1848, liberal nationalists attempted a revolution. They wanted a constitution and a united nation, demands similar to those voiced by Italians and by many people in eastern Europe. They failed. In the crisis of their efforts, the revolutionaries debated a central theme of German history— where were the German borders to be; what were to be the dimensions of the new Germany? Who among those who spoke German were to be part of the national German state? Otto von Bismarck realized the "little Germany" solution, creating a German Empire that excluded those Germans who lived in Austria-Hungary. A "greater Germany," including those fourteen million in Austria-Hungary, was not then possible. But the German Empire did not bring tranquillity to Europe. After two world wars in the twentieth century, Germany's neighbors were concerned about the impact of a united Germany on continental peace and security.[2] Thus, when ultimately the Federal Republic of Germany was established in the western occupation zones, initial French reaction to a prospect of West German rearmament was often described as attempting to ensure that German forces were large enough to deter the Soviets but not large enough to endanger France.[3] The German question is, therefore, a European question.[4] German unity may be accepted by Germany's neighbors if they are convinced that no danger arises from it. The German question is also an issue of strategic importance, because the two German states belong to different alliance systems. What has been characterized by former West German Chancellor Helmut Schmidt as Soviet "defensive imperialism" has long been viewed as a threat to all of Western Europe. Germany is strategically so pivotal, and economically so significant, that not only European, but global issues are involved in the German question. Hence, the United States sees the German question amidst both European and global ramifications. Secondly, the German question is about freedoms and self-determination. Today's two German states not only have different governments, but they have different social, political, and economic systems reflecting the division of Europe. There are fundamental issues of freedom and human rights, recognized by Western nations as a part of their philosophical framework and value systems.[5] Freedom is an essential element. In the western occupation zones, decisions for local self-government led to interzonal cooperation and, ultimately, to the establishment of the Federal Republic of Germany in 1949. The Soviet Union then moved to create the German Democratic Republic in its zone. The entire founding process of the Federal Republic of Germany reveals a deep concern about making decisions that could lead to Germany being permanently divided.

The founders took careful steps. They declared that they were not going to write a constitution, but a "basic law," announcing that a constitution would have to be postponed until there was a reunited Germany. The Basic Law served to stress this temporary situation. It proclaims its provisional status in the preamble, and looks forward to the reunification of the German people in free self-determination. The choice of a capital revealed the same concern. With Berlin under four-power occupation, a temporary capital in one of the Western zones was necessary. Frankfurt was deliberately not chosen. That city had hosted the parliament of the revolutions of 1848–1849, and it could be viewed as a potential legitimate national capital. Many of the founders wanted a clearly provisional capital, nothing that would threaten the sought-after reunification. Eventually, Bonn, a small city south of Cologne, was selected. The Basic Law contains other provisions which affirm that the Federal Republic of Germany is a provisional state within Germany. All Germans have German citizenship. Thus, residents of the former Soviet zone, the German Democratic Republic, are not considered to be foreigners, but Germans, just as entitled to a passport in the Federal Republic of Germany as Germans born in the West. A German who comes to the Federal Republic of Germany may, therefore, receive a passport.

The legal points are not technical or idle details. Lacking a formal peace treaty with a united Germany, the victor powers established their relationship within Germany and their respective rights according to a number of arrangements and treaties. If not consistently maintained, these are subject to erosion and elimination, threatening the security of vital relationships. The most dramatic test of the rights of the Western allies was the Berlin Blockade of 1948, when the Soviet Union cut off land access to the western zones of the City of Berlin. The United States defended the Western position by mounting a massive airlift, ferrying supplies into the beleaguered city around the clock until the Soviets reopened the land routes. Berlin, itself, is an artificial case, enmeshed in legal and treaty arrangements. The Soviet effort of 1948 was followed by other attempts, each in a different way, to force the United States, France, and Great Britain out of their sectors in the city and to strip the city of its special status, paving the way for its incorporation into the German Democratic Republic. Thus, although there is now a mayor in West Berlin, and one in East Berlin, the territory assigned to the Soviet zone, there is legally no city of West Berlin. The mayor in West Berlin is Mayor of Berlin, not West Berlin. Although the Soviets and East Germans no longer participate in the all-city elections, and a separate mayor is chosen in the East, this does not change the legal status of the Mayor. The Soviet Union has also attempted to have the western zones recognized as a separate entity, a city of West Berlin. These attempts have always been rejected. Several times, the German Democratic Republic, which states that Berlin is its capital, has attempted to deal with the Western allies for various aspects relating to Berlin. These efforts have also been rejected. Passport and visa issues on the occupation lines within the city have been predicated on the rights of the former victors. If the Western allies permit the German Democratic Republic to have jurisdiction, or the Soviet Union to succeed in having the western sectors of Berlin acknowledged as a separate entity, the very presence of the Western allies in Berlin itself may be endangered. Thus, the legal questions and highly technical issues, including as well the question of who checks which forms, have become vital to the overriding principle—the presence of the United States, France, and the United Kingdom in Berlin, and the maintenance of the free governance of the western sectors of that still-divided city.[6] It is a patchwork quilt, stabilized by a treaty of 1952, called by the West Germans the *Deutschlandvertrag*, which led to the termination of the occupation regime and laid down relations between the three Western powers and the Federal Republic of Germany, plus the Quadripartite Agreement on Berlin of 1971, but still resting on the division of Germany at the end of the Second World War.[7] The western sectors of the city have a flourishing life, and an economy that has made significant strides. Access is guaranteed by the Four Power Agreement, and rail, highway, and air routes serve growing numbers of citizens and tourists. As the war recedes into ever more distant memory, the status of Berlin remains a symbol of the German question.

Ultimately, the Federal Republic of Germany has itself only limited sovereignty, and this, too, is tied to the City of Berlin. If the Federal Republic of Germany were completely sovereign, that might call into question the permanence of Western allied rights in the western parts of the City of Berlin, which are based on the occupation of divided Germany pending a general peace treaty. Nor are those western sectors a part of the Federal Republic of Germany in every way. They, in turn, have only limited status as a part of the Federal Republic of Germany, by international agreement. The limited sovereignty of the Federal Republic of Germany is further reflected in the existence of special teams of the Allied powers who have rights to observe each other. Soviet soldiers in the Federal

Republic of Germany are offset by teams of Western soldiers in the German Democratic Republic. The Soviet Union emphasizes the importance of the legal issues by officially describing its troops in the German Democratic Republic as "Soviet forces in Germany," and not "Soviet forces in the German Democratic Republic," much to the continued displeasure of the government of the GDR.

The provisional and artificial nature of the division has left open the German question, and the first years after the establishment of the two governments within Germany gave no indication when a reunification might be accomplished. In 1952, the Soviet Union appeared to offer the Western powers an opportunity for reunification of the two remaining parts if the resultant Germany would be neutral. This offer, whether genuine or not, and historians differ in their interpretation of that, was rejected. Most believe that this was a ploy to prevent the Federal Republic of Germany from joining the North Atlantic Treaty Organization, but some insist that there were reasons for accepting Russian sincerity. Rolf Steininger has maintained that this was a lost chance for reunification, but his analysis has been spurned by several who were in prominent positions at the time.[8] Werner Weidenfeld contends that the Soviet Union had no intention of permitting free elections under international supervision. Stalin, in any case, had referred to the two German states, and regarded the former eastern territories, those parts of prewar Germany annexed by the Soviet Union and Poland, and from which almost all of the German inhabitants had left, as a closed issue. For many years, the Western allies refused to accept that annexation in all aspects, pending the peace treaty. With the Soviet Union and Poland in possession, and most of the original population gone, Western diplomacy did not seriously consider recovering them for Germany, but the matter was left officially unresolved in part to retain some pressure towards an ultimate peace treaty for Germany as a whole. The renunciation of force treaties implicitly and de facto recognized the Oder-Neisse line as the German eastern border, but further and comprehensive reinforcement was provided by the Helsinki Accords of 1975. The status of the frontier is enmeshed in the legal framework of the postwar years. In effect, the territories are gone, no return is considered, both German states have entered into agreements which accept their current status, and both have signed accords which guarantee this, but many Germans maintain that the situation still must be endorsed by the future government of a united Germany. In their view, this gives Eastern Europe an interest in reunification.

Meanwhile, the Federal Republic of Germany responded to the needs of Western Europe, including those of its own citizens, and accepted the new requirements of a new role for Europe and European countries in the world. The Basic Law foresaw the surrender of sovereignty within a European entity, and the Federal Republic of Germany moved anxiously to expand the European Coal and Steel Community established after the war into what has become the European Community. The EC was originally a limited economic union, but has moved steadily in the direction of greater and greater economic unity and even political union for Western Europe. Expanding from six member countries to twelve, with a total of 320 million people, the European Community has a gross national product larger than that of the United States and dwarfing that of the Soviet Union. It has a foreign trade which makes it an economic world power. Former passport and visa requirements have been dropped, and travel within the EC by citizens of EC countries has been made so free of restrictions that a European consciousness has emerged. The Franco-German Treaty of 1963, a success of Charles de Gaulle and Konrad Adenauer which contributed to laying old enmities to rest, has further aided in the integration of the Federal Republic of Germany into Western Europe. The NATO alliance with the United States, providing for common defense, has also bound the Federal Republic firmly into a system which guarantees its security and ensures broad support for the maintenance of the shared and common values embraced in its Basic Law. Cooperation and integration in Western Europe has brought economic benefits not only to the Federal Republic of Germany, but also to the German Democratic Republic.

The German Democratic Republic was not to be regarded as outside the pale. German-German trade is not considered as foreign trade, but internal trade under special conditions. Thus, the German Democratic Republic has special privileges in trade with the Federal Republic of Germany which grant it access to one of the countries of the European Community, a situation from which it clearly benefits.

One of the goals of the GDR is to expand this trade benefit to include other countries in the European Community.[9]

The Federal Republic of Germany has been easier for its population to accept than the German Democratic Republic has been for its people. The West German "economic miracle" after the war and the abundant freedoms guaranteed by that democratic state served as a magnet to those less fortunate across the Elbe. The German Democratic Republic had not been established by popular consent, and its government was seen as an extension of Soviet power. The years after the Second World War were hard for Germans in the GDR, and economic progress lagged far behind that of the West. East Germans, therefore, voted "with their feet," and left their homes by the millions to settle in the Federal Republic of Germany, where both individual freedom and economic advantage awaited them. This situation deprived the GDR especially of skilled and young people (between 1949 and 1961 about 2.7 million fled the German Democratic Republic) and made planning and development difficult, if not impossible. In addition, it tended to undermine the very legitimacy of the East German state. To stop it, the Berlin Wall was built, and emigration from the German Democratic Republic was severely restricted.

The construction of the Berlin Wall, and the extension of brutal frontier barriers, including a "shoot-to-kill" policy, effectively cut down the flow of emigrants to a trickle. The German Democratic Republic then renewed its efforts to build an economy along a socialist path with an absence of the freedoms enjoyed in the West, and under the disadvantages of unequal trade agreements with the Soviet Union. Faced with the virtual closing down of possibilities of emigration after the construction of the Berlin Wall and the tighter sealing of frontier areas, Germans in the GDR turned their energy to economic progress, albeit under the difficulties imposed by the very system that wanted such progress to provide legitimization. The German Democratic Republic sought to build loyalty to itself, partly as a device to aid economic development and partly as a means to ensure legitimacy in the minds of its people. While many West Germans looked forward to the eventual dissolution of the GDR and the absorption of that territory and its population into a democratic Germany, East Germany moved at a fast pace to strengthen the foundations of its own, separate, existence. This did not necessarily mean, however, that the German question was a closed matter for the German Democratic Republic. Its people continued to regard the Federal Republic of Germany as a free state on German soil, and many would have emigrated if they could. In the first half of 1988, more than 5,000 found ways—including via third countries—to reach the west.

In the years immediately after the Second World War, the initiative in German reunification was necessarily in the hands of the Allied powers. By the mid-1950s, they had failed to restore Germany, and the subsequent agreements that they reached were more in the nature of preserving the status quo than in rearranging the European structure. At that point, the initiative passed to the Germans themselves. Zbigniew Brzezinski later wrote that the Allies would never "impose" reunification on the Germans. They would have to want it and strive for it. By that time, however, the Federal Republic of Germany had become firmly embedded within both the European Community and NATO, and the German Democratic Republic had become equally absorbed into the Soviet-led economic and military alliances in Eastern Europe. The Federal Republic, with the Hallstein Doctrine, sought to discourage other countries from recognizing the German Democratic Republic. Reunification seemed to await a dismantling of the GDR, and that was not in the offing.

Two developments opened new opportunities for the Germans. One of these was détente.[10] As President Richard Nixon moved the United States into détente, the confrontation between the two systems eased. Parallel with this, the Federal Republic of Germany began its own détente with Eastern Europe. West German abandonment of the Hallstein Doctrine was already clear by 1967, and a program of building contacts and relationships in Eastern Europe, known as Ostpolitik, opened opportunities for communication with the German Democratic Republic.

The Federal Republic of Germany accepted the fact that the German Democratic Republic existed, but refused to acknowledge it as a foreign country. With the legal underpinning in place, the two German states gingerly began to develop closer relations. This was encouraged by the two settlements of 1971, a "Quadripartite Agreement" signed by the four World War II Allied powers on the status of Berlin and a 1972 "Treaty on the Basic Relations Between the Federal Republic of Germany and the German Democratic Republic," by which the German states agreed to establish permanent missions in each other's seat of government and, effectively, to acknowledge each other. To the latter end, Bonn insisted upon adding a letter, stating that the treaty did not conflict with the political aim of the Federal Republic of Germany to work for German unity through free self-determination. Relations between the two German states improved, and more travel was permitted.

In the almost two decades since the 1972 treaty, three significant developments have taken place. First, the population percentage has shifted, with more Germans alive who were born after the Second World War and after the division of their country than before. Second, the population as a whole, including these new generations, has not become satisfied with the status quo and continues to regard Germany as a divided country. Third, as Western Europe has become more closely integrated, and expanded its relationship with Eastern Europe, the German Question does not become less, but more acute.

The policy of détente, and continuing Ostpolitik, has intensified contacts between the two German states. Germans from the German Democratic Republic have traveled in the West, in increasing numbers, and returned home. They have seen a West Germany with a common heritage, a common culture, and many common interests (emigration pressure, therefore, has failed to ease). The same has been the case for West Germans visiting the East. Not only have older citizens visited relatives, but large groups of younger West Germans have taken every more frequent visits to the GDR, and returned with a sense of commonality. Far from the years driving the two Germanies apart, the new generation in the West, far freer to express its opinion and to travel, has rejected permanent division in Europe. Younger West Germans have traveled all over Western Europe, and also in much of the world. Within the western part of their own continent, they have seen visa restrictions disappear, passport regulations dropped, and borders almost reduced to signposts before which one may not even have to halt an automobile. When one can travel to France or Belgium without a second thought, the artificial nature of the border within Germany has become increasingly apparent to a younger generation, some of whom see the continental division on the Elbe, between East and West Europe, as equally illogical. There has also been a recognition that long-term developments in both Germanies have led to some differences in perspective among the populations of the two states.

With the emergence of new generations has come a new form of identity discussion in the Federal Republic of Germany. As in the nineteenth century, German borders may well lie beyond the frontier posts. Identifying as West Germans, younger citizens see themselves also as Germans, and many raise the question of what this means for their relationship to East Germans. They also see themselves as Europeans. The historic dimension of the German question surfaces with the continuing debate over German identity.

This has contributed to a renewed discussion in the Federal Republic of Germany about the role of the German question in government policy. There has been general agreement that the two German states should not drift further apart, that the Germans in the West have an obligation to assist the economic well-being of those in the East, and that Bonn should do all things possible to enhance freedom in the East. This has led to some friction with the United States, where Ostpolitik was not viewed without suspicion. Henry Kissinger was critical of Ostpolitik under Chancellor Willy Brandt, and a revival of American concerns erupted at the end of the 1970s when there was a new apprehension about potential West German neutralism. The term "Finlandization," then current in many articles and public statements in the United States, expressed American concerns that West German Ostpolitik might lead to neutralism in the Federal Republic of Germany in return for better relations with the Soviet Union and the possibility that Moscow might offer a form of reunification in return. West Germany, it was feared, might adopt a neutralist foreign policy in the hope of such better relations. As that anxiety passed, new stages nevertheless emerged in contact between the Federal Republic of Germany and the German Democratic Republic.

In the ongoing Ostpolitik, Bonn has sought agreements on a variety of mutual concerns, ranging from environmental matters to cultural affairs.[11] The two Germanies do not exchange ambassadors, but each has a representation in the other's capital. In September

1987, Erich Honecker, chairman of the Council of State of the German Democratic Republic paid the first visit to Bonn by an East German leader, returning visits of West German chancellors to East Berlin. A movement has grown recently to develop sister city relationships between cities in West and East Germany. In addition, the Social Democratic Party of the Federal Republic of Germany has held talks with the Socialist Unity Party, the governing party of the German Democratic Republic and the two have issued joint declarations.[12] The West German Ministry for Intra-German Affairs has taken the lead in negotiating a cultural agreement between the two, and leading political figures have exchanged visits and been present at public functions. Nearly all of the German Democratic Republic can receive West German television, and border areas of the Federal Republic of Germany can receive East German broadcasts. Bonn has promoted visits by young people and social groups to the GDR, and tried to encourage reciprocal visits. The GDR, needing Western currency, has been careful not to restrict tourism too severely, and maintains special shops in which only hard currency may be used. The contacts between East and West Germany are growing, and the number of visitors on both sides is increasing. This is being encouraged by all political parties in the Federal Republic of Germany, and some observers in Washington, D.C., were surprised when Franz Josef Strauss, leader of the Christian Social Union, played a key role in bringing a large loan from Bonn to the East Germans.

Economic support for the Germans in the East has also been a major goal of the Federal Republic of Germany. Large payments for building, maintaining, and modernizing highways leading to Berlin, contributions by the West German public to building and rebuilding churches in the East, as well as payments for a variety of purposes have helped to support the East German economy and aided in raising the standards of living of the people. Goods produced in the GDR are sold in West Germany, further improving the economy. Other aspects of the relationship include environmental protection and culture. With respect to the former, both states have an interest in cleaning up the environment, but the GDR has asked for West German financial aid and technology for a series of major projects. Some blackmail is also involved. The cleaning up of the Elbe, for example, brings GDR demands that the border between the two be moved to the middle of the river instead of the east bank. Filters and scrubbers on smokestacks, materials and money for sewage control, and various waste water control devices, are all needed by the German Democratic Republic to deal with its environmental problems. Even culture is a part of the general quality of life. A cultural agreement between the two German states permitted an exhibit of expressionist works in the GDR, which then sent some of the treasures of Dresden for viewing in West Germany. Both economic and cultural exchanges are intended to raise the standard of life in the East, while simultaneously creating a relationship so advantageous to East Berlin that a gradual improvement in basic freedoms and rights may be realized.[13]

Modification of GDR police conduct has been most difficult to encourage and the most elusive of all West German efforts. East Berlin has been more relaxed about letting its people travel in the West in recent years, but still shows no sign of tearing down the Wall. Whole families still cannot travel, in order to ensure that those individuals who do will return. Periodically, renewed crackdowns have earned disappointment in Bonn. Nevertheless, the efforts continue, and signs of opening and reform are earnestly awaited.

Whether the continuous efforts from Bonn stem from a new recognition of German identity or a feeling that the people of both German states would share common problems in the event of an armed conflict between NATO and the Warsaw Pact, there has been no doubt in recent years that the German question has retained its meaning and is still alive.[14] Germans have accepted the fact that it will not be solved soon. They understand that it is not a matter for Germans alone. On the other hand, there are two avenues in which it the German question is influencing the future of Europe.

First, there has been a reluctance in the Federal Republic of Germany, and in the German Democratic Republic, for different reasons, to cut one another adrift. While the GDR insists on full West German recognition, and acceptance of GDR citizenship, the West has not let go, and East Germans see themselves as sharing a heritage as well as having much in common with those in the West. West German foreign policy continues to consider the GDR as a state within Germany, worthy of a special relationship. The GDR does not reject many of the features of this policy. Even a downplaying of the German question in favor of closer relations between the West and East in Europe, submerging the future of Germany into the future of Europe, is seen by some as accepting the realities without sacrificing a future reunification in a different form. The 1950s still held the hope of reunification in a national state, but the future now means to some a striving toward a close relationship between the two Germanies that would bridge the political and social frontiers. Some discussions of the future of the German question turn on solutions other than the reestablishment of a German nation-state.

Second, the Federal Republic of Germany, a strong economic power, plays an increasingly important role in Europe. The appointment of a German as secretary-general of NATO underscores a new status for Bonn. Previously decried as an economic giant but a foreign policy pigmy, the West German state is quietly taking more of a leadership role. As all political parties talk about Europe, and the German stake in Europe, West German chancellor Helmut Kohl assumed the six-month presidency of the European Community in 1988 with a popular view of him as a "Euro-chancellor." The European Community has emerged as a major world economic force, and despite its internal problems, it has expanded its influence. The weakness of the Soviet economy, and the related problems in Eastern Europe have encouraged the development of better relations between the East and West in Europe. In any such development, the relationship between the two German states becomes a factor.

Thus, the German question has become even more a European question, in which the Soviet union can still make another offer.[15] This is a new dimension for the United States, and for West and East Europeans as well. The Soviets hold a number of possibilities open, and researchers carefully dissect and analyze each new emanation from Moscow. The Federal Republic of Germany has not found a solution to the German question, but neither has it put the issue to rest. There is no reunification on the horizon, but the differences between the German states have not yet led clearly to the point that each considers the other as foreign, despite those on both sides of the Elbe who believe that the two have drifted so far apart that there will be no return. The question of German identity is a significant part of the German question itself. Germany has left the postwar period, and the German question is a part of the new Europe.

NOTES

1. Wolf D. Gruner. *Die deutsche Frage: Ein Problem der europäischen Geschichte seit 1800* (Munich: C. H. Beck, 1985), 155–206 and Wolfgang-Uwe Friedrich, "The German Question Between West and East," *Aussenpolitik* 3 (1987): 224–57.
2. Günther Wagenlehner, ed., *Die deutsche Frage und die internationale Sicherheit* (Koblenz: Bernard und Graefe, 1988).
3. Ernst Weisenfeld, *Welches Deutschland soll es sein?—Frankreich und die deutsche Einheit seit 1945* (Munich: C. H. Beck, 1986), 29–49.
4. Speech by Foreign Minister Hans-Dietrich Genscher on November 13, 1980, as cited in Hans-Dietrich Genscher, *Deutsche Aussenpolitik* (Bonn: Aktuell, 1981), 290–305.
5. "Remarks by President Reagan Concerning the Federal Republic of Germany and Western Security, April 25, 1983," *Documents on Germany, 1944–1985* (Washington: United States Department of State Publication 9446, 1986), 1362–63.
6. *Dokumente zur Berlin-Frage 1967–1986* (Munich: R. Oldenbourg, 1987).
7. *Dokumente des Geteilten Deutschland*, vol. 2, *Seit 1968*, ed. Ingo von Münch (Stuttgart: Alfred Kröner, 1974), 94–108, 301–46.
8. Rolf Steininger, *Eine vertane Chance: Die Stalin-Note vom 10. März 1952 und die Wiedervereinigung* (Berlin: J. H. W. Dietz, 1985) and the opposing view by Wilhelm G. Grewe, *Die deutsche Frage in der Ost-West Spannung* (Herford: Busse Seewald, 1986).
9. *Materialien zum Bericht zur Lage der Nation im geteilten Deutschland 1987* (Bonn: Bundesministerium für innerdeutsche Beziehungen, 1987), 626–35.
10. Klaus Lange, ed., *Aspekte der deutschen Frage* (Herford: Busse Seewald, 1986).
11. *Innerdeutsche Beziehungen: Die Entwicklung der Beziehungen zwischen der Bundesrepublik Deutschland und der Deutschen Demokratischen Republik* (Bonn: Bundesministerium für innerdeutsche Beziehungen, 1986).
12. "Gemeinsames SPD-SED-Papier: Die Streit der Ideologien und die gemeinsame Sicherheit," *Texte zur Deutschlandpolitik*, Series 3, vol. 5— 1987 (Bonn: Bundesministerium für innerdeutsche Beziehungen, 1988), 171–181.
13. Helmut Kohl, Speech on the Occasion of the Visit of Secretary Honecker on September 7, 1987, as cited in *Texte zur Deutschland politik*, Series 3, vol. 5—1987 (Bonn: Bundesministerium für innerdeutsche Beziehungen, 1988), 149–199 and Dorothee Wilms, Speech at the Consortium for Atlantic Studies at Arizona State University on September

24, 1987 (Bonn: Bundesministerium für innerdeutsche Beziehungen, 1988).

14. Werner Weidenfeld, *Die Identität der Deutschen* (Bonn: Schriftenreihe der Bundeszentrale für politische Bildung, 200, 1983), 13–49.

15. Wolfgang Pfeiler, *Deutschlandpolitische Optionen der Sowjetunion*, Forschungsbericht 63 der Konrad-Adenauer-Stiftung (Melle: Knoth, 1987).

2
ANTI-AMERICANISM AND THE STRUGGLE FOR A WEST GERMAN IDENTITY

Andrei S. Markovits

THE PROBLEM

1986 represented a major watershed in the political culture of German-American relations. For the first time since 1945, more German citizens liked and trusted the leader of the Soviet Union than the president of the United States. While all surveys have to be interpreted with a grain of salt and this particular one may say more about the popular appeal of Mikhail Gorbachev and Ronald Reagan as individuals rather than the feelings engendered in the German population by their respective countries and political systems, there can be no doubt as to the significance of this finding in the German context. Mikhail Gorbachev seems to have won his popularity contest with Ronald Reagan in virtually every West European country, and yet nowhere has this created astonishment and apprehension among European and American elites comparable to the West German findings. The reasons for this "German exception" are quite evident. Whereas in the case of Britain, France, Italy, as well as the Scandinavian and Benelux countries these findings—though startling and somewhat disturbing to American officials—remained discrete and self-contained, in the context of the Federal Republic they embodied only part of a much larger whole best described by what the French so aptly have called *les incertitudes allemandes*.

It is the argument of this essay that Gorbachev's victory over

Reagan for the affection of the West German public is deeply linked to the still unresolved "German question" and the continued search for "German identity." In contrast to *any* other European country where the Gorbachev-Reagan popularity contest *never* attained any deeper implications for that particular country's political culture and relationship with the United States, this is not the case for the Federal Republic. Beneath the visible tip of changed percentages in the West Germans' perception of and affection for America and Americans lies a murky and huge iceberg of unresolved German history whose thawing over the next few decades will cause a lot of flooding and turmoil for all involved in navigating these uncharted and troubled waters. As a consequence of the Third Reich's destruction and Germany's broken national identity ever since, the United States has assumed a very special role in the formation and weaning of the political reality known as West Germany, something the United States has not replicated anywhere else in Western Europe and perhaps not even in Japan as a consequence of that country's continued cohesion as one sovereign entity.

The special nature of German-American—as opposed to British-American, French-American, or Dutch-American—relations clearly lies in the broken nature of Germany's national identity and historical legacy. For just as in West Germany, so, too, has the United States continued to exert a hegemonic authority in military and political relations vis-à-vis virtually all Western European countries since the end of World War II. Again, in a clear parallel with the German situation, the United States emerged all over Western Europe as the first and foremost economic and cultural power since 1945. And yet, American missiles and Coca-Cola embodied a very different symbolic—thus political—texture in West Germany as compared to any other West European country. Both have been appreciated or rejected by different people at different times in France, Britain, or Italy; in no instance, however, did American missiles or Coca-Cola play a key part in the post–World War II identity formation of the French, British, or Italians. One could take or leave either (as in the case of the French who decidedly opted for Coca-Cola and spurned American missiles as early as 1966) or both without any of the choices implying something beyond the manifest nature of the choices themselves. In other words, in contrast to the German case, there never existed a meta level of understanding and experience beyond the manifestly political and cultural in America's relations with the countries of Western Europe. Without a doubt, the creation of the cold war and Germany's position as a frontline state in an antagonistically divided Europe made American penetration of the Federal Republic's political, military, economic, and cultural life a lot more pronounced than anywhere else in the West. But more than geography, it was the broken continuity of German history and the ensuing uncertainty of German national identity which lent the United States willy-nilly a role in Germany's post-1945 existence that in this form exists nowhere else in Europe. The United States has been qualitatively different toward the Federal Republic than toward any other political and military ally, just as Americanism as a sociocultural phenomenon has meant different things to post–World War II Germans than to other Europeans. This essay argues that the current re-definition by West Germans of their relationship to the United States has to be analyzed in the context of the Federal Republic's search for a national identity. As such, this "anti-Americanism" is quite different from its more common variety ubiquitously found elsewhere in Western Europe. Thus, a mere comparison of percentages as to how many people like or dislike America in West Germany in contrast to other European countries simply misses the point because it cannot help but fail to account for the different qualitative textures which these anti-Americanisms entail. In the German context, anti-Americanism is part of a larger search for German—*and* "federal republican"—identity of which the *Historikerstreit*, the Bitburg incident, the Fassbinder controversy, the peace movement, neutralism, and pacifism form disparate, contradictory, even mutually exclusive and hostile, yet integral components. At the time of writing it remains completely unclear as to where this incipient search for national identity will lead the Federal Republic, Germans, and Europeans in the years to come. There can be no question, however, that recent years have witnessed an increasing shift in intellectual interest and political debate in the Federal Republic from the republic to the nation which—hardly by chance—was accompanied by a parallel shift from the prominence of the social sciences (notice, for example, the telling identification of political science in the Federal Republic as "democratic" science) primarily to that of history. Suffice it to say that forty years after the establishment of the Federal Republic and forty-four years following the end of World War II, the "German question" continues to remain alive and well on Europe's political stage. For the remainder of this chapter, I propose to analyze merely the negative aspects of German-American relations in this process. In a short-handed, thus flawed, manner, I will hereafter refer to this complex web of negative attitudes and wary positions by the Germans vis-à-vis the United States and things American as "anti-Americanism."

ANTI-AMERICANISM: A HISTORICAL ANALYSIS

Feelings about America have riled Europe at least since the establishment of the United States in 1776. While there obviously always existed a lot of admiration for the "New World," negative attitudes and opinions prevailed, especially among the Old World's intellectuals of the left and the right. Europeans always felt very ambivalent toward this transatlantic European extension which, in so many ways, was quite similar to their own world, yet in other respects represented something completely new and alien. Few European intellectuals remained neutral toward America. America, whether good or bad, simply mattered and, as such, engendered debate, controversy, and passion.

Because America mattered, it always symbolized a lot more than it actually represented in reality. Americanism has stood for modernity, modernization, mass democracy, mass production, mass culture, and mass communication, just to mention a few of the most common associations it has created in European intellectual thought in the course of two centuries. Depending on the normative orientation which one developed in relation to these phenomena, one held pro- or anti-American feelings, opinions, and attitudes which, as a consequence, had little to do with actual knowledge of or experience with Americans, the United States, or things American. Thus developed certain preconceived notions about America which continue to color Europeans' view of the United States to this day.

From the late eighteenth century (i.e., the founding of the United States), throughout the nineteenth and well into the twentieth century, a strongly negative assessment of things American outdistanced any positive views of the United States and its inhabitants on the part of German intellectual elites. Both rightist and leftist thinkers placed German "Kultur" above American "civilization." From virtually opposite vantage points, critics of the left and the right constantly decried this American civilization as overly materialist, vulgar, uncouth, instrumental, isolationist, and provincial, yet at the same time also as expansive, predatory, irresistible, and thus dangerous.

Beginning with Hegel, virtually all pre–twentieth-century German intellectuals condemned what they perceived as the political immaturity of the United States, as manifested by its lack of a European-style state. As long as it failed to establish such a state—and the prognosis looked bad given the size of the country as well as its civil turbulence (which was an outgrowth of its immigrant and multiethnic population)—the United States, Hegel concluded, would remain forever peripheral to world history. Accordingly, Heine wrote of America: it was a "colossal jail of freedom" where "the mob, the most disgusting tyrant of all" exercised "its crude authority." Heine continued: "You dear German farmers! Go to America! There, neither princes nor nobles exist; there, all people are equal; there, all are the same boors!" Jacob Burckhardt equated what he and many European intellectuals perceived as the a- and anti-historical nature of American society with barbarism. Bruckhardt discussed the "ahistorical *Bildungsmensch*" who, so Burckhardt argued, dominates the New World and creates its materialist blandness, monotony, mediocrity, and uniformity, and whose only escape, therefore, lies in an inevitable—and pathetic—imitation of the Old World's mores and values. Nikolaus Lenau, a major America enthusiast before his trip to the United States, was so disappointed in all things American after his arrival to the New World that he returned to Germany in a completely dejected state, informing his countrymen that there were "serious and deep reasons why there were no nightingales and no singing birds at all" in this awful country of "worn out people" and "scorched forests." Whether these intellectuals had actually visited the United States, as had Lenau, or whether they made their judgments from afar (as did Heine, Burckhardt, and Nietzsche), mattered little in terms of their negative assessment for the German *Bildungsbürgertum* well into the twentieth century. This view saw America as a soulless juggernaut, threatening *Kultur*, beauty, and authenticity—which only a long history could bestow upon a people—with crassness, materialism, and cheap imitation. The very essence of this upstart country was the destruction of its own *Kultur* as evidenced by the gradual genocide of the native Americans.

It would, of course, be remiss not to mention the existence of a strongly pro-American attitude among German intellectuals of the nineteenth and twentieth centuries. Johann Wolfgang von Goethe's famous "Amerika, Du hast es besser" denoted unquestioned respect on the part of certain German elites for the novelty, originality, and dynamism which informed the "New World's" existence as opposed to the tradition-bound conventionalism of Europe. It should be noted that both Karl Marx and Friedrich Engels spent considerable time analyzing and interpreting events in the New World for Europe's bourgeois readership, most often in a favorable light. These two, as well as a number of their socialist followers and co-ideologues, rejoiced in America's bourgeois republicanism and its material populism, very much hoping that Europe's working classes would be encouraged in their political struggles by the liberating experiences which they detected in American social developments. For Marx and Engels the victory of the Union over the Confederacy represented an event of world historical proportions in which progress clearly prevailed over reaction, hardly the case on an autocratic European continent dominated by the Habsburgs, Hohenzollerns, and Romanovs.

In addition to Marx, Engels, and many of their socialist disciples, it was mainly a small group of German liberal republicans who extolled the virtues of the New World. Fascinated by America's federalism, some of these individuals voiced their pro-Americanism in 1848 during the national assembly in Frankfurt. To German liberals, the constitutional arrangement of the United States remained a model well into the twentieth century. With the complete victory of the conservative political and cultural order following the ill-fated Paulskirche movement, these liberals—and a few non-Marxist radical democrats—faded into Germany's political and cultural background. Some of them took their admiration of the United States sufficiently seriously to emigrate to the New World. While in the Weimar Republic a strong cult of pro-Americanism continued to influence a number of intellectuals (such as, for example, Bertolt Brecht and Siegfried Kracauer), with it subsequently attaining nearly hegemonic proportions in certain academic circles of the Federal Republic's early years, there is no doubt in my mind that a negative (at best an ambivalent) as opposed to a positive assessment of the United States and things American has continued to prevail in German intellectual discourse to this day. I see little evidence of this changing in the near future.

From the latter part of the nineteenth century through the Weimar Republic and well into the present day of the Federal Republic, one can distinguish four major types of anti-Americanism in the public discourse of German intellectual life. As depicted in fourpart table 2.1, one has to distinguish between the anti-Americanism of the left and the right, just as one has to differentiate between what I have labeled "cultural" and "political" anti-Americanism.

For the Left, America is dangerous and negative by virtue of its power as the leading capitalist actor in a capitalist-dominated world. The United States is seen as dominating, domineering, and intimidating by virtue of its might and its willingness to use it virtually without abandon. By being the world's leading capitalist power, the United States—for the German Left—cannot but be imperialist, thus predatory, bellicose, and brutal. By virtue of the primacy of political economy as opposed to culture for any Left, there can be no doubt that the German Left focused its criticism of the United States on the political as opposed to the cultural. In addition to a structural critique of the general political arrangements in the United States, the German Left also paid considerable attention to particular American policies which it saw as prima facie evidence for America's unsavory role in the world. Yet, the Left, too, addressed the cultural dimensions of Americanism in a negative way. Rather than dwell on the qualitative inferiority of American culture in comparison to European (specifically German) as the Right has continued to do, the Left centered its rejection of American culture in the context of American capitalist hegemony. Thus, for German leftist intellectuals, Coca-Cola and McDonald's ought to be rejected not primarily as a consequence of their inherent qualitative inferi-

ority (though I continue to be amazed at the high level of unadulter-
ated elitism among West German leftists) but as an expression of the
ubiquity and uniformity of American capitalism.

Contrast to this the German Right's anti-Americanism. In the political realm, rather than perceive the United States as too powerful
and imposing as does the Left, the Right has consistently viewed the
United States as a paper tiger which is all talk and no action. For
the right, the United States has always been unable and unwilling
to assume world leadership which would behoove its size and overall importance and which the rest of the world so desperately needs

Table 2.1
Schematization of Anti-Americanism in Germany Since the Late
Nineteenth Century

	The Left	The Right
Political	America, as the world's fore-most capitalist country, is en-gaged in imperialism. It is the leader of world reaction. America is a predatory power which is bent on totally con-trolling the world. Vis-à-vis the Federal Republic of Ger-many as a whole, the United States is viewed as an actor which strove for the estab-lishment of West Germany at the direct expense of a united, demilitarized, and neutral Germany. While the '68ers saw the capitalist Fed-eral Republic as an accom-plice of the United States, the left of the 1980s sees the FRG increasingly as America's vic-tim.	America, because of its es-sentially vulgar nature, is not equipped to be the much-needed leader of the free, white, and Western world. Because of its lack of tradi-tional elites and its permis-siveness, America's political system is disorganized, con-fused, and completely inap-propriate to govern the United States adequately, let alone the world. Thus, Euro-peans and Germans would do well not to trust the United States because it is structur-ally and historically incapa-ble of furnishing serious po-litical leadership. America, ultimately, is weak, shallow, naive, inexperienced, and no match for the adversaries of the free world.

	The Left	The Right
Cultural	American culture is seen as the expression of an alienated, brutal capitalist society which has produced soulless, plastic, and inauthentic artifacts solely for the profits of huge companies. The American "culture industry" produces cheap, essentially worthless things for a quick fix in a mass market populated by misguided, manipulated, and exploited individuals who are stripped of their collectivity by the inherent divisiveness of a capitalist-dominated society. McDonald's, Dallas, Dynasty, and Coca-Cola do not only lack intrinsic worth, but serve the capitalist class by making it lots of money while at the same time keeping the American population duped, inactive, and divided.	American culture is not worthy of the name. The United States, because of its vulgar nature, has never been capable of producing anything of lasting value. Worse, it has used its newly acquired financial might to buy real, that is, European, culture and/or imitate it in a crass style behooving the nouveau riche that the United States basically will always remain. The danger of American culture, however, is its mass appeal which has made it so successful among Europe's masses as well. Thus, American culture is not only worthless and shallow, but also dangerous and corrupting by virtue of its universal appeal.
The U.S.	Basically dangerous because of its power	Basically dangerous because of its weakness

in a postcolonial, essentially rudderless age threatened by chaos and communist expansion. The Right never trusted the populist, egalitarian, essentially democratic aspects of American life which it always regarded as vulgar, plebeian, and profoundly weak. To the German Right, the chaotic nature of American politics represented merely another symptom of the weak, immature, and permissive character of a country without traditional elites and established statecraft. German rightists have always regarded the United States as an inadequate replacement of the old European powers in leading the world. They continue to view Americans as confused, uneducated, unsophisticated, gullible, naive, provincial, and essentially weak political actors in an increasingly complex and dangerous world. Just as politics and economics dominate culture for the Left, the inverse is the case for the Right. American politics, in the view of German rightists, cannot help but be in a shambles because American culture is inferior and shallow. Adding insult to injury, it is precisely the inferiority and shallowness of American culture which makes it so acceptable to the masses of the world. Thus, the German Right does not only bemoan the inadequate quality of Coca-Cola and McDonald's, but it casts a fearful eye on how effectively and irresistibly these products—in addition to many others—have become part of contemporary West German culture, as well thereby perhaps permanently undermining the superior values of authentic German *Volkskultur*.

For both, the Left and the Right, America lacks true soul, understanding, and authenticity. It seems artificial, plastic, and fake. In addition to being inauthentic, the United States appears to its German critics devoid of solidarity. Whatever the context and whoever the observer, the centerpiece of German anti-Americanism sooner or later rests on a view of American life as anomic, artificial, and without much-needed solidarities, be they those of class, religion, culture, or Volk. Clearly, little good could emanate from such a construct for its own well-being, let alone for that of Germany and the rest of the world.

Whereas much of the content of these four categories of anti-Americanism also exists outside Germany, there is another dimension which has made the history of anti-Americanism in the Federal Republic quite unique in the post–World War II European context. I am referring to the particularly German confluence of all aspects of the just-described anti-Americanism on the one hand with the strong post-1949 urge to identify with America and things American on the other. Nowhere in post-1945 Europe did the United States assume such a central and existentially fundamental role in the conduct of everyday life and the construct of political identity as it did in the Federal Republic. Of course, the Marshall Plan left its imprint on countries such as Italy, France, and Austria, to name but a few. And undoubtedly, the thorough Americanization of contemporary British life, though facilitated by a common cultural heritage and the strong bonds of a common language, began in earnest with the invasion of the "Yanks" during World War II. The two world wars had irrevocably defeated the Old World and beckoned the American Century. But only in Germany was there a *Stunde Null*. Only in Germany did a gaping hole emerge which still remains far from filled forty-four years after the war and forty years following the establishment of two sovereign German states. It was *faute de mieux* that the United States and Americanism stepped into this hole from which they are now being gradually displaced in a process that will be lengthy and is already painful for Germans and Americans alike. For if West German public life had primarily been dominated by the anti-American sentiments and attitudes described above, there would not have been any conflicts and complications. Instead, on the surface the Federal Republic became engulfed by a pro-Americanism which was probably second to none in its fervor anywhere in post–World War II Europe while the old—and renewed—anti-Americanisms coexisted. America and Americanism, already evoking complex emotions for all Europeans, entered the murkier realm of identity formation only for the West Germans. Thus, in the Federal Republic, a qualitatively different degree of complexity was added to the old "America" problem among European intellectuals, in the sense that the United States and things American became inextricably linked to the search for a new German and/or "federal republican" identity, with nothing comparable occurring anywhere else among America's allies in Europe, possibly the world. Nowhere in Europe—with the possible exception of Australia—was the common belief in the evils of communism as essential to the formation of postwar political identity as was the case in the Federal Republic. Indeed, this commonly shared distrust of the Soviet Union and communism created an important bond between the United States and the Federal Republic and formed a major pillar of what was to become the much-vaunted "specialness" of German-American relations. While this "specialness" continues to survive into the fifth decade of the Federal Republic's existence, it is confronted with increasingly demanding strains which test the patience and perseverance of both partners to the detriment of the hitherto mutually beneficial relationship. It bears mention, of course, that this "special" relationship was from its very inception profoundly unequal

in America's favor which is not to say that the West Germans did
not derive major benefits from it on all levels. But therein lay many
of the problems which have since emerged. Had the United States
only been repressive and exploitative vis-à-vis the Federal Republic,
there would not have developed any conflict and ambivalence by
the Germans toward the United States and Americans. A relatively
straightforward aversion would have arisen with little need for explanation and analysis. The United States, however, resembles a
rich uncle with annoying foibles, much generosity, and definite
demands who is admired *and* needed by an initially poor, young,
and talented nephew. The nephew may even appreciate the uncle
and emulate him. But would he love him? Would he accept him
without any resistance and resentment always knowing—and being
reminded of—the uncle's initial generosity with material and spiritual support? Would there not be constant jockeying for more control on the part of the uncle and greater autonomy on the part of the
increasingly independent nephew? It is in this dynamic, unique to
German-American relations in the context of postwar European history, that anti-Americanism attained a special quality in West
Germany. I will now briefly turn to a discussion of strains in German-
American relations on a state level which I see as structurally important corollaries to the growing anti-American sentiments in virtually all segments of the Federal Republic's citizenry. Since governmental relationships have major effects on popular attitudes and
opinion, a brief sketch of the lasting troubles between the Federal
Republic and the United States is necessary for an appropriate con-
textualization of anti-Americanism in the West Germany of the 1990s.
The chapter will conclude with some speculative assessments regarding future developments.

THE GOVERNMENTAL CONTEXT

Let us not forget that the starting point of the political relationship
between the Federal Republic and the United States began with the
two countries being on opposite ends of a power continuum: The
United States enjoyed a hegemonic position in the world perhaps
never before attained by any country; Germany, in contrast, lay

destroyed, morally defeated, politically weak and—so it seemed—permanently cowed. The last forty years have witnessed a gradual but certain rapprochement between these two countries on the previously mentioned imaginary continuum of power, with the Federal Republic slowly approaching the midpoint "from below" and the United States "from above." While it is clear that the respective trajectories by the two countries are only in small part a result of the changing nature of their mutual relationship, there can be no doubt that these trajectories have altered the objective position of each country vis-à-vis the other and concomitantly changed each country's perception of the other. With the Federal Republic's emergence as Europe's leading political and economic power, it was simply inevitable that significant rifts developed in German-American relations. Add to that the United States' moral decline as a consequence of its Vietnam fiasco, Watergate, and Irangate, as well as a continuing record of scandalous involvements in other parts of the world, and it is not hard to see why even such devoted (by necessity *and* by choice) allies as the West Germans have developed a certain wariness regarding their relationship to America. The following areas of dispute will continue to provide constant strain in German-American relations for the foreseeable future.

Détente and Ostpolitik

The Social Democrats' most successful and lasting legacy has been without any doubt the permanent institutionalization of détente in Central Europe by means of Ostpolitik. Nowhere have the tangible benefits and genuine gains of détente been more visible on a daily and human level than in the Federal Republic. While Germans experienced détente as an improvement in their everyday existence, Americans—at best—maintained a detached and intellectual relationship to this political construct. Briefly put, détente and Ostpolitik have worked without qualifications for the Germans; they did not for the Americans. Thus, every West German government—regardless of party composition and coloration—will continue to foster détente, ever mindful of seizing any opportunity which could potentially improve the Federal Republic's relations with the East, most notably East Germany.

At the core of Ostpolitik lies Deutschlandpolitik. Whereas virtually nobody in the Federal Republic—excepting the political Right's most revanchist and also unrealistic wing—yearns for an actual reunification of the two Germanies, there exists a broad political consensus (from green to black) for a continued intensification of West Germany's relations with the German Democratic Republic, culminating perhaps in some sort of association or condominium in the future. The road to such a rapprochement with the GDR, as every West German government fully knows, leads through Moscow. Hence, regardless of the particular charm of a specific Soviet leader and his genuine popularity with the West German public where "Gorbymania" clearly attained its peak in the Western world, there are compelling structural reasons for the Federal Republic to continue improving the already good relations with the U.S.S.R. This courting of the Soviet Union will not "neutralize" the Federal Republic. Nor will this process lead to West Germany's "Finlandization." It will, however, accentuate Germany's long-standing tradition of "Zwischenkultur" which will hardly endear it to its Western allies, most notably France and the United States. To the extent that the United States will continue its global rivalry with the Soviet Union even in a period of mutual coexistence and respect, any of the Federal Republic's maneuvers to improve its standing with the Soviets will incur at least the Americans' suspicion if not their ire. As the Federal Republic pragmatically enhances its instrumental relationship to Moscow, the old bogeymen of the Soviet enemy and of communism will increasingly fade into the background. This demystification of an old enemy will lead to the furthering of an already existent hiatus between the American and the West German political cultures regarding the role of communism in the world. With American attitudes not expected to change, it seems likely that the mutually bonding "Feindbild" will have vanished from the West German scene in the course of the next decade.

One need not be an economic determinist to mention the central importance of Osthandel to Ostpolitik. With the Federal Republic's eminent position as the West's leading trader with the Soviet Union and Eastern Europe likely to continue—perhaps even expand— there exist ample economic reasons for the West Germans to improve their relations with the East. COMECON (the communist equivalent of the European Community)-imposed embargoes or not, economic rivalry provides yet another point of friction which is most likely to burden German-American relations in the foreseeable future.

Economic Rivalry and Differences

It would be well beyond the scope of this chapter to analyze the reasons for the peculiar situation in which the two defeated powers of World War II, Japan and Germany, find themselves today in the role of being America's most successful economic challengers. Surely, however, this fact has no been lost on any of the three participants. For the duration of America's unquestioned political hegemony, economic discord between the Federal Republic and the United States could easily be sublimated by the former's adherence to the "economic giant political dwarf" syndrome. This has become increasingly untenable with the actual and perceived decline of American hegemony in the world, most certainly in Europe, in the course of the 1970s and 1980s, and the partly concomitant rise of the Federal Republic as a major political actor on the European continent, especially in the area of East-West relations. Moreover, the internationalization of global economic relations in which a number of epicenters (Tokyo, London, Zurich, Frankfurt, and Hong Kong, in addition to New York) have developed, has added yet another dimension to the weakening of the United States vis-à-vis its allies, particularly the Federal Republic and Japan.

Conflicts between the United States and West Germany in economic matters are far from novel and are bound to be exacerbated in the years to come. One can expect them in a number of already existing areas: First and foremost, serious tension will arise around the growing American tendency toward protectionism. With the Federal Republic's economy anchored in a forty-year tradition of export orientation in which the American market has played an increasingly prominent, though far from preeminent, role, any intensification of protectionist tendencies on the part of the United States will meet with the Federal Republic's certain disapproval, perhaps even eventual retaliation. With every fourth job in West Germany fully dependent on the country's export prowess, it is rather unlikely to expect any change in the Federal Republic's long-held strategy of free-market-based export as the centerpiece of its economic stability and material well-being. This is not to say that the West Germans cannot be accused of considerable hypocrisy on the issue of protectionism. Ask any American producer of telecommunications equipment when they last succeeded in breaking the quasi-monopolistic and highly protected collusion between Siemens and the Bundespost for the Federal Republic's lucrative multibillion-dollar communications market. Surely the answer will be laced with sentiments of disappointment, derision, and hopelessness. Suffice it to say that while past bilateral trade relations between the United States and the Federal Republic were far from constantly harmonious, they were on the whole amicable and devoid of serious, disruptive conflict. With the increasing presence of protectionism in the generally accepted discourse of trade relations between the United States and its major trading partners, among which the Federal Republic plays a preeminent role, German-American relations will be certain to experience an additional strain in the years to come.

Inextricably tied to the issue of protectionism is the uncertainty of the exchange rates between the mark and the dollar. The fluctuations of the dollar have long been irritating to many Germans, and indeed have reinforced the growing anti-American sentiment which in a wholesale fashion blames the United States for all economic difficulties incurred by West Germany in its global trade relations. Thus, it is interesting to note that whatever the course of the dollar was over the decade of the 1980s, many Germans saw in its particular value the major culprit of their own economic ills. When the dollar was extremely low vis-à-vis the mark at the beginning of the 1980s, many people in Germany saw in this an attempt by the United States to displace the Federal Republic's exports from the American market and their general weakening vis-à-vis the American competition in the world as a whole. When the dollar's fortunes reversed themselves by the middle of the decade and reached plateaus which were the highest since the breakdown of the Bretton Woods compact in the early 1970s, many Germans blamed the United States' policy of high interest rates for diverting German investment to the more lucrative American money markets. Furthermore, a high dollar also meant a considerable increase in the Federal Republic's energy bills, since virtually all of West Germany's oil has to be imported and paid for in dollars. Thus, the strong dollar suddenly became the Federal Republic's bane by adding to the lack of domestic investment and consumption in a period of growing unemployment which had well exceeded the shameful number of over two million registered persons by the middle of the decade. With the Plaza agreement of September 1986 once again reverting the fate of the dollar from highflier to pedestrian, Germans resumed blaming the United States for backdoor protectionism since they viewed the Treasury's strategy of letting the value of the dollar drop as a direct attempt by the United States to weaken exports to that country, a measure certainly destined to affect West Germany's export sector in an adverse manner. In short, whatever the Americans do with the dollar's value, the Germans grumble. A high dollar is seen inimically as is a low dollar—or no dollar opposing any substantial reform of the world's currency system which would replace the dollar's present position as the lead currency (*Leitwährung*) with a basket of currencies in which the mark would inevitably be accorded center stage. Thus, as in so many aspects of America's presence in West German reality, the United States remains betwixt and between: While still needed it becomes increasingly unwanted.

Different Vantage Points in Global Politics

Ultimately, of course, the long-existing cleavage between the fact that the United States is a global power and the Federal Republic a European one will continue to dictate the often conflicting strategies pursued by each of these two countries vis-à-vis each other and the rest of the world. But more than in the past, this conflict will be burdened by mixed messages and an always-present cluster of contradictory and mutually exclusive wishes and hopes about each other which, however, will remain confined to a meta level of communication. Thus, while one part of the Federal Republic's political reality would undoubtedly like to see the United States continue— even intensify—its hegemonic role as the leader of the Western world, an equally important part would rejoice in a less omnipresent, dominant, and interventionist America. What complicates matters is the fact that it would be far too simplistic to associate the former position with the political Right and the latter with the Left in the Federal Republic. Rather, these mixed messages and contradictory wishes cut across conventional party allegiances, increasingly forming alliances on a case-by-case basis. Since part of these reactions in the Federal Republic arises in response to American measures, the fact that things are equally murky on this side of the Atlantic only furthers the contingent nature of the situation. For just as the consensus of what the Germans really want from the Americans has gradually evaporated in the course of the 1980s, so, too, it has become unclear what the Americans want from the Germans. While on the one hand there exists an influential strain in American wishes and thought which would like to give the Germans a lot more global power and responsibilities than they currently have, this, on the other hand, is countered by an equally strong belief that any such developments would come at the expense of the United States' hegemonic role in the world and its receding position vis-à-vis the Soviet Union in Europe. Moreover, one still finds a certain reluctance among some Americans to augment the Germans' already substantial power which in turn is also echoed among many Germans themselves. Paralleling the murkiness of the situation in the Federal Republic, in the United States, too, it seems quite futile to align any of these views with the support of either of the two major political parties. In short, perceptions and expectations of each other's roles—if not the roles themselves—have become increasingly blurred over the last few years with no discernible signs for any clearing up in the near future.

All in all, America's role as a global power and its concomitant neglect of Europe in German eyes will continue to irk policymakers in the Federal Republic. At the same time, a growing number of West German citizens will in fact push for an even greater neglect by the United States, which in this case will be labeled "noninvolvement," "noninterference," even "decolonization" by the fringes of the Left and the Right. There is no doubt, however, that to the United States the Federal Republic will continue to be only one among many global commitments which makes West Germany's presence in the daily lives of American politicians and citizens quite marginal. That the same does not pertain to America's presence in Germany is prima facie evidence of the United States' existence as a global power throughout the forty-year existence of the Federal Republic. While this is unlikely to change, it remains an open question as to how the Federal Republic's political public will continue to relate to this rather extraordinary post–World War II arrangement.

CONCLUSION

This chapter has argued that the special nature of America's position in the Federal Republic has largely been a corollary to and consequence of the interrupted and complicated development of a German identity in a post–World War II Europe. It is in the context of this "German exceptionalism" that relations with the United States and all things American have experienced a qualitatively different existence in the Federal Republic as compared to elsewhere in Europe. Thus, Americanism and anti-Americanism are rather *sui generis* in their texture and meaning to the political culture of the Federal Republic. After placing this very particular phenomenon in its historical setting, the chapter then delineated some areas of tension on the state level which will undoubtedly continue to strain German-American relations for years to come.

Ultimately, of course, anti-Americanism in the Federal Republic is a political construct. Its manifestations, appeals, and relevance depend entirely on the political situation wherein they occur. Thus, just as it is virtually impossible to predict the future political developments of a country as complex as the Federal Republic, it is equally futile to hazard predictions concerning anti-Americanism's future role, form, and content in the Federal Republic's fifth decade. Nevertheless, in line with the argument presented in the preceding pages, it seems quite likely that the complex of anti-Americanism will remain closely tied to the increasingly pertinent debate in the Federal Republic about German identity, nationalism, patriotism, and federal republican consciousness—in short the West Germans' emotional and political self-perception vis-à-vis Western Europe, Eastern Europe, the German Democratic Republic, and the Soviet Union. Thus, in the Federal Republic, more than anywhere else, the parameters of Americanism and anti-Americanism will continue to be formed well beyond the immediate confines of a bilateral relationship with the United States proper. It seems certain, though, that in the Federal Republic America as an image, construct, and discourse will remain a lot more than the United States actually embodies in its material and tangible presence. America will continue to stand for progress, growth, technological wizardry, and unbound opportunity, but also for crime, delay, recklessness, and immaturity. As to which of the two sides will prevail for which group under what conditions remains an empirical question closely tied to the concrete conduct and actual outcome of the political process in the Federal Republic's future.

3
A CHANGING SOCIAL CONSCIOUSNESS

Russell J. Dalton

The German culture and social consciousness are an enduring scholarly interest for students of modern Europe because of the intriguing nature of the culture and its influence on the course of history. In part, this fascination is based on the complexity of the German social fabric. This is, after all, the birthplace of Karl Marx as well as the nation that brought Adolf Hitler and his Nazi ideology to power. It is a nation renowned for its writers and composers, but is equally known for its political excesses. In answering the question "What does it mean to be German?" *federal president* Richard von Weizsäcker cites the rich diversity of the German cultural heritage:

German Classicism hoped to redefine us into a people of poets and thinkers. In the Biedermeier period, a politically impotent dullness and naivete was held to be a German characteristic. At one time people regarded the passion and force of the 'Sturm und Drang' as typically German; at another, Eichendorff's resonant songs of the soul and of Nature. Sometimes our special talent for music is seen, at others our alleged capacity for industry and discipline, which is applied to good ends as to very bad ones. Some deny us any capacity for elegance . . . while others detect the German spirit precisely in the polished language of Lessing, Heine or Nietzsche.[1]

Is it any wonder that the Germans remain uncertain about their cultural and political heritage?

Despite this diversity, research on the German social consciousness has focused on the aberrations of social values that supposedly contributed to the political failures of modern German regimes. For at least half a century this "German question" has been one of the central issues in the study of German culture and politics. The German question linked the frailty of Weimar democracy and the political excesses of the Third Reich to negative characteristics of

German culture. Social scientists inside and outside of the Federal Republic noted parallels between the authority relations within the traditional German family and individual orientations toward the state. The political intolerance of German politics was supposedly due to intolerance in German social relations. The apolitical and undemocratic orientations of postwar Germans appeared as a persisting trait in German culture.

While attempts to develop a national stereotype should always be suspect, empirical studies during the early postwar period found substantial justification for many of the negative characterizations of the German public. German social life was closely scrutinized by HICOG and OMGUS surveys during the period of Allied presence, and the picture they painted of the German social consciousness was often unflattering.[2] German attitudes toward politics reflected the legacy of prior authoritarian regimes, displaying disturbingly high levels of residual sympathy for the Nazi ideology and open doubts about democracy. Other studies found that more general social relations were tainted by intolerance, distrust, and social isolation.[3]

Ralf Dahrendorf's landmark study, *Society and Democracy in West Germany*, provided the most thorough description of the German social consciousness at the beginning of the Federal Republic, discussing both the general social norms and the specific political beliefs that were the basis of the "German question."[4] Although Dahrendorf was skeptical of attempts to explain German political development primarily in terms of national culture, a tautological exercise in his opinion, he nevertheless maintained that individuals adopt the "social roles" prescribed by prevalent social customs. Dahrendorf saw German norms as stressing private values and personal self-interest to the neglect of public values and community-mindedness. While his description of these norms contained many negative traits—indifference toward the weak, traces of authoritarianism, a strong preference for social order, an anxiety about competition and conflict, and a preference for hierarchic and bureaucratized patterns of social relations—Dahrendorf also felt that social and political change could redefine theses norms.

Perhaps even more amazing than the Wirtschaftswunder has been the transformation of many of these negative social norms over the past forty years. The closed, hostile, and inward-looking society that Dahrendorf and others described changed in fundamental ways. Individual values and the norms governing social and political behavior shed many of their premodern characteristics. Although no subsequent work has equalled the conceptual breadth of Dahrendorf's early study, an accumulation of evidence suggests that important aspects of the social norms he outlined are indeed changing.

This transformation of the West German social consciousness is part of an ongoing process of social and political change in the Federal Republic. During the first phase of this process the nation experienced the modernizing forces of Western culture that had, at least in part, bypassed Germany for much of the past century. The aristocratic tradition of the past was largely destroyed by the end of World War II, and a new social order grew up in its place. A democratic political system and more egalitarian social structure created a new standard for social relations. In short, the development of a relatively modern, open, and pluralist society inevitably changed many of the premodern social norms that Dahrendorf had observed, and moved the West German social consciousness closer to the norms expressed in other West European democracies.

A second factor redefining the German social consciousness was the Federal Republic's development of the characteristics of an advanced industrial society. Unprecedented affluence eventually lessened the salience of economic and security issues that had long been the primary goals of governments and the public. Growing access to information from the media and expanding educational opportunities broadened cultural horizons. The nation experienced one of the longest periods without war in modern German history. Changes in the social structure eroded traditional divisions, just as new bases of social stratification came to the fore.

These advanced industrial forces are introducing new elements into the German social consciousness, especially among younger generations. Having grown up in an affluent, pluralist social setting where economic well-being, personal security, and social stability seem assured, the values of many young people are changing to reflect an alternative view of life and societal goals. These so-called "postmaterial" values—self-expression, personal freedom, social equality, self-fulfillment—are markedly different from the economic and security concerns that still preoccupy many older Germans. The values provide an alternative social consciousness, or an *Alternativkultur,* that differs in fundamental ways from the dominant norms of the German social consciousness.

Few disagree that the Federal Republic has experienced fundamental cultural change during the postwar period, and the extensive writings on the topic by German authors attest to their awareness that German society and the public are changing. As many as a dozen books and innumerable articles have been written on this subject since 1980; the German literature on culture and value change is probably more extensive than in any other Western democracy. Certainly there are differences in interpreting the evidence, and differences in drawing implications—but nearly all agree that fundamental changes are occurring. This chapter reviews some of the basic questions of German social norms, first raised by Dahrendorf, to assess how much these aspects of the social consciousness have changed. Then, we consider how advanced industrialism and the value changes it stimulates are continuing the process of cultural change.

BECOMING MODERN

Germany is one nation where the stereotype of the culture is well known; in fact, too well known in some ways. German culture has been analyzed in extensive detail, with attention focused on the negative culture norms inherited from earlier periods. Dahrendorf's description of the social consciousness in postwar Germany provided the most comprehensive view of the German psyche, and the problematic traits that others had noted. For example, he observed that most individuals stressed private values over community-mindedness. These sentiments reflected a negative orientation toward others, leading to feelings of interpersonal distrust and social estrangement. At the same time, individuals relied on the advice of social institutions, such as the churches and unions, to set social norms and guide individual behavior. The combination of self-interest and reliance on external authority represents some of the basic characteristics of a premodern social consciousness.

While these negative characterizations of popular values and cultural norms were widely applicable during the immediate postwar years, many aspects of this social consciousness changed in the new environment of the Federal Republic. By examining the prominent features of the culture that Dahrendorf noted, we can determine how much change has occurred.

One of the traits most often associated with German culture is an unquestioning acceptance of authority. Scholars such as Theodor Adorno, Erich Fromm, and Erik Erikson maintained that authoritarian tendencies permeated German society, and began with social relations within the family. Authority patterns learned in the home carried over to politics, business, and other social relations. Dahrendorf observed that the authoritarian German father furnished a model for citizen acceptance of the Kaiser or the Führer:

The German father is, or at least used to be, a combination of judge and state attorney: presiding over his family, relentlessly prosecuting every sign of deviance, and settling all disputes by his supreme authority.[5]

Dahrendorf felt that the authoritarian values taught by the family were one of the reasons for the pathology of liberal democracy in Germany. While the model of the authoritarian family was more applicable earlier in this century, researchers observed traces of these tendencies during the early years of the Federal Republic. Gabriel Almond and Sidney Verba, for example, found that West Germans were less likely than either Americans or Britons to say that they participated in family decision making during their youth.[6] Furthermore, these childhood experiences were related to feelings about the contemporary political process. Other early opinion surveys depicted lingering authoritarian tendencies within the West German culture: excessive deference to authority, a failure to exercise individual responsibility, and a preference for strong leaders.

This authoritarian legacy was inconsistent with the postwar social system, and social norms gradually changed to reflect the new reality. For instance, data from the well-known public opinion institute, Allensbach, indicate that in 1951 few people (28 percent) named independence and free will as traits parents should emphasize in raising their children; these same two traits were the most common response (51 percent) in a 1976 replication of the question.[7] Among young adults in their twenties, those who are likely to actually have children, two-thirds said they would stress these two values. Conversely, the importance placed on obedience in child rearing declines over this same time period. Gerda Lederer's study of adolescent values documents a marked trend away from authoritarian values between 1945 and 1979.[8] By this latter time point, moreover, German adolescents appear less authoritarian than American youth. Adult opinion surveys display a similar pattern. A recent international study of adults indicates that the West German public is significantly less likely than Americans or other Europeans to feel that greater respect for authority is desirable.[9]

West German culture now encourages its citizens to be more independent and less deferential toward all forms of authority. In fact, many analysts conclude that these resocialization efforts were overly successful; social observers are now more likely to lament the lack of respect for authority in contemporary West German society than its continued excess. Skepticism of authority is especially pronounced among the young and better educated who were the focus of these resocialization efforts. Among a large number of young people, the authoritarianism of the past has been replaced by antiestablishment tendencies of the present. These youthful doubts about authority influence family affairs, social relations, and political actions.

The question of social tolerance is often discussed in the same context as the authoritarian aspects of the German culture. Intolerance was a prominent feature of German political culture and general social norms under previous regimes. Dahrendorf sensed the continuation of these attitudes in postwar West Germany. He characterized the culture as indifferent toward the weak—citing the treatment of children, expectant mothers, and the ill—and not merely toward social and political minorities. This lack of understanding and empathy for others affected even the simplest social interaction; the queueing instinct so prominent in the British was entirely absent, disapproving stares greeted unusual social behavior, and social conformity was encouraged. The lack of tolerance in such mundane matters raised doubts about the possibility of developing public tolerance of dissent, political opposition, and social minorities.

A mass of public opinion data documents the growth of civic

tolerance among the West German public. The open expression of racial or religious hostility is no longer accepted within the culture, even if some individuals remain prejudiced. David Conradt's work on the changing political culture finds a growing acceptance of democratic political procedures.[10] Other research indicates a substantial increase in political tolerance within the West German public. Divergent political views are tolerated, even if not accepted. Greater tolerance is also evident in other aspects of the social consciousness. For instance, opinion surveys indicate that more parents now believe that tolerance should be stressed in raising a child; people say that tolerance is an important part of the citizen's role. Probably the strongest evidence of change is the large body of public opinion surveys documenting greater tolerance among the young.

While levels of *civic* tolerance have improved, this still remains a questionable aspect of German *social* norms. Opinion trends show only modest temporal change in a variety of measures that directly or indirectly tap feelings of tolerance in nonpolitical interpersonal relations. For instance, the percentage of the public that feels that one can trust another person who holds opinions completely different from one's own is virtually unchanged from 1956 to 1977. Most social observers note that patterns of everyday behavior still frequently reflect elements of intolerance in personal relations. This aspect of German cultural norms has not, as yet, completely been remade.

Distance in interpersonal relations was another characteristic of the social consciousness noted by Dahrendorf. Social relations encouraged a reserved and inwardly oriented pattern of individual interaction. Dahrendorf felt that private social relations led to the development of private values, where egocentric needs take precedence over social needs. These norms are a long-standing aspect of German culture, reflecting the traditional stress on family ties and primary social networks as well as the uncertainty of the world beyond. These sentiments developed a less benign content as a result of the traumatic events of the Second World War. The postwar emphasis on privacy is often linked to the wartime *Bunkermentalität* necessary to survive in dire circumstances—withdrawal into a close circle of friends that can be depended upon entirely. Privacy also signaled a distrust of one's fellow man and an unwillingness to rely upon strangers. Opinion polls conducted during the immediate postwar years documented the very negative image that Germans held of each other. If others are seen as spiteful, selfish, and not worthy of trust, who would want to socialize with these people? The Germans accepted Goethe's famous dictum that Germans "are so worthy as individuals, so wretched in the mass."

The negative values underlying this pattern of social relations slowly moderated as West German society became more open and more tolerant. Images of one's fellow Germans grew more positive. The Allensbach Institute has asked a number of trend questions dealing with interpersonal relations. In 1949 a plurality of the public (46 percent) thought other people tended to be spiteful, but by 1976 only 16 percent of the public expressed this sentiment. Other items display a growing willingness to discuss personal problems with others and to develop a wider friendship network. Similarly, the research firm, Infratest, found a dramatic shift in a measure of social isolation that asked whether there were others one could turn to in time of an emergency.

The transformation of this aspect of the culture is, however, also incomplete. The majority of West Germans still say that most people cannot be trusted, even though distrust is less common than it was in the early 1950s. Personal relations are still primarily oriented to a small circle of close friends rather than extensive social networks. But even if a restrained pattern of social relations remains part of the culture, it is less dependent on a *Bunkermentalität* and social distrust.

In discussing the German social consciousness it is almost obligatory to consider the importance placed on industriousness and hard work. Weber's *Protestant Ethic* described an attitude toward work and life that was familiar to most Germans. The Protestant ethic was intended to explain the pattern of economic development among Western societies, but the work ethic also instilled a sense of discipline, order, and efficiency in the population. Citizens of the Federal Republic openly embraced this work ethic, especially during the postwar reconstruction period. Over the past three decades, "industriousness and efficiency" are cited most often by the Germans themselves as their best qualities, mentioned by about two-thirds of the public in Allensbach opinion surveys. The value of *Fleiss* is a legendary characteristic of the West German worker.

A hard look at the evidence, however, casts doubts about the continuing applicability of these norms. A generation ago, most employees said that they enjoyed their time on the job more than their leisure time; opinion polls found that the balance had shifted to leisure activities in the mid-1970s.[11] When labor union officials claim that six weeks paid vacation is necessary to maintain the health of the workers because the present five-week period is insufficient, one must question the continuing applicability of Weber's description. The limited German support for the work ethic appears most clearly in international comparisons. Stephen Harding and his colleagues developed a measure of work orientations partially derived from Weber's concept of the Protestant ethic; the West Germans are the next-to-lowest on this scale among the ten nations surveyed, behind the Italians and Spanish workers and surpassing only the French.[12] The West German work force is also third from the bottom in overall job satisfaction. And again, studies indicate that these trends in work values are most pronounced among the young.

The public's exceptional commitment to work will probably remain a widely held myth of West German culture. This is seen as a desirable trait to possess, and it adds an aura of quality and craftsmanship to German products. But the specific norms underlying this cultural myth are unraveling. To the extent that the Protestant ethic contributed to social rigidity and a sense of discipline within society, the erosion of these norms will encourage a broader definition of self and less rigid social relations. These changing norms will primarily affect the economic system, which must reassess labor incentives and adapt to these new norms.

The evidence presented here suggests that many of the negative aspects of West German social norms noted by Dahrendorf have improved in the past forty years. The nation has shed much of its premodern social consciousness. Citizens are more trustful of each other, more tolerant of diversity, and more open in social relations than they were during the immediate postwar years. The West German social consciousness is now more compatible with the open, pluralistic, and modern features of comtemporary society.

Despite this progress, however, the transformation of social norms has been incomplete. Although feelings of trust have improved, many people continue to be critical of their fellow citizens. Most Germans remain distinctly individualistic in their personal values; this is especially true among older cohorts. Interpersonal relations are still focused on small personal networks, even though social interaction is broadening. To some extent, these developments represent a continuation of the German priority on private values over public values that Dahrendorf noted, but with an important difference. Instead of ego-centered behavior being a defensive reaction to a hostile world, individualism now is seen as an opportunity to develop according to one's own priorities.

The partial change in social norms also contrasts with the rich literature documenting a fundamental transformation in the political culture over the past forty years.[13] This imbalance between social and political change reflects the unequal pattern of socio-political development in the Federal Republic. The institutions of the new state focused their efforts on remaking the political culture through denazification and subsequent reeducation programs, and by linking the prosperity of the Wirtschaftswunder to the new political system. Political attitudes changed dramatically and extensively as a consequence. These accomplishments and the evolving structure of the socioeconomic system affected social norms more gradually and less completely. Changes in social norms thus have lagged behind the changes in political norms. Citizens learned to be tolerant of political views and minorities before they learned tolerance in their social relations. Individuals were initially more likely to challenge the authority of political figures than to question personal authority relationships. Thus, while analysts proclaim that the political culture has been remade, social norms are still evolving.

POSTMATERIAL VALUE CHANGE

The modifications in the social norms identified with the "German question" are the most important changes in the German social consciousness during the past four decades, but in recent years a new aspect of social change has become apparent. Once substantial progress was made in addressing traditional socioeconomic needs, the public broadened their interests to include a new set of personal and political goals. The first evidence of these changing values came from among university students during the mid-1960s. What began as leftwing attempts to reform the universities and as demonstrations against the Vietnam War, the rightwing Springer press chain, and police terror tactics, soon grew to question a broad array of prevailing social values. To an extent, this new social consciousness challenged the traditional norms of German society; less attention was placed on economic success than on the quality of life, hierarchic social relations were replaced by an emphasis on participatory decision making, and traditional moral values were supplanted by a concern for individual freedom and alternative life-styles.

These new values became a cultural force through the creation of a distinct social milieu where individual values were translated into social norms. Counterculture districts emerged in several large cities, with natural food stores, bio-bakeries, cooperative businesses, leftist bookshops, vegetarian restaurants, and youth-oriented cafés, offering a life-style attuned to the new values. An extensive social network provided an environment where an *Alternativkultur* could develop. The support of intellectuals, academics, and an alternative press helped diffuse these new norms throughout West German society. The proponents of these new values became active participants in the political process; their political thrust is supported by the actions of numerous citizen action groups (*Bürgerinitiativen*), new social movements (the environmental movement, women's groups, the peace movement, etc.), and *Die Grünen*.

The development of these new value orientations is generally linked to a broad theory of value change proposed by Ronald Inglehart.[14] Inglehart maintains that a person's value priorities are heavily influenced by the family and societal conditions of one's early formative years. In a time of depression or civil unrest, *material* values such as economic well-being and security receive primary attention. If a society can make significant progress in addressing these goals, then some people may shift their attention toward higher-order *postmaterial* values such as individual freedom, participation, and the quality of life.

Some postmaterial goals—freedom of expression, participation, and personal freedom—represent an expansion of traditional European liberalism to a broader popular base. This process of value change therefore continues the modernizing trends noted above. But in addition, other postmaterial goals—orientations toward social relations, life-styles, and environmental quality—represent the newly emerging concerns of advanced industrial societies that are not addressed by traditional liberal ideologies. Value change along the material-postmaterial continuum thus subsumes some of the same social trends discussed in the context of the "German question," but with an additional postindustrial element.

The value change theory is based on a process of sociopolitical development occurring within most advanced industrial democracies. Affluence, the growth of the welfare state, expanding communication and transportation networks, domestic order, and international stability create the conditions in many Western nations that allow new political interests to come to the fore. Moreover, because basic value priorities tend to be socialized relatively early in life, these changing social conditions exert the greatest impact on the values of younger generations socialized in the postwar era.

This general theory of social and value change is especially relevant in West Germany. The social, economic, and political changes within German society are probably the largest of any West European nation, and have produced vastly different life experiences for succeeding generations. Older generations socialized before World War II lived at least partially under an authoritarian government, experienced long periods of economic hardship, and felt the destructive consequences of world war. Given these experiences, it is not surprising that many older individuals retain a relatively high priority for *material* values despite thirty years of the economic miracle and political stability.

Younger Germans, in contrast, have grown up in a fundamentally different environment. Present-day living standards are several times higher than Germans ever experienced prior to World War II. The development of the modern welfare state now protects most citizens even from major economic problems. Postwar generations also possess a broader worldview, reflecting their higher educational levels, greater access to a rich media environment, and more diverse cultural experiences. Furthermore, the past four decades are one of the

Table 3.1
The Distribution of Value Priorities

	Relative Emphasis on Goal
Material Goals	
Money and material possessions	81
Social and professional status	45
Accumulate wealth and property	42
Dress and manners	42
Hard work	28
Personal achievement	20
Respect for authority	20
Sense of duty	0
Law and order	−3
Patriotism	−16
Postmaterial Goals	
Personal freedom	−15
Developing new life-styles	−44
Regard for minority interests	−53
Social justice	−57
Equality of opportunity	−63
Citizen participation in politics	−65

Sources: 1979 survey of German youth aged 19–37 (N = 1,103) conducted by the United States Information Agency. Table entries are the percentage difference between those saying that society places "too much emphasis" versus "too little emphasis" on each goal.

longest periods of international peace in modern European history. Under these conditions, the security concerns that preoccupied pre-war generations diminished in urgency. As a result, some members of the postwar generation are broadening their interests to include new *postmaterial* goals.

A public opinion survey of German youth conducted in 1979 can help refine the meaning of materialism and postmaterialism as well as illustrate the generational basis of value change (table 3.1). A sample of young people was asked whether society placed "too much" or "too little" emphasis on a variety of personal goals. Two clusters of goals emerge from these evaluations.[15] Materialist goals include such items as "money and material possessions," "social and professional status," "hard work," and "respect for authority."

Young people not only see these as interrelated goals, but also feel that German society places too much emphasis on these objectives. For instance, 84 percent state that money and material possessions receive too much emphasis and 3 percent say that these goals receive too little emphasis, producing a percentage difference score of 81 points. The young believe this surfeit of attention applies to most other material goals.

An alternative, postmaterial cluster of social goals includes items such as "personal freedom," "developing new life-styles," "social justice," and "participation in politics." Not only are these goals seen as distinct from material objectives, but the young feel that each of these goals is presently underemphasized by contemporary society.

Many of the values promoted by postmaterialists have earlier roots in the political culture. Germans have always held nature in high regard, and the forests possess almost mystical qualities in literature and folklore; some of these same elements are seen in the appeals of the modern environmental movement. The unconventional, nonmaterialist, and romantic tendencies among contemporary youth also evoke images of the *Wandervogel* movement of the early 1900s. Despite these historical precedents, postmaterialism represents a qualitatively new development for West German politics. The *Wandervogel* never numbered more than a few thousand participants, the alternative Green party has nearly 40,000 members and received over three million votes in the 1987 federal elections. Popular support for many New Politics issues is even more extensive. Earlier alternative movements held antidemocratic and *völkisch* views;[16] the supporters of the contemporary alternative movements lie at the opposite end of the political spectrum. Finally, earlier movements were a reaction to a social and political context that bears little relevance to contemporary West Germany.

The breadth of value change can be seen most clearly in public opinion trends spanning the postwar socioeconomic recovery. The Emnid Institute has asked a question that measures the priority given to four basic human freedoms: freedom of worship, freedom of speech, freedom from fear, and freedom from want.[17] In the harsh economic environment of postwar Europe, a plurality of Germans felt that freedom from want was most important. As the success of

Table 3.2
The Trend in Material/Postmaterial Value Priorities

	1970	1973	1976	1979	1982	1984	1987
Material	46	42	42	37	32	23	19
Mixed values	44	50	47	52	54	58	67
Postmaterial	11	8	11	11	13	20	34
	100%	100%	100%	100%	100%	100%	100%
PDI[a]	35	34	31	26	19	3	−15

Source: European Community Studies, 1970, 1973; Eurobarometers 6, 12, 18, 20, 27.
[a]The Percentage Difference Index (PDI) is the difference between the percentage with material values versus those with postmaterial values.

the economic miracle lessened these basic needs, there was a long-term shift away from this materialistic goal and a growing emphasis on freedom of speech.

Inglehart devised another measure of value priorities that classifies postmaterialists as those respondents who believe that "protecting freedom of speech," and "giving people more say in government decisions" are the two most important social goals; materialists are those who stress "fighting rising prices" and "maintaining order in the nation" as their primary goals. This four-item index is an admittedly crude measure of the complex value changes occurring in West German society, but the index has the advantage of being asked continuously in public opinion surveys since 1970. This measure of value priorities shows a fairly steady trend toward postmaterial values over the past two decades (table 3.2). These new value orientations have been surprisingly resilient in the face of major economic recessions of the 1970s and the currently high levels of unemployment. The plurality that once stressed only materialist goals has now been replaced by a majority expressing interest in a mix of material and postmaterial goals. The number of postmaterialists increased from 11 percent in 1970 to 34 percent in 1987—despite the difficult economic conditions of the intervening period. In the most recent survey the "pure" postmaterialists actually outnumber materialists for the first time. Furthermore, there are marked generational differences in value priorities. Materialists predominate in the older generations reared during the Second Empire and

Weimar Republic, while postmaterialists are more prevalent among the youngest age groups. Thus generational turnover has fueled the gradual extension of postmaterial values, and this trend has been accelerated in recent years by the mobilizing influence of *Alternativ* organizations such as *Die Grünen*.

A Clash of Cultures

With the development of postmaterialism the unique concerns of the "German question" are joined by a postindustrial debate similar to that occurring in other European democracies. The social forces driving West German society are no longer focused solely on the cultural legacy of the past, but are also concerned with emerging social issues as the Federal Republic becomes an advanced industrial society.

As is the case in most other European nations, the postmaterial movement has not won open acceptance from the establishment. Even two decades after the first waves of the student movement, these new interests often generate division and tension within the social system. To some critics, postmaterialism represents a rejection of the values that brought economic and political security to the Federal Republic. Having reached a significant level of economic progress, materialists fear that the pro-environment, postmaterial political movements could undermine the nation's economic achievements. The protests and radical appeals of postmaterial groups also conjure up images of political instability that worry many Germans. Indeed, there are radical and antidemocratic elements of the alternative movement that bear monitoring, but this is a distinct minority.

The clash of values is a visible aspect of interpersonal relations. It is evident in everyday life as elderly Germans look askance at young people who dress and act in unconventional ways; between parents who want their children to share their concerns for financial and personal security, and children who want more personal fulfillment. Older people who remember the economic and social instability of Germany's past cannot understand why the young do not share these concerns. Moreover, the rhetoric of the young often puts their elders on the defensive. The street graffiti of the alternative movement voices its alienation from Germany's past: "Better a demonstration by democrats than a nation of Nazis," "You are everything, the *Volk* means nothing." These new social tensions will test the growing tolerance of the German public that was discussed above.

The tension between old and new is also a visible feature of contemporary West German politics. Over the past decade numerous confrontations have occurred between the alternative movement and political authorities. Occasionally these confrontations led to clashes with police, as some protestors used violence. Opponents of *Startbahn West*, an expansion of the Frankfurt airport that would destroy a large forested area, were forcibly removed from the site by police after months of confrontation. The opposition to the deployment of INF weapons in the Federal Republic pushed protest activities to a postwar high. Violence by radicals at a 1987 environmental protest resulted in the death of a police officer and tighter government restrictions on protestors. Antinuclear demonstrations and clashes with police have surged in the wake of Chernobyl. This scenario is being played out over and over as new social and political controversies arise. Moreover, *Die Grünen* have brought this anti-establishment style into the halls of the Bundestag and Land parliaments. Thus the West German public sees a continuing conflict between old and new that often exceeds the conventional boundaries of social discourse.

Several leading sociologists have discussed these tensions between old and new as a conflict between cultural norms and the economic system.[18] In other words, the materialist, hierarchic order of industrial society is being challenged by the nonmaterialist, pluralist order of an emerging advanced industrial society. They see the political system as the only institution able to balance these contending forces and reconcile the differences. From this perspective the actions of the polity will determine the Federal Republic's future course.

This conflict between cultures reintroduces some instability and uncertainty into the West German political system. While West German democracy will undoubtedly remain one of the most stable in Europe, it no longer may be as tranquil or as predictable as it has been in the past. Increased polarization on traditional social and economic issues is already visible between the established political parties, and these trends are most noticeable among younger party elites. A running series of battles between New Politics adherents and the political establishment also can be expected in the years ahead. These conflicts may even take an occasional violent turn, though this should be the exception.

At the same time, the changing social consciousness signified by postmaterialism can represent a positive development for West German society. Postmaterial values emphasize democratic norms. Several New Politics groups have pressed for the Federal Republic to live up to its democratic rhetoric and expand the citizen's role in the political process. In addition, the postmaterial movement represents an openness to change and recognition of unmet social needs that many established political figures acknowledge were lacking. One SPD leader called the alternative Green movement a sign of creativity in the Federal Republic which is not present to the same extent in France or the United Kingdom, and added that German politicians should welcome the challenge they present. Cultural change represents a challenge to the political status quo, but it is a challenge that evolves from society's past accomplishments.

CULTURAL CHANGE AND SOCIETY

The first lesson to be learned from the Federal Republic is that a static view of an unchanging (or unchangeable) culture should be avoided. The social and political norms of postwar Germany have undergone substantial change in the past forty years. The images of an authoritarian, intolerant, and socially isolated public that Dahrendorf described have been reshaped, or at least substantially modified, over the last four decades. While the social culture has not been transformed as fundamentally as the political culture, the positive trends for most of the social traits identified with the "German question" are substantial.

Despite these developments, we still cannot say that these trends have run their course. Substantial potential for change still exists. The social institutions—churches, unions, community networks— that normally perpetuate the dominant social values now exert less influence on the public's social consciousness.[19] These institutions are not as able as they once were to perpetuate prevailing social norms. An increasing proportion of the population is no longer integrated into these social networks, therefore making these individuals more susceptible to new cultural appeals.[20] Traditional social institutions are themselves becoming less monolithic, debating alternative social goals and alternative values rather than projecting a single cultural model.

This potential is also heightened by the continuing socioeconomic development of the Federal Republic. The social forces driving West German society no longer are focused on the cultural and socioeconomic legacy of the past, but on the emerging problems of an advanced industrial society. With this development, West German culture has moved closer to the pattern of other Western democracies. The concerns of the "German question" are joined by those of an advanced industrial society.

The diversity of the present culture creates the potential for greater pluralism in individual beliefs. A dominant social consciousness can now more easily coexist with distinct subcultures maintained by their own support networks. In addition, just as societal institutions and political parties are attempting to influence popular norms, the public's changing values are exerting pressure for change within these institutions. The multiplicity of social influences and separate cultural milieus suggests that social norms are not as firmly entrenched as in a society in which tradition dictates values and these values are reinforced by societal institutions. Thus the potential for further evolution and growth in the West German social consciousness is still substantial.

NOTES

1. Richard von Weizsäcker, *A Voice from Germany* (London: Weidenfeld and Nicholson, 1985), 71.
2. Anna Merritt and Richard Merritt, *Public Opinion in Occupied Germany: The OMGUS Surveys, 1945–1949* (Urbana: University of Illinois Press,

1970); Anna and Richard Merritt, *Public Opinion in Semisovereign Germany: The HICOG Surveys, 1949–1955* (Urbana: University of Illinois Press, 1980).

3. Elisabeth Noelle-Neumann and Erich Neumann, *The Germans, 1947–1966* (Allensbach: Institut für Demoskopie, 1968).
4. Ralf Dahrendorf, *Society and Democracy in Germany* (New York: Doubleday, 1967). First published in German in 1965.
5. Dahrendorf, *Society and Democracy in Germany*, 139; also see chapter 23.
6. Gabriel Almond and Sidney Verba, *The Civic Culture* (Princeton: Princeton University Press, 1963).
7. Elisabeth Noelle-Neumann and Renate Köcher, *Die verletzte Nation* (Stuttgart: Deutsche Verlags-Anstalt, 1987).
8. Gerda Lederer, "Trends in Authoritarianism," *Journal of Cross-Cultural Psychology* 13 (1982): 299–314; Gerda Lederer, *Jugend und Autorität* (Opladen: Westdeutscher Verlag, 1983).
9. Noelle-Neumann and Köcher, *Die verletzte Nation*, 321.
10. David Conradt, "The Changing Political Culture." In *The Civic Culture Revisited*, ed. Gabriel Almond and Sidney Verba (Boston: Little, Brown, 1980).
11. Elisabeth Noelle-Neumann and Burkhard Strumpel, *Macht Arbeit krank? Macht Arbeit glücklich? Eine aktuelle Kontroverse* (Munich: Piper, 1984); Noelle-Neumann and Köcher, *Die verletzte Nation*.
12. Stephen Harding, David Philips, and Michael Fogarty, *Contrasting Values in Western Europe* (London: Macmillan, 1986), chapter 5.
13. Kendall Baker, Russell Dalton, and Kai Hildebrandt, *Germany Transformed* (Cambridge: Harvard University Press, 1981); Conradt, "The Changing Political Culture."
14. Ronald Inglehart, *The Silent Revolution* (Princeton: Princeton University Press, 1977); Ronald Inglehart, "Postmaterialism in an Environment of Economic Insecurity," *American Political Science Review* 75 (1981); Ronald Inglehart, *Culture Shift* (Princeton: Princeton University Press, 1989).
15. The clusters were based on a factor analysis of the value measures; see Russell Dalton, "The Persistence of Values and Life Cycle Changes," *Politische Psychologie*, special issue of the *Politische Vierteljahresschrift* (December 1981).
16. For instance, the large *bündisch* youth movement of the 1920s had a distinct racist, antidemocratic, and nationalistic orientation.
17. See Russell Dalton, *Politics in West Germany* (Glenview, Ill.: Scott Foresman/Boston: Little, Brown, 1989), chapter 4.
18. Claus Offe, "New Social Movements: Challenging the Boundaries of Institutional Politics," *Social Research* 52 (1985): 817–68; Richard Lowenthal, *Change and Cultural Crisis* (New York: Columbia University Press, 1984).

19. See the more extensive discussion of the changing role of social institutions in Russell Dalton, *Culture and Politics in West Germany* (Ann Arbor: Institute for Social Research, 1988).

20. Wilhelm Bürklin, "Governing Left Parties Frustrating the Non-Established Left," *European Sociological Review* 3 (1987): 109–26.

4

FEMINISM IN FOUR ACTS: THE CHANGING POLITICAL IDENTITY OF WOMEN IN THE FEDERAL REPUBLIC OF GERMANY

Joyce M. Mushaben

Unrecht gewinnt oft Rechtscharakter
allein dadurch, dass es häufig vorkommt.
—Bertolt Brecht,
Geschichte des Herrn Keuner

Die Frauenbewegung wird aber niemals ihr
Ziel—die Gleichberechtigung der
Geschlechter—erreichen, wenn die Frauen
sich nicht bei allem Festhalten an ihren
Sonderinteressen untereinander verbunden fühlen.
—Mina Cauer, Lily von Gizycki,
Die Frauenbewegung 1,
no. 1, 1 January 1895

The relationship between the prevailing socioeconomic status of women and the extent of their direct participation in the exercise of political power in industrial society is not necessarily a symmetrical one. Nor do the imbalances between the two variables always lean in the same direction, as demonstrated by the differential gains made by women's groups in the United States and the Federal Republic over the last four decades. As a participant-observer in both movements since the early 1970s, I have been struck many times by the importance of political cultural factors in relation to the type of progress that has been made in securing women's rights in the political and economic arenas. Political cultural variations moreover play a critical role in the determination of resource mobilization *strategies*, as well as in the establishment of different organizational *networks*, the common goals of feminist activists in the two countries notwithstanding.

It is no secret that American citizens, in general, are more "apolitical" than their European counterparts, and that they are historically much less inclined to call upon "the state" to remedy deep seated socioeconomic imbalances. At the same time American feminists have realized that rugged individualism has its limits, and they have actively sought to redress gender-based inequities through legislatures and the courts, even without the benefit of the proverbial leg of a constitutionally explicit guarantee of equality upon which to stand. In addition to a more widespread and often more intense interest in things political, German women have been more directly affected by politics—through the hardships of two world wars, through the loss of property and the separation of families imposed by the nation's division. They can call upon the welfare state (*Sozialstaat*) to provide some measure of economic security; and the "state of law" (*Rechtsstaat*) has, in theory, equipped them with a potentially formidable constitutional instrument, Article 3 of the Constitution, for use in their struggle for political-juridical equality.[1] While American feminists might look to West German legal and welfare state guarantees with a measure of respect and envy, it is clear that, even under these conditions, the proverbial battle of the sexes is far from over. Constitutional mechanisms alone have not served to eliminate many deep-seated sociocultural biases that have rendered the struggle an even more difficult one, in certain respects, for women in the postwar German state.

The political identity of women in the FRG has undergone a number of dramatic changes over the last forty years, although the transformation is by no means complete. At times the process has been hampered by the lack of a positive, movement-internal consensus, as well as by the resulting stop-and-go character of various movement initiatives. Developments of the 1980s, however, seem to have infused political activists and feminist groups with new energy and a new sense of urgency: there is a need to guard against a potential "roll-back" of hard-won opportunities in light of the pressing economic problems now facing all advanced industrial states.

With regard to the role of women, each decade of the West German state seems to manifest a politically distinctive character; its profile derives from the cumulative influence of changes in the general sociopolitical climate, the emergence of new "women's" issues, and from the cultivation of new, movement-linked strategies in the pursuit of gender equality. As is true of women's rights movements everywhere, advocates and activists need to study where they have been, based on a critical evaluation of their own past weaknesses and strengths, in order to determine where they need to go and how to get there most expeditiously. Consequently, this survey of women's political growth and social movement activism during the first four decades of postwar West German history offers both an analysis and an appeal.

KINDER—KÜCHE—KIRCHE: THE RECONSTRUCTION OF THE PATRIARCHAL ORDER, 1949–1959

November 12, 1988, marks the seventieth anniversary of women's suffrage in Germany. The road to meaningful political participation, as voters, candidates, and officeholders, has been a very rocky one for women, their journey fraught with a number of unique historical perils. Promulgated in 1850, the Prussian Law on Associations (*Vereinsrecht*) barred "female persons, the mentally ill, schoolchildren and apprentices" from membership in any political organization or assembly, a ban not rescinded by the Reichstag until 1908.[2] Having attained the right to vote with the support of Communists and Social Democrats in 1918, women, in effect, burned their own bridges before they could cross them, beginning with the election of 1919. The first women to enjoy the right of franchise headed for the local polls, at rates equivalent to those of participating men (82.3%), largely in order to cast their ballots for center and rightwing forces. The net effect of the female vote in subsequent elections was not limited to a passive undermining of the Left; a slightly higher turnout among women in 1933 attested to their active support for the emerging NSDAP.

It was more than a lack of political experience that accounted for this ill-fated vote of confidence in right-wing radicalism. Women's acquiescence and support for the Nazis, for the most part, derived from the extreme economic insecurity and political fragmentation attributed to Weimar; economic conditions were critical in determining the *direction* of both the male and female votes cast. On the other hand, the *strength* of the latter's psychological preference for the Right no doubt rested with the pervasiveness of traditional religious and social beliefs that rendered women more susceptible to Hitler's promises to glorify motherhood (and to link it to a "higher purpose") than to the Weimar feminists' arguments against the repressive division of labor and gender-specific self-sacrifice so characteristic of women's existence in the industrial age. Neither their own political innocence nor unquestioning compliance with role-obligations dictated from above would shelter women from the consequences of the reign of terror that followed, however.

The early years of occupation by more democratic forces subsequent to Nazi capitulation were no kinder to women. In fact, their lot worsened considerably as a result of postsurrender rapes by victorious Russian soldiers, forced quartering, and the sudden breakdown of the rationing system.[3] The important political questions for women after 1945 focused not on the distribution of power (*Machtfrage*) but rather on the distribution of scarce food resources (*Magenfrage*). Daily consumption levels fell from an average per capita count of 2000 calories during the last months of the war, to official lows of 775–794 calories in the American and French occupation zones through 1947. Many women were compelled to "hamster" their way through the countryside and black markets in search of adequate nutrition for themselves and their dependents.

The personal survival strategies pursued by women were not without political content. In fact, as Freier argues, the occupational powers consciously relied upon such typically female nurturing activity in their calculations for resource distribution and recovery:

The Allies and the German authorities could make use of the German tradition, in that housework, cooking preserves, collecting food, making financial ends meet with regard to groceries, had already passed the general test of adding a subsistence amount to the all-too-low income bases. The housework tradition, executed without pay by the woman for the family, expanded the room for the maneuvering open to political strategies. . . . Women's work bridged over the breakdown resulting from industrial demolition, limitations on production, bans on export trade and the Allies' policy of "waiting out" the effects of shortages in the provisions sector. (Kuhn, vol. 2 p. 52)

Millions of *Trümmerfrauen* (rubble women) were mobilized to work outside the home, according to the principle "s/he who works, must also eat"; for three years they labored to dig the former Reich out of its own ruins—sometimes as conscripted laborers, often in order to increase their official rations to nourish their dependents. The provisional Economic Council, officially charged with recommending steps for scarcity management, was expanded in February, 1948; of the 104 half-appointed, half-elected members, only 5 were women. Not a single woman was to serve on the Committee for the Equalization of Burdens (*Lastenausgleich*)—although women were most directly affected by its rulings. Within days after the initiation of currency reform in June, 1948, residents in the western zones saw a wide range of goods "miraculously" reappear on the market—for those who could afford to pay. Money carefully hoarded through the war years was devalued overnight at the rate of RM 100: DM 6.5; by December prices had risen by 14 percent.

To counteract the power vacuum experienced during the early postwar years, women created their own local antifascism committees, over 6,000 in the eastern zone; their counterparts in the western zones quickly reestablished formal and informal relations with British and American women's organizations. They convened an assembly of 5,000 participants to address prisoner-of-war questions, and mobilized regular cooking courses to compensate for missing ingredients. Another 2,000 banded together to found the Union of German Democratic Women (*Demokratisher Frauenbund Deutschlands*) in 1947. Local cooperation in these various committees transcended party lines until 1948, when the reconstituted CDU, SPD, and FDP decreed that future collaboration between party members and female Communists (many of whom had suffered incarceration under the Nazis) was forbidden.

A degree of ideological division among women's groups had preceded this ban on sororitization by many decades, to be sure. But the fifty-year prohibition on female membership in political associations under Prussian rule meant that diverse women's groups of the 1800s had been free to work toward the same or similar goals without directly entangling themselves in the formalized, internecine warfare being waged between the parties. The fact that women, despite their partisan differences, had cooperated effectively enough to allow for economic "normalization" by 1948, points to the patriarchal character of the parties' anticollaboration ban in two respects. First, the work of the women's committees, which focused on predominantly life-preserving functions, was officially rendered "superfluous" as soon as economic conditions appeared to have stabilized. Secondly, women's issues and female grass roots activism, thus reclassified as "low politics," were deliberately subordinated to higher party concerns—a measure almost guaranteed to keep the women's movement split along partisan lines for the next three decades.

The promulgation of the Basic Law (*Grundgesetz*) in May, 1949, institutionalized a return to business and politics as usual: the sixty-one Founding Fathers comprising the Parliamentary Council significantly outnumbered the four Founding Mothers. Anne Haag's hard-driving initiative in Baden-Württemberg led to the eventual inclusion of Article 4, Paragraph 3 (the right to conscientious objection against service with a weapon) in the final draft. Long-standing Social Democrat Elizabeth (Rohde) Selbert waged and won a protracted battle to ensure that the sexual equality and equal rights mandate found in Article 3, Paragraphs 1–3 would not be anchored to a "special protection" clause for women, although her appeal for a reform of the Civil Code in conformance with the new constitution went unheeded.

Among the women of "the first hour" who assumed seats in the newly elected Bundestag in 1949 were many who had acquired formal political experience in the National Assembly and the Reichstag prior to 1933: Louise Schroeder, former acting mayor of Berlin; Christian Democrat Helene Weber, and Social Democrat Helene Wessel, both former Center party officials. They were joined by others who had entered party politics by virtue of their social welfare professions, Martha Schanzenbach, trade unionist Liesel Kipp-

Kauel, and Käte Strobel, later to become the first SPD minister of health in 1966. The first female president of the Bundestag, Anne-Marie Renger (1972–1976), entered Parliament in 1953.

Frauenpolitik (both in the sense of women's politics and policies for women) revolved around the issues of economic security for widows, dependents, and the disabled, youth welfare and education, and the allocation of scarce housing during the reconstruction era. Their formal equality as citizens notwithstanding, women's status in terms of statutory law continued to rest on their primary obligation to household and family; indeed, the preamble to the 1957 Equalization of Rights Law specified the importance of men's responsibilities as "preserver and provider," complemented by women's duties as "the female heart of the family." The legal basis for women's adherence to *Kinder, Küche* and *Kirche* roles would remain intact until the 1977 adoption of the reformed Marriage and Family Law.

The return to a life focusing exclusively on the three "K's" for most of the fifties was perceived by many women as a well-deserved respite from the double burdens of family maintenance and low-paid labor during the war and its aftermath. Employment rates among married women in general fell to roughly 25 percent in 1950, while the rate for single women (over 15) remained high at 82.4 percent. Of the eight million women in paid employment, 20 percent (1.6 million) had children under fifteen; an additional 1.4 million managed households consisting of at least one other person.[4]

The prevailing orientation to politics, characterized by the slogan *ohne mich!* (without me), was not confined to women, as survey results from the period illustrate: 73 percent of those interviewed in March, 1949, expressed "little or no interest" in the *Grundgesetz;* one-half of the males and two-thirds of the female respondents questioned shortly after its promulgation in May knew nothing about its contents. Only one-fifth of those surveyed by June 1954 could explain the abbreviation "NATO."[5]

The elitist nature of the higher educational system offered few prospects for either the short-term, socioeconomic advancement of women or their incorporation into the political power structure over the long run. By the mid-fifties, female students comprised about one-third of the enrollments at West German universities, which continued to function as the primary recruitment channel pursuant to careers in the legal, medical, and academic fields, as well as in state administration; their numerical presence did not translate into an even distribution across the more powerful professions, however.

Regarding their direct participation in the political process, the number of women sworn in as members of the Bundestag (MdBs) rose from 28 to 38 (9 percent) between 1949 and 1953, and from 45 to 52 (10 percent) during the second legislative term, 1953–1957, as shown in table 4.1. Less than 5 percent of those seats were the result of direction election, that is, based on the single-member district vote comprising the first half of the dual ballot; most of the women entered Parliament by virtue of the party lists drawn up for the second, proportional vote cast. Although the SPD had adopted a proportionality principle analogous to a quota system at its 1908 Nuremberg Party Congress, its application was declared "no longer necessary" after 1949. Usually one or two "women's places" were reserved on party lists in more cosmopolitan districts, but not necessarily for safe seats (table 4.1). The list vote also accounted for a larger number of women at the end of the legislative periods; included among this group were the "replacements" (*Nachrückerinnen*, not widows!) for members who had died or resigned during the four-year term; Beate Hoecker notes that male MdB's were inclined to label these later entrants "the coffin hoppers".

The "without me" orientation receded into the background over the proposal for German rearmament in the early fifties. Party cleavages intensified in conjunction with the "Fight Against Atomic Death" campaign, 1957–1959, which had been triggered by NATO's proposal to deploy nuclear weapons in the western zones, especially after it was revealed that deployments had already taken place with the secret consent of Defense Minister Franz Josef Strauss in 1957. This significant, extended display of public opposition ended the era of apoliticism and moreover introduced many members of the not yet "civic culture" to the concept of unconventional political participation. Women's groups allied themselves in protest with religious activists and trade unionists, but they played no independent role in these campaigns. Cold war tensions reinforced women's

Table 4.1

Women in the Bundestag

Election Period	Parliamentary Seats Held by Women[a]						
	Beginning of Term		End of Term		Directly Elected, Single-member Constituency		Ratio of Directly Elected to List-election Members
	Total	%	Total	%	Total	%	
1. 1949–1953	28	6.8	38	9.0	12	5.0	1:1.3
2. 1953–1957	45	8.8	52	10.0	9	3.7	1:4.0
3. 1957–1961	48	9.2	49	9.4	9	3.6	1:4.3
4. 1961–1965	43	8.3	49	9.4	7	2.8	1:5.1
5. 1965–1969	36	6.9	41	7.9	8	3.2	1:3.5
6. 1969–1972	34	6.6	32	6.2	6	2.4	1:4.7
7. 1972–1976	30	5.8	36	6.9	4	2.0	1:6.5
8 1976–1980	38	7.3	41	7.9	7	2.8	1:4.4
9. 1980–1983	44	8.5	45	8.7	11	4.4	1:3.0
10. 1983–1987	51	9.8	—	—[b]	10	4.0	1:4.1
11. 1987–	75	15.4	83	16.0[c]	17	6.8	1:4.4

Source: Adapted from Peter Schindler, *Datenbuch zur Geschichte des Deutschen Bundestages, 1949 bis 1982* (Bonn: Nomos, 1984) and *Datenbuch zur Geschichte des Deutschen Bundestages 1980–1984* (Baden-Baden: Nomos, 1986); 1987 data were graciously provided by the Informationsdienst des Landtags Baden-Württemberg.
[a] As a percentage of all directly and proportionately elected seats.
[b] Not available.
[c] As of June 1988.

mainstream electoral support for the Adenauer government under the conservative mottos of "negotiation through strength" and "no experiments."

In view of what had gone before and in contrast to what was yet to come, the first decade under the new constitution was a relatively quiet one. The traditional division of labor into gender-based private and public spheres was reestablished with little opposition, as women became the trickle-down beneficiaries of an economic miracle in the making. The heightening of cold war tensions reaffirmed women's partisan inclination to stay the course with Adenauer—at higher rates than men—through the elections of 1957 and 1961. The dialectic of international relations imposed a new set of harsh political

Table 4.2
Bundestag Elections

	Percentage Party Vote Cast on Second Ballot ("List")[a]								
Election Year	CDU/CSU		SPD		FDP		Other[b]		Greens	
	Women	Men	Women	Men	Women	Men	Women	Men	Women	Men
1953	47.2	38.9	27.6	32.5	10.4	11.7	14.8	16.9	—	—
1957	53.5	44.6	28.9	35.3	7.4	8.6	10.2	11.5	—	—
1961	49.6	40.4	32.9	39.7	12.2	13.6	5.3	6.4	—	—
1965	51.7	42.1	36.2	44.0	9.2	9.7	2.9	4.3	—	—
1969	50.6	40.6	40.4	45.6	5.3	6.1	3.7	7.7	—	—
1972	46.0	43.0	45.7	46.9	7.7	8.8	0.6	1.3	—	—
1976	48.8	42.2	43.1	43.6	7.6	8.1	0.5	1.2	—	—
1980	43.7	44.2	38.4	43.1	10.8	10.5	0.3	0.6	1.2	1.6
1983	49.2	47.7	39.4	38.4	6.3	7.2	0.3	0.7	4.8	5.9
1987	46.1	42.5	37.8	38.5	8.3	9.2	1.2	1.6	7.7	8.3

Source: Adapted from Ursula Feist, "Die Amazonen sind noch fern. Das Wahlrecht der Frauen: Enttäuschungen und Chancen" in Feministische Studien 5, No. 2 (November 1986): 5; further, Statistisches Bundesamt Wiesbaden, Wahl zum 11. Deutschen Bundestag, 25. Januar 1987, Heft 11 (Stuttgart: Kohlhammer, 1987), pp. 16–17.
[a]Excludes absentee ballots; figures for 1953 do not include Rheinland-Pfalz, Bavaria, or the Saarland; 1957 figures also exclude the Saarland.
[b]Figures for 1980, 1983, and 1987 exclude Greens.

realities upon those women, and men, suddenly cut off from family and friends by the Berlin Wall in August 1961.

One can argue, retrospectively, that the Wall signaled the commencement of a new era in postwar politics, although many of the trends evinced during the fifties would persist through the mid-sixties. By the end of the next decade, however, many a daughter would turn against the role-identification of her mother, just as many a son would turn against the political identification of his father—both rejections resting in part on the New Left's collective questions as to what daddy had done during the war, and why mother still refused to talk about it.

FINE DISTINCTIONS, MAJOR CONSEQUENCES: THE 1960s

At another time, in another place, parental interrogations of the New Left sort might have gone the way of other classical cases of generational conflict; when coupled with the Young Socialists' demands for radical democratization, and growing opposition to the Vietnam War however, the rejection of parental mores acquired a new political significance that extended well beyond campus boundaries. New Left mobilization unwittingly brought to light a number of gender-based discrepancies that would eventually set the parameters for change and thus redefine women's political identity in the FRG over the next decade. Dialectical materialism, as reflected in the antithetical gap between constitutional guarantees of equality and opportunity, on the one hand, and the postwar distribution of personal wealth and unpaid labor, on the other, would become both less tenable in theory and less tolerable in practice for women of the next generation.

Willy Brandt's 1969 exhortation to voters to "dare more democracy" did not unleash the forces of student protest; rather, it served to legitimize an increasing pressure for democratization-from-below that had been gathering momentum since the onset of the Grand Coalition in 1966. Student demands nonetheless differed in their quality and intensity from those advanced by the SPD. The 2 June 1967 death of Berlin student Benno Ohnesorg (during a protest against the Shah of Iran), as well as the April 1968 assassination attempt against Rudi Dutschke, led to a fusion of many disparate protest causes and groups, exponentially increasing both the participants' sense of political fury and their potential for sustained mass action.

Comprising at best one-third of the university enrollments, women attempted to carve out a niche for themselves inside the larger movement, but their effectiveness was limited by a number of fitful starts and stops. They began, innocently enough, with the "children problem." In January 1968, seven female members of the West Berlin Socialist Student Federation (SDS) created their own Action Council for the Liberation of Women (Aktionsrat zur Befreiung der Frau), "in recognition that authoritarian behavioral structures had already entrenched themselves even within the ranks of those who characterized themselves as wanting to struggle against such [authoritarianism] worldwide."[6] Translation: These married women students were no longer willing to contain their frustration, once they realized that *they* had to stay home tending young children while their radical men were free to march out the door to pursue higher causes, such as demonstrating and masterminding the revolution.

Rather than resign themselves to surrogate forms of participation, a number of women brought their children along to the next major protest "happening," the February 1968 Congress on Vietnam. They rotated responsibility for some forty children sent out to play in the foyer of the Technical University, thereby inspiring the initiation of the Berlin *Kinderläden* (child-care cooperative) movement that quickly spread throughout the city. As Kontos argues, many (mostly male) researchers focusing on the "postmaterialist" mobilizations of the seventies have tended to overlook or, at best, to undervalue the conceptual as well as the strategic/tactical contributions that emerged from this campaign to the betterment of later movements.[7] In addition to recognizing the inherently discriminatory nature of the traditional "family order," these early parental activists issued the call for "anti-authoritarian education," a battle cry that would soon work its way through the schools and into a university system still proudly upholding an academic mission established by Humboldt in 1807. Child-care organizers moreover coalesced to create the first "citizen initiative" groups, a very effective brand of do-it-yourself politics that would become the hallmark of the "new social movements" over the next decade. The *Kinderläden* campaign nevertheless backfired in a least one respect: even with the possibility of sharing parental responsibility, female coordinators were so busy locating and renovating suitable facilities, in addition to their lobbying for state subsidies, that no time or energy remained for direct involvement in *other* political work.

In September 1968, women took their cause to the twenty-third (SDS) Delegate Conference in Frankfurt, where they insisted on the need to end exploitation in the "private sphere" as well as in the public realm, and called upon radical men to undergo a change of consciousness themselves. Male leaders apparently saw little contradiction between their own promises to liberate the world and their expectations that the women at their sides would continue to make their coffee, engage in free (heterosexual) love, and attend to the children in their communal apartments. When the convening "authorities" dismissed the women's demands for "lack of a theoretical basis," one incensed appellant made it clear to all-male panel that the "personal is the political" with a few well-targeted tomatoes from her lunch bag: the move was "seconded" by other females in attendance. Within weeks, independent women's groups sprang up in a number of cities and university towns.

Unfortunately these groups were no more immune to the perils of fractionalization than were their male-dominated counterparts in the student movement at large. In addition to not being taken seriously by the most influential movement organizations, the women's relatively elitist university affiliations resulted in their social isolation vis-à-vis mainstream wives and mothers. The extreme positions they represented were far removed from the daily realities facing the majority of women in the FRG, and moreover clashed with the pervasiveness of strong "anticommunist' sentiments—especially in the city where the Wall served as an ever-present reminder of conditions in the "so-called GDR." Their own anti-authoritarian stance made them inimical to formal organization and instilled in them a scorn for coalitions with elements of "the establishment" (e.g., parties and trade unions) which they shared with the movement as a whole. Many groups were formed, disbanded, and recreated, unable to find or forge a consensus on the (ir)reconcilability of "family" and "socialism," on the one hand, and incapable of agreeing on whether to adopt a separatist approach based on personal consciousness-raising or to rely on a more collectivist, class-struggle approach to consciousness-raising, on the other.

These divisions would later establish themselves as two separate wings of the movement. Neither configuration applied the term "feminist" to its activities prior to 1970, at which point individual groups began to absorb the thinking of Betty Friedan, Simone de Beauvoir, Kate Millett, and others through literature imported from abroad. The socialist wing began to rediscover the protofeminist theories of earlier German radicals, such as Rosa Luxemburg, Clara Zetkin, and August Bebel. The West German analogue to *The Feminine Mystique*, namely, Alice Schwarzer's work on *The "Little Difference" and Its Major Consequences (Der "Kleine Unterschied" und seine grossen Folgen)* did not appear on the market until 1975.

Larger and usually more moderate women's organizations, such as the Democratic Women's Federation of Germany (DFD), along with clusters of female party members from the Left (e.g., the German [DKP] Communists) did join in the escalating protests against the emergency powers legislation, nuclear deployments, the anti-Springer campaign, and, later, the Vietnam War. These solidarity displays notwithstanding, the spirit of intergroup cooperation did not become self-sustaining. The tragedy of the women's movement during the critically formative years of the late sixties was that some participants had been prematurely politicized by their own early association with particular factions of the student movement at large, for example, with the Spartakists, Maoists, Trotskyists, or with other communist "K-groups." Their common identity as an "oppressed minority" within a larger (albeit also minority) radical movement failed to transcend or supercede their primary identification with the "grander" political causes—a dilemma shared by women's movements throughout history.

Moreover, since revolutionary movements, by definition, entail all-or-nothing propositions (in contrast to reform movements), female activists tended to internalize the pursuit of an all-encompassing "ideological" or theoretical framework, the search for a *Gesamtkonzept*, from whence a consensus on strategy and tactics would automatically flow. Short of discovering that "comprehensive concept," they would not allow themselves to be bought off or co-opted with partial reforms that failed to challenge and overthrow the capitalist/patriarchal order *per se*. Theirs would remain a predominantly antistrategy strategy until the end of the next decade, with "consciousness-raising," "equal opportunity," and "monopoly-capitalist exploitation" as its axial themes. Polarization and fragmentation among the more radical groups intensified to the point of total rupture, leaving behind a political landscape strewn with many personally scarred and professionally wounded leftists, as well as many ostensibly unbridgeable trenches between and among partisan women's groups (as experienced by this participant-observer of the Women's Summer University convened annually at Berlin's Free University since 1976).

A new political identity defined primarily in negative or "demarcation" terms was unlikely to produce positive results for West German women. Indeed, feminist stirrings among the radical fringe could do nothing to alter the relative share and distribution of places for women in higher education. Nor did their substantive message and ideological affiliations promise to open any doors to female graduates seeking employment in state administration or in the corporate world during the *Berufsverbot* (career blacklisting of leftists) period that followed.

For the more moderate wing of the movement, the Grand Coalition was an era infused with an optimism that gave birth to a new generation of women leaders eager to combine elements of feminist theory with political action. The end of the decade saw a number of veterans, such as Hildegard Hamm-Brücher (FDP), Helga Wex (CDU), and Käte Strobel (SPD), assuming prominent posts in party and government. The federal elections of 1969 resulted in the first, postwar victory for the Social Democrats, whose promise of sweeping social reforms and rapprochement with "the other Germany" drew many newly enfranchised voters into the party fold; the recruits included an unprecedented number of moderate but nonetheless politically conscious women with varying levels of protest experience. The SPD's calls for more radical democracy notwithstanding, the percentage of seats occupied by women in the Bundestag actually declined between the fourth and fifth legislative periods, ranging from 43 to 49 (or 9.4 percent) through the 1961–1965 term, to a total of 36 to 41 seats (7.9 percent) between 1965 and 1969; their relative share dropped to a record postwar low of 6.2 percent during the first three years of the social-liberal coalition.

By 1971, politicized feminism rediscovered a measure of common cause in the struggle over abortion reform, but cooperation once again proved to be short-lived. In fact, the defeat that was incurred on this particular single-issue front ultimately reinforced the self-righteous, anti-coalition orientation of separatist groups, resulting in a second definitive split. It took a second changing of the generational guard, along with a dramatically transformed political-economic environment, to weld the many feminist factions and focus groups back together again.

RETRENCHMENT THROUGH AUTONOMY: PROJECT-FEMINISM AND THE 1970s

The new social-liberal coalition under Brandt was not the first to push for a decriminalization of the antiabortion strictures contained in the 1871 Criminal Code. Efforts by the Weimar Independent party (USPD), Socialist party (SPD), and German Communist party (KPD) to eliminate Paragraphs 218 and 219 from the Code had resulted in a slight mitigation in the terms of punishment for violators by 1926. The intense debates waged in the period 1946–1948 produced no direct changes in the law itself, although hard labor and the death sentence were formally struck from the sentencing rules in 1953. After 1969, Käte Strobel's initiation of a countrywide program for sex education and family planning, under the auspices of the expanded Ministry for Youth, Family, and Health, opened the door for a new legalization campaign.

While the SPD and FDP parliamentary caucuses wrangled internally over the acceptability of abortions in the first trimester of pregnancy, more radical feminist groups found tactical inspiration in a number of comparable campaigns being waged abroad. A self-incrimination campaign conducted by 343 French feminists in April 1971 provided the model for the June 1971 "speak out" action in which the names of 375 prominent West Germans who had illegally terminated pregnancies were made public in *Stern Magazine* (issue no. 74). In addition to ending a long-standing taboo on public debate over the abortion issue, these "confessions" generated a wave of summer demonstrations and a delegate conference in Düsseldorf and Frankfurt, attracting representatives from twenty-five women's groups. Together they initiated "Action 218," a petition drive calling for an end to criminalization through the complete removal of 218 from the Code; they further demanded insurance coverage for abortions, contraceptives, and additional sex education programs. In July 1971, they presented a Solidarity Declaration containing 86,500 signatures and 3,000 self-indictments to the federal minister of justice (an action followed by repeated police raids on groups headquarters). Munich, Frankfurt, and Berlin served as sites for mass demonstrations in the fall, followed by a major Women's Tribunal against Paragraph 218 in Cologne during May 1972. A variety of groups staged disturbances at professional medical congresses and saw to the scheduling of "Action Weeks against 218" in all major cities through 1974.

Existing law, the same paragraphs that had become the vehicle for "procreation hygiene" abuse under the Nazi regime, proscribed women's access to legal abortions; but by 1969 *de jure* penal sentences were reduced or suspended for abortions performed on the basis of specified "indicators" (classified after 1974 in terms of medical, eugenic, criminal, and "hardship" factors). Women's demands for a trimester approach, viz., a guaranteed right to abortion "on demand" during the first three months of pregnancy, found major support within the German Trade Union Federation (DGB), the DKP, the FDP, the Association of Socialist Women (ASF), the Jusos, and the national SPD caucus. The social-liberal parliamentary majority adopted trimester legislation in April 1974, which the conservative majority in the Bundesrat immediately sought to block. Bolstered by strong church opposition to the new law, the CDU/CSU Länder joined parliamentary conservatives in taking the case to the Constitutional Court. In its 5-to-12 decision of 25 April 1975, the same year as the official commencement of the United Nations' Decade of Women, the court upheld the state's obligation to see pregnancy carried to full term, declaring that "many women . . . reject a pregnancy because they are not willing to take on the natural duties of motherhood and the self-denial connected with [that role]." The court induced the Bundestag to pass a new law in May 1975, legalizing the procedure only when the need for abortions under one or more of the four indicators had been certified by a doctor. Once the law took effect in June 1976, independent women's groups began to organize chartered buses to Holland where provisions were comparatively more liberal; the practice continued until 1978, when activists decided to replace symbolic (and futile) gestures with a new push for counseling and referral services, for outpatient clinics, doctors' surveys, and a renewed emphasis on public debate and protest.

The lapidary character of the court's decision had a devastating impact on the movement, both in light of the emotional intensity that had characterized the campaign and in view of the tremendous effort that had been poured into forging a coalition among still deeply factionalized groups. This campaign marked the first time that a "feminist" cause had joined radical and reformist forces by clearly transcending class-elitist boundaries. But the issue did not provide a sufficiently firm foundation for common political identity, especially in the face of defeat. More militant groups moved quickly toward separatism, while reform-oriented activists returned to a concentration on party and coalition politics.

The legislative efforts undertaken by a second wave of female parliamentarians in the early seventies had a dramatic impact on the social and legal status of mainstream women in the Federal Republic. Included among the ranks of those who entered the Bundestag between 1969 and 1976 were Marie Schlei (parliamentary state secretary to Chancellor Schmidt, and later minister for economic cooperation); Katharina Focke (SPD minister for youth, family and health); Antje Huber (Focke's ministerial successor after 1976); legal specialist Herta Däubler-Gmelin, consumer advocate Anke Martiny, and FDP-Presidium member Liselotte Funcke. Their combined efforts resulted in a number of critical statutory reforms, namely: changes in marriage, family, maternity, and adoption laws; pension, social assistance, youth welfare, and parental sick leave legislation; alterations in the payment of child-support and housing subsidies, as well as reforms regarding foreign workers and the probate rights of women in agriculture. They moreover lobbied for "co-determination" in industry and for a major overhaul of the higher education system under the banner of "equal opportunities." The cumulative effect of these reforms, though not immediately obvious, was a gradual accomodation of West German social policy to the equal rights and equal protection requirements of the Basic Law. Still dependent upon backdoor (list system) access to political office, women closed out the decade with only 7.9 percent of the Bundestag seats at the end of the eighth electoral period. Others, like Anke Fuchs, nevertheless began to move into national ministerial, party executive, or state government offices.

The mid-seventies moreover witnessed a wide variety of initiatives geared toward self-discovery and self-identification, set in motion by the proliferation of "autonomous groups" (*Die Autonomen*). The first *Women's Year Book* (intended as an anthology of the movement but markedly devoid of themes about working women) appeared in 1974, as did the first *Frauenkalender*. The 1976 *Yearbook* turned to counterculture, body consciousness, and violence against women, parallel to the creation of the first women's shelter in West Berlin. The same year brought the opening of the annual Women's University at the Free University of Berlin, as well as the first issue of the magazine *Courage* in September. The second feminist magazine, *Emma*, commenced publication in February 1977, and a spirit of "market competition" was also implicit in the 1978 appearance of a second women's calendar, "Day-by-Day." For every new idea that was spawned, there arose an "initiative"; Women against Rape, Housework for Pay, Women in Technical Professions, and Aid for Turkish Women were but a few of the areas covered, next to the creation of Viva (a feminist publishing house), women's cafés, bars, art courses, and galleries. A growing body of indigenous feminist literature also went to press under the autonomous label, including the works of Alice Schwarzer, Verna Stefan, Marie Louise Janssen-Jurreit, and Sylvia Plogstedt.

With so much struggling yet to be done on so many fronts, diversity could have had a *positive* mobilizing effect, had each group been willing to recognize the unique contribution made by others. Instead, the autonomous emphasis on project activism among feminists tended to institutionalize divisions, making it ever more difficult to establish a least common denominator. Social-liberal reformists who argued "it's not the men, it's the system" met with radical countercries that "equal rights defined by patriarchy are not worth the struggle."

The development of the women's shelters provides a case in point. Inspired by the British experience and moved by a 1974 film over local spouse and child abuse problems, a small group of Berlin feminists established a shelter that soon became the basis for a three-year "model" project adopted and subsidized by the Federal Ministry of Youth, Family, and Health at an annual level of DM 450,000. Over 615 women and 730 children sought refuge in 9 houses during the first 12 months of operation (now financed directly by the Berlin Senate). Other shelters followed in Cologne, Bielefeld, and Hamburg, many of which have remained dependent on private contributions—with noticeable differences in the quality of housing afforded. Of the 120 shelters in existence by 1986, 87 could be classified as "autonomous" homes, added to 14 more autonomous "initiatives."[8] Not all have remained ideologically pure, however; many have found it necessary to drop their admant opposition to federal, state, or municipal involvement and to join the growing queue for public funds. They nevertheless insist on non-hierarchical, grass-roots–democratic management, exclude marriage counseling from their psychological systems, and generally reject direct cooperation with men. When religious and charity organizations began to establish their own centers to meet the extraordinary demand (24,000 users in 1986, including asylum-seekers at eighteen Catholic homes against marital violence in Bavaria), they were promptly denounced by autonomists for having created "counter-shelters," potentially aimed at driving the latter (often lesbians) out of the market. The autonomists faced counterattacks from the reformist flank as well, which charged that separatists worked as accomplices by relieving the state of its constitutional responsibility and, thus, its fiscal burden for the special protection of mothers and families.

The rise and spread of autonomous projects was paralleled by the rapid profusion of the so-called *Sponti* groups (spontaneous ones) on university campuses, set in motion by a new, anti-ideological, anti-intellectual, yet issue-critical student generation. I concur with Doormann that the radical feminist groups are not as unique as they think—"they have much in common with the Sponti and Alternative movement, and also share its symptoms: 'the novel expedition into the [realm of the] irrational,' . . . the animosity towards theory and organization, self-restriction to the private sphere, refusal and rebellion, instead of challenge and 're-volution.' "[9] The overlap remains incomplete, however. While autonomous groups did share many of the negative ("anti-") Sponti symptoms, they were far removed from the live-and-let-live approach that made it possible for the latter to join in other protest coalitions. Institutional memory, as well as the personal experiences conveyed by older siblings, rendered the new wave of student activists very wary of the highly organized, overtly cerebral, "no-fun", and ultimately self-destructive character of the sixties' movement defined along ideological lines. Prior to the 1980 birth of the Greens, the *Spontis'* affinity for small-is-beautiful thinking led them to prefer loose coalitions with neighborhood "citizen initiatives" over mass meetings with trade union or party representatives. These neighborhood groups mobilized primarily around environmental protection issues, and opened their membership to anyone, from radical ecologist to liberal pastor, from concerned housewife to conservative bird-watcher, willing to work for the common cause.

The setbacks inflicted upon the women's movement by the over-politicization of the 1960s found little cure in the virtual depoliticization of the late seventies. The withdrawal of the radical-feminist groups from the public sphere coincided with a major economic downturn, which left reform issues vulnerable to the "red pen politics" imposed by the Schmidt government, for example, programs encouraging young women to enter traditionally male professions, followed by subsequent cutbacks in university funding. The opening up of the universities under the social-liberal rubric of "equal opportunity"—and the energy crisis—unfortunately coincided with the coming of age of the West German baby boom. First-semester enrollments among women registered a significant increase, from 26.7 percent in 1969 to 36.6 percent in 1975 and 38.8 percent in 1979, as a higher percentage of females who had completed the Abitur at rates almost equivalent to males decided to pursue higher education. Yet even with the hurdle of formal qualification behind them, the new graduates discovered the door to professional and economic opportunity suddenly closed by a dramatic jump in academic unemployment rates, in particular: the ninefold increase in joblessness for all academics between 1973 and 1984 amounted to a twenty-fivefold increase for female graduates.[10]

By deliberately choosing to step outside the boundaries of conventional politics, the autonomous project feminists were effective in bringing many new "women's issues" and spheres of activity to public consciousness. They overlooked the extent to which parliamentary politics itself could be used as a vehicle for overcoming a gender-based lack of power and resources. Theirs was a separate political identity that could not be sustained as a model for the movement as a whole.

The end of the 1970s brought a fusion of antinuclear energy and weapons protests under various extraparliamentary roof organizations, the driving force for the "new social movements." Involvement in feminist projects and local citizen initiatives had afforded many women the chance to acquire basic organizational skills outside the home, and conveyed many lessons about public relations, formal decision making, state-administrative and resource mobilization processes. As co-founding members of a "party of the new type," they would finally undertake their own long march through the institutions after 1980. No longer content with the role of the critical consumer, women would take on a new identity as policy producers and party executive officers.

THE TURNING POINT: PRAGMATIC FEMINISM AND THE 1980s

Like its Republican counterpart in the United States, the conservative government of Chancellor Kohl first discovered the West German gender gap in connection with the very election that brought it back to power after thirteen years of social-liberal rule. While women's rates of electoral participation have closely approximated those of men since 1972 (a year also significant in terms of partisan realignment), they constituted 53.8 percent of the eligibles and 53.1 percent of the actual voters in the March 1983 elections. Demographics have compelled the parties to undergo a democratic change of heart regarding the incorporation of "women's issues" into campaign platforms and also in relation to the placement of many more female candidates on the respective party ballots. The Christian-liberal government has discovered women's politics and policies as an important component of the conservative "turnaround" (*Wende*).

What is new about the conservative agenda is not its proclivity for applying cutbacks to those areas traditionally of greatest concern to women, for example, education and social polity. Rather, what distinguishes "the New Partnership between Man and Woman" decreed in the CDU's (CDA) 1981 and 1985 Essen Principles is the recognition and acceptance of women's participation in the paid labor market (totaling 52 percent or 10 million adult women). They quickly add, however, that female work-force participation should remain "flexible" (read: part-time, with low or no benefit requirements for employers), that true "freedom of choice" must be guaranteed to women who stay with or return to *Kinder* and *Küche*, and that homemaking and childrearing are also recognized (but not paid) as careers. While conservatives claim to be responding to a relatively high demand for part-time employment opportunities among married women and mothers of small children, they are less eager to address the argument that this demand is, more often than not, a function of the "double burden," that is, based on the persistence of traditional role expectations and the inequitable distribution of family and household responsibilities among women and men engaged in paid labor. Even the CDU women have publicly protested Norbert Blüm's attempt to pin problems of juvenile delinquency, poor school performance, and divorce on mothers' unwillingness to place "their sacrifices on the altar of self-actualization."[11]

Contradictions in the CDU/CSU's answer to the "Women Question" are especially evident in the case of two recent policy developments:

Example A: In response to a perceived "population deficit" (a fear that "the Germans are dying out!" due to a "post-pill" drop in the birth rate) the Federal Educational Subsidy Law of January 1986 provides a monthly payment of DM 600 to either parent who stays at home up to twelve months after childbirth; it offers no guaranteed return to one's former, full-time job. The monetary provision will hold little attraction for men, who usually earn more; the lack of job security is unlikely to inspire women with hard-won professional training to trade their career satisfaction for "the soft power of the new motherhood" (*die neue Mütterlichkeit*).

Example B: In reaction to a troubling budget deficit, the January 1986 law regulating supplemental "Baby Year" pensions will save the government an estimated DM 4–6 billion (coinciding with a DM 40 billion tax cut). Those excluded are the 4.6 million women born before 31 December 1920, the *Trümmerfrauen* who bore and raised 11.2 million children in addition to digging the fledgling state out of the fascist rubble—this generation includes the mother of Helmut Kohl (born 1930), Heinrich Geissler (1930), and Norbert Blüm (1935)!

Critical female reactions to policy developments of the eighties, including mobilizations against the Pershing II and cruise missile deployments and against a tightening of abortion regulations, have retained their partisan overtones. Efforts to formalize women's inter-party cooperation have been modest at best: among the notable exceptions are the intraparliamentary discussion group known as the "Monday Club" (now 400 members strong after two decades of existence), the legislative initiative sponsored by the women of all parties to strengthen labeling and testing requirements for food products in the mid-seventies, and the more recent effort to block a further tightening of abortion regulations. More striking is the extent to which women have asserted themselves *within* their respective parties, for example in support of quotas for candidacies and internal offices.

In spite of, or because of, their *enfant terrible* status, the Greens have been the most successful in opening party offices to female members, as well as in placing a wide range of women-focused issues on the electoral agenda. Both the modified "rotation" principle and the "zipper principle" (the alternation of female-male candidates as "listed" on the party's second ballot) have catapulted such women as Petra Kelly, Antje Vollmer, Waltraud Schoppe, and Jutta Ditfurth into positions of prominence at state and national levels over the last eight years. These gains have not always met with enthusiastic support from Green males, however, who still talk about their own "willingness to sacrifice" for the very rights of women that should be taken for granted. The more spectacular examples attesting to women's political competence, the 1984 all-female parliamentary executive committee *[das Feminat]* and the all-female slate, the "impudent women of Hamburg," who tallied one of the Greens' largest land-level vote counts to date (10 percent), are still perceived as "a totally crazy experiment."[12] The seven-article "Antidiscrimination Law," drafted by Green women in autumn 1985, is unlikely to see promulgation by 1990, as are the 19 articles of their proposed Quota Law (at the level of 50 percent). Their citation of more than fifty-eight passages from existing statutes which explicitly discriminate against women, however, offers an excellent example of how feminists can/should utilize the parliamentary process to remove barriers to gender equality. The key question for constitutional experts is whether Articles 3, 6, 20, and 33 of the Basic Law do, in fact, oblige the leaders of the West

Table 4.3

Women in Government in the German Federal Republic at the
Federal Level (December 1987)

A. Cabinet Members: 2
B. Bundestag:

		December 1987			March 1983	
Party	*Total*	*Women FRG*	*% FRG*	*West Berlin*	*Women FRG*	*%*
CDU/CSU	223	17	7.6	11	17	6.6
SPD	186	31	16.6	2	21	10.4
Greens	42	21	50.0	2	10	37.0
FDP	46	6	13.0	2	3	8.6
Total	497	75	15.0	22	51	9.8

C. Bundesrat: December 1987
   Regular Members: 4 of 45 full (*ordentliche*) members
   Acting/Representative Members: 14

Source: Statistisches Bundesamt

German state to intervene actively in all segments of society to
counteract forty-year-old patterns of discrimination against those
who now comprise the demographic majority.

Renate Schmidt, Inge Wettig-Danielmeier and other Social
Democratic women have been quite active in pushing for implementation of the resolution to promote women within the party passed
by the 1984 Essen Congress (containing no specific percentages); the
(ASF) has called for a minimum quota of at least 40 percent for all
party offices. The pros and cons of intraparty quotas are still being
hotly contested, not only between national political elites and the
less enlightened rank and file groups, but also among female parliamentarians of the first, second, and third generations. Renger's ve-
hement opposition contrasts sharply with the qualified-to-enthu-
siastic support exhibited by those who entered the Bundestag in the
years 1969–1980; acceptance is virtually unanimous among the
women whose mandates began with the 1983 and 1987 elections,
according to personal interviews conducted by this author.

Rita Süssmuth's* popularity as the minister for youth, family,

* Süssmuth, a professor by occupation, is now president of the Bundestag.

Table 4.4

Female Representation in the State Parliaments

Landesparlament	On 9 June 1988			On 6 August 1985		
	Elected Members Total	Of Those, Women	%	Elected Members Total	Of Those, Women	%
Baden-Württemberg	125	12	9.6	126	8	6.3
Bayern	204	25	12.3	204	15	7.3
Berlin	144	23	16.0	140	23	16.4
Bremen	99	27	27.3	100	17	17.0
Hamburg	120	36	30.0	120	18	15.0
Hessen	110	18	16.4	110	12	10.9
Niedersachsen	155	20	12.9	171	12	7.0
Nordrhein-Westfalen	227	26	11.5	227	25	11.0
Rheinland-Pfalz	100	14	14.0	100	12	12.0
Saarland	51	6	11.8	51	6	11.7
Schleswig-Holstein	74	9	12.2	74	9	12.2

Source: Data were graciously provided by Dr. Otti Stein, Leitstelle zur Durchsetzung der Gleichberechtigung der Frauen, Staatskanzlei, Saarland.

health and women tends to rise and fall on an issue-by-issue basis, as does the level of female activism within CDU/CSU ranks in general. Conservative women have been especially vocal in relation to government proposals for AIDS testing and treatment, and have publically opposed a negative reinterpretation of Paragraph 218 rules. Of all the parties, the FDP has proved least effective in attracting the women's vote, although it evinces a higher percentage of female MdBs than the CDU/CSU (see table 4.3).

Putnam's Law of Increasing Disproportions is alive and well in the FRG—the higher the rung on the political ladder, the smaller (and more isolated) the number of women appointed and elected— despite unquestionably high levels of motivation and formal-educational qualification among prospective female policymakers (compare tables 4.3 and 4.4). A recent survey of members of the Bundestag indicates that women have demonstrated greater mobility than men —or that they have been forced to pay a higher price for empowerment: Four-fifths of the female MdBs comprising the Tenth Bundestag had higher educational degrees, as opposed to two-thirds of the men; 43.1 percent of the women were single, divorced, or widowed, while 82 percent of the male MdBs were married with children.[13]

The 1987 elections produced a dramatic increase in the share of seats held by female MdBs, from 9.8 percent (in 1983) to 15.4 percent. But even with a 3.5 million voter surplus, Hoecker has calculated that if women continue to rely upon the traditional methods of attaining office at the same rate that has characterized their progress over the last four decades, they should not expect to achieve full parity in government or equal representation in Parliament before the year 2107 (the SPD's task force on the equality of women and men reckons with 2113)!

According to the Federal Statistical Office, women comprised 24.3 percent of the full-time mid-level civil service employees in 1963, 29.4 percent in 1975, and 30.5 percent in 1983. The proportion of women within the subset of judges and administrators amounted to 13.3 percent (1969), 18.9 percent (1975) and 20.5 percent (1983); the share of part-time positions held by women in public service at the federal level rose from 82.3 percent to 92.2 percent to 93.1 percent over the same periods.[14] Enlightened parliamentarians succeeded in amending the 1976 Framework for Higher Education Law (HRG) to address the question of institutional(ized) discrimination in the hiring, tenure, and promotion of female academics. They could not prevent the lowering of state-exam grade requirements for would-be judges, once women began to outscore male applicants in ever larger proportions, however. Nor have they waged an effective crusade against the age-32 cut-off rule for civil service entry, which is prejudiced against the realities of female biology and biography.

The feminists of the eighties have adopted a more pragmatic approach to participation in the political power structure, for example, calling for quotas but sending in numbers of candidates whenever and wherever they can. They have moreover begun to cultivate a positive consensus regarding the need for new strategies and tactics in pursuit of greater socioeconomic equality for women. They have sought to adapt American concepts of affirmative action (*Frauenförderung*) and comparable worth to West German structural and legal constraints. Although they lack the powerful "class action suit" mechanism that has been a mainstay of women's and minority rights

Table 4.5
Supplementary Women's Affairs and Equal Opportunity Offices in the FRG (December 1987)

A. Federal Level
   • Ministry of Youth, Family, Women, and Health (current minister: Professor Rita Süssmuth)
   • Department of Women's Affairs, situated within the above ministry (current director: Dr. Hanna Beate Schöpp-Schilling)
   • Federal Working Group of Local/County Women's Bureaus (9 members in the current speakers' committee)
B. Land Level (as of July 1987)
   • *Frauenbeauftragte* and *Gleichstellungsstellen*
     Total: 11 (1 per state)
   • Ministers in state government
     Total: 15 ministers/senators (cabinet level)
           8 state secretaries (higher administration)
C. Common Level
   There are approximately 235 offices that have now been created at the local, municipal, and county level, dealing specifically with women's/equal opportunity issues; the total includes part-time and nonpaid (*ehrenamtlich*) as well as paid and/or full-time positions.
D. City or Municipal Government
   Approximately 2.761 (16%) of some 17,108 elected city council seats are occupied by women (December 1987 figures).
E. University Level
   There are 1,537 women holding the title of "professor" (all ranks) who are currently employed at institutions of higher learning in the FRG; the number of female full professors relative to all full professors stands at roughly 3%. In addition, there are 251 female academic assistants (*Hochschulassistentinnen*), 10,242 scientific and artistic technical aides (*Wissenschaftliche und künstlerische Mitarbeiterinnen*) and 1,197 women instructors for special assignments (December 1987 figures).

Source: Data were graciously provided by Dr. Otti Stein, Leitstelle zur Durchsetzung der Gleichberechtigung der Frauen, Staatskanzlei, Saarland, and by Renate Schmidt, member of the Bundestag who currently heads the SPD's parliamentary Arbeitskreis Gleichstellung von Frau und Mann.

groups in the United States, FRG activists have developed their own network of legal advocates through the creation of over 230 highly visible Women's Affairs and Equal Opportunity Offices (*Frauenbeauftragte* and *Gleichstellungsstellen*) spread throughout the political, administrative, and academic landscapes (see table 4.5.) They have begun to generate their own data bases through Women's Studies projects (*Frauenforschung*), professional conferences, and Bundestag inquiries, and have opened themselves to coalitions, albeit temporary ones, with other partisan and societal groups. While they accept MdB Anke Martiny's dictum, that "s/he who does not struggle, has already lost," the new pragmatic feminists are more self-confident, more self-reflective and, therefore, less susceptible to the polemical confrontations and the all-or-nothing perceptions of power that afflicted the feminists of earlier eras—qualities perceived by the actors themselves as "typically German."

VALUE CHANGE AND FUTURE PERSPECTIVES

It is highly unlikely, given the combined influences of structural factors (e. g., the nature of the postwar electoral system) and political-cultural factors (e. g., the deep-seated affinity for "imperative mandates"), that women in the FRG will seek to establish their own clearing-house equivalent to the U.S.-National Women's Political Caucus for the promotion of feminist candidates and officeholders across party lines. Their direct affiliation with a variety of new social movement organizations has nonetheless helped to assuage a long-suffered sense of "contact anxiety," in addition to providing a wealth of experiences vis-à-vis conventional and unconventional forms of participation. The critical question for contemporary feminists is whether they will be ready and willing to abandon old preferences for ideological purity in favor of more pragmatic coalition politics, in view of the demographic and electoral opportunities likely to emerge in the 1990s.

   In the process of mobilizing support for the new social movements, West German women of all political colors have internalized many of the so-called "postmaterialist" values professed most openly (and often in a monopolistic tone) by the Greens, namely, a commitment to ecological preservation, social justice, grass roots democracy, and structural as well as personal nonviolence. It is unclear what special relevance the dichotomy materialist/postmaterialist holds for women: on the one hand, the historical, gender-based division of labor has always rendered women responsible for material and physical (re)production processes; "homemaking" has long compelled them to find a balance between self-actualization, material resources, and the common good of the family. On the other hand, material wealth has rarely been a source of individual power for women—property ownership having long been defined as a male right—hence their greater willingness (thus socialized) to spend money in the service of others, or to work for low pay or no pay at all. What is clear is that value changes have begun to permeate the consciousness of younger, mainstream women, especially in regard to the traditional division of male and female labor: as one March 1986 Infas poll revealed, only 12 percent of those under 35 envision *Küche und Kinder* alone as their ideal future.

In addition to exhibiting higher levels of education and political interest than the generations preceding them, the daughters of the sixties and seventies have also begun to project a new self-image and a more progressive "understanding of politics" across class and party lines. A 1980 *Emma* survey found that 98 percent of its readers perceived West German political parties as "inimical to women" (*frauenfeindlich*). In 1982 Hoecker asked 363 male and 197 female activists in Bremen to imagine the likely effects of a majority female membership upon their own party: 16.1 percent of the women thought things would remain "the same," 56 percent foresaw "some" change, 27 percent "many changes;" the figures for men were 14.1 percent, 52.9 percent and 33 percent, respectively.[15] The important point is that ever more women are taking it upon themselves to influence or redirect the course of West German politics. The last four decades have witnessed a steady increase in the number of women actively campaigning for election to the Bundestag; accounting for 8.9 percent (207) of all candidates in 1949, 9.5 percent (249) in 1969, and 20.1 percent (592) in 1980, their numbers reached an all-time high of 685, or 25.4 percent, by January 1987.[16]

There remains the problem of a "consensus deficit," especially among feminist-fundamentalists who continue to oppose compromises of the pragmatic-feminist sort. Jansen stresses the "quintessential lack of a broadly anchored, widely supported, political and strategic comprehensive concept [*Gesamtkonzept*], of a complete overview of the objective and subjective interest configurations of women . . . as well as [the lack of] an appropriately broad and politically relevant comprehensive union or means of cooperation."[17] The discovery of an all-encompassing strategy, interest profile, or grand coalition is unlikely, and perhaps even undesirable. The struggle for equality indeed requires that West German women become active in all segments of society, in all aspects of public policymaking; but not all groups have to be involved on all fronts simultaneously! This is not to say that single groups should insist on the cultivation of issue monopolies—nor is it a call for the Autonomists to abandon their "principles." In fact, every movement needs its fundamentalists, if only to test periodically the consistency of its goals and the purity of its conscience. Feminist obstructionism, on the other hand, contributes little to the common cause; it merely reinforces those who would preserve the prevailing gender-specific division of labor and its consequent maldistribution of power and opportunity. As new social movement participants have learned, organizational overlap ensures a transfer of learning experiences, a transmission of effective strategies and tactics from group to group, from one cause to another. Empowerment is a cumulative process.

The issues confronting women in the next decade will be many and varied. There is nonetheless an important distinction to be made, between policies defined as especially relevant *to* and *for* women, the issue orientations of women *in* politics, and the pursuit of *feminist* values and objectives. The catalogue of issues and policies judged to be of special interest to "women" has expanded considerably over the past forty years. Women's environmental concerns are no longer limited to hearth and playground; they now include problems of radiation exposure, toxic pollution, and the existence of potential nuclear battlegrounds. It is only by virtue of the accomplishments of the founding mothers of the reconstruction age that the daughters of the social reform era have been able to move on to new fields of political action. It is likewise the women of the nineties who will raise a more fundamental challenge to gender-specific divisions of labor and power, based on the gains of the second generation who recognized—in theory and practice— the limits imposed by the "double burden."

The feminist theme for the 1990s, as defined by parliamentarian Renate Schmidt, has an ironic twist: "the women's question is now

a men's question." Without fundamental changes in the consciousness and behavior of men, beginning with the equitable distribution
of family and household responsibilities, there can be but limited
progress in the campaign to secure women's constitutional rights.
There are hopeful signs that the legitimacy of "quotas" and other
"positive discrimination" measures will cease to be the focus of
heated debate by the end of the decade, enabling elected officials to
move on to the real questions of social change. Those issues will
include the opening of new career doors for women in traditionally
male professions; workplace guarantees, as well as reintegration and
retraining programs for women after childbirth; the push for a shortened workweek (35 hours), in addition to expanded part-time employment opportunities for men; equalization of pensions and the
provision of adequate child-care facilities; and, last but not least, the
liberalization of abortion laws. Prospects for the promulgation of a
sweeping antidiscrimination law are less than rosy.

Equally important for women will be the problems of acid rain
and pollution, toxic and nuclear waste disposal, the potential hazards of genetic research and biotechnology, and the overdeployment
of chemical and nuclear weapons in their own backyards—in short,
the very questions of science and technology, war and peace traditionally comprising "a man's world." It is the latter set of issues that
is drawing ever more women into the political arena. There moreover exists a growing body of parliamentary veterans evincing "distinctly ministerial qualities," notes MdB Peter Conradi; the list includes Anke Fuchs, Herta Däubler-Gmelin, Birget Breuel, Hildegard
Hamm-Brücher, along with current ministers Dorothee Wilms and
Rita Süssmuth.

The search for a positive, political postwar identity is not a search
confined to women of the Federal Republic; in this respect, the
value changes that have taken hold within the equal rights and
feminist movements are representative of value changes that are
being internalized by the political culture at large. Forty years in the
making, their long march through the institutions may not be a
sufficient condition for the realization of a broad range of constitutional rights and ideals. But it is certainly a necessary one, and the
women of the Federal Republic are finally on their way.

NOTES

1. Article 3 of the *Grundgesetz* holds "(1) All persons shall be equal before the law. (2) Men and women shall have equal rights. (3) No one may be prejudiced or favored because of his *[sic]* sex, his parentage, his race, his language, his homeland and origin, his faith, or his religious or political opinions." The equality mandate is strengthened further by several other constitutional rights including Art. 1 (the inviolability of human dignity); Art. 6 (protection of marriage, family, children, and mothers); Art. 12 (freedom to choose one's trade, profession, place of work, and place of training); Art. 20 (democratic and social state): and especially Art. 33, "(1) Every German shall have in every land the same political rights and duties of citizenship, (2) Every German shall be equally eligible for any public office according to his *[sic]* aptitude, qualifications, and professional achievements."

2. All electoral data presented in this section are taken from Joachim Hoffman-Göttig's work, *Emanzipation mit dem Stimmzettel. 70 Jahre Frauenwahlrecht in Deutschland* (Bonn: Verlag Neue Gesellschaft, 1986). Unless otherwise noted, my historical survey of the occupation and reconstruction years derives from two often-cited collections: Annette Kuhn, ed., *Frauen in der deutschen Nachkriegszeit*, vol. 2 (Düsseldorf: Schwann, 1986) and Anne-Elisabeth Freier and Annette Kuhn, eds., *Frauen in der Geschichte*, vol. 5 (Düsseldorf: Schwann, 1984). Page numbers of direct citations appear in parentheses, according to volume.

3. An estimated 80 percent of "several ten of thousands" of rapes that were registered in Berlin are reported to have occurred between 24 April and 3 May 1945, according to Ingrid Schmidt-Harzbach, "Eine Woche im April. Berlin 1945-Vergewaltigung als Massenschicksal," *Feministische Studien* 3, no. 2 (November 1984): 51–65.

4. Figures are cited from Peter Merkl's chapter, "The Politics of Sex: West Germany," in *Women in the World: A Comparative Study*, ed. Lynn B. Iglitzin and Ruth Ross (Santa Barbara, Calif.: ABC-Clio, 1976).

5. Elisabeth Noelle and Erich Peter Neumann, eds., *Jahrbuch der Öffentlichen Meinung, 1947–1955* Allensbach: Institut für Dewrskopie, 1956), 159, 94.

6. Lottemi Doormann, ed., *Keiner schiebt uns weg, Zwischenbilanz der Frauenbewegung in der Bundesrepublik* (Weinheim/Basel: Beltz, 1979), 23ff.

7. Silvia Kontos, "Modernisierung der Subsumptionspolitik? Die Frauenbewegung in den Theorien neuer sozialer Bewegungen," *Feministische Studien* 2 (1986): 34–49.

8. Bundesministerium für Jugend, Familie und Gesundheit, *Hilfen für*

Misshandelte Frauen. Abschlussbericht der Wissenschaftlichen Begleitung des Modell-projekts Frauenhaus Berlin (Stuttgart: Bundesministerium für Jugend, Familie und Gesundheit, 1981); and Kathrin Kramer and Claudia Pai, "Frauen auf der Flucht," *Die Zeit,* 17 January 1986.

9. Doormann, *Keiner schiebt uns weg,* 69.
10. Petra Drohsel, "Schule, Berufe, Hochschule." in *Frauenwiderspruch— Alltag und Politik,* ed. Mechtild Jansen (Cologne: Pahl-Rugenstein, 1987), 117.
11. Marliese Dobberthien, "Zur Konservativen Familien- und Sozialpolitik der Wende." In Jansen, *Frauenwiderspruch,* 84.
12. See Heide Simonis's chapter in Otto Kallscheuer, ed. *Die Grünen— Letzte Wahl? Vorgaben in Sachen Zukunftsbewältigung* (Berlin: Rotbuch Verlag, 1986).
13. Beate Hoecker, *Frauen in der Politik. Eine Soziologische Untersuchung* (Opladen: Leske & Budrich, 1987), 87.
14. Statistisches Bundesamt, *Personalstandsstatistik,* special series 14, no. 6 (Wiesbaden 1985).
15. Hoecker, *Frauen in der Politik,* 222.
16. Ibid., 75.
17. Jansen, *Frauenwiderspruch,* 24.

5

THE PROTESTANT CHURCH IN DIVIDED GERMANY AND BERLIN

Richard L. Merritt

This chapter explores the place of the German Protestant church in the often dramatic struggle among different temporal and spiritual powers to control the German soul.[1] Of central concern are the tension between organizational and individual goals, sharp differences in political perspectives, and the consequences of all these for political community in postwar Berlin. Particularly in the first years after 1948, when ecclesiastical structures in Germany spanned territories housing separate and mutually antagonistic political systems, the spiritual and political values inherent in the triangular relationship state-church-individual were potentially explosive. They went to the very heart of the church itself.

QUEST FOR UNITY

German Protestantism has been fragmented virtually from its beginnings in the early sixteenth century. After Martin Luther's break with Rome, independent spirits, including some of his earliest supporters, began advancing their own views on Christianity. Fed by struggles for political power among princely patrons, personality clashes among strong-willed men of the cloth, and doctrinal disputes among Lutherans, Zwinglians, Anabaptists, and myriad others on such matters as the Holy Eucharist, sectarianism flourished. Nor did the growing possibility of armed conflict between Protestants—some inspired by religion, others by German patriotism and resentment against Rome's claim to secular authority—and Catholics diminish this sectarianism. To avert bloodshed, Europe's princes met in 1555 in Augsburg. What they produced, however, was less a resolution of the burgeoning conflict than a stabilization of the status quo, one that legitimized Protestantism and the territorial lord's right to prescribe the form of religion to be followed throughout his own lands (*cuius regio, eius religio*). Mutual distrust and deeply embedded antagonisms stymied subsequent efforts to unite Protestants.

The late eighteenth and early nineteenth centuries saw some (often halting) steps toward unification. For one thing, with the growing size of Germany's territorial units came larger administrative offices to organize religious life. Most Länder or provinces, however, maintained separate church structures. For another thing, some German leaders, with political goals in mind, exerted pressure on the churches.

The end of World War I changed the very nature of the Evangelical churches in Germany. Before 1918 each provincial church had stood under the protection of the government or ruler of its own province (or, in some cases, provinces). The collapse of the Wilhelmine empire and formation of the Weimar Republic meant the separation of church and state in Germany. To be sure, the state continued to support religion—financially, for instance, by imposing a church tax on every individual belonging to a religious community. The church was nonetheless, and for the first time, on its own.

The League of German Evangelical Churches, founded in 1922, was sorely tested when the Nazis came to power and promoted a centralized church structure based on their appeal to the so-called German Christians. The internal struggle that ensued practically tore apart the German Evangelical churches. Alarmed at Nazi inhumanities, and disturbed by the apparent inability of provincial church administrations to withstand the enforced coordination (*Gleichschaltung*), individual pastors and church communities banded together to form an underground "Confessing Church" (*Bekennende Kirche*). The state persecuted its leaders, in some cases throwing them into concentration camps, in still others simply executing them.

Their effectiveness in undermining Nazi authority in the church and their martyrs qualify the leaders of the Confessing Church as authentic heroes of the resistance to Hitler. At the same time, however, they helped to destroy the newly formed German Evangelical church. When in the spring of 1945 the Nazi regime collapsed in the rubble that had been Berlin, Protestantism in Germany was without formal leadership, but the collapse of nazism generally left those who had resisted it in a good position for reorganizing postwar German life.

Reorganization proceeded most rapidly in the provincial churches, such as that in Berlin-Brandenburg. The long history of this church province, which comprised the municipal diocese of Berlin and three further dioceses in the Brandenburg March, was characterized by an organic unity that extended down into the individual parishes. It was this quality, along with extensive wartime planning by the Prussian Council of Brethren, that permitted quick, but thorough, action. Reorganization began less than a week after Berlin's capitulation to the Red Army on 2 May 1945. By the end of July the first postwar synod of the Confessing Church of Berlin-Brandenburg had ratified the new organization and confirmed Otto Dibelius in his position as the first bishop. Before the year's end, the Evangelical Church in Berlin-Brandenburg (*Evangelische Kirche in Berlin-Brandenburg,* or EKiBB), possessed a well-articulated structure for making and implementing decisions, and, through its weekly newspaper, *Die Kirche,* for addressing a wider public.

Reconstituting an Evangelical church for Germany as a whole was quite a different matter. Given their experience under nazism, the leaders of some provincial churches dragged their heels. Then, too, the first months of the occupation encouraged decentralization by forcing provincial churches and parishes to rely on their own organizational and other resources. Meetings nonetheless began among representatives of the provincial churches and the Confessing Church, and aimed at creating an overarching organizational structure for all German Protestants. By July 1948, in Eisenach, they had adopted a constitution for the Evangelical Church in Germany (*Evangelische Kirche in Deutschland,* or EKD) and set in motion a wide range of other common activities. Once again the country seemed to be on the path toward a united church.

POLITICAL DIVISION

Even while church leaders were meeting in Eisenach, however, the political rifts that would divide Germany into two countries were beginning to complicate the EKD's promising beginning. Almost from the very outset of the occupation, the wartime Allies had discovered that their views of how the postwar "democratized" Germany should look diverged sharply. Differing perspectives turned into contrary policies by 1947; and by the beginning of the following year the cold war was in full swing. Separate currency reforms in June 1948 in the three western zones of occupation (plus the western sectors of Berlin) and the Soviet zone (plus the Soviet sector of Berlin) forced the church to establish separate institutions and procedures in East and West to handle the two currencies. The subsequent blockade of West Berlin and counterblockade imposed by the Western Allies on territories under Soviet control restricted the travel of all Germans, including church leaders. By the fall of 1949, after the creation of separate governments in East and West, the EKD found itself one of the very few organizations bridging the boundary between the two countries.

The fact that the EKD thrived in the restored framework of political liberalism in the West is not especially remarkable. The Federal Republic took seriously its constitutional guarantees of individual and organizational liberty in matters religious. The new chancellor, Konrad Adenauer, was himself a deeply religious man who, though a Catholic, was insistent on securing the full representation of Protestants in the political affairs of the republic. Church leaders accepted the liaison as natural. Few were the critics at the time who commented on the implications of a church and political regime working hand in hand.

The EKD faced greater problems in the East. The GDR's communist ideology had no room for organized religion, especially a church that resisted the state's efforts to mobilize it on behalf of political goals. Threats to isolate and suppress the church turned into policies in mid-1952, after the FRG had reached agreement with its Western Allies on a future path of development that included West German rearmament. With the death of Stalin in early 1953 and the

GDR's recognition that its overall policies were seriously alienating its own population came a more relaxed attitude toward the church. Renewed hostility toward all West German organizations, including the church, came after agreements in 1954–1955 gave the Federal Republic almost complete autonomy—which meant, among other things, the right to create a defense force linked to the North Atlantic Treaty Organization (NATO).

The year 1957 was the watershed as far as the East German government was concerned. In February of that year, without having brought the matter before the church's synod, the EKD Council contracted to provide pastoral services to the newly established West German *Bundeswehr*. East German officials, who had rejected out of hand the EKD's proposal to provide the same service to members of the GDR's People's Army, interpreted the step as final proof of the church's subservience to what they saw as West German militarism and imperialism, and began to insist that the church on East German soil dissociate itself from the EKD. In April 1957 the government's Office for Contacts with the Church was transformed into a State Secretariat for Church Questions, whose director sought contacts only with church officials resident in the GDR. A year later Prime Minister Otto Grotewohl denied a request for a meeting made by the Conference of Church Leaders in the GDR, chaired by Bishop Otto Dibelius of Berlin-Brandenburg who lived in West Berlin and who, as chairman of the EKD Council, had led the battle of words against the GDR. In his response, Grotewohl said that, in the future, he would only receive delegations all of whose members lived in the GDR or East Berlin, and recommended as the leader of such a delegation the bishop of Thuringia and deputy chairman of East Germany's Conference of Church Leaders, Moritz Mitzenheim.

Resisting Totalitarianism

The EKD thus faced a dilemma. If the East German state was intent on barring Western church officials from any activity in the territory under its control, then the church's insistence on retaining its existing structure and leadership would simply mean its exclusion from East German life. This in turn meant that, in all probability, state officials would continue to bear down on the activities of pastors in their parishes, and make life difficult for active Christians in the GDR. Yet, to relinquish the unified structure that German Lutherans had worked so hard to create would at the very least be bowing to state demands that resembled those of Nazi totalitarianism, at worst exposing Protestants in the GDR to further pressure by a state bent on a new form of *Gleichschaltung* that would ultimately destroy any sense of individual religious liberty.

At the outset the church chose the path of resistance. The argument, phrased so well by Bishop Dibelius in 1949, was that any state seeking to restrain the free exercise of religion was acting immorally and was destined to fail in its endeavors (Dibelius 1949:85–88). Resisting any such effort was therefore the command of the day. Indeed, it is undeniable that the church's steadfast opposition to the GDR's restrictiveness gave many the courage to resist its inroads into the private sphere. Individual pastors and lay persons stand out as bulwarks who comforted and inspired those buffeted by political storms and state demands. Then, too, the EKD's central office channeled funds and other forms of support to parish and provincial churches in East Germany. The result of these and other measures was that the church structure in the GDR could provide a basis for passive resistance and other forms of pressure that sometimes forced the government to modify its position. It also enabled the church to maintain a unified structure across the territories of East and West Germany.

Ultimately, however, the EKD's stance yielded little more than tactical shifts on the part of the state in its dealings with the church. Even to those unwilling to recognize its legitimacy, the position of the Soviet and East German Communists must have been clear. Perhaps not at the outset, but certainly later, they were seeking to reorganize German life in accordance with the principles of Marx and Lenin. As long as the church was willing to participate in the creation of this new society, it would be tolerated, even encouraged. But should the church see and reject such a role as undesirable "political" activity, then the government would restrict its freedom of movement and undermine its position in society.

Religious Liberty in the GDR

Shortlived tactical retreats notwithstanding, the East German government's reaction to the church's resistance was to tighten the reins. Its ability to manipulate the legal and political context within which the church operated, no less than its control over financial institutions and foreign exchange and especially domination of the mass media, gave the state powerful weapons. While many of the steps it took seemed aimed at aspects of the church's organizational structure, it must be added, each of them and others besides struck more or less directly at the individual's religious liberty. Active church members and their families were harassed in a multitude of ways. Petty regulations and licensing procedures either prevented church meetings or made it difficult for anyone not part of the church's inner circle to find out about them.

The church's response to such measures frequently exacerbated the very conditions it was designed to ameliorate. Typical was the dispute over membership in the Free German Youth (FDJ). Beginning in 1954 the GDR undertook a major campaign to recruit young people for this organization of activists, the initiation ceremony for which required the teenagers publicly to profess the atheistic principles of Marxism-Leninism. Bishops in the GDR no less than the more general EKD leadership took the position that membership in such an organization was inconsistent with membership in the church. They thereupon forbade confirmation to any child who had been initiated into the FDJ. For religious families in the GDR, this meant that their children had to choose between the church and what amounted to a normal citizen's life—for advancement in school and preferred jobs were frequently denied to those who refused to join the FDJ, and even their parents might suffer at their workplace and in their private lives.[2]

The issue of children dedicating themselves to socialism through membership in the FDJ versus confirmation went to the heart of the triangular state-church-individual relationship in the GDR. The government and the bishops had in effect declared war on each other. The position of the state was that even Christians had a civic obligation actively to support the development of socialism in the GDR. That of the church stemmed from the belief that the future of Christianity rested upon unyielding resistance to "Godless communism" in any of its forms—a tactic that had saved German Protestantism under nazism. But the war itself, although accompanied by ideology-laden declarations fired at each other by hardened exponents of contrary positions, was in reality carried out in the bosom of the home by anguished families which had to choose between mutually exclusive options that affected every aspect of their daily lives.

The dispute also revealed an emergent bifurcation of thinking within the church itself. The EKD leadership and most church leaders in the GDR continued to hew to a hard line. Increasingly, however, pastors and the laity alike, especially those who had been too young to participate in the Confessing Church or who held a liberal view of politics and/or religion, pointed out that this hard line was having disastrous consequences. For one thing, it was not moving the state to modify its position. State officials were simply ignoring the church, when they were not harassing it. The idea of an underground church, critics also argued, was romantically attractive, to be sure, but guaranteed a future in which the church could have no influence in public life. More seriously, by putting families and especially young people on the firing line in the cold war, the church was failing to fulfill its primary mission: to bring Christianity to the individual. It was time, they concluded, to recognize the fact that socialism would dominate the GDR for a long time to come, and to learn how to be Christians in a socialist state.

Legitimacy of the GDR

The climax of the refusal within the EKD's leading circles to recognize the new realities of German politics came in October 1959 with the publication of Bishop Otto Dibelius's letter to another provincial bishop, Hans Lilje.[3] The courage of this seventy-nine-year-old chairman of the EKD Council cannot be doubted. During the Nazi years Dibelius had been a founder and guiding light of the Confessing Church, and both then and after 1945 he had helped to draft numerous statements championing the cause of the church in its battle against an all too overweening state. The church, Dibelius had written a decade earlier,[4] cannot accept unconditionally the primacy of the state, and limit itself to being a division of religious affairs in the state bureaucracy. . . . Living Christian faith will never permit itself to be used as an instrument of propaganda for state power. Accordingly, it can never give up opposition to a dictatorship of the state in matters of faith.

The church, he concluded, is the single most important "bulwark against the tyranny of the state."

The eleven years during which he had chaired the EKD Council had not softened his attitude but merely given him a new target. These years, after all, had been marked by the division of Germany and the emergence of a state in its eastern region that was basically inimical to the principles for which he and so many others stood. These years also saw the emergence of the FRG's doctrine that it alone represented the legitimate interests of the German people. The West German refusal to recognize *de jure* or *de facto* the existence of the German Democratic Republic, and such measures as the Hall-stein Doctrine which were designed to discourage other countries from according such recognition, found a strong echo among many church leaders facing the threat of a divided church as well.

Dibelius focused his letter to Lilje on the controversial question of authority, raised by St. Paul in his letter to the Romans (13: 1–2). Paul said:

Every person must submit to the supreme authorities. There is no authority but by act of God, and the existing authorities are instituted by Him; consequently anyone who rebels against authority is resisting a divine institution.

Does this mean submission to any and every regime? Or should we not be speaking rather of "legitimate" authority, that is, authority (or regimes) instituted by God? "We have experienced the totalitarian state," Dibelius wrote, "and are experiencing it still." Such a state determines social norms, "what is good and what evil." The GDR was doing just that. It followed that, when Prime Minister Otto Grotewohl said that "whatever furthers the interests of the regime is good; whatever damages the regime is bad," he was turning Paul's concept of authority on its head and rendering it meaningless.

Authority in the GDR, Dibelius wrote, is not legitimate. Hence he personally did not feel obligated to obey its laws. If caught speeding on the highway between Berlin and West Germany, he would pay his fine silently but be utterly free of any sense of guilt. "Why is that so?" he asked.

It is so because I know that any regulation in the domain of a totalitarian state is decreed under conditions that deliberately exclude God, that deliberately exclude everything that I as a Christian am able to call moral, but which stem from the grasp for power of the totalitarian regime—a regime that I, for the sake of God and our Lord Jesus Christ, would like to see overcome.

Dibelius closed the letter by saying that he would like to interpret the concept which Luther had translated as "authority" (*Obrigkeit*) as an order sanctified by "legitimate force" (*rechtmässige Gewalt*).

The immediate effect of this letter, when its contents became known publicly, was stunning. It seemed to be saying to the sixteen million citizens of the GDR: Since you live under the thumb of an illegitimate regime, that is, illegitimate in the eyes of God, you have no moral obligation to obey its laws. Dibelius's later explanation that his was a private letter rather than an official position paper of the church he headed, and that he was not calling for actual civil disobedience in the GDR, did little to allay the hue and cry in both parts of Germany. Neither did an official church press release stating the EKD's correct position, which was that no state could claim absolute authority over individuals. Dibelius himself fanned the flames further at the end of October when, in a service at the American church in the West Berlin suburb of Dahlem, he thanked West Berlin's mayor for "the gift of freedom." Meanwhile, church leaders in the GDR were called on the carpet to assure state authorities that what Dibelius had said carried no official weight, and that the church did not intend to stir up any hornets' nests in the state's domain.

Dibelius's letter forced the church to come to grips with the issue of its relationship to the East German state. The controversy it aroused in top-level councils of the EKD made the bishop's subsequent announcement (in January 1960) that he intended to resign from his leadership positions both more probable and welcome. More significantly, by demonstrating the logical consequence of lines of thought questioning the fundamental legitimacy of the GDR, the letter raised in a very sharp form the long-standing question of priorities: organizational unity across the territory of the two Germanies versus a political perspective resting solely on moral considerations. The church could not have it both ways. It could not attack the right of the GDR to exist and continue to expect the GDR to cooperate with the church. Noncooperation—on the assumption that pressure from the West or other political circumstances did not topple the East German regime—would surely make more difficult the lot of Protestants in the GDR, attenuate their religious liberty still further, and lead in the long run to the EKD's division if it wanted to remain active in that country.

End of Structural Unity in the EKD

The value of structural unity *per se* was increasingly questioned. An organizational structure cutting across the boundary lines separating the GDR from the FRG was *ceteris paribus* a good idea. Until relatively recently in the church's history, however, a unified church for Germany had been the ideal, not the norm. Most church leaders at the end of the 1950s could remember a time, before the creation of the League of German Evangelical Churches in 1922, when territorial decentralization was the rule; and since then, except for the Nazi interlude, what unity existed was marked by strong strains of *de facto* decentralization across a wide range of church matters.

Was the church willing to insist on structural unity at the cost of organizational freedom and religious liberty in the GDR? As it turned out, increasing pressure from the East German government resolved this question by making continued unity virtually impossible. This was clear at the latest by August 1961, when the GDR built a wall around West Berlin. Residents of that city, including Bishop Dibelius, were denied access to the East (although West Germans could continue to travel between East and West Berlin). A virtual ban on travel for GDR citizens from the East into West Berlin and West Germany meant that it was no longer possible to hold EKD synods or leadership conferences there. Even so, the organizational unity of the EKD remained standing, at least on paper. And the use of West German couriers and other devices permitted extensive coordination of activities across the boundary between the two Germanies. Physical separation, together with the need to deal separately with their own governments and problems, nonetheless split the church effectively into an EKD-West and EKD-East.

The final push for formal separation came in 1968.[5] Early in that year the GDR revised its criminal code to eliminate any special protection for the church (for example, against blasphemy) and declared it to be a private association like any other, it also wrote a new constitution spelling out the position of the church in society. Although, at the request of the church, freedom of religion and conscience was included in the new constitution, the key passage (Art. 39.2) declared that "the churches and other religious communities will organize their affairs and exercise their activity in a manner consistent with the constitution and law of the GDR."

The Conference of Church Leaders in the GDR understood the writing on the wall. In June 1968 it set up two committees, one to develop a new structure for the provincial churches in the GDR, and the other to explore possible arrangements with the government which could regulate the details of state-church relations. Three months later the first committee produced a draft constitution for the Federation of Evangelical Churches in the German Democratic Republic (BEKDDR or, more simply, BEK) that took only eight months for all provincial churches in the GDR to ratify.

Yet formal separation of the two territorially based churches did not mean the end of informal unity. Its new constitution enabled the BEK to establish fairly good working relations with the East German government. But, as one BEK report phrased it, "renunciation at the institutional level expanded maneuverability at the functional." Both churches acted explicitly to uphold the symbols of united German Protestantism. Article 4.4 of the BEK's constitution, for example, not only committed the Federation to be part of a "special community" comprising the "whole of Evangelical Christianity in Germany," but went on to assert the BEK's preparedness, "in the freedom born of partnership," to act accordingly on "issues which affect in common all Evangelical churches in the German Democratic Republic and in the Federal Republic of Germany." Moreover, top-level meetings continue to ensure a maximum of coordination on theological, liturgical, and practical matters; and in a variety of ways the EKD and its member churches provide financial and moral support for beleaguered Christians in the GDR. The result has been a fragile unity emphasizing the spiritual community of the EKD and BEK, without threatening the autonomy of either.

Splitting the Church in Berlin-Brandenburg

The history of the Evangelical Church in Berlin-Brandenburg (EKiBB) shows even more dramatically the costs and consequences of splitting the church along territorial lines. The newness of the EKD as an organization, especially when contrasted to the long-standing organizational integrity of the provincial churches which made it up, contributed to the relative ease with which it could be divided, and so did the fact that, except for the special situation in Berlin-Brandenburg, a neat line of demarcation could be drawn between the church provinces in the GDR and those in the West. What to do about the EKiBB was a more problematic question. Its organizational integrity had deep historic roots, to be sure, but one of its four dioceses originally comprised the entire city of Berlin, split since 1948 under two governments. Whereas Bishop Dibelius from the outset had had to live with the loose federalism of the EKD, his position as bishop of the EKiBB rested on an organic unity.

The Evangelical Church in Berlin-Brandenburg felt the effect of the cold war much more keenly than did the EKD as a whole. The creation of separate currency areas, for instance, meant keeping separate books, and it meant that the financial office of the church, located in West Berlin, had to set up a branch in East Berlin. Other branch offices with other functions soon followed. Their purpose was to facilitate the activities of an integrated church rather than to split it apart, and to ensure that the church could meet the specific demands of increasingly different legal systems in the two halves of the city. Overall planning, budgeting, and ecclesiastic legislation nevertheless remained the responsibility of the central institutions whose offices, in turn, saw to it that the interests of parishes and church leaders throughout Berlin and Brandenburg were adequately taken into account. Personnel for the various offices, too, came from throughout the province rather than being assigned to offices in the currency area in which they lived. To fulfill its various missions, and to maintain its overarching organizational unity, the EKiBB was prepared to put up with virtually any number of technical inconveniences.

Pressures on the provincial church from GDR authorities, which began in early 1950, continued with greater or lesser intensity over the course of the next two decades. These officials greatly disliked the fact that offices in West Berlin were making decisions affecting day-to-day life in East Berlin and the GDR, and greatly distrusted the provincial church's top leaders—especially Bishop Dibelius, who was intimately linked with policy making in the EKD and in West Germany more generally. Little that the church did made it seem likely that even those of its branches on Eastern soil were prepared to accept a new definition of their role in socialist society. By early 1959 the situation had become sufficiently touchy that the EKiBB began planning for the eventuality that the GDR would sever the rest of the church province from its core in West Berlin.

That contingency occurred in August 1961 with the construction of the wall. The immediate effect was to deny Easterners access to West Berlin; and only days later the reverse also became policy. The EKiBB's plan of 1959 had called for the bishop's representative in East Berlin, Kurt Scharf, to assume a more active leadership role in such an eventuality, but a sly trick on the part of GDR authorities soon left Scharf stranded in West Berlin as well. Scharf's *de facto* expulsion was doubly problematic. For one thing, it left the eastern region of the church province without clear lines of day-to-day authority. Protestants there had to rely on indirect communications with the chancellery in West Berlin and their own governing committee of twelve leading East German church officials (including the superintendents general of the three dioceses in Brandenburg). This worked well enough, as the organizational work for simultaneous but separate synods in March 1962 showed, but was clearly not a long-term solution.

Second, the expulsion compounded the EKiBB's problem of succession. Early in 1960 Bishop Dibelius had asked to be relieved of his responsibilities. The committee set up to find a successor settled on Scharf, in part because, as a long-standing resident of East Berlin, he seemed to be acceptable to the GDR's government, and also in part because his recent election as chairman of the EKD Council placed him a key role in the church as a whole. But, the day before the committee was to meet to make final its selection, Scharf was denied reentry into East Berlin. The EKiBB felt it had no choice but to prevail on Dibelius to remain in office.

It took almost a dozen years to resolve the succession problem and, with it, the future of the provincial church in Berlin-Branden-burg. Scharf continued as the bishop's administrator even though he could not enter the East (but in 1963 Superintendent General Günter Jacob of Cottbus was deputized for the easter region), and regional offices became adept at communicating through third parties and setting up divided synods under the motto, "Separate, but we be-long together!" In 1966 Dibelius announced his retirement again. This time, despite the GDR's stern warning that any new bishop for East Berlin and Brandenburg would have to come from the eastern region, Scharf received substantial majorities at synods held in both parts of the city and thus became the EKiBB's new bishop. The official East German announcement that Scharf's election would be without effect in the GDR gave a clear sign that the provincial church was far from being out of the woods.

Mutual accommodation was nonetheless in the offing. Church leaders on both sides of the wall, each fighting off challenges from their own hardline "conservatives" and "liberals," moved toward a *modus vivendi*. They developed a perspective that emphasized and even built on the degree of community between the two regions (though requiring mutual agreement for structural changes, for ex-ample), denied that recent events had damaged the capacity of the regions to operate as a single structural entity, and declared that, even if they were forced to go their own ways organizationally, it would not mean the end of their unity in fulfilling the Christian mission. By 1973 they had created separate bishoprics, without, however, dissolving the formal juridical ties on which the EKiBB as a whole rests.

The modus vivendi has worked well in practice. East German officials, who had already permitted the provincial bishopric in the eastern region to join the Federation of Evangelical Churches in the GDR, chose to interpret the existence of the two offices as evidence of separate organizations; officials in the West persist in stressing the continuation of formal unity. Meanwhile, especially after the Quadripartite and inter-German treaties of the early 1970s reopened the gates to East Berlin and the GDR, church leaders in both regions have found that the new arrangement provides them with extensive opportunities for interaction and even coordination in fulfilling their spiritual tasks.

SPATIAL ORGANIZATION AND RELIGIOUS LIBERTY

The division of Germany and the sharply divergent paths taken since then by the two German states have posed a double threat to the conception of religious liberty held by the country's churches. The first pertains to the scope of their activities in the German Democratic Republic. Although hostile to the very idea of religion, the East German state guarantees constitutionally both freedom of conscience and the churches' right to exist as social entities. It has not sought to interfere with doctrinal or liturgical matters, nor has it undertaken a systematic program of religious persecution. The state nonetheless makes total claims on the loyalty of its citizens and those social organizations it tolerates. This has meant substantial pressure exerted from time to time on the churches and other bodies which resist state demands for adherence to political norms and which provide a basis of social support for citizens reluctant to adopt the East German version of communism as their own way of life. However rewarding in other ways, it is not easy being a Christian in the GDR.

More directly germane to this chapter is the second threat. At one time the Protestant church insisted that organizational unity across the whole of Germany was vital for maintaining its religious liberty. Throughout the 1950s, and in some respects even later, it refused to recognize the legitimacy of territorial changes made in Europe from 1945 to 1949. It argued that the church has an absolute right to organize its own affairs as it sees fit, even if this means organizational structures transcending political boundaries, and that its ability to fulfill its spiritual mission rests on this organizational integrity. The religious liberty of individuals thus depended on the extent to which the church enjoyed such liberty as social structures.

It was precisely this equation of individual and organizational liberty that the East German regime rejected. As the 1950s progressed and the prospects for German reunification grew dimmer—indeed, some analysts have argued that leaders in neither the East nor the West were seriously interested in reuniting the country given then-current world conditions—the GDR was increasingly firm about the need for individuals and organizations under its jurisdiction to accept the authority of the state, to break off all formal ties to the West, or else accept the consequences. The church learned it could defy the state's demand for spatial reorganization, but that doing so had its price. What is more, it would be individuals, members of the flock, who would pay the lion's share of the price.

Perhaps the climax of resistance came with the publication of Bishop Dibelius's letter on legitimate and illegitimate authority, which spelled out fairly clearly the logical consequences of such a stance. Realizing that the costs of resistance were too great, the EKD agreed to separate structures for East and West Germany; and eventually the provincial church in Berlin-Brandenburg followed suit in fact if not form.

The GDR, for its part, has shown toward the church a degree of flexibility uncharacteristic of its overall policies. For example, it has tolerated slow-moving decision-making processes that progressed toward changes in substance, and did not insist that every i be dotted and every t crossed on the issue of formal division. Thus the EKiBB still has not rewritten its constitution to reflect the fact that bishops and synods in West Berlin and the rest of the church province operate separately from each other. Seldom does the state intervene in the procedures by which the church maintains a high degree of effective coordination across the boundary in Berlin. The East German regime has also tolerated a great deal of public criticism from church officials in the GDR on such matters as paramilitary training for schoolchildren and the Warsaw Pact's reluctance to take significant steps toward disarmament.[6]

The rationale for such flexibility on the part of GDR officials may well be the feeling that time is on their side. Year by year the churches and their members in East and West get more involved in the political system of their own state—Ernest Renan's "plebiscite of daily living." In the earthly realm there is ever less to coordinate. Then, too, for most church members, especially in the West, the church does not play a paramount role in their lives.[7] Although sentimentally they may prefer a church structure unified across the whole of the former church province, practically it may make little difference to them. They belong to their own parish churches and seldom have significant contacts with neighboring ones. Even those Protestants in West Berlin who are sufficiently close to the EKiBB-West that they read its weekly newspaper only rarely obtain information about church matters in the East.[8] The clergy and laic active in church governance who take a lively interest in cross-boundary linkages are increasingly inclined to focus their energies on things they can affect rather than on the *fata morgana* of a truly united church in East and West.

Such changes suggest several conclusions. First of all, the tension between trying to meet individual versus institutional goals can, in the absence of clear priorities, be destructive of both. Second, in the church and elsewhere, the most efficacious way to change organizational policy is frequently through personnel changes. People in power tend to repeat their first successes. Their failure to recognize changed contextual circumstances, and the inability of their lieutenants to make them aware of such changes, can lead to tragic consequences (such as unbearable pressure on individual Christians in the GDR).

Then, too, every passing year makes state boundaries more determining for the German churches. For the GDR to push more strongly toward formulas embodying the real changes that have already been made would be counterproductive. It could arouse public controversy that would show the GDR not to have completely subdued the churches, and it might force church officials to take public stances that could only slow down that process. It could strengthen a popular image of the church as a spiritual refuge for those who would escape the task of coming to grips with life in a socialist state. It could also fuel the arguments of those outside the country who feel that the GDR's regime oppresses its own citizens. The GDR's better tactic is to wait until the full effects of spatial change have taken place. In the meantime, by tacitly accepting their division, the churches can better shore up religious liberty for their structures in East and West and the individual religious liberty of the congregations they serve.

NOTES

1. For discussions of these various dimensions, see Richard L. Merritt, *Political Community in Divided Berlin* (forthcoming). Unless otherwise noted, the information in this paper stems from various editions of the yearbook of the Evangelische Kirche in Deutschland (EKD), *Kirchliches Jahrbuch für die Evangelische Kirche in Deutschland* (Gütersloh: Gütersloher Verlagshaus Gerd Mohn, 1948–1981); various editions of A. Lampe, H. R. Reichhardt et al., *Berlin.—Chronik der Jahre* (Berlin: Heinz Spitzing Verlag [7 vols to date, covering 1945–1960], 1961–1978); H. Brunotte, *Die Evangelische Kirche in Deutschland: Geschichte, Organisation und Gestalt der EKD* (Gütersloh: Gütersloher Verlagshaus Gerd Mohn, 1964); discussions with church officials in East and West Berlin; and newspaper clippings and other material in the archive of the Evangelische Kirche in Berlin-Brandenburg as well as, for the years since 1960, my own files.

2. See, for example, Richard W. Solberg, *God and Caesar in East Germany: The Conflicts of the Church and State in East Germany since 1945* (New York: Macmillan, 1961).

3. Otto Dibelius, *Obrigkeit: Eine Frage an den 60jährigen Landesbischof* (Berlin: n.p., 1958).

4. Otto Dibelius, *Grenzen des Staates* (Tübingen: Furches-Verlag, 1949), 85, 88.

5. For the political context of this development, see A. James McAdams, *East Germany and Detente: Building Authority after the Wall* (Cambridge,: Cambridge University Press, 1985).

6. The BEK has staunchly supported a peace movement that the GDR government has sought unsuccessfully to suppress. The government has forbidden the wearing of the movement's symbol—a button depicting the statue, "Swords into Plowshares," donated by the Soviet Union to the United Nations and prominently displayed before the latter's headquarters in New York City—but the police frequently look the other way rather than arrest every young East German wearing such a symbol. In this and similar matters the EKD scrupulously avoids taking a stance, for to do so would be to give ammunition to GDR ideologues who argue that the Protestant Church in the East continues, at least implicitly, to take its marching orders from "reactionary circles" in the West.

7. In West Berlin on a typical Sunday in 1980, only 2 percent of the nominal members of the Evangelical Church actually attended services (Evangelische Kirche in Berlin-Brandenburg, Konsistorium, *Statis-*

tiches Bericht 1982 [Berlin: EKiBB, 1982], 33). This figure was up from 1.7 percent in 1976.

8. For a quantitative content analysis of attention patterns from 1946 to 1980 in the *Berliner Sonntagsblatt: Die Kirche,* see Merritt, *Political Community in Divided Berlin.*

II

THE POLITICAL RULES OF THE GAME

6

THE BASIC LAW OF THE FEDERAL REPUBLIC OF GERMANY: AN ASSESSMENT AFTER FORTY YEARS

Donald P. Kommers

On 23 May 1989, the Basic Law became forty years old. Designed as a political framework for a new experiment in constitutional democracy, it has survived the vagaries and vicissitudes of the postwar period as well as the buffeting of its critics both left and right. It may not have fulfilled all the promises of its founders—what constitution has?—but under the usual standards for measuring the success of a constitution it has stood the test of time. Yet, as the designation "Basic Law" (*Grundgesetz*) implies, it was framed originally, as the preamble declares, "to bring a new order to political life for a transitional period." The term "constitution" (*Verfassung*), a more dignified appellation, would be reserved for the document that would govern a reunified Germany. Time, however, has erased the significance of the distinction between these terms, and they will be used interchangeably throughout this chapter. In sum, the Basic Law has been firmly woven into the fabric of West German society and politics; it has become the fertile source of an ever-deepening and widening constitutional tradition.[1] Today, as the fortieth anniversary of the document has arrived, the Basic Law enjoys the status of a genuine constitution framed to last in perpetuity.

HISTORICAL NOTE

Any assessment of the Basic Law after forty years should, at the outset, recall the circumstances of its creation. Like other European constitutions adopted in the immediate postwar period, the Basic Law was anything but a visionary document. It was hammered out instead by seasoned politicians on the anvil of experience and against the backdrop of a totalitarian age. As Carl Friedrich noted, they crafted a "negative revolution" that said "no" to all grandiose schemes for the reconstruction of the political order.[2] Mindful of their dismal past and drained of the ideological fervor that marred the history of their times, they quietly set about to establish peace and stability. They were remarkably successful in achieving both: the Federal Republic's commitment under Article 24 to a supranational framework of collective security and its willingness under the same provision to relinquish certain powers of national sovereignty helped to secure the peace, while in other parts of the Basic Law institutional innovations designed to repair the deficiencies of the Weimar Constitution brought a high measure of stability to the new polity.

The Basic Law's emphasis on stability and repair made it look as if the framers were engaged in a work of restoration. In a sense they were. They wanted to stem the tide of change, curtail the power of the state, and suppress dangerous political movements. Moreover, in reconstituting their political order, they turned to Germany's own models of constitutional government, models that were to be found in certain nineteenth-century state constitutions, the short-lived Frankfurt Constitution of 1849 and, most notably, Weimar's Republican Constitution of 11 August 1919.[3] Study of the Bonn and Weimar Constitutions reveals a close genetic relationship between the two charters. Indeed, several major articles of the 1919 Constitution were fully grafted onto the Basic Law. Even the Basic Law's provisions on the judicial control of constitutionality, attributed by many commentators to American influence, trace many of their antecedents to Germany's own tradition of constitutional review, just as Bonn's Federal Constitutional Court (*Bundesverfassungsgericht*) finds its nearest historical analogue in Weimar's High State Court (*Staatsgerichtshof*).[4]

Yet, at the same time, the Basic Law marks a radical break with previous German constitutions. Previous constitutions in the republican tradition were largely statements of political ideals and guidelines to political action. The Basic Law, by contrast, is a law of superior force and obligation and is directly enforceable as law by a judicial establishment crowned by the power and majesty of the Federal Constitutional Court. In broadest outline the gulf between Weimar and Bonn represents a major shift from a constitutional *democracy* to a *constitutional* democracy. This decided emphasis upon constitutionalism sets the Basic Law apart from the democratic theory underlying the Weimar Constitution, an easily amendable charter notoriously subject to majoritarian change and manipulation. Even though the Weimar Republic had a tribunal armed with limited powers of constitutional review, the historic norm then and before was that legislatures rather than courts would enjoy the preeminent role in the protection of constitutional guarantees. Today, however, consistent with the framers' intent, democratic theory and constitutionalism find themselves locked in a permanent embrace of mutual tension. Democratic theory is obviously still immensely important in German constitutionalism, but political democracy is now subject to the superior law of the Constitution. Thus, far from being restorative, the Basic Law is in truth revolutionary, although perhaps in the negative sense suggested by Friedrich.

THE NEW CONSTITUTIONALISM

Rights and Values

Articles 1 and 20 contain the core values of Germany's new constitutionalism. Article 1, the cornerstone of the Basic Law, declares: "The dignity of man is inviolable. To respect and protect it is the duty of all state authority." In Paragraph 2 of Article 1 the "German people acknowledge inviolable and inalienable rights." Paragraph 3, finally, declares that the basic rights enumerated in the Constitution (Articles 1–18) "shall bind the legislature, the executive, and the judiciary as directly enforceable law," a provision added to

Article 1 in 1956 to remove any doubt that the executive as well as the legislature and the judiciary would be bound by the law of the Constitution.[5]

The notion of "inviolable and inalienable" rights—a major ingredient of constitutionalism—is largely opposed to the language and spirit of earlier German constitutions. Many of the Basic Law's guaranteed rights provisions are word-for-word reproductions of corresponding articles in the Frankfurt and Weimar Constitutions. The Bonn Constitution, however, "acknowledges" the preconstitutional existence of these rights. Contrary to the prevailing legal positivism of the Weimar period, fundamental rights are not the creations of law. Rather, they are natural rights grounded in the concept of "human dignity" (Article 1). General or positive law may limit, where indicated in the Basic Law, the exercise of certain fundamental rights, but for the first time in German constitutional history positive law itself can be measured by the higher law of the Constitution.

The rights enumerated in the Basic Law (Articles 1–18) include all the classical freedoms (e.g., expression, assembly, religious exercise, privacy, property, and equal protection) associated with the Western liberal tradition, together with certain rights in the spheres of family relations, education, and choice of employment. Article 19, paragraph 2, underscores the preeminence of these rights by prohibiting any encroachment upon "the essential content of [a] basic right" and by the cognate right of all persons under paragraph 4 to appeal to the judiciary when a basic right is infringed by public authority.[6]

The constitutional system of the Federal Republic also differs from past regimes in its refusal to treat individual freedom as positively expressed through the functions of the state. Indeed, the very notion of the state (*Der Staat*) has undergone substantial change in German constitutional theory. In Kant, the *Staat* forged a perfect synthesis between freedom and the objective authority of law; in Hegel, it sired a moral organism in which individual liberty was perfectly realized in the unified will of the people, not arbitrary will but rather "the power of reason actualizing itself in will." In short, the German "state" was treated historically as a superior form of human association and as a unity of individuals and society in a higher synthesis of freedom and solidarity. Some features of the Basic Law, particularly its communitarian values, are more readily understood in the light of these traditional German notions of liberty and state, notions suggestive of aspects of the Aristotelian polis and the early American tradition of civic republicanism. Nevertheless, as Leonard Krieger has pointed out in his monumental history of the concept of German liberty, the framers of the Basic Law discovered in the light of the Nazi experience the "bankruptcy of the state as a liberalizing institution." "Dominant now," he concluded "is an attitude which views the state as a morally neutral, purely utilitarian organization of public power."[7]

Krieger's assessment, while containing some truth, needs to be qualified. As a modern twentieth-century constitution, the Basic Law captivates our attention precisely because it appears in some respects to blur the distinction between law and morality. The constitutional text binds the polity to law but at the same time subjects law to a higher moral order which is expressed constitutionally in such notions as "moral code" (Article 2), "concept of international understanding" (Article 9), "justice" (Article 20), and certain views of man and society found by the Federal Constitutional Court to be implicit in the concept of "human dignity" (Article 1).[8] To be sure, the Basic Law's list of fundamental rights protects the political and social diversity of the German people, but its higher values of community and ordered liberty supposedly keep it from lapsing into a destructive and uncivilizing anarchy of moral and ideological discord. The point to be made here is that these higher values infuse the Basic Law with a normative character resistant to a purely utilitarian interpretation.

The normativity of the Basic Law owes much to the three legal traditions that helped most to shape it. These traditions, so rich in moral theory, are contained within Germany's heritage of classical-liberal, socialist, and Christian natural law thought. Each of these traditions has played a formative role in German legal history. Each was powerfully represented in the constitutional convention of 1949. Each finds many of its central values present in the text of the Basic Law. Each is currently and importantly represented in German political life. The Free Democratic Party (FDP) represents the classical-liberal tradition; the Social Democratic Party (SPD) the socialist

tradition; and the Christian Democratic Union (CDU) and its Bavarian affiliate, the Christian Social Union (CSU) the Christian natural
law tradition. When drafting the Basic Law, the representatives of
these parties shed their historical antagonisms and, in a remarkable
display of communal concord, they drew willingly from the humanistic content of each tradition and managed to create a constitution
that combines the main values of each in a workable if not always
easy alliance.

At the risk of oversimplification, the liberal tradition might be
said to inhere in the classical freedoms listed in several articles of
the bill of rights; the socialist tradition in certain social welfare
clauses, including provisions concerning duties of property and the
socialization of economic resources; and the Christian tradition in
articles on social morality, religious education, and the institutional
prerogatives of the established churches and rights associated with
marriage and the family. Philosophically and politically these traditions diverge significantly from one another, yet converge around a
common core of belief about the nature and needs of the human
personality. Article 2, for example, which guarantees "the right [of
everyone] to the free development of his personality," subject only
to certain norms of civic obligation, is one of several key rights
provisions around which all three traditions could rally.[9]

Structures and Relationships

Article 1, as we have seen, embodies the Basic Law's core value of
human dignity. Article 20, the other central linchpin of the Constitution, sets forth the basic principles of the new polity: paragraph 1
defines the Federal Republic as "a democratic and social federal
state;" paragraph 2, after proclaiming that "[a]ll state authority em-
anates from the people," asserts that this authority "shall be exercised by the people by means of elections and voting and by specific
legislative, executive, and judicial organs." Thus does the Basic Law
create a representative democracy undergirded by the doctrine of
separation of powers. But then paragraph 3 yokes democratic theory
once again to constitutionalism with these words: "Legislation shall
be subject to the constitutional order; the executive and the judiciary shall be bound by law *and justice*" (italics added). So crucial are

these core values that Article 79 (3) of the Basic Law actually bars any amendment that would limit or infringe "the basic principles laid down in Articles 1 and 20."[10]

The machinery of government created by the Basic Law also reflects the new constitutionalism. Political institutions are arranged in such a way as to shield the new polity against being overwhelmed by the excesses of popular democracy. The Constitution reaffirms the principle of popular sovereignty, but now it would manifest itself in representative rather than plebiscitary institutions, including the indirect election of the federal president; the new government would embody a strong chancellor unremovable save by a constructive vote of no confidence; federalism would be placed entirely beyond the power of the people to amend; separation of powers would include the judicial control of constitutionality; majority rule would be overlaid with a complex system of checks and balances, including the corporate right of the *Länder* to participate in the national legislative process; and finally, in still another break with German constitutional tradition, political parties would be recognized as principal organs of political representation, but the Federal Constitutional Court would be authorized to declare them unconstitutional if "by reason of their aims or behavior of their adherents, [they] seek to impair or abolish the free democratic order or to endanger the existence of the Federal Republic of Germany" (Article 21).

Most of these institutional features and regime principles attach themselves to one or more of the four perspectives on the state that have over the last four decades achieved authoritative status in German constitutional law. These perspectives are captured in the concepts of *Parteienstaat* (political party state), *Sozialstaat* (social welfare state), *Rechtsstaat* (state based on the rule of law), and *streitbare Demokratie* (militant democracy). (The polity is, of course, also a *Bundesstaat*.) Each of these concepts, around which a large and meaningful jurisprudence has been crafted, imposes certain obligations on the state.[11] The *Parteienstaat* mandates a central role for political parties and a limited degree of public financial support of parties during election campaigns; the *Sozialstaat* requires affirmative action on behalf of the general welfare; the *Rechtsstaat*—the traditional touchstone of constitutionalism in Germany—demands clear, reasonable, equal, and predictable rules governing the relations between the state and individual citizens; finally, *streitbare Demokratie* requires the sturdy defense of democratic values under the supervision of the Federal Constitutional Court. Like the liberal, socialist, and Christian traditions that nourish German constitutionalism, these perspectives on the state are often in conflict. In combination, however, they encapsulate what several provisions of the Basic Law refer to as the "free liberal democratic basic order."[12]

A close reading of the Basic Law, as already suggested by the foregoing discussion, reveals a document marked by compromise and conflicting values. A detailed constitution of 146 articles woven from antagonistic political and legal traditions could hardly be anything less. But this should not be taken as a blemish. Even a lapidarian text like the U.S. Constitution represents a bundle of not altogether compatible provisions. The real meaning of a constitution is often found in its overall structure and underlying aspirations, or in what Edward McWhinney characterized as the "judicial quest for constitutional first principles that gives a certain coherence and order and rationality to otherwise rambling and interminable constitutional documents."[13] The Federal Constitutional Court has been engaged in precisely such a quest from the moment of its creation, repeatedly underscoring the internal coherence and structural unity of the Basic Law, even describing it as a "logical-teleological entity,"[14] a concept which in itself suggests a fusion of the positivistic and natural law traditions in German legal history.

The centerpiece of this interpretive theory is the concept of an "objective order of values." The Constitution is said to incorporate the "basic value decisions of the founding fathers," the most basic of which is their choice of a "free democratic basic order" crowned by the principle of human dignity. These basic values, including the right to life and the inviolability of the human person (Article 2), are objective not only because they are frozen in perpetuity into the text of the Basic Law but also because they are said to have an independent reality under the Constitution, thus imposing upon all organs of government an affirmative obligation to see that they are realized in practice—that is, rendered a manifest objective reality. One consequence of this doctrine, which is rooted very clearly and at various places in the constitution, is that severe limits can validly be imposed on persons and movements actively opposed to the substantive values of the Basic Law, particularly those regime principles (e.g., federalism, separation of powers, multipartyism, rule of law, popular sovereignty, independence of the judiciary, and free and equal elections) embodied in the concept of a liberal democratic order. And so, as German judges and commentators are fond of saying, the Basic Law is anything but neutral toward values. They commonly agree that the Basic Law is a constitution of substantive values, embracing both rights and duties that the state is obliged to enforce. The state, in sum, is a militant democracy empowered actively to defend its most cherished values against all enemies, both internal and external.[15]

THE DOCUMENT: OF THINGS ORDINARY AND FUNDAMENTAL

Chief Justice John Marshall, speaking about the nature of a constitution in the celebrated case of *McCulloch v. Maryland* (1819),[16] said "that only its great outlines should be marked [and] its important objects designated." He sharpened the point in *Cohens v. Virginia* (1821) by saying that "a constitution is framed for ages to come, and is designated to approach immortality as nearly as human institutions can approach it."[17] In measuring the Basic Law against the Marshallian standard of "great outlines" and "important objectives," we confront a document far less elegant or inspiring than the foregoing description of the new constitutionalism might suggest. In its original form the Basic Law consisted of 146 articles (151 if we include the five articles of the Weimar Constitution on church-state relations absorbed into the Basic Law under Article 140). By 1980 it had swelled into a document of 171 articles, almost four times the length of the United States Constitution. Thus, while Germans might be proud of the blessings wrought by their constitution, they could hardly marvel at its artistry or its durability as a self-contained whole.

The Basic Law, in short, lacked the "timelessness" that might be said to inform the United States Constitution. While it embodied the core principles of liberty and democracy one would wish to see in a modern constitution, it was not confined to those "great and transcendental objects of all legitimate government." It was very much a seasonal document, drafted quickly and under pressure in the face of mushrooming hostility between East and West and against the backdrop of conflicting signals received by the framers from the Allied powers. It was also the product of a divided and occupied Germany, reflecting the absence of sovereign nationhood and requiring transitional provisions on such matters as citizenship, refugees, elections, former Nazis, the status of Berlin, and the organization of the federal territory.

An Amendable Charter

That the Basic Law was a document framed in many of its parts to meet the special conditions of the postwar period was underscored by the frequency with which it has subsequently been amended. In a short space of twenty-five years (1951–1976) parliament had amended the Constitution in sixty different places for the ostensible purpose of filling perceived gaps and correcting flaws in the framers' handiwork. In addition, major amending statutes created thirty-two new articles, inserted twenty-three new paragraphs into old articles, and repealed five articles, adding up to an immense amount of constitutional tinkering. Most of the repair work, however, took place in1956, 1968, and 1969. The 1956 revisions adjusted the Basic Law to the restoration of German sovereignty and remilitarization. The 1968 changes, reflecting West Germany's very great concern with national security, created a new section (consisting of 11 articles) dealing with the steps to be taken in defense of the nation in the event of an attack or the imminent threat of an attack from outside the country's borders. The package included several related amendments to existing articles, the most controversial of which was the restriction imposed on the basic right of privacy of posts and telecommunications under Article 10.[18] In 1969, finally, and in part the consequence of the grand coalition, constitutional change was directed toward social and economic concerns. Numerous amendments expanded the powers of the national government over the domestic economy, loosened certain restrictions on budgetary planning, realigned the federal-state relationship, and modified guidelines for the apportionment of tax revenue and financial assistance to the various states.

In viewing the Basic Law as a whole, however, we find that its prolixity is mainly because of its federal provisions. Seven sections and no fewer than sixty-five articles of the Constitution are devoted to spelling out in meticulous detail the nature of the Basic Law's federal structures and relationships. These provisions specify the legislative powers of the Federation and the Länder, the authority and composition of the Bundesrat, the structure of public administration, the financial relationship between levels of government, and even the sources of revenue on which each level of government is to depend for its maintenance. The Basic Law also distinguishes between five types of public administration, identifying what laws can be administered by what level of government and in what manner. Finally, in 1969, West Germans added a new section on cooperative federalism (Section VIIIa) to the Basic Law, authorizing federal and state governments to undertake certain tasks jointly, one of these being planning and research in the field of higher education.

An American critic committed to a "great outlines" approach to constitutional craftsmanship would find most of these provisions uninspiring, unnecessary, and unworthy of constitutional recognition. Our critic would certainly be correct in suggesting that provisions of such specificity invite frequent amendments to the Constitution, posing the danger of trivializing fundamental law. From the German perspective, however, such specificity is essential if West Germany's brand of administrative or "vertical" federalism is to function as intended. In a polity where nearly all legislative power is concentrated at the center and where the power of the Länder to levy and collect taxes is severely limited, the Constitution must delineate—in far greater detail than would be necessary under a system of "horizontal" federalism—the structure and principles of public administration, the process of tax administration, and the division of revenue sources between the Federation and the Länder.

The framers also learned from the Weimar experience that the only way to safeguard the primary responsibility of the Länder in the administration of national law "as a matter of their own concern" (Article 83) was to itemize those selected functional areas over which the Federation would have exclusive administrative authority and in other policy areas specifically to bar the creation of parallel federal agencies at state and local levels. The framers also wanted to avoid gaps or loopholes in the document that would cast the Federal Constitutional Court in the kind of major interpretive role historically played by the United States Supreme Court. Fearing the erosion of Länder authority through judicial review, they consciously set out to leave as little as possible to interpretation. In the Basic Law's scheme of things the Bundesrat was to serve as the balance wheel or guardian of federalism. For this reason, the Constitution lists no fewer than thirty-nine issue areas or situations in which the consent of the Bundesrat is required for legislative or governmental action. (In all other matters the Bundesrat enjoys a suspensive veto.) Save for one development to be noted later, German federalism has worked pretty much as the framers envisioned, a tribute to their success as constitution-makers.[19]

Federalism aside, our American critic would be likely to find other superfluous provisions in the Basic Law. He would probably object to all of the 1968 amendments relating to the defense of the nation against aggression. These provisions—totaling eighteen new articles and major additions to eight others—express an old German tendency to be thorough in all things. Germans seem to want to provide for all contingencies and to close every loophole in any legal structure. The Germans wrote the 1968 provisions to insure that human rights and the rule of law would be preserved to the maximum extent possible during an emergency, even though the American experience has shown that such emergencies can be dealt with by ordinary law and within the framework of the existing constitutional order. By ratifying the 1968 amendments, however, Germans have made emergency powers a part of their constitutional order, opening up the disquieting possibility, however remote, that the exception may swallow the norm.

It is probable, too, that most Americans would be uncomfortable with the many references to duties and responsibilities in the Basic Law, including the obligation of the state to grant "special protection" to marriage and the family (Article 6[1]), not to mention the "natural right of" and the "duty primarily incumbent on parents" to provide and care for their children (Article 6 [2]). Such matters, like the nationalization of natural resources (Article 15), the duties of property (Article 14), liability to military service (Article 12a), the rights and duties of civil servants (Articles 33, 131, and 132), and the legal status of judges (Article 98), could easily be relegated to and regulated by law. The problem, again from an American perspective, is whether future generations should be bound by the values and practices found to inhere in such provisions.

Limitations on Basic Rights

Americans would also be ill at ease, I believe, with all the qualifications imposed upon the exercise of basic rights and liberties. Freedom of expression, for example, may be "limited by the provisions of the general laws, the provisions of law for the protection of youth, and by the right to inviolability of personal honor" (Article 5 [2]). The right to personality is constrained by the "moral code" as well as by specified norms of civic obligation. Other specified limitations bracket such rights as freedom of association (Article 9 [2]), privacy (Article 10 [2]), and the inviolability of the home (Article 13 [3]). Under the terms of Article 18, an individual may even have to forfeit certain fundamental rights if he or she uses these rights "to combat the free democratic basic order," just as political parties can be declared unconstitutional if their activities "seek to impair or abolish the free democratic or basic order" (Article 21 [2]).

Finally, Americans are likely to disagree with Germans over what should be counted as a constitutional right. The Basic Law, for example, has constitutionalized the right of parents to have their children educated in the public schools in the faith of their choice (Article 7 [2] and [3]). It also confers on religious bodies organized under public law the power "to levy taxes on their members in accordance with Land law on the basis of civil taxation lists" (Article 140). Free choice of one's trade, profession, and place of work (Article 12) is also guaranteed, as is conscientious objection to military service (Article 12a) and the right to establish private schools (Article 7 [4]). Many of these provisions are fully explicable in terms of historical circumstances unique to Germany.

On the other hand, Germans may assert that their Constitution, particularly in its fundamental rights provisions, is in the mainstream of contemporary constitutionalism. The Basic Law's catalogue of rights and duties, its normative rules of conduct, together with certain communitarian restraints imposed upon the exercise of fundamental rights, and its broad commitment to the principle of nondiscrimination are squarely in alignment with the constitutions of most modern democracies, including international instruments such as the International Covenant on Civil and Political Rights and the European Convention on Human Rights.[20]

In addition, Germans are not prepared to apologize for the many reservation clauses written into the Basic Law's fundamental rights provisions, or for expanding the concept of rights beyond what many Americans would approve. Indeed, a number of German rights policies found in the written constitution have been adopted in the United States through judicial interpretation. But there is something to be said in favor of the German reservation clauses. Above all, they provide constitutional interpreters with broad guidelines in terms of which fundamental freedoms are to be reconciled with communitarian social values. In some instances the Basic Law itself requires an interest-balancing approach to constitutional interpretation, the healthy consequence of which is to limit the policy-making role of the courts, insuring that their decisions will be rooted in the constitutional text or at least in purposes that can reasonably be inferred from it.[21]

One of the purposes of a constitution is to identify the deeply shared values of a people, to express what they prize most as a community, and to put future generations on notice that certain enduring values rank higher than others. In addition to limiting the exercise of political power, a constitution may appropriately seek to create a consensus on things held most dear by a people. The combination of individual rights and communitarian values found in the Basic Law is a reasonably adequate expression of the temper and spirit of the German people. One of the functions of the Federal Constitutional Court in interpreting the Basic Law is to safeguard and promote that temper and spirit.

We Americans, I think, have tended to underestimate the extent to which judicial review, particularly when exercised in opposition to conventional values, can break down the shared understanding on which the wholeness of a community depends. Another purpose of a constitution is to remove some questions of value from the arena of public debate, to minimize conflict, to promote consensus, and to channel human activity into predetermined ends. The previous statement is not intended to throw cold water on those who would emphasize individual rights over social norms. What is being suggested here, although perhaps in less precise language than I would wish, is that a bill of rights such as the Germans have incorporated into their fundamental law blunts the capacity of the judiciary to impair the political culture and undermine consensus on certain issues.[22]

The Enquête Commission

Contemporary Germans do seem satisfied with their inherited Constitution. By 1976, as already mentioned, they had overhauled the Constitution in numerous places, repairing many flaws and omissions in the original document. There have been no constitutional amendments since 1976. Major constitutional conflicts between high federal organs continue to arise under the Basic Law but these have been resolved more or less adequately by judicial interpretation. In addition to its record in safeguarding basic rights, the Federal Constitutional Court has played a central role in defining the authority of other constitutional organs and holding them to the roles specified in the Basic Law. In the well-known *Bundesrat case*, for example, the Court rejected the coequality or coresponsibility theory that the "upper house" had begun to assert vis-à-vis the Bundestag.[23] More recently, in the *Bundestag Dissolution case*, the Court reminded the chancellor and the federal president that the dissolving power is limited and can only be undertaken in circumstances where, arguably, the government has lost its original mandate.[24] It suffices to remark that the Court's own role in the creation of consensus and a durable constitutional tradition is one of the remarkable features of postwar German constitutionalism.

Finally, and despite general satisfaction with the Basic Law's evolution in the postwar period, the Federal Republic has given considerable attention to general constitutional reform. A special twenty-one-member constitutional revision commission set up by the Bundestag in 1971 (the Enquête Commission) devoted five-and-a-half years to the study of the Basic Law. Its final report—a document of 700 typewritten pages—lacked any recommendation for fundamental constitutional change.[25] It concentrated rather on strengthening various aspects of the existing document. Its most important recommendations pertained to intergovernmental relations and finance. Proposals to place the national government's legislative powers more decidedly in the hands of the Bundestag were to be offset by an expansion of the Bundesrat's consent power.[26] Satisfied with the current relationship among the states, the Commission rejected a proposal to establish a *Länderrat,* a new major organ of government composed of Länder officials and designed to constitutionalize the process of interstate cooperation that had been carried on for years by specialized multistate agencies and committees.

The Commission also considered various proposals to strengthen or reform Parliament. While rejecting a proposal to expand the electoral term from four to five years, it recommended an amendment that would allow one-fourth of the Bundestag's membership to introduce a motion for dissolution, in which case a vote of two-thirds in favor of the motion would result in new elections. In the Commission's view this proposal, if accepted, would avoid any repetition of 1972, when the opposition failed to dissolve the Bundestag under Article 67 even though the government had lost its working majority. Past experience with interbranch conflict over parliamentary investigations into political corruption also prompted the Commission to propose an amendment permitting the Bundestag to establish an investigative committee on the motion of one-fourth of its members and to compel the government and administrative officials to cooperate with it.

None of these proposals has resulted in an amendment to the Basic Law. Two of its earliest recommendations, however, had already been implemented by the time of the final report's submission. The first was a minor amendment to Article 39, approved in 1976, eliminating the uncertainty that had previously existed with respect to the start and finish of a parliamentary term. The second was the insertion of Article 45c into the Basic Law, providing for the appointment of a Petitions Committee in the Bundestag to act on complaints received under the right-to-petition provision of Article 17. It is of interest to note, finally, that except for a minor proposal to amend Article 14, the Commission left untouched the entire bill of rights. Nor has the Commission proposed any amendment that would reverse or undermine existing constitutional doctrine as proclaimed by the Federal Constitutional Court.

DEMOCRACY AND THE CONSTITUTIONAL STATE

This assessment of the Basic Law would not be complete without considering recent critiques of state and society in West Germany. These critiques, emanating from both the Right and the Left of the political spectrum, agonize over the so-called crisis of legitimacy that is said to beset Western liberal democracies in general and West Germany in particular. The criticism from the Right has advanced the concept of "ungovernability" to describe the malaise of modern democracy. The malaise has been caused by the politics of mass participation and the politicalization of just about everything. What mass democracy has done in their view is to clog the engine of the state, making it impossible for any government to satisfy the numberless demands and expectations of the electorate, leading in turn to a loss of confidence in representative institutions and disillusionment with the capacity of political parties under the Basic Law to perform any kind of steering or integrating role in the system.[27]

The criticism from the Left, rooted mainly in Marxist critiques of late capitalism, turns the neoconservative diagnosis on its head. One of its major precepts is the domination by capital of Parliament, bureaucracy, and the political parties. This rather crude Marxist view shades, however, into a much more sophisticated analysis in the hands of commentators like Jürgen Habermas, Ulrich Preuss, and Claus Offe. Their critiques are based on the proposition that modern liberal democracy has failed to break down the pattern of subordination and hierarchy that holds sway over a passive citizenry dominated by self-perpetuating elites. Their solution is to restructure democracy by creating a truly informed and active citizenry, empowered to decide for themselves the direction of their lives and the socioeconomic conditions under which they shall live.[28]

One nevertheless discerns an interesting point of convergence in these critiques. Both Right and Left appear to reject the structural principles of modern German constitutionalism. These principles include separation of powers, checks and balances, and perhaps even judicial review. They also reject certain features of modern parliamentarianism, such as the principles of pluralism and consensus associated with the representation of party and group interests. The Right, in putting forth what might be called a Burkean view of representation, envisions a Parliament composed of independent legislators free of all allegiances except the pressure of their own consciences. The Left, in putting forth an egalitarian view, appears to look beyond existing political structures to decision-making procedures that would involve direct popular participation in public policy making. This comparison, however, should not be driven too far. After all, the criticism of the Right is rooted in respect for traditional structures of social morality, regard for authority, and partiality toward the *Rechtsstaat*. The criticism on the Left, on the other hand, stems from a philosophy of emancipatory individualism rooted in various forms of participatory democracy.

The criticism from the Left is of more interest to us here because it is the dominant critique of contemporary German constitutionalism. There is, of course, nothing essentially new about this critique. We find the argument laid out in full force in Karl Jaspers's *Wohin treibt die Bundesrepublik?*[29] published in 1966, seventeen years after the promulgation of the Basic Law. This popular book was a savage attack on the condition of West German democracy. The attack was directed toward the political culture as well as the constitutional order. Jaspers realized, of course, that there is often a large gap between constitutional norms and political reality. The Basic Law is in many ways a model democratic constitution that is based on the formation of an informed and virtuous citizenry. Yet no constitution is capable of saving a people from its own complacency, from the politics of drift, or from the corruption of political officials.

Jaspers is nevertheless severely critical of certain features of the Basic Law which in his estimation has helped to block the rise of popular democracy. The absence of any provision for popular referenda, the constructive vote of no confidence, the indirect election of the federal president, the ban on unconstitutional political parties, and the limits imposed on opposition to the constitutional order have contributed in his view to a paralysis of political life in the Federal Republic. He also deplores two other long-lasting features of the political order that have achieved near constitutional status by judicial interpretation. These are the 5 percent clause and the public financing of political parties.

In the aggregate, according to Jaspers, these features have entrenched the power and domination of the governing parties to such an extent that the "existing oligarchy of parties may lead to an authoritarian state, and this in turn to dictatorship."[30] Party financing, too, has contributed to the "oligarchy of parties," just as the 5-percent minimum for representation was designed to protect the ruling parties from new parties."[31] Jaspers was, of course, writing on the eve of the grand coalition which eliminated any effective parliamentary opposition. In due course, even with the renewal of major party opposition in 1969, Jaspers's analysis seemed right on target. By the mid-1980s West Germany was deep in public scandals involving the influence of money in politics. Public subsidies for the parties, which had skyrocketed in the previous decade, appeared not only to have entrenched the established parties' bureaucracies but also to have fostered a climate of loose political morality, the kind of morality that produced the Flick affair and other "conspiracies" to circumvent party finance laws.[32]

These flaws in the system are not, however, the product of a faulty constitutional design. That design sought to combine democratic with effective government. The five percent clause was still another way of achieving this result. Party financing too was rooted in democratic theory and stems from the German *Rechtsstaat*'s pervasive distrust of the *Verbändestaat* (an interest group state). The Basic Law regards political parties as the chief agencies of political representation. Indeed, one of its innovations is the wedding the *Parteienstaat* to the concept of the *Rechtsstaat*. The constitutional theory of the *Rechtsstaat* and the nineteenth-century idea of parliamentarianism with which it was associated does not imply mass democracy. The *Parteienstaat*, on the other hand, affirms the reality of mass democracy and the cognate principle of political equality. Under this theory—one most closely associated with the writings of Gerhard Leibholz, an influential member of the Federal

Constitutional Court for twenty years—the only effective way of informing and determining the will of the people is through the medium of mass membership political parties capable of electing a government and disciplined enough to translate its pledges into public policy.[33] Party finance was thought necessary, as was the case in the United States, to "purify" the electoral process and to keep parties uncontaminated by the influence of political interest groups.

In any event, Jaspers looks wistfully back to the Weimar Constitution for a more appropriate model of democracy. The framers of the Basic Law, in rejecting its plebiscitary institutions and procedures, were motivated by a "distrust of the people" that is no longer justified in his view by modern political conditions. Interestingly, these procedures and institutions were rejected again in the 1970s by the Enquête Commission on Constitutional Reform. The Commission turned down all proposals for referenda and endorsed anew the indirect election of the federal president and the constructive vote of no confidence.

The Commission was nevertheless responsive to a number of complaints and frustrations found in Jaspers's critique and echoed by more recent critics of the Basic Law. In addition to his attack on certain institutional features of the Basic Law, Jaspers pleaded for more public disclosure of governmental proceedings, stronger parliamentary control over the government, greater parliamentary regard for constituency complaints, an ombudsman to hear complaints against the bureaucracy, and more political independence for the federal president. To break up the oligarchies in control of the established parties he advocated more democratically organized parties, an open nomination process—here he pointed to American primary elections as a model—and a greater display of independence on the part of the chancellor in appointing cabinet officials.[34]

The Commission responded to these concerns by recommending (1) a method by which the Bundestag might dissolve itself, (2) the establishment of investigative committees on the motion of a parliamentary minority, and (3) the establishment of a parliamentary petition committee. The last recommendation, as already noted, is now a part of the Basic Law. The need for an ombudsman, on the other hand, seems unnecessary in view of the constitutionalization, in 1970, of the constitutional complaint procedure. Three years earlier Parliament enacted the Political Parties Act, a measure that finally implemented the constitutional provision requiring political parties to organize themselves democratically and publically to account for their funds. And while the 5 percent clause remains in effect, the Federal Constitutional Court has held that any political party capturing as little as 0.5 percent of the total vote in a parliamentary election is entitled to public funding.[35] Public funding, incidentally, was adopted partly in response to an earlier Federal Constitutional Court decision which invalidated, as violating equal protection, a tax exemption for contributions to political parties.[36] The Court, in fact, proposed public financing as a valid means of fostering the independence of political parties.

The Enquête Commission received a large number of proposals to further strengthen the role of political parties and at the same time to open the parties to more grass-roots influence. For example, one proposal would have allowed voters to change the order of candidates appearing on the second or list ballot, an ordering which the Federal Constitutional Court has declared cannot be changed by party leaders after an election. This proposal and others designed to strengthen the corporate role of parties in the German system did not win the Commission's majority approval.

Democratic representation is a problem at the level of constitutional theory precisely because the Basic Law contains two alternative visions of the political process. One view envisions political parties as the chief agencies of political representation. The other view envisions parliamentary delegates as independent decision-makers. The first view is rooted in Article 21, the second in Article 38. Article 21, which recognizes the critical role of political parties, is the basis for proposals to solidify the influence of parties in forming the political will of the people. Article 38, on the other hand, declares parliamentary delegates to be "representatives of the whole people, not bound by orders . . . and subject only to their conscience." The two articles blend the juridical theory of the *Parteienstaat* and the parliamentarianism of the *Rechtsstaat* into an uneasy alliance. These views matter in constitutional interpretation. Must a parliamentary delegate forfeit his seat if he changes parties? Can a party—the Greens for example—recall a delegate if he fails to abide by instructions? May a party rotate its delegates within the period of a single legislative term? These are examples of problems that could easily arise under these provisions.

THE BASIC LAW: A CONSTITUTION VALIDATED

What validates the Basic Law as a whole? The question has been fervently debated among German constitutional theorists. The preamble refers to the "German people" as the "constituent power" responsible for the Basic Law. In 1949, however, state legislatures, not the whole German people, chose the delegates to the constitutional convention (Parliamentary Council) just as they and not the people ratified the Constitution. For these reasons, the Basic Law has been said to lack *formal* legitimacy in German constitutional theory. In the prevailing view, however, the Basic Law's legitimacy depends on the correspondence between popular will and existing constitutional values. The Federal Constitutional Court itself has espoused a theory of the *inherent*—as opposed to *formal*—legitimacy of the Basic Law. In the *Communist Party* case, the Court wrote: "[The political] system in the Federal Republic is legitimate ... because it is an expression of the social and political convictions reflecting the current cultural condition of the German people."[37] One could add that even from the perspective of formal legitimacy the Basic Law has been confirmed overwhelmingly, again and again, in federal elections. Thus, as Gunnar Schuppert remarks, "the subsequent elections to the Federal Parliament and the high turnout of voters at these elections provided, as it were, retrospective legitimation for the *Grundgesetz.*"[38]

The legitimacy debate, however, seems terribly artificial and abstract in the light of forty years of experience under the Basic Law. A constitution should be judged not by the validity of historical or judicial theories underlying its origin but, as I think Professor Schuppert is suggesting, by the stability and durability of the democratic political order it has created. Longevity is one sign of good constitutional engineering. In addition, the institutions of governance created by the Basic Law work today much as the framers intended them to work.

The Basic Law sets up a democratic government founded on the rule of law. Government by consent has been achieved in the Federal Republic through representation by elected officials. Although the system does not satisfy the broad participatory demands of Bonn's severest critics, it surely incorporates a vitally important element of democratic theory. The rule of law likewise finds its institutional manifestation in the judicial control of constitutionality. Here the Federal Constitutional Court has played a crucial and active role in defending and promoting constitutional values in the Federal Republic. In addition, the Court's decisions have generated a steady stream of scholarly commentary fully equal to the sophistication and fertility of constitutional scholarship in the United States. Its influence on German public life, like that of the increasing numbers of learned commentaries on the Basic Law, not to mention literally thousands of monographs, reports, and articles on particular aspects of the Basic Law and the Court's work, is well-nigh irreversible.

Another measure of the effectiveness of a constitution based on the rule of law is the extent to which guaranteed rights are observed and enforced. In this respect the Federal Republic's record is as solid and impressive as that of any other liberal democracy in Western Europe, a reality that should not be obscured by episodic occurrences such as the prohibition of an extreme left- or right-wing party, the Spiegel affair, the *Berufsverbot*, or even the activities of the Constitutional Protection Office. The courts are readily and freely available to any citizen who feels himself injured under the law of the Constitution. Indeed, the right to a judicial hearing before one's lawful judge is one right that has been vigorously and uniformly enforced throughout the Federal Republic. Germans also seem aware of their basic rights under the Constitution. More than 80,000 of them—the large majority without the aid of a lawyer—have exercised their right to file a complaint with the Federal Constitutional Court on the ground that one of their liberties had been infringed by public authority. Public support for the constitutional complaint procedure, like the high rating the Federal Constitutional Court continually receives in public opinion polls, is one measure of the breadth and depth of the constitutional consciousness prevalent today in the Federal Republic.

This assessment of the Basic Law and the constitutionalism fostered by it in no way suggests that all is well politically in the Federal Republic. The ills of West German politics cannot be cured by constitutional law. Even Karl Jaspers perceived this truth. "Today," he said, "we are lucky to have this constitution, despite its flaws."[39] He described the Basic Law as "a fine piece of work, meticulously framed by thinking politicians and political scientists. It contains the traditional basic ideas of parliamentary democracy, and it proclaims the basic rights of man as inalienable, not to be changed by future parliamentary majorities."[40] Germans, he suggested, would have to show themselves worthy of the Basic Law. "On this rock alone," he concluded, "stands our free federal state."[41]

NOTES

1. Several authoritative commentaries on the Basic Law reflect this tradition. See, for example, Maunz-Dürig-Herzog, *Grundgesetz* (Munich: C. H. Beck, 1971 [currently in four volumes]); Gerhard Leibholz and Han Justus Rinck, *Grundgesetz für die Bundesrepublik Deutschland*, 6th ed. (Cologne: Verlag Dr. Otto Schmidt KG, 1980); Ingo von Münch, *Grundgesetz-Kommentar* (Munich: C. H. Beck [vol. 1, 3d ed. (1985); vol. 2, 2d ed. (1983); vol. 3, 2d ed. (1983)]); Bruno Schmidt-Bleibtreu and Franz Klein, *Kommentar zum Grundgesetz für die Bundesrepublik Deutschland*, 5th ed. (Neuwied and Darmstadt: Hermann Luchterhand, 1980); and Axel Azzola et al., *Kommentar zum Grundgesetz für die Bundesrepublik Deutschland* (Neuwied and Darmstadt: Hermann Luchterhand, 1984 [two vols.]). See also Ernst Bend, Werner Maihofer, and Hans-Jochen Vogel, *Handbuch des Verfassungsrechts* (Berlin: Walter de Gruyter, 1984 [two vols.]).
2. See Carl J. Friedrich, "The Political Theory of the New Democratic Constitutions." in *Constitutions and Constitutional Trends Since World War II*, 2d ed, ed. Arnold J. Zurcher (New York: New York University Press, 1955), 15. See also John F. Golay, *The Founding of the Federal Republic of Germany* (Chicago: University of Chicago Press, 1958).
3. Elmar M. Hucko, *The Democratic Tradition* (Leamington Spa: Berg Publishers, 1987). This book contains the text of the Frankfurt (1849),

Imperial (1871), Weimar (1919), and Bonn (1949) Constitutions as well as the author's commentary.

4. See Donald P. Kommers, *Judicial Politics in West Germany* (Beverly Hills, Calif.: Sage Publications, 1976), 30–42.

5. Ingo von Münch, *Grundgesetz-Kommentar*, 3d ed. (Munich: C. H. Beck, 1985), 1: 102–3.

6. For discussions of basic rights and the principles underlying the Basic Law, see Ulrich Karpen, ed., *The Constitution of the Federal Republic of Germany* (Baden-Baden: Nomos Verlagsgesellschaft, 1988). This book includes chapters on equality, free speech, and property rights. See also Donald P. Kommers, *The Constitutional Jurisprudence of the Federal Republic of Germany* (Durham: Duke University Press, forthcoming 1989).

7. Leonard Krieger, *The German Idea of Freedom* (Boston: Beacon Press, 1959), 470.

8. Kommers, *Constitutional Jurisprudence*, chapter 7.

9. For a discussion of these traditions, see Koppel Pinson, *Modern Germany* (New York: Macmillan, 1966), 12–22, 173–218.

10. Karl Doehring, "The Limits of Constitutional Law," in Rudolf Bernhard and Ulrich Beyerlin, eds., *Reports on German Public and Public International Law* (Heidelberg: C. F. Müller Juristischer Verlag, 1986), 35–37.

11. Klaus Stern, *Das Staatsrecht der Bundesrepublik Deutschland*, 2d ed. (Munich: C. H. Beck, 1984), 1: 206–18, 456–69, 776–92, and 877–914.

12. See Karl Doehring, "The Special Character of the Constitution of the Federal Republic of Germany as a Free Democratic Basic Order" in Karpen, *Constitution of the Federal Republic*, 25–44.

13. Edward McWhinney, *Supreme Court and Judicial Law-Making: Constitutional Tribunals and Constitutional Review* (Dordrecht and Boston: Martinus Nijhoff Publishers, 1986), 168.

14. Judgment of December 14, 1965, 19 *Entscheidungen des Bundesverfassungsgerichts* [Decisions of the Federal Constitutional Court] (1965): 206, 220 (hereafter cited as BVerfGE).

15. for a detailed and critical discussion of this interpretive theory, see Helmut Goerlich, *Wertordnung und Grundgesetz* (Baden-Baden: Nomos Verlagsgesellschaft, 1973).

16. McCulloch v. Maryland, 17 U.S. (4 Wheat.) 316 (1819).

17. Cohens v. Virginia, 19 U.S. (6 Wheat.) 264 (1821).

18. This amendment permitted state officials to tap telephone lines without informing the persons affected by such taps. It also prevented such persons from seeking recourse in the courts; complaints arising from invasions of privacy under Article 10 (2) were to be heard by a special review panel appointed by Parliament. The Federal Constitutional Court sustained the constitutionality of this amendment in the *Privacy of Communications* case. For an English translation of this case, see Wal-

ter F. Murphy and Joseph Tanenhaus, *Comparative Constitutional Law* (New York: St. Martin's Press, 1977), 659–66.

19. The work and status of the Bundesrat are treated in Gebhart Ziller, *Der Bundesrat*, 7th ed. (Düsseldorf: Droste Verlag, 1984). For an excellent treatment of the Federal Constitutional Court's role in settling federal-state conflicts, see Philip M. Blair, *Federalism and Judicial Review in West Germany* (Oxford: Clarendon Press, 1981).

20. See Paul Sieghart, *The International Law of Human Rights* (Oxford: Clarendon Press, 1983).

21. See, for example, Kommers, *Constitutional Jurisprudence*, chapter 7.

22. See Eckart Klein, "The Concept of the Basic Law," in Christian Starck, ed., *Main Principles of the Basic Law* (Baden-Baden: Nomos Verlagsgesellschaft, 1983), 20–21.

23. Judgment of 25 June 1974, 37 BVerfGE 363.

24. Judgment of 16 February 1983, 62 BVerfGE 1.

25. See *Beratung und Empfehlungen zur Verfassungsreform*, Part I, "Parliament und Regierung" (1976) and Part II "Bund und Länder" (1977) (Bonn: Presse- und Informationszentrum des deutschen Bundestages).

26. One major recommendation would have repealed Article 75 which lists those subjects concerning which the federal government may enact general or skeletal laws. These subjects were added in turn to the federations's list of concurrent powers under Article 74. In addition, the Commission proposed to extend the Bundesrat's absolute consent power to additional subject areas, including certain matters relating to foreign policy. For a complete list of the Commission's proposed amendments to the Basic Law, see ibid., 250–71 (part I).

27. See, for example, Wilhelm Hennis et al., eds., *Regierbarkeit: Studien zu ihrer Problematisierung*, vol. 1 (Stuttgart: Klett-Cotta, 1975).

28. See Claus Offe, "Ungovernability: on the Renaissance of Conservative Theories of Crisis" and Ulrich Preuss, "Political concepts of Order for Mass Society," in Jürgen Habermas, ed., *Observations on "the Spiritual Situation of the Age"* (Cambridge, Mass.: The MIT Press, 1984), 67–119.

29. In translation, the book appears as *The Future of Germany* (Chicago: The University of Chicago Press, 1967). All citations from this edition.

30. Ibid., 78.

31. Ibid., 8.

32. For a recent study of party financing, see Arthur B. Gunlicks, "Campaign and Party Finance in the West German 'Party State,' " *The Review of Politics* 50 (1988): 30–48.

33. See Gerhard Leibholz, *Strukturprobleme der modernen Demokratie*, 2d ed. (Karlsruhe: C. F. Müller Verlag, 1964).

34. Jaspers, *The Future of Germany*, 10–16 and 73–84.

35. Judgment of 3 December 1968, 24 BVerfGE 300.

36. Judgment of 24 June 1958, 8 BVerfGE 51.
37. Judgment of 17 August 1956, 5 BVerfGE 85, 379 (1956).
38. Gunnar F. Schuppert, "The Constituent Power" in Starck, ed. *Main Principles*, 45.
39. Jaspers, *The Future of Germany*, 58.
40. Ibid., 57.
41. Ibid., 58.

7

WEST GERMAN CORPORATISM
AT FORTY

Michael G. Huelshoff

Since the founding of the Federal Republic, West German corporatism has evolved into a complex set of formal and informal relationships among capital, labor, and the government. This chapter is mainly concerned with two issues—to place the Federal Republic in the context of corporatist theory, and to trace the development of German corporatism since 1949. After a short review of corporatist theory, we will argue that the establishment and development of corporatist institutions in the Federal Republic was a result of complex political processes, with both domestic and international actors and events playing significant roles. Additionally, it will be argued that German coalition politics made it difficult to maintain momentum toward strengthening corporatist institutions at the macro or micro levels during the 1970s. Under the current center-right coalition, it is unlikely that further steps will be made to expand or strengthen corporatist institutions at these levels, although this situation enables the regional (Land) governments to play a more significant role in economic affairs.

While this chapter focuses primarily upon the institutional arrangements that constitute corporatism, it is important to note the social context within which such institutions operate. In comparison to most other advanced industrial democracies, the Federal Republic exhibits considerable cooperative behavior among major social actors, often involving the state. To suggest that little progress on strengthening the institutions of German corporatism is likely in the near future does not imply that politics in the Federal Republic is not today heavily influenced by social norms of cooperation, or that the center-right coalition can ignore organized interests on the left.

CORPORATIST THEORY AND THE FEDERAL REPUBLIC

Before discussing the theory itself, a word regarding definitions is necessary.[1] Charles Meier defines corporatism as the "broad concertation between employer and employee representatives across industries, which is usually established and sometimes continually supervised under state auspices."[2] Many theorists emphasize institutions when defining corporatism, while others have emphasized the importance of a broad social understanding among classes. Peter J. Katzenstein, for example, defines corporatism as the "ideology of social partnership" found in many advanced industrial societies today.[3]

Mainstream corporatist theory is based upon a few, simple assumptions, including the relevance of class-based analysis of social activity, and a view of the state as an independent actor in society, pursuing its own ends. From these assumptions a process model is developed, which can be summarized as:

1. Class interests are aggregated via peak associations, representing most or all members of a given class;
2. Bargaining among peak associations and sometimes the state is common, and is designed to manage industrial conflict, leading to stable social relations. This bargaining is often institutionalized;
3. As a rough equivalence of power is said to exist among the participants, bargaining outcomes consist of equivalent compromises among the interests of the participants, and
4. The outcomes of such bargaining are said to be binding upon the members of the peak associations.

Further, distinctions are made between the structures or institutions of interest intermediation (what Philippe C. Schmitter calls corporatism 1), and the mode of making and implementing policy that results from these structures or institutions (corporatism 2).[4] For example, in the Federal Republic, the institutions of corporatism

(corporatism 1) include Concerted Action, the national information exchanges between capital and labor that took place between 1967 and 1976, and codetermination in the supervisory boards of most firms. Corporatist modes of making and implementing policy (corporatism 2) also exists in Germany, including the informal consultative arrangements that were common in the Schmidt government, and the broad norms of cooperation that are said to characterize German society.

Another important element in the corporatist scheme is the role of political parties. A number of authors have noted the link between social democracy and the establishment of corporatist institutions, arguing that the institutions arise largely when social democratic governments are in power.[5] This raises issues of the distribution of power between capital and labor in corporatist arrangements, and the stability of corporatism when economies undergo considerable stress and when social democrats are not in power.[6] Some scholars have also stressed the apparent instability of corporatist institutions and policy processes.[7] In response to this instability, new concepts have been introduced to explain the mixed pattern of social relations that result. Distinctions have been drawn between micro corporatism (or corporatism at the plant or firm level), meso corporatism (at the regional level), and macro corporatism (at the national level).

With regard to the Federal Republic, Peter J. Katzenstein has argued that policy-making exhibits considerable stability, with change occurring only in incremental steps.[8] Kenneth Dyson has also suggested that political parties play a minor role in economic policy.[9] If correct, this view of German politics would suggest a relatively stable pattern of relations in corporatist institutions and policy processes. Jutta Helm, in contrast, has argued in her case study of industrial adjustment in the Ruhr that policy processes with regard to the coal and steel industries underwent a significant adjustment after the "Wende" of 1982.[10] This view is also consistent with the arguments of those who note the instability of corporatist processes, and the lack of equivalence of power among participants in such arrangements.

Empirically, the development of the institutions of corporatism (that is, corporatism 1) in the Federal Republic has, with one important exception, occurred only when the Social Democratic Party (SPD) has been in power in Bonn. These institutions have been established primarily at the micro level. Micro corporatist institutions, including codetermination and the works councils, are relatively stable as they are based upon federal legislation. While the Christian Democratic Union/Christian Social Union (CDU/CSU) has important interests in maintaining the "ideology of social partnership" in the Federal Republic (corporatism 2), their version of how this social partnership is to work is significantly less cooperative as regards labor than that suggested either in corporatist theory or by the SPD. The "Wende" of 1982 did move the Federal Republic somewhat closer to Lindbolm's notions of the privileged position of capital,[11] but did not eliminate the overarching "ideology of social partnership" from German politics. This situation has made more visible the activities of regional governments which engage in increasingly effective meso corporatist activities. This chapter, then, falls somewhere between the stability in policy making noted by Peter J. Katzenstein, and the changes due to the "Wende" noted by Jutta Helm.

Finally, as a "medium" corporatist society,[12] the Federal Republic does not exhibit all the characteristics of classic corporatism. There is no single peak association representing capital, and labor's peak association has relatively little real power over its constituent unions. Additionally, while the unions have considerable influence over the plant-level works councils, they are not strongly influential across all industries, and recently disagreements have arisen between the unions and the works councils with regard to both management of restructuring and flexible working rules. Full federal participation in corporatist arrangements is limited by its long-standing commitment to free market principles. The division of power between the federal and regional levels of government also constrains the ability of Bonn to participate in macro corporatist arrangements, but does provide the regional governments with the resources and opportunity to encourage cooperation between capital and labor. Corporatist theory also fails to account for the role of the financial community in economic policy making, a particularly significant actor in the German political economy.

THE DEVELOPMENT OF CORPORATISM IN THE
FEDERAL REPUBLIC

In examining the complex system of corporatism in the Federal Republic, distinctions will be drawn between the institutions of German corporatism, and the social environment within which they exist (that is, corporatism 1 and corporatism 2 respectively). It will be shown that while progress remains to be made with regards to institutionalization, cooperative decision making, particularly in comparison to other advanced industrial democracies, continues to be common in Germany.

The creation of national-level corporatism was historically not on the agenda of the German labor movement or its political ally the Social Democratic Party. With the exception of the period of the Weimar Republic, the dominant factions in the Left argued for the creation of socialism in Germany, and the nationalization of industry. The road toward socialism, however, was paved with various institutions that today are associated with corporatism. As long as demands for the nationalization of industry and the creation of socialist institutions went unrealized, progress was limited to creating forms of economic democracy, within a clearly capitalist economic structure. These institutions of economic or industrial democracy include works councils and parity codetermination, and constitute what is today known as micro corporatism.

Notions of economic democracy and cooperation between capital and labor have deep roots in German industrial history. The oft-cited reforms of Emperor Wilhelm II included the possible establishment of works councils in factories. Small-scale, privately initiated cooperation between capital and labor had occurred in Germany in the early period of industrialization, and might best be explained by pressures of "backwardness." The move toward economic democracy gained new momentum during the First World War in industries vital to the war effort when right-wing elements of the Majority Socialists agreed with military leaders to create works councils in exchange for uninterrupted production of war goods. In the political chaos following the war, workers forced some industries to establish works councils and codetermination. The Weimar Republic's codification of the first part of these efforts, the 1920 Works Councils Law, was, however, an attempt by labor leaders and the SPD to reassert control over the radicalized rank and file. Worker participation in decision making was restricted, although works councils were extended throughout the economy.

The Weimar Constitution included some provisions for establishing corporatist institutions at the national level. Article 165 called for national works councils and national economic councils, but these bodies were inactive. The Nazis destroyed the independent labor movement upon their seizure of power in 1933, forcing workers to accept on authoritarian (and highly circumscribed) version of corporatism. Thus, the German labor movement in 1949 suffered from a rather confused inheritance. While on the one hand capital and labor had occasionally come to cooperative arrangements to regulate class conflict, state intervention had been either ineffectual or excessively harsh, and had generated cleavages between labor leaders and the rank and file. This experience would contribute significantly to the development of corporatism in the Federal Republic: labor would distrust government intervention in class conflict at the national level, due not only to the Nazi repressions, but also to the ineffectual interventions of the Weimar regime. Economic democracy via micro corporatism would also be seen as a mechanism for avoiding right-wing extremism in the New Germany.

Initial Limited Gains: 1945–1966

Industrial democracy was a key element among the postwar goals of labor. Codetermination in the workplace, though, took a back seat to policies emphasizing the creation of socialism in the FRG, via the nationalization of major industries. Micro corporatist institutions were largely seen as an important step on the way toward a more egalitarian society based upon socialist principles. While it is debatable how much the unions really felt that the creation of socialism was possible, the issue remained near the top of their agenda until 1963.

Demands for the nationalization of industry and the creation of socialism were unacceptable to the occupying powers, particularly the United States. Codetermination, though, enjoyed some support from the occupying powers as a means of constraining capital's political influence. In the newly formed FRG, heavily influenced by postwar U.S. hegemony and led by the conservative parties, calls for nationalization made little headway. Labor would find its demands for codetermination and other issues largely frustrated until it dropped its insistence on nationalization in 1963, and until it had a strong ally in Bonn after 1966.

Between 1949 and 1966, the labor movement scored only one success in its efforts to build industrial democracy. The 1951 Codetermination Act for the Coal and Steel Industries (Montan Mitbestimmung) established parity codetermination in the coal and steel industries, giving one-half of the members of the supervisory boards of firms in these industries to labor. The law also required that a labor director be appointed to managing boards to oversee labor issues, with the workers enjoying a veto over this appointment.

The compromise leading to the 1951 legislation can be attributed partially to external pressures.[13] Chancellor Adenauer saw American calls for increased German output of war goods to support U.S. intervention in Korea as an opportunity to improve Germany's standing with its most important ally. Production of war goods, however, was quite controversial in the Federal Republic, and the German Trade Union Federation (DGB) seized upon this opportunity to demand progress on codetermination in exchange for support for Adenauer's efforts to accommodate the Americans. Under threat of a general strike, an eleventh-hour deal was struck in direct negotiations between the chancellor and the DGB, leading to parity codetermination in coal and steel. While it supported the union demands, the SPD played a small role only since it opposed German production of war goods.

While the 1951 legislation was a partial success in the drive for economic democracy, it was the only real success between 1949 and 1966. The 1952 Works Legislation Act was a failure for the unions, and slowed the establishment of micro corporatism in the Federal Republic. While the 1952 act reintroduced works councils, the extension of codetermination was limited to the election by workers of only one-third of the members of the supervisory boards of all firms outside the coal and steel industries. Additionally, the election of the labor director was not subject to worker veto, as in the 1951 legislation.

Why did the unions enjoy little success in building German corporatism during this initial period? The 1952 Works Legislation Act did little more than reestablish works councils along the lines of Weimar legislation. As long as the unions continued to insist on nationalization of German industry, and as long as the SPD supported these demands, little progress on economic democracy was possible. Rejecting a market-oriented society might have been popular with party and union stalwarts, but it did not attract public support, enough votes, or potential coalition partners except from the extreme Left. In the context of American political and economic hegemony, such a clear rejection of American ideals was unpopular with many voters and parties. This also strengthened the resolve of business leaders and the conservative regime in Bonn to oppose expansion of codetermination. With American economic ideology at its strongest, and with a federal government striving for international recognition via its alliance with the United States, nationalization was unlikely to win support from bourgeois political parties or social classes. Codetermination, in turn, could be easily labeled by these groups as a step toward nationalization and socialism.

The SPD, in turn, was clearly not strong enough to force the issue. The party won only 29.2 percent of the vote in the 1949 election. Membership had been dropping since 1948, and did not stabilize until 1956. The party also suffered setbacks in the elections of 1953 and 1957. During the 1950s, the SPD found itself unable to fully throw off the legacies of the past: its continued adherence to historical determinism, its distrust of government, and a "pseudo-revolutionary, emotion-inspired radicalism" which did not translate into the ability to organize mass movements to affect political developments.[14] After the death of Kurt Schumacher in 1952, ideological splits between radical leftists and several, rival groups of reformers heightened the party's difficulties. As a result, the SPD was unable to translate its opposition to government policy on rearmament, European cooperation, German reunification, or economic policy into votes, and hence political power.

The establishment of economic democracy in the Federal Republic during its first seventeen years was greatly hampered by the Left's poor bargaining position. The SPD, unable to break out of its Weimar experiences and split by infighting, could not generate sufficient political pressure to force such reforms on the German political economic system. In the context of an American economic and political hegemony that emphasized free market principles, the bourgeois forces—capital and its political allies the CDU/CSU and the Free Democratic Party (FDP)—were able to largely reject the demands of the Left. As the German economy grew through the 1950s, the Left's view of the future of German society grew increasingly irrelevant. Only with both the SPD's and the DGB's explicit rejection of socialism and acceptance of the legitimacy of the market, in the Godesberger and Düsseldorfer Programs of 1959 and 1963, respectively, and in the context of the Federal Republic's first real recession in 1965, would both succeed in establishing micro corporatist institutions and limited economic democracy for the whole of the German economy.

Coalition Politics and Corporatist Expansion: 1967–1976

The first postwar German recession in 1965 helped to bring the SPD to power. While the CDU had been slowly moving toward a more or less Keynesian approach to the economy and informal macro corporatist discussions between capital and labor, the Great Coalition of 1966–1969 accelerated this process. Three major steps were made toward establishing and strengthening the institutions of macro and micro corporatism in the Federal Republic during this period: the 1967 Law on the Promotion of Stability and Growth, the 1972 reform of the works councils legislation, and the extension of parity codetermination outside the coal and steel industries in 1967.

Macro Corporatism. The foundation of German macro corporatism is the Law to Promote Economic Stability and Growth. The 1967 law formally recognized a neo-Keynesian role for government in the Federal Republic. It also created Concerted Action, the national-level coordination mechanism among capital, labor, and government that most closely approximated macro corporatism for the Federal Republic.

Concerted Action, however, never grew into the sort of national-level collective bargaining envisioned in corporatist theory. Participation in Concerted Action was neither compulsory nor were the results binding upon the participants. Neither capital nor labor faced compelling incentives to formalize the relationship. Capital could maintain the maximum flexibility in its control of wage costs by keeping Concerted Action informal, avoiding constraints on its approach to wage bargaining that might have been imposed in a formal arrangement. For the unions, formal, binding negotiations would necessitate strengthening the DGB at the expense of its constituent unions, particularly in the area of wage negotiations. Labor's long-standing distrust of government and business also suggested a cautious approach to close cooperation with capital and government, and the unions might have feared that institutionalized national-level cooperation would curtail their already limited right to strike. More importantly, the arrangement seemed to work as it was, and was not a traditional goal of the labor movement anyway. In the context of German social partnership demands for a strengthened Concerted Action would have unnecessarily provoked capital.

Neither of the main political parties, the CDU/CSU or the SPD, was particularly interested in formalizing Concerted Action. Both major parties favored some sort of national cooperative arrangement between capital and labor, but the CDU/CSU's slow drift toward neo-Keynesianism through the 1960s never went far enough to embrace macro corporatism. The SPD's formulations at the macro level remained rather vague through the Great Coalition, and not much different from the type of information-sharing envisioned in the conservative government before 1966. The Free Democrats, in opposition between 1966 and 1969, opposed Concerted Action as an infringement upon property rights.

For macro corporatism to have grown in the Federal Republic, it would have to have had the active support of the unions and the SPD. With the unions seemingly uninterested in a strong, centralized institutional arrangement between capital and labor, the SPD was under little pressure from its main constituent to strengthen Concerted Action. In the run-up to the 1972 election, the SPD, trying to win an absolute majority, saw no need to change a relationship that was functioning reasonably well, and in which its most important constituent, the labor movement, had expressed no interest in changing. Hence, there was little serious discussion of formalizing Concerted Action.

Micro Corporatism. In contrast to the situation with Concerted Action, significant steps were taken after 1969 to strengthen micro corporatism. The reform of the works councils legislation of 1952 was the first of these efforts. The Works Councils Act of 1972 greatly expanded the powers of the councils. It required the establishment of works councils in all firms employing over five workers, and strengthened the powers of the councils in the areas of hiring, firing, promotions, transfers, and work allocation. The law required the drawing up of "social plans" in cases of large-scale layoffs. These plans would guarantee severance pay, retraining, and other benefits for laid-off workers.

The 1972 act was the result of compromise between the SPD and the FDP. In exchange for tabling codetermination proposals, the FDP supported the strengthening of works councils legislation. The act represents the high point of the drive to establish economic democracy in the FRG. It also contributed to conflict between the SPD and the Free Democrats over economic policy generally, and over codetermination in particular. These conflicts plagued the center-left coalition until its demise in 1982.

After the 1972 election the SPD renewed its efforts to realize parity codetermination. Draft bills presented in cabinet meetings generated a storm of protest from the FDP. The FDP, which had opposed codetermination since the 1951 compromise between Chancellor Adenauer and the DGB, resisted all effort to expand parity codetermination and called on German business for support. The Federation of German Industry (BDI) issued a series of warnings about the effects of the draft legislation that projected a collapse of the German economic "miracle" if the legislation was adopted. But the SPD could not back down. Its prestige and special relationship with labor was on the line, particularly after its attempt to stimulate the economy to combat the 1974 recession through use of neo-Keynesian policy tools was frustrated by the Bundesbank's tight money policy.

In this political context, the resulting Codetermination Act of

1976 pleased no one. It provided for parity codetermination in all firms employing over 2,000 workers, but with some significant reservations. These reservations included white-collar representation in labor's supervisory board delegation, a weakening of labor's control over appointment of the labor director, and the election of board chairs by shareholders alone, with the provision of two votes to break ties for the chair. While this was the best that the SPD could do, the act pleased neither labor, which viewed the compromise bill as a sellout to capital, nor capital, which feared that a loss in competitiveness would result. Capital responded immediately with a civil suit questioning the constitutionality of the 1976 codetermination legislation. While the suit would be rejected by the Federal Constitutional Court several years later, labor seized upon this to walk out of Concerted Action, arguing that in this context cooperation with capital could not be contemplated. While informal consultations continued in the Schmidt government, institutionalized cooperation at the macro level was terminated.

From 1966 until 1972, labor made steady progress toward achieving economic democracy in the Federal Republic. After 1972, though, progress was less than satisfying. FDP and business opposition to codetermination led to a bill that can only be considered a partial victory for labor. Institutionalizing micro corporatism in the Federal Republic was stalled, and has yet to regain momentum. Further, macro corporatism was weakened as a result of the battles over micro corporatism.

German Corporatism Since 1976

The legislative record on corporatism since 1976 is short. The only real attempt by the Schmidt regime to maintain some political momentum, the effort to stop firms from reorganizing themselves to avoid the strong parity codetermination in the coal and steel industries, failed to do more than slow the transition of some firms (notably Mannesmann AG) out of the provisions of the 1951 legislation. No efforts to correct the weaknesses of the 1976 legislation were possible in the latter years of the Schmidt coalition, although Chancellor Schmidt often used his personal power to bring together capital and labor in informal gatherings to coordinate policy. Not only was Bonn rife with political conflict after 1976, but also the second oil crisis of 1978–1979 signaled the end of the Federal Republic's successes in avoiding much of the economic crises that plagued other advanced industrial democracies. Beginning in the late 1970s, long-term, structural unemployment in many industries grew. Most basic manufacturing industries faced pressures to structurally adjust, including steel, textiles, shipbuilding, and consumer electronics.

On the union side, there has been a significant redefinition of union goals. In the context of limited growth, and in response to a decline in blue-collar employment, the unions have shifted their focus somewhat to issues other than codetermination. Humanization of the workplace and other goals are replacing codetermination at the top of labor's political agenda, at least in part due to the growing influence of white-collar workers in the unions. Additionally, the 35-hour workweek has been the focus of two painful strikes in the Federal Republic. The 1978 strike failed to achieve the 35-hour week, and while the 1984 strike was able to win a compromise 38.5-hour workweek, both damaged the image of the union movement in the eyes of the conservative parties. The Neue Heimat affair further weakened the political position of organized labor, and contributed to the electoral weakness of the SPD in 1987.

After the confirmation of the center-right coalition in the 1983 election, the new government moved quickly to redefine Bonn's role toward the economy. The fiscal conservatism that marked the latter years of the Schmidt coalition was strengthened with calls for tax cuts and tax reform, curtailment of social spending, and the easing of regulation of the economy. While progress on these issues has been particularly slow, in this political atmosphere significant progress on strengthening the institutions of corporatism is unlikely.

Chancellor Kohl did temporarily restart Concerted Action in 1985, but his attempt to reintroduce informal national level consultations was in part shrewd preelection positioning. The CDU/CSU-FDP coalition had poor relations with organized labor for the first three years of its tenure, and its legislative slate was hardly designed to attract labor votes. Government hostility during the 1984 strike, and its attempts to modify Paragraph 116 of the Labor Promotion Law after the strike added to the hostile atmosphere. The recent series of initiatves on the part of Arbeitsminister Bluem, including modifica-tion of work rules, can be interpreted in part as an attempt to split the labor movement. Additionally, Bonn's attitude toward industrial adjustment has been decidedly anti-union. Even when capital and labor could agree on industrial restructuring, as in the case of the Ruhr steel industry during early 1987, the center-right coalition refused to participate. Strengthening corporatist institutions is clearly unlikely in such an atmosphere. The CDU/CSU cannot, however, abandon the labor movement. Such a policy would be inconsistent with the broad notions of "social partnership" that characterize German society, and probably cost the CDU/CSU votes. Also, the left wing of the CDU would oppose a more aggressive anti-union pro-gram, weakening the party and the center-right coalition. Given these constraints, it is likely that the stop-and-start relationship between the conservative parties and the unions common in the last few years will continue.

In contrast, with the demise of institutionalized macro corpora-tism, the stagnation in the expansion of micro corporatist institu-tions, the meso or regional level of cooperation has grown in impor-tance in recent years. Many regional governments have become active in attempting to stimulate investment, particularly in "high tech" industries. The most notable successes have taken place in Baden-Württemberg and Bavaria. Additionally, as industrial decline has become increasingly concentrated in a few regions, affected state governments have been active in attempting to assist firms and workers to adjust to the new conditions. While this often includes attempts to attract new investment and "high tech" industries, much of the focus of such regional cooperative schemes has been upon the management of decline. Both North Rhine-Westfalia and the Saar-land, among others, have been active in encouraging regional coop-eration to ease economic transitions. While state governments have historically supported cooperation between capital and labor, these endeavors have grown more significant as national level cooperation has been increasingly difficult. As long-standing institutional con-straints have decreased moreover in significance and labor solidar-ity has weakened in the face of industrial crises, the region has in some instances proven itself as an economically effective level of intervention.

German corporatism, then, is clearly influenced by political factors. Which party is in power does make a difference. Expansion of micro institutions is largely possible only when the SPD is in power, or when specific crises and opportunities suggest to the conservative parties that compromise is necessary. Additionally, it seems likely that the "Wende" had a significant impact upon the atmosphere within which the corporatist institutions function (corporatism 2), by weakening the ties between the federal government and labor. The Kohl government has been able to resist calls for expanded corporatism because labor and the SPD have been weakened by both internal strife and structural changes in the German economy. Kohl's tilt toward capital, though, remains significantly constrained by both the existing institutions of German corporatism, and the somewhat tattered "ideology of social partnership."

GERMAN CORPORATISM IN THE NEXT DECADE

The experience of the Federal Republic suggests several observations regarding the future. First is the importance of political allies. Significant progress in institutionalizing micro corporatism in the Federal Republic has been attained only with a strong ally in Bonn. External events can occasionally force some compromise on the bourgeois parties—such as the importance of the Korean War in passage of the 1951 codetermination law—but a strong political ally in the federal government is crucial. Another observation derives from the importance of coalition politics in the Federal Republic. German voters are known to prefer coalitions to single-party governments. Progress toward strengthening corporatist institutions in the Federal Republic will be constrained by the internal dynamics of coalition governments, particularly those including the Free Democrats.

Finally, as the structure of the union movement has changed, so have its goals. The growth of white-collar union membership, and the corresponding decline of blue-collar employment as jobs are lost to foreign competition and upgraded through automation, has led to a softening of some traditional union demands. Humanization of the work environment and other new goals have come to replace codetermination at the top of labor's agenda. The differential pressures of restructuring, furthermore, have weakened the centralization of the labor movement. Until the labor movement can fully absorb these changes, significant progress toward strengthening micro level corporatism is unlikely.

It is doubtful that the German labor movement fully desires the creation of a macro corporatist society along the lines of Sweden or Austria. Labor distrust of capital and government is still strong. As its ambivalence toward Concerted Action suggests, the labor movement may well prefer to maintain the strength of individual unions, and the right to strike, if at the expense of national-level cooperation. Without a significant softening of the CDU's attitude toward the labor movement, progress on institutionalizing macro corporatism is unlikely.

It seems likely, as well, that meso corporatism will continue to be a significant element of German corporatism. The successes of the southern German states have attracted attention elsewhere. Additionally, as the Federal Republic approaches the full integration of the Common Market in 1992, new demands upon the German economy will undoubtedly be met in part with assistance from the state governments, and may well encourage the federal government, regardless of which party or parties are in power, to reconsider some form of Concerted Action.

NOTES

The author wishes to thank Arthur Hanhardt, Peter Merkl, and Ferdinand Müller-Rommel for comments on earlier drafts of this chapter.

1. The term "corporatism" appears in a variety of forms in the literature. Such terms as "neocorporatism" and "democratic corporatism" have been used to distinguish patterns of social organization in advanced industrial democracies from those found in fascist or authoritarian

states. For simplicity's sake this paper will use the generic "corporatism," as the context here is quite clear. See Peter Katzenstein, *Corporatism and Change* (Ithaca, N.Y.: Cornell University Press, 1984), 27.

2. C. Meier, "Preconditions for Corporatism," in John H. Goldthorpe, ed., *Order and Conflict in Contemporary Capitalism* (New York: Oxford University Press, 1984), 40. See also P. Schmitter, "Still the Century of Corporatism?" *Review of Politics* 36 (1974); P. Schmitter, "Modes of Interest Intermediation and Models of Societal Change in Western Europe," *Comparative Political Studies* 10 (1977); and Leo Panitch, "The Development of Corporatism in Liberal Democracies," *Comparative Political Studies* 10 (1979).

3. Katzenstein, *Corporatism and Change*. See also W. Korpi, *The Democratic Class Struggle* (London: Routledge and Kegan Paul, 1983).

4. Philippe C. Schmitter, "Reflections on Where the Theory of Neo-Corporatism Has Gone and Where the Praxis of Neo-Corporatism May Be Going," in Gerhard Lehmbruch and Philippe C. Schmitter, eds., *Patterns of Corporatist Policy Making* (Beverly Hills, Calif.: Sage, 1982).

5. Panitch, "The Development of Corporatism"; and Gerhard Lehmbruch, "Liberal Corporatism and Party Government," in Philippe C. Schmitter and Gerhard Lehmbruch, eds., *Trends Toward Corporatist Intermediation* (Beverly Hills, Calif.: Sage, 1979).

6. See, for example, Panitch, "The Development of Corporatism"; and Andrew Martin, "Is Democratic Control of Capitalist Economies Possible?" in Leon Lindberg et al., eds., *Stress and Contradiction in Modern Capitalism* (Lexington, Mass.: Lexington Books, 1975).

7. Panitch, "The Development of Corporatism"; see also Gerhard Lehmbruch, "Problems for Future Research on Corporatist Intermediation and Policy Making," in Schmitter and Lehmbruch, eds., *Trends Toward Corporatist Intermediation*; and Jutta Helm, "Coping with Economic Change: Managing Industrial Crises in the Ruhr Valley," paper presented at the Meeting of the German Studies Association, St. Louis, Mo., 15–18 October 1987.

8. Peter J. Katzenstein, *Policy and Politics in West Germany* (Philadelphia: Temple University Press, 1987).

9. Kenneth Dyson, "The Politics of Corporate Crisis in West Germany," *West European Politics* 7 (XXXX): 24–46.

10. Helm, "Coping With Economic Change."

11. Charles Lindblom, *Politics and Markets* (New York: Basic Books, 1977).

12. See Gerhard Lehmbruch, "Concertation and the Structure of Corporatist Networks," in John Goldthorpe, ed., *Order and Conflict in Contemporary Capitalism* (New York: Oxford University Press, 1984) and Kerry Schott, *Policy, Power, and Order* (New Haven: Yale University Press, 1984).

13. There is some controversy on this point. See A. Baring, *Ausenpolitik in*

Adenauers Kanzlerdemokratie (Munich/Vienna: R. Oldenbourg, 1969), and H. Thum, *Mitbestimmung in der Montanindustrie. Der Mythos von Sieg der Gewerkschaften* (Stuttgart: Deutsche Verlagsanstalt, 1982).

14. See H. Grebing, *The History of the German Labour Movement.* (Munich: Nymphenburger Verlagshandlung, 1966), 162.

8

THE AMBIVALENT INSIDER: THE DGB BETWEEN THEORY AND REALITY

M. Donald Hancock

Since its inception in 1949, the German Trade Union Federation (Deutscher Gewerkschaftsbund, or DGB) has confronted sharp ideological criticism from both right and left. Restorative economic and political forces have viewed the DGB as a potential threat to the sanctity of private ownership, whereas neo-Marxist critics have repeatedly chastised union leaders for their failure to promote "consequential socialism"(defined minimally as social ownership of the means of production and distribution). Neither view accurately encapsulates either the DGB's ideological vision of active system change or its political-economic role in postwar German society.

PROGRAMMATIC PRINCIPLES

Radical critics are correct to the extent that the DGB eschews the orthodox Marxism of its counterpart organization in the German Democratic Republic, the Free German Federation of Trade Unions (FDGB). Like its Social Democratic, Catholic, and liberal trade union predecessors in Imperial and Weimar Germany, the DGB views itself more as the advocate of the economic, social, and political interests of the working classes than as a revolutionary vanguard. "We are part of the capitalist order," a DGB official candidly asserted in a private interview, "and we affirm the established state."[1] Accordingly, the DGB and its constituent union officials accept as a matter of ideological principle the legitimacy of diverse group interests on the labor market and open competition among political parties in local, state, and national elections.

Nonetheless, the DGB is far from an uncritical apologist for industrial capitalism. With the adoption of their initial catalog of "fundamental demands" at the DGB's founding congress in Munich in 1949, union leaders expressed a potentially radical strategy of economic democratization. The central tenets of the first postwar program called for the "codetermination of organized workers in all personnel, economic, and social questions of economic leadership and organization," as well as the "nationalization of key industries, especially mining, iron, steel, chemicals, energy, the important transportation enterprises, and credit institutions." Central economic planning, in the view of first-generation DGB officials, would prove the most expeditious means to achieve an economic policy that would ensure "full employment, the most suitable utilization of all productive resources, and the satisfaction of economically important needs." Economic planning, the 1949 program reads, "is wholly compatible with the basic rights of human freedom. The most important freedom for the majority of people—freedom from need and fear of need—can be achieved only through it."[2]

Political realities in the form of Christian Democratic executive dominance from 1949 to the mid-1960s and a rising tide of anticommunism during the same period, which tended to equate democratic socialist goals in the West with forced collectivization in the East, inhibited DGB aspirations to achieve its hopes for a "new economic order" during the formative years of consolidation of the Federal Republic's economic system. With the exception of the DGB's impassioned engagement on behalf of codetermination legislation in the early 1950s (see below), union leaders consciously restricted their demands to immediate bread-and-butter issues. An example of ideological retrenchment was the DGB's first postwar action program in 1955. In contrast to the Munich declaration of 1949, the 1955 program contained a relatively modest litany of union objectives: a shorter workday, a five-day workweek, higher wages, and improved social benefits.

Appearances were deceptive, however, and the DGB adopted revised programs of principle (*Grundsatzprogramme*) in 1963 and 1981, reasserting and expanding its initial vision of economic democratization. As fundamental values the DGB affirms, as expressed in the 1981 document, the political and social equality of all citizens; principles of parliamentary democracy and political pluralism; the right of all citizens "to work and to education . . ."; the right to social security; solidarity among all wage earners in defense of their rights of freedom and equality; the unity of industrial workers, salaried employees, and officials in a single trade union movement (the *Einheitsgewerkschaft*); and the political independence of the DGB "from government, parties, churches, and employers."[3]

In their "tireless struggle" on behalf of citizen rights since "the beginning of industrialization," Germany's trade unions constitute —in the eyes of the DGB—"a crucial integrative factor of democracy and an indispensable force for the further democratic development of the economy and society." It is from this system-affirmative perspective that the DGB proclaims its principal ideological critique of established West German society:

The general improvement in the standard of living, which is due above all to the productivity and diligence of workers and . . . the struggle of the trade unions [on behalf of] social and economic reforms, has made it possible for many workers to achieve a new way of life. Yet insecurity at the workplace, the inequitable distribution of income and property, unequal educational opportunities, and dependence on economic power have not yet been overcome. Additional burdens have arisen as a result of a deterioration of the environment and the intensification of work due to . . . the application of new technologies and new forms of work organization.

Developments in the Federal Republic have led to the restoration of old property and power relations. The concentration of capital advances steadily onward. Small firms are continually pushed back or subordinated economically to larger companies. Workers—the overwhelming majority of the population—remain largely excluded from control over the means of production.[4]

To remedy these perceived deficiencies the DGB advocates as the unions' first priority a series of measures designed to make working life more secure and humane. Chief among them is "an extension of codetermination (*Mitbestimmung*) by the workers [to permit their] equal participation in all economic, social, and cultural decisions." Concretely, the DGB urges the further development of works councils, the creation of a uniform system of codetermination that would accord equal representation to labor and capital on the company boards of all larger firms, and the establishment of a network of state, regional, and national Economic and Social Councils to achieve macro-level economic coordination. Additional means to promote "social control of economic power" would include a reform of the banking system to prevent banks from dominating firms through their ownership of shares, increased economic competition by publicly owned companies, government influence over investments (*Investitionslenkung*), the formation of a comprehensive "general economic plan" (*Rahmenplan*), and "the transfer of key industries and other market-dominating enterprises into collective property." Coupled with these institutional reforms, in the view of the DGB, should be a commitment by both public and private economic actors to "qualitative growth that serves the attainment of the right to work, an improvement in work and living conditions, an equitable distribution of income and property, and an increase in social welfare."[5]

Second in the DGB's catalog of priorities—albeit comprising significantly less space in the current program than its economic aspirations—is the preservation and refinement of existing social security benefits. Claiming partial credit on behalf of organized labor for the historical attainment of comprehensive health, accident, and retirement benefits, West Germany's trade union spokesmen urge the further extension of welfare services to families and "problem groups," including the long-term unemployed.

The principal ideological thrust of the DGB's program is thus oriented toward a system of economic democracy characterized by an extension of state and worker influence over the productive process. Conservative apprehensions notwithstanding, the DGB's proposals do not constitute a blueprint for authoritarian rule in the form of a "trade union state." For one thing, the DGB's program is more rhetorical than substantive; it is by no means clear, for instance, *who* should determine the general economic plan or *how* the state should prevent the "misuse of economic power" or "guide" investments. In addition, and most importantly, DGB officials have consistently been reluctant to press for the wholesale realization of their postwar programs in the absence of a supportive parliamentary majority. At the same time, the DGB's political engagement on behalf of codetermination and its contemporary economic prescriptions indicate that organized labor in West Germany is more of an advocate of active system change than its radical critics would allow.

THE DGB's QUEST FOR PARITY CODETERMINATION

Of all the items on the DGB's inventory of sociopolitical reform objectives, *Mitbestimmung* stands out as the most important. Member unions have seen to the material and social interests of workers throughout postwar economic and political development; the central DGB leadership in Düsseldorf has taken upon itself the more comprehensive task of defending and broadening their rights as economic citizens.

The DGB's quest for participatory rights by workers in company and broader economic decisions is rooted in the effort by revolutionary Social Democrats to establish works councils in the wake of Imperial Germany's collapse at the end of World War I. Originally conceived as a means to unify economic and political decision-making power in the hands of the working classes, the works councils were institutionalized in a diluted form as consultative company boards or councils (*Betriebsräte*). The councils, which were sanctioned by constitutional as well as statutory law, functioned with reasonable effectiveness throughout the years of the Weimar Republic. They were subsequently dissolved following the National Socialist rise to power.

Early postwar union activists promptly resurrected the concept of works councils and added the demand for worker participation in economic decisions. As Hans Böckler, later chairman of the DGB, declared at the first postwar union conference in March 1946 in Hannover: "German workers may not experience again what happened in 1920/21, namely that despite their best efforts they were ultimately betrayed. . . . We have to be represented *equally*, not only in individual companies, not only in economic councils, but throughout the entire economic process."[6] Occupation officials proved responsive to the union demands for codetermination, not the least because of their own interest in decartelizing German industry and punishing Nazi war criminals. Accordingly, the wartime Allies jointly sanctioned the reestablishment of works councils throughout Germany in April 1946. A year later, the British introduced a more radical experiment in economic democracy in the form of parity representation by workers and employers on company boards in the iron and steel industries in their own zone of occupation.[7]

These early achievements prompted DGB leaders to seek legislation that would extend parity codetermination on a national basis following the formation of the Federal Republic in 1949. Thus, the DGB submitted a draft proposal in May 1950 calling for the "equality of capital and labor in the decisions of both individual companies and the economy itself."[8] The federal government's initial response, however, fell far short of labor's expectations. Charged with the task of formulating authoritative guidelines for implementing an Allied directive to restructure Germany's coal-mining, iron, and steel industries, the newly formed Federal Ministry of Economics actually envisioned a restrictive law on codetermination that would abolish the parity provisions already in force in the former British zone. In response, members of the DGB's largest and politically most militant union—IG Metall—voted overwhelmingly to stage a nationwide strike, scheduled to begin on 1 February 1951. To avoid a bitter and disruptive social conflict at a time of increasing international tension, Chancellor Konrad Adenauer personally intervened in subsequent consultations among employers, DGB representatives, and cabinet officials to help forge a more acceptable arrangement. The upshot was an agreement to retain parity codetermination in the iron and steel industries and to extend it to coal as well.

The law on codetermination in the iron and steel industries, which went into effect on 21 May 1951, constituted a major if only partial victory for organized labor in its efforts to transform socioeconomic power relations in the fledgling Federal Republic. It provides for the appointment of an equal number of representatives of workers and shareholders on the supervisory boards of the larger coal, iron, and steel companies along with an additional "neutral" member to ensure majority decisions. In addition, each board of directors is empowered to appoint a labor director (*Arbeitsdirektor*) who must enjoy the confidence of a majority of the workers' representatives on the board. The labor director is charted with overseeing "personnel management, [the] organization of work in accordance with human needs, performance and remuneration, matters concerning collective agreements, training and further training, labour and social law, industrial safety, housing." The act stipulates further that the responsibilities of the labor director "require a close cooperation with the works councils."[9]

Although the 1951 bill encouraged DGB leaders to work for the extension of parity codetermination to other industries throughout the Federal Republic, they promptly encountered resistance on the part of employers and the CDU-led majority in Parliament. As a policy consequence of the deepening mood of political conservativism in the wake of the cold war, the Bundestag endorsed a revised (i.e., German) version of the earlier Allied directive on works councils in 1952 that provided for only one-third worker representation on the supervisory boards of the remaining industrial firms. The DGB and its member unions launched a public protest against what labor officials considered a regressive move in relation to the 1951 law, but to no avail. By then the West German "economic miracle," based on social market principles of competitive capitalism, had begun in earnest, and the Adenauer government was enmeshed in complex negotiations with Allied officials concerning West German rearmament and European integration. As a result, the federal government demonstrated little inclination to respond to further DGB lobbying efforts which were antithetical to the Christian Democrats' own ideological preferences. The futility of DGB efforts to extend the principle of parity codetermination or to influence national policy in controversial areas of rearmament and nuclear weapons ultimately induced union leaders to adopt a lower political profile during the remainder of the decade.

Only after Adenauer's resignation as federal chancellor in 1963 and the beginning of an electoral shift in the balance of political forces between the Christian Democrats and the Social Democrats did prospects improve for an extension of codetermination rights. Simultaneous with the formation of the CDU-SPD Grand Coalition in 1966, the DGB affirmed at its seventh national congress "that a genuine democratic order is only possible when working men and women not only have the right as citizens to influence Parliament, the government, and the administration, but can also exercise an equal voice in economic life. This influence should be felt at the workplace, in the company, in the industrial branch, throughout the nation, and in the European institutions."[10] To mobilize informed opinion in support of parity codetermination on an industrywide basis, the DGB undertook an extensive public relations campaign that culminated in a mass meeting in Cologne in March 1968 at which union leaders unveiled their version of appropriate legislation. According to the DGB proposal, parity codetermination should be extended from the coal, iron, and steel industries to include all companies with capital reserves of 75 million marks or more, an annual turnover of 150 million marks, and/or 2,000 or more workers.

All three of the parties in Parliament responded with proposals of their own. Among them only the SPD endorsed the concept of equal representation of workers and capital on supervisory boards. Both the CDU and the Free Democratic Party (FDP), in contrast, advocated lesser thresholds that would ensure the continued numerical superiority of shareholder interests. This discrepancy initially precluded an agreement between the SPD and the FDP on a codetermination bill after they formed a national coalition government in 1969. By the beginning of their second ministry in 1972, however, the two parties had tentatively concurred on a compromise measure. After protracted committee deliberations in Parliament, which revealed continued strong opposition to the parity principle among employers as well as legal testimony questioning its very constitutionality, the SPD-FDP cabinet introduced a joint legislative proposal in December 1975.

The government's bill approached but did not quite achieve full parity between labor and capital. It called for ostensible equality in that workers and shareholders would each be entitled to elect one-half of the members of the supervisory boards of joint stock companies employing 2,000 or more workers; nonetheless, the measure accorded owner representatives de facto controlling interest over company affairs. This would be achieved, first, through a provision that each supervisory board must elect its chairman and managing board by a two-thirds vote; and, second, through the absence of a neutral member to arbitrate conflicts between worker and shareholder delegates. Instead, the board chairman was accorded a double vote to break potential ties between the two blocs.[11] Since neither he nor the managing boards themselves could be chosen in opposition to the representatives of capital, the practical effect would to ensure the continued dominance of private ownership in the West German productive process.

Despite DGB reservations about precisely the latter implications of the cabinet's proposal, the Bundestag endorsed the new codetermination law on 18 March 1976. It went into effect on 1 July, with the provision that any affected party would have a year to challenge its legal status through the court system. Union leaders greeted the measure as a progressive step, although they vowed they would continue their efforts to achieve full parity in the future. Efforts to achieve this goal have been frustrated, however, by a convergence of political and economic factors that marked a new stage in the political and economic evolution of the Federal Republic.

CONFLICT AND ECONOMIC CRISIS

The DGB's qualified success in achieving near-parity codetermination in Germany's nonsteel, iron, and coal industries was abruptly challenged when thirty employer associations and nine firms filed suit with the Federal Constitutional Court on 29 June 1977 (one day before the expiration of the statutory deadline), alleging that the 1976 bill infringed constitutional rights of private property.[12] As spokesmen for the Federation of German Employers Associations (BDA) declared in Cologne: "The codetermination law thereby undermines the capacity of shareholders to function effectively. . . . [It] is, [moreover,] incompatible with the basic constitutional principles and guidelines governing the legal order and nature of the economy and labor relations today."[13]

The DGB chairman, Heinz-Oskar Vetter, angrily responded by declaring that he would not participate in the next session of high-level economic policy consultations with federal officials and employer representatives—known as Concerted Action (*Konzertierte Aktion*)—that was scheduled to begin in July in Bonn. The sessions had been initiated by the federal government in 1967 as a mechanism to mobilize support among employers and unions for the Grand Coalition's economic stabilization policies in response to the recession of 1966–1967.[14] During the subsequent decade, "Concerted Action" meetings had assumed a more general consultative nature, with key spokesmen for Germany's principal labor market partners convening periodically each year with cabinet and Bundesbank officials to discuss national economic policy. Employer groups had generally affirmed the utility of Concerted Action as a device to facilitate wage stability and increased productivity, whereas DGB spokesmen had become increasingly critical of the sessions. Especially irksome from their perspective was the tendency by government and employer representatives to cite official statistical data as a basis for urging unions to practice wage restraint, whereas employers were allegedly not expected to reciprocate by restricting their "price increases and rate of profit growth."[15]

Vetter's decision to boycott *Konzertierte Aktion* in July 1977 thus reflected a deepening schism on West Germany's labor market. In a *Spiegel* interview published in the immediate aftermath of the employers' legal action, Vetter expressed fear that the employer groups had filed the suit less to test the constitutionality of the 1976 bill itself than to induce the Federal Constitutional Court to question the legality of parity codetermination as codified in the legislation of 1951. It would not be necessary for the Court to do so directly, he suggested. Instead, "it would be sufficient if it ruled that this law (i.e., that of 1976) is just barely constitutional, and then perhaps adds in passing: incidentally, our task was not to determine whether codetermination in the coal and steel industries is or is not constitutional." In such a case, Vetter added, the inevitable result would be open political conflict. He implied that if the courts—prompted by the employer suit—should rule against parity codetermination, West Germany's workers would "take to the streets to defend it."[16]

The dispute between employers and unions prompted tension between the coalition partners as well. The Social Democratic minister of labor, Herbert Ehrenberg, demonstratively joined Vetter in shunning the July 1977 session of Concerted Action, whereas the Free Democratic minister of economics, Hans Fridrichs, was present. This divergent reaction was symptomatic of a larger partisan conflict between the SPD and FDP that had begun by then to emerge over appropriate government action in the wake of the successive international oil price "shocks" during the 1970s that fueled inflation, a rise in unemployment, and growing budgetary deficits throughout the industrialized world.

Vetter's apprehensions were allayed in March 1979 when the Federal Constitutional Court upheld the constitutionality of the 1976 law—as well as, by implication, the 1951 bill on parity codetermination.[17] By then, however, economic factors loomed ever larger as a source of escalating party and group controversy over economic and social policy. The oil crisis had caused West Germany's annual growth rate to plummet from nearly 5.0 percent in 1973 to −2.3 percent in 1975. During the same period, unemployment had jumped from 1.2 percent to 4.7 percent. Following a partial recovery in 1976, economic performance once again slumped following a second round of oil price increases in 1977. Throughout the second half of the decade the unemployment rate doggedly persisted at an annual average of 4.4 percent—by far the highest level since the onset of postwar economic recovery in the early 1950s.

As early as 1977 union officials had begun to criticize the government's economic measures as insufficient to cope with the country's worsening economic doldrums. Vetter and others targeted particularly the FDP because of the party's reluctance to endorse more than a marginal increase in public appropriations to combat unemployment.[18] DGB and union spokesmen also criticized the Free Democrats for their refusal to concur in the abolition of overtime hours in industry as a means of encouraging the employment of additional workers.

In an effort to induce cabinet officials to adopt a more interventionist economic stance, the DGB issued a comprehensive catalogue of "Recommendations . . . for the Restoration of Full Employment" in July 1977.[19] Among its principal proposals are an expansion of the public sector and state investments in social housing, health, education, public transportation, and environmental protection; increased public support for "future-oriented industrial branches"; the introduction of a mandatory tenth school year and an eleventh year of vocational training; and a reduction in the flexible retirement age to sixty for both men and women. Asserting that "the realization of a basic right to work . . . must have precedence in a social *Rechtsstaat* over the interests of private profit, . . ." the DGB reasserts in the catalog of recommendations its long-standing programmatic demand to introduce macroeconomic codetermination.[20]

In practice, the DGB's exhortations proved more an exercise in rhetoric than a stimulus to action. The Free Democrats utilized their pivotal position as junior coalition partner to veto the interventionist measures advocated by organized labor in favor of a policy of fiscal and monetary restraint as their preferred strategy for coping with the domestic effects of stagflation. Disagreement between the FDP and the SPD over details of economic policy management—including the size of the budget deficit and public expenditures on unemployment compensation—became progressively more intense as the decade wore on.

Exacerbating policy conflict within the coalition was the onset of a temporary period of FDP electoral decline. Beginning with the Landtag election in Lower Saxony in 1978, the Free Democrats failed to mobilize the requisite 5 percent of the popular vote for representation in ultimately six of Germany's eleven states—and thereby confronted the discomforting prospect that they might disappear altogether as a viable political force. The combination of growing disagreement with the SPD over economic management and their sagging electoral fortunes thus prompted the Free Democrats to instigate the dramatic coalition breach in October 1982 that resulted in the election of Helmut Kohl as head of a new CDU/CSU-FDP federal government.

The restoration of Christian Democratic ascendancy in national West German politics marked a decisive interruption in organized labor's reform agenda. For the remainder of the 1980s, the DGB and its member unions have been relegated to a subordinate political role reminiscent of their status during the Adenauer years.

ASSESSMENT AND PROSPECTS

Throughout the postwar period both the expansion and contraction of the DGB's political influence can be attributed to a variety of factors. Foremost among them are the vicissitudes of coalition politics. While the SPD serves as the principal political ally of organized labor in the legislative process, the DGB's success or failure in implementing programmatic reforms has consistently been dependent on tactical support proffered alternately by the Christian Democrats and the Free Democrats. Such was the case with the passage of codetermination legislation in both 1951 and 1976.

The intensification of cold war tensions during the 1950s and escalating differences over economic issues between the SPD and the FDP during the 1970s and early 1980s signaled a decline in the capacity of organized labor to sponsor subsequent reform initiatives. Reinforcing the diminution of DGB influence in the late 1970s was the employers' suit against the codetermination law of 1976—a move that expressed a stiffening resolve by business interests to resist system-changing reforms that promised to alter the balance of economic and political power in West Germany.

A third factor contributing to the DGB's loss of political influence was Vetter's own decision to boycott concerted action from July 1977 onward. His action had the practical effect of ending formal tripartite policy consultations on key economic issues.[21] As a consequence, the DGB and its leading unions deprived themselves of an important opportunity to participate in policy discussions at a time when their voice might have helped ameliorate Germany's worsening economic conditions.

The change of government in 1982 has reinforced the subordinate role of organized labor in the contemporary West German polity. The DGB and its member unions have not abandoned their programmatic commitment to an extension of codetermination rights in the face of continuing employer opposition.[22] Neither have they forgone periodic militancy on the labor market, as evidenced by a protracted strike by steelworkers and printers in 1984 on behalf of a shorter workweek.[23] Nonetheless, constraining political and economic realities of the 1980s have compelled the labor movement to accept, however grudgingly, an unemployment rate that rose above 9.0 percent by mid-decade and mounting evidence of industrial stagnation in the face of increasing international economic competition.[24]

West Germany's trade unionists thus remain ambivalent insiders as the Federal Republic enters its fifth decade. They are sufficiently a part of the established capitalist-pluralist order to forswear antidemocratic tactics in pursuit of their prescriptive vision of economic democracy. Yet the programmatic tenets of the labor movement sustain a critical awareness among union activists of different policy priorities and alternative forms of economic governance to those that characterize the Federal Republic "at forty." In the absence of a supportive parliamentary majority, however, the DGB and its member unions must of necessity resort to their accustomed historical strategy of postponement.

NOTES

1. Interview with the author at DGB headquarters in Düsseldorf.
2. *Die Grundsatzforderungen des DGB 1949*, reprinted in Dieter Schuster, *Die deutsche Gewerkschaftsbewegung*, 5th rev. ed. (Düsseldorf: DGB-Bundesvorstand, 1976), 84–86.
3. *DGB-Grundsatzprogramm 1981* (Düsseldorf: DGB-Bundesvorstand, 1981), 1–3.
4. Ibid., 3–4, 9–10.
5. Ibid., 15–16.
6. Quoted in Schuster, *Die deutsche Gewerkschaftsbewegung*, 76.
7. J. Kurth, *Geschichte der Gewerkschaften in Deutschland*, 4th rev. ed. (Hannover: Norddeutsche Verlagsanstalt O. Godel, 1965).
8. Quoted in Schuster, *Die deutsche Gewerkschaftsbewegung*, 86.
9. Bundesminister für Arbeit und Sozialordnung, *Codetermination in the Federal Republic of Germany* (Bonn: 1978), 48.
10. Quoted in Schuster, *Die deutsche Gewerkschaftsbewegung*, 16.
11. *Codetermination in the Federal Republic of Germany*, 12–18.
12. Article 14 of the Basic Law stipulates that "Property and the right of inheritance are guaranteed."
13. *Frankfurter Allgemeine Zeitung*, 30 June 1977.
14. The consultative meetings were mandated by the 1967 Law to Promote Economic Stability and Growth. For a summary and assessment of concerted action, see Hancock, *West Germany: The Politics of Democratic Corporatism* (Chatham, N.J.: Chatham House, 1989).
15. Klaus von Beyme, *Gewerkschaften und Arbeitsbeziehungen in kapitalistischen Ländern* (Munich: R. Piper, 1977), 255.
16. Quoted in *Der Spiegel*, 11 July 1977, 22.
17. The court ruled that the employers' claims were groundless since shareholders exercised majority control on company boards. It noted that if the law in fact led to negative consequences, an appropriate remedy should be sought through legislative channels. Vetter hailed the decision as conforming "to a great degree [to] the main points in the legal

192 The Political Rules of the Game

stand of the unions." Employer spokesmen were less enthusiastic but said they would accept the Court's ruling.

18. At the cabinet's behest, the Bundestag endorsed an emergency appropriation of 430 million marks in November 1976 to stimulate employment. The expenditure had little discernible effect on the economy.

19. DGB-Bundesvorstand, *Vorschläge des DGB zur Wiederherstellung der Vollbeschäftigung* (Düsseldorf: DGB-Bundesvorstand, 1977).

20. Ibid., 6, 10.

21. The tripartite discussions were replaced by less formal bilateral discussions with leading union and employer group representatives. The bilateral talks were initiated by former SPD chancellor Helmut Schmidt and have been continued by individual members of the Kohl cabinet.

22. Conglomerates such as Mannesmann AG, a manufacturer of diverse industrial products, have sought through diversification to escape the jurisdiction of the 1951 law on parity codetermination in favor of the less stringent provisions of the 1976 bill. In 1980, former chancellor Helmut Schmidt proposed that Mannesmann and similar concerns remain subject to the 1951 regulations for a period of six years. The suggestion was criticized by both management and union officials.

23. The striking unions sought a reduction in the workweek to 35 hours in an effort to create new jobs for unemployed workers. A compromise agreement was reached on a 38.5-hour workweek.

24. For an informed critical assessment of an alleged "national epidemic of inertia" in the Federal Republic, see "Rich and Comfortable, West Germany Also is Ominously Stagnant," *Wall Street Journal,* 1 August 1988, 1, 4.

9

STRUCTURAL CHANGE IN THE RUHR VALLEY: WHAT PRICE SOCIAL PEACE?

Jutta A. Helm

Today the Ruhr Valley is generally thought of as the biggest "problem area" in West Germany's otherwise robust economy. With the highest unemployment rates, the lowest growth rates, and a declining population, the area between Wesel in the West and Hamm in the East, Hagen to the South and Haltern in the North looks like an aging industrial colossus whose products are no longer needed. But it is not easy to relegate an area encompassing a population of 5.1 million people, almost a third of North Rhine-Westphalia, to the dustbin of history. Questions about the fate of the area, once Germany's and even Europe's largest and most dynamic industrial center, have been on the West German political agenda since the late fifties. Forty years after the creation of the Federal Republic laid the foundation for a stable political order and economic prosperity, the Ruhr is in the throes of a major "structural crisis," its second since the end of the war. How did this happen? Were the people of the Ruhr betrayed, let down by managers and politicians, as steelworkers often claimed during the wave of protests that has accompanied new closures and rationalizations in their industry? Is the region finished, exhausted, a victim of a process of economic restructuring that is global in scope and hence beyond the reach of regional or national policymakers? Or is the Ruhr area a sleeping giant, poised for a comeback that will be based not on the monoculture of old—steel and coal—but on the area's tremendous resources in science and learning, the nation's most developed infrastructure, and a highly qualified work force? Clearly, the fate of the Ruhr is of more than regional importance. At least once, in 1966, a crisis in the region contributed to the downfall of a national government. That, in itself, would justify a close look at the Ruhr, its problems, and potential. In the past, national governments have always responded to the problems of the Ruhr, marshalling often considerable resources to finance a mixture of economic adaptation and political compensation to the social and economic costs of change. This is the essence of the social market consensus as it emerged after 1949: the victims of economic change could count on often generous assistance to cope with the consequences. But the magnitude of the recent crisis has stretched both the willingness and the capacity of national political actors to continue past assistance packages to ease the pain of change. This raises the question about new solutions to take their place.

This essay examines the three most difficult challenges the Ruhr has faced during the last forty years: the crisis of reconstruction in the immediate postwar years; the coal crisis, beginning in the late fifties; and finally the steel crisis, which currently engulfs the region. Each of these challenges will be examined in the light of political, social, as well as economic events which shaped the region.[1] In the limited space available, it is not possible to provide a comprehensive history of the region. But the focus on crisis periods will tell us much about the region and its connections with national political developments.

POSTWAR DEVASTATION AND RECONSTRUCTION

The end of hostilities in 1945 brought the people of the Ruhr Valley face to face with tremendous problems. Economic collapse, devastated cities, massive homelessness, and famine were the new reality. The Allied occupation forces—notably the British—were eager to revive the region's economy sufficiently to reduce its dependence on Allied assistance, as well as to initiate the delivery of German goods to her neighbors to compensate for the devastation caused by the German military onslaught. In the German economic revival, the Ruhr economy, with its concentration of coal and steel industries, which were remarkably intact considering the years of Allied aerial bombing, figured prominently. The challenge was enormous. How could coal miners, to mention just one example, do a full day's work on a ration of 1200 calories? (The peacetime ration for work of this sort had been 3200 calories.) Not surprisingly, productivity per man shift dropped to half of its 1936 level. There was a drastic shortage of qualified workers; managers and owners were often in prison or hiding, leaving their firms to be run by labor-dominated factory committees. Allied policies contributed to the difficulties and contradictions of the early postwar years. The goal of maximizing German production conflicted with the reparations policy which tore up entire production facilities, often never to be rebuilt. This conflict was finally resolved in 1949. Until 1952 the Allies discussed various forms of "restructuring" of German industry, designed to break up trusts and cartels which had featured so prominently in the prewar economy. The socialization of heavy industries was also discussed. While these issues were debated, the industrialists in the Ruhr had little interest in investing in or even maintaining their production facilities. This resulted in frequent breakdowns and low productivity. Bottlenecks in transportation delayed coal and steel products from reaching their intended customers, leading to blackouts and power failures. Mine workers struck repeatedly to demand improved rations and the socialization of heavy industries—one of their central political demands. Overall, not the future of Germany, but strategies of survival—food, shelter, and other necessities—dominated life in the Ruhr Valley during these difficult years.

In spite of all these problems, economic normalization began in late 1947, accelerated by the currency reform in 1948 and then the Korean War. Rationing, regulation, and planning were gradually eliminated. But there is more to the immediate postwar years than a desperate effort to achieve a degree of economic normalization. Three significant developments were begun in those difficult years, all of which continue to influence the Ruhr and West Germany as a whole to this day. The first of these developments—the introduction of company-level codetermination—started in the steel industry in 1947. The demand for a far-reaching democratization of the economy had been an integral part of union demands since 1945. In principle, the British occupation authorities had agreed to this. But the first steps toward its realization were taken in 1947 by the Klöckner steelworks. A group of farsighted managers offered employees equal representation with capital on the company's supervisory board. Other firms followed suit. Their motives were mixed. Some, no doubt, accepted the challenge of a new era in industrial relations involving some sort of social partnership between capital and labor. Others were persuaded that Allied reparation plans and schemes for the restructuring of the basic industries might be influenced more successfully if labor and capital closed ranks. In 1951 the initially informal arrangement received the sanction of law when the Bundestag approved the Codetermination Act for the Coal and Steel Industries, granting labor parity with capital on corporate boards. The law was only passed after considerable maneuvering on the part of Ludwig Erhard, the minister of economics, and Chancellor Adenauer, both of whom initially opposed an equal role for labor on the boards. Strike votes had already been taken, showing near-unanimous support for the concept among labor's rank and file, with a showdown only averted at the last moment. By the late fifties, parity codetermination had become one of the most successful innovations that was achieved in the Ruhr Valley. Labor-management relations lost much of the adversarial tone that characterized them elsewhere. In the words of an early admirer, Abraham Shuchman, codetermination established "a new course between capitalism and collectivism that leads to a more rational and just social order."[2] This was to become obvious during subsequent economic crises, at first in the coal and later in the steel industry. In 1952 a more diluted version of codetermination gave employees in other industries the right to be represented on corporate boards. Participation rights were extended to public sector employees in 1955 and strengthened in new legislation in 1976. For the workers of the Ruhr" basic industries, it remains a matter of considerable pride that this new and popular system of industrial relations was invented by them, in their firms. Today, workers and managers alike invoke the term "social partnership" to describe its innovative content.

A second issue that deserves mention in the postwar period was the shift in political affiliations in the Ruhr Valley. Contrary to the image of the "red Ruhr" that originated during the 1920s, the Social Democratic party did not have a well-established base in the region. Instead, the Center Party and its message of Catholic social action dominated the politics of the Ruhr. This left the Social Democratic party at a disadvantage in the postwar years, and the Christian Democratic Union dominated North Rhine-Westphalian politics until 1966. After the Bad Godesberg conference, the Social Democrats were, however, in a much stronger position to appeal to Ruhr voters. Social historians credit the link between factory-based works councils (union-dominated), trade unions, and the party with this turnaround. It was this network of employee organizations which led Ruhr voters to the SPD in growing numbers. In 1966 the Social Democrats became the largest party in state elections, paving the way for the formation of a social-liberal coalition government in Düsseldorf. And in 1969 the SPD overtook the CDU in the state for the first time in a federal election, largely on the basis of the strong SPD showing in the Ruhr Valley. The loyalty of Ruhr voters held fast even in the 1983 federal election when the SPD lost the state to the Christian Democrats again. It carried the Ruhr districts, however, and statewide its losses were below the national average.

It is probably also an indication of this loyalty that the region's party activists and leaders can generally be counted on to follow the national party's leadership and to refrain from participating in public quarrels over party positions and leaders. Some have concluded that this attests to the conservatism of the Ruhr's Social Democrats and the strength of the "Kanalarbeiter" faction in its ranks. Be that as it may, it is difficult to envisage a scenario which would dislodge the party from its strong position in the Ruhr. Today the region's political identity is closely tied to the Social Democratic Party.

A third factor to be discussed is the impact of the Korean War on the Ruhr economy. Overall, the Korean War is usually credited with the acceleration of economic growth in West Germany. This was certainly the case, and the Ruhr Valley profited from this growth wave. It was only later that experts began to ask whether the war-induced boom in the coal and steel industries did not result in a premature freezing of the Ruhr's economic structures. The boom solidified the importance of the traditional sectors and discouraged the development of a more diversified regional economy. With Allied (primarily American) pressures, the federal government was directed to alleviate bottlenecks in coal and steel production. This prompted a host of federal subsidies as well as the creation of an industry-financed investment fund, most of which was directed to the Ruhr's basic industries. A large proportion of Marshall Plan aid also flowed in that direction. All of this was contrary to the intentions of the federal government. Ludwig Erhard favored a broad-based economic recovery program in which the lighter consumer industries took the lead. But Erhard and Adenauer saw no way to maintain this approach without seriously complicating relations with the United States. There is no doubt that these policies had long-term consequences. In the words of Werner Abelshauser, "[t]he politically induced boom in the basic industries became an obstacle for an industrial reorientation of North Rhine-Westphalia during the period of reconstruction."[3]

THE ECONOMIC MIRACLE AND THE COAL CRISIS

After a difficult beginning, the Ruhr area enjoyed eight years of growing prosperity between 1950 and 1958. Unemployment levels were well below the national average and wages were rising. However, the bloom of the region's economy was short-lived. By 1958, when the earlier investments in the coal industry were beginning to yield higher levels of production, coal sales declined for the first time and miners were laid off. For the miners, this was little short of traumatic. They could not believe that after years of struggle and sacrifice a new crisis shattered their hard-won prosperity. In addition, the crisis came as a complete surprise. Only months earlier the European Community of Coal and Steel had predicted a coal shortage. The downturn in coal demand was not a cyclical phenomenon, however. The Industrial Union of Mining and Energy Workers (IGBE) discussed the possibility of a structural crisis as early as 1958, but made few converts. But we now know that the crisis was indeed structural; German coal was gradually displaced by two new competitors: cheap imported coal (including American coal) and oil which became increasingly popular for heating.

Government policies during the following years were characterized by a piecemeal approach. A sales tax for heating oil was imposed in 1959, an import tax for heating oil was raised and lowered repeatedly, voluntary restraint agreements with oil companies were negotiated, and long-term delivery contracts for imported coal were canceled, at some cost to the Federal Treasury and the oil companies. In 1963 employers and the federal government agreed to subsidize the closure of uneconomic mines. This enabled the companies to finance severance pay and pensions for laid-off miners. By early 1964, twenty-seven large and approximately one hundred small mines had been closed and forty-eight mines had been merged. When, by 31 October 1964, another thirty-one large mines and twenty small mines were registered for closure, even the federal government was jolted into shock. IGBE took the initiative and called on the federal government to assist with the formulation of a long-term plan to consolidate the mining industry. Specifically, the union suggested the formation of a commission, chaired by the minister of economics, with an equal number of industry and union representatives. Again the union's call for a concerted response to the crisis went unheeded. Two initiatives from the mining industry were also rejected. Chancellor Erhard reiterated his belief that the mining industry itself should accomplish whatever reorganization was needed. As it turned out, this was the last gasp of laissez-faire in federal policy toward the coal industry.

During the summer and fall of 1966 the situation deteriorated rapidly. The first postwar recession continued unabated. State elections in North Rhine-Westphalia briefly returned a weakened CDU to government. Coal sales dropped further and more miners were on reduced work schedules. Even so, over 90 percent of the mine workers voted to strike in the face of meager wage offers from the employers. Once again the federal government offered a stopgap measure—just before the state elections. But the crisis followed its own momentum. In November, Veba, a federally owned energy and chemical conglomerate, announced the closure of a large mine. The resulting uproar was tremendous. Churches held services to pray for the prevention of further closures; mayors, miners, and ministers marched in the streets; the mine companies appealed to the federal government to take steps to restore public order and prevent the spread of a growing panic. The dominant mood was ably expressed by Rainer Barzel, a prominent CDU politician: "When the Ruhr burns, the waters of the Rhine will not suffice to put out the fire."[4]

In this setting, the Federal Ministry of Economic Affairs finally agreed to reexamine its coal policy, nine days before the collapse of the Erhard government in late November.

Almost simultaneously with the birth of the Grand Coalition in Bonn the political complexion of the Land government in Düsseldorf changed as well; the CDU-FDP coalition broke up and was replaced by an FDP-SPD coalition. The new governments gave high priority to the solution of the coal crisis. Accordingly, a new series of proposals surfaced in 1967. The Mine and Energy Workers Union took the lead with a draft plan for a "German Ruhr Coal Association." It would consolidate the existing companies under private ownership—a significant departure from its earlier proposals. On the industry side, things were also moving in a new direction. Increasingly, the initiative had shifted from the Ruhr employers association representing the mining companies, to prominent spokesmen of the steel industry and the Federation of German Employers Associations (BDA). They were very concerned to find a solution that combined industry access to cheap energy (oil, imported coal) with the safety of domestic energy supplies. During 1967 and 1968 this group sponsored an action committee to initiate "self-help for the solution of the coal crisis," which financed seventeen additional mine closures. Soon known as the Rheinstahl Circle, the group included among its members the banker Hermann J.Abs, Fritz Berg, president of the Federation of German Industry (BDI), Ernst Schneider, president of the German Industry and Trade Association (DIHT), and Hans-Günther Sohl, director of the Thyssen steel conglomerate.

Following several bilateral meetings with union and mining company representatives, the new minister of economics, Karl Schiller, convened the first meeting of the Concerted Action Coal, or coal talks, in March. Mining company and union officials, along with officials of the state governments of North Rhine-Westphalia and Saar and economists from several research institutes, met in what was to become a characteristic feature of Schiller's leadership style. While trilateral coordination of policy itself was not new, Schiller's institutionalization of this approach was the innovation of economic policymaking in 1967. The purpose of this approach was to incorporate economically powerful groups into the framework of government policy and thereby steer them in the direction of the collective good.

What did the coal talks yield? First, the talks produced a basic consensus about the long-range goal of a reduced but economically viable coal industry in private ownership. The second result was agreement on a three-phase program and timetable to adapt and consolidate the coal sector. Numerous difficult and rather technical matters had to be resolved quickly, because Schiller threatened a legislative fiat if the negotiators could not achieve a consensus. It took a little over a year to draft a coal bill which was acceptable to all participants. The bill provided for the consolidation of all mining operations in one big conglomerate; the federal government and the state of North Rhine-Westphalia guaranteed its assets up to DM 3.3 billion. Ruhrkohle AG (RAG) was officially founded on 27 November 1968. Starting 1 January 1970, it owned and operated the fifty-two mines, all in the Ruhr Valley, which had joined the corporation. The previous owners became stockholders in RAG in proportion to the assets they contributed. Separate agreements were signed with the steel and utility industries, the major consumers of coal. As it turned out, both agreements were rather unfavorable for RAG. The steel industry, for one, was required to buy its coal from RAG, which in turn was obligated to supply coal at prices no higher than those paid by its foreign competitors. At the time, however, the twenty-year delivery contracts seemed to guarantee a certain stability to Ruhrkohle. Another provision of the agreements was the requirement that funds which were now available to the steel and utility industries (via the federal and state guarantees) be invested in the Ruhr area. Table 9.1 summarizes the long-term results of the coal crisis.

The rescue of the coal industry has all the features of a neocorporatist deal that became a central feature of policymaking under the Grand Coalition and subsequently under social-liberal coalition governments. The participants were committed to an ideology of social partnership. The steel bosses knew they could not just off-load a troubled industry, leaving the government treasury to cover the social costs. This was reflected in the acceptance of a Social Plan as part of the restructuring package. The Social Plan guaranteed rather generous benefits to every laid-off miner, giving them the reassur-

Table 9.1

Coal Mining in the Ruhr Area

	1950	1957	1969	1978	1982	1988 (target)
Mines	140	122	52	28	24	22
Employees	366,000	398,000	182,000	136,000	126,000	111,000
Production (millions of tons)	105	122	85	61	63	55

Source: Andreas Schlieper, *150 Jahre Ruhrgebiet* (Düsseldorf: Schwann, 1986), 166, and Werner Abelshauser, *Der Ruhrkohlenbergbau seit 1945* (Munich: Beck, 1984), 192ff.

ance that they would be taken care of. Housing and pension plans were secured. The plan was financed jointly by the European Community, the federal government, and Ruhrkohle. It became a classic example—now emulated in many other industries—of protecting workers from the harsh dictates of the market. In turn, the steel and utility companies were assured domestic coal supplies at competitive prices. But as stockholders in Ruhrkohle, they remained responsible for the company's liquidity. Repeatedly they joined with federal and Land governments to provide Ruhrkohle with badly needed cash infusions. Moreover, the deal forcefully reminded the parent industries of their responsibility for the region's economic future; hence the obligation to invest in the Ruhr area. Other features of the rescue deal also show neocorporatist features: the process itself revealed a pattern of voluntary and informal coordination of conflicting objectives through continuous bargaining between groups (which were highly centralized and concentrated), government officials, and parties. Surely the experience of nearly twenty years of codetermination in the Ruhr area facilitated this process.

The solution of the coal crisis restored the social peace. Among labor leaders especially, there were many expressions of satisfaction that the rescue package had succeeded in providing for an orderly shrinkage of the coal industry, that no one was forced to join the ranks of the unemployed in the process, and that this was accomplished in the wake of the Federal Republic's first recession in 1966–1967. The "Concerted Action Coal" became a model for other troubled industries; the concept of the Social Plan was copied widely and became part, in 1972, of the revised Works Constitution Act.

Again, there was the proud feeling that the people along the Rhine and Ruhr had mastered a crisis creatively.

The coal crisis was certainly the dominant issue in the Ruhr Valley during the 1960s and while other issues pale in significance, two of these issues should be discussed briefly. The first is a demographic shift, including the growing presence of foreign workers, or guest workers, as they were initially called. The second issue is the discovery of the "quality-of-life issue" in the Ruhr Valley.

Population statistics for the Ruhr area show a period of steady growth between 1950 and 1960 with over a million newcomers settling there. The population peaked in 1965 at 5.75 million and has declined ever since to the current level of 5.1 million inhabitants. Like North Rhine-Westphalia and the Federal Republic as a whole, the area has shown a negative birthrate for some years. In addition, it has experienced considerable outmigration as workers moved elsewhere (mostly south) in search of jobs and economic opportunities. Actual population decline was partially compensated by the arrival of foreign workers. This started in the 1960s after the Berlin Wall closed off the migration of East Germans who had been "voting with their feet" during the late forties and fifties. But the labor shortage persisted, and employers started to recruit foreign workers in Southern Europe. Italians and Spaniards arrived by the thousands during the sixties; later Yugoslavs and Turks became the largest groups. Their jobs in the German economy have mostly been the low-grade, unskilled jobs that German workers increasingly deserted during the boom years. Even so, every recession prompted majorities of German public opinion to demand their repatriation, charging that they "take jobs away from German workers." Since 1973 the influx of foreign workers has declined steadily (except for 1979–1980), but the number of foreign residents has increased to 4.5 million as workers have been joined by spouses and children. In the Ruhr Valley, foreign workers have also established their presence. Ruhrkohle employed 21,000 foreigners in 1983 when they represented 17 percent of its work force. Among the employees who actually work in the pits, the foreign contingent is even higher (26 percent). Over 80 percent of them come from Turkey. Like many other companies, Ruhrkohle now devotes considerable resources to the training and social integration of its foreign workers, many of whom are second-generation Ruhrkohle employees. The case of Ruhrkohle is not typical, however; the large foreign contingent in its work force is due to its image as a declining industry which has made the recruitment of German workers difficult. Overall, foreigners represent only 8 percent of the Ruhr area's work force.

In the Ruhr (as elsewhere), foreigners were not easily integrated into German society. Turks especially are often tolerated rather than accepted. Nevertheless, many of them plan to stay in Germany indefinitely. Schools and local governments are now making more of an effort to accept their responsibility for the foreign residents. Citizen initiatives, churches, and the Green Party have also worked to integrate them into neighborhoods as well as social and cultural activities. The fact that there now is a debate about how best to accomplish this—rather than to question the need for integration— must be seen as a sign of progress.

Another development with long-term implications was the discovery of quality-of-life issues in the Ruhr Valley. Perhaps it all started with Willy Brandt's statement at a campaign rally in Dortmund in 1961, where he predicted that someday the skies above the Ruhr would be blue again. Certainly the new issues emerged out of a general reorientation of West Germany's priorities after the economic miracle of the fifties and sixties had restored high levels of economic security and prosperity. During the sixties, the people in the Ruhr Valley still worked longer hours, experienced more sickness, a shorter life span, and enjoyed fewer recreational and educational resources than people in other regions of the country. Public concern over the "educational crisis" (*Bildungsnotstand*) in the sixties was particularly relevant to the Ruhr area. Up to 1965, this densely populated area with over five million inhabitants did not have a single university! This was remedied in 1965 with the founding of the University of Bochum; during the seventies four additional universities followed. Their impact was dramatic. While the region contributed a mere 6 percent of all North Rhine-Westphalian university students in 1965, its share rose to 25 percent by 1980. Secondary school attendance has also risen, leaving the area now with a well-qualified work force. Deficits in other areas were systematically reduced with the help of several development programs that were initiated by the state government. The first of these, the Development Program Ruhr of 1968, concentrated on infrastructure and social service delivery. Subsequent programs have continued these efforts. As a result, the quality of medical care has improved; environmental damage has been reduced. The urban environment has been upgraded through a combination of measures which include the development of parks, recreational facilities, land-use policies, and a regional rapid transit network. Most West Germans continue to think of the Ruhr area as unattractive, unhealthy, and congested. Public perceptions ignore the Ruhr's tremendous progress in urban planning and cultural offerings. In the eyes of most, the Ruhr continues to be shaped by economic determinants, but this is no longer true. The long crisis has given the region a political and cultural identity that was lacking before state and federal governments became increasingly active in the region. There is a consensus that these steps have improved the quality of life in the region.

THE PERMANENT CRISIS

The participants in the reorganization of the coal industry hoped for the stabilization and eventual recovery of the regional economy. This was not to be, however. Three related factors account for this: the continuing coal crisis, the emerging steel crisis, and finally, the unfavorable structure of the Ruhr economy. These will be taken up in turn.

Ruhrkohle never achieved the hoped-for stability (table 9.1). Heating oil became even more popular; with more nuclear power plants coming on line in the seventies, coal sales declined even though a long-term agreement with utilities guarantees a certain level of German coal consumption—at some cost to German taxpayers. The crisis of the steel sector also depressed coal sales. Even though the company has continued to improve productivity and trim its work force and production capacity, its losses have accumulated. Several "coal rounds" with industry and union representatives and officials from Land and federal governments were needed to put together new financial rescue packages. So far, these rescue operations have functioned in the manner of the high-level coal talks that led to the creation of Ruhrkohle in 1967–1986. Coal's continuing importance as the region's second-largest employer, as well as concerns about the preservation of a secure source of domestic energy, have persuaded policymakers to provide additional subsidies. Until now, the company has been able to keep its promise that no miner will lose his job and join the ranks of the unemployed. Reductions in the work force have been achieved through early retirement. For several years, nobody over fifty-five has worked in the pits, and the retirement age continues to drop.

The steel crisis started in 1975 after the worldwide recession induced by the first oil embargo. Declining demand for capital goods and the arrival of new producers with state-of-the-art production facilities forced drastic production cutbacks. It also intensified worldwide competition for market shares. Nations like West Germany which had been exporting up to a third of their output were hard hit. Steel production peaked in 1974 with fifty-three million tons; by 1982 it had plummeted to thirty-six million tons, even though the German industry had pursued modernization and rationalization of plant and equipment more aggressively than its European competitors. Between 1970 and 1980 German steel producers shed 90,000 jobs—about half of them in the Ruhr area—apparently without much social tension. IG Metall, the powerful metal workers' union, agreed that German steel only had a chance if it modernized to remain competitive. The corporations in turn provided generous compensation for workers who became redundant, based on the model of the coal industry. By 1980 the magnitude of the crisis grew precipitously, however, and political intervention was required.

Two developments forced the federal and state governments' hand. The European Community established production quotas for the steel industries of member states in 1980. Furthermore, a subsidy code was negotiated to regulate and curtail the growing practice of member governments providing massive operational subsidies to keep national steel firms afloat. The code only approved subsidies that were designated for restructuring and reduction of production capacity. By 1985 steel capacity was to shrink by 30 percent. German producers welcomed the subsidy code, but objected to cutbacks in production capacity. The prevailing view is that such across-the-board reductions would penalize West Germany, whose industry has for some time modernized and reduced excess capacity. Disagreements about the distribution of the cutbacks continue today. German steel companies now argued that they needed government help to keep up with their subsidized European competitors. And both state and federal governments stepped in with an array of subsidies for research and development, emission control investments, tax-favored investments, social assistance to redundant workers, and job-creation programs for former steel workers. All of this was negotiated in corporatist crisis-management deals with industry, union, and government participation. According to reports by several participants, partisanship did not enter these negotiations. Even the market-oriented ministry of economic affairs in Bonn, headed by the Free Democrat Count Lambsdorff, was broadly supportive of these adjustment measures.

Another development which forced government intervention was the regional impact of the steel crisis. With over half of all steel capacity concentrated in the Ruhr area, the continuing restructuring was bound to have a profound impact. In the city of Dortmund, home of the Hoesch corporation, unemployment rose from 7.8 percent in January 1981 to 11.5 percent in April 1982. Since 1984 it has not been below 15 percent. As was the case earlier in the Saarland, aid was necessary to prevent the collapse of the regional economy. The Land government of North Rhine-Westphalia was extremely concerned about the "knock-on" effect of reductions in steel output and employment. It was estimated that one steel job guaranteed two additional jobs in other sectors. With the disappearance of 1,000 steel jobs per month, governments could not stand by and allow the logic of the market to run its course. It is important to note, however, that government intervention did not replace market-oriented decision making by the steel companies themselves. They remained the central actors who determined how to restructure the industry, what capacities to modernize or eliminate, and where to reduce work forces. At no time did governments pressure the steel companies to maintain inefficient production sites. Quite the contrary; government aid was tied to the centralization of capital to form larger, more productive units *and* to the elimination of inefficient sites, which entailed manpower reductions. Labor went along because of its political and economic integration in the larger social order.

In spite of these adjustment efforts, the steel industry (and the

Ruhr as a whole) is not yet in a position to see the light at the end of the tunnel. Last year Thyssen, the largest steel conglomerate, closed two mills, shedding almost 6,000 workers. Krupp is closing its large crude steel mill in 1988, leaving several thousand men without work. In the long run, industry spokesmen estimate that somewhere between 20,000 and 35,000 jobs will be eliminated. Not surprisingly, steel workers have become very cynical and no longer believe that any steel worker has a secure job. When Krupp announced the closure of its mill in Duisburg, workers took the unprecedented step of blocking a few major highways and bridges for several days, thereby paralyzing traffic in the entire region. The Ruhr has not seen this type of worker militancy for some time, prompting many to ask whether the social consensus of the past was giving way to dangerous levels of confrontation and cynicism.

At this point, it is quite clear that the Ruhr's troubles are the result of an unfavorable economic structure. The coal and steel sectors still provide close to 40 percent of the region's employment and virtually tie its economy to their fortunes. This is not a new development. In the sixties, it was already obvious that the Ruhr economy was lagging behind other regions in terms of productivity and growth. One figure is particularly telling: in 1964, two-thirds of the region's labor force were employed in industries with below-average growth rates. Of all the states (excepting Saar and West Berlin), North Rhine-Westphalia achieved the lowest rates of economic growth between 1950 and 1964. Turning to the eighties, it is obvious that the economic gap between the Ruhr area and the rest of the Federal Republic has widened. The region remains particularly vulnerable to economic crises. This is shown by its unemployment levels which are now well above those of the difficult postwar years (see table 9.2).

The Land of North Rhine-Westphalia has made tremendous efforts—starting with the Development Program Ruhr in 1968—to overcome the Ruhr's vulnerability. The Westphalia Program 1975 and the Action Program Ruhr in 1979 poured large mounts of money into the region, mostly for infrastructure and public investment projects. The federal government provided further assistance through the Joint Program for the Improvement of Regional Economic Structures, a constitutionally mandated program that is administered jointly by the Land and federal governments. The original hope that

Table 9.2
Unemployment Rates (in percent)

	1949	1970	1985	1988
Ruhr area	n.a.	1.4	15.0	16.1
NRW	4.2	0.8	11.8	10.2
Fed. Republic	8.8	0.3	9.8	9.9

Source: Kommunalverband Ruhrgebiet, ed., *Arbeitsmarkt Ruhrgebiet* (Essen: Kommunal-verband Ruhrgebiet, several recent editions), and Abelshauser, *Der Ruhrkohlenbergbau*, 166.

these programs could achieve a rapid transformation of the region had to be abandoned, however. Experts now underscore that structural economic change is inherently slow. Some also point to remaining obstacles that discourage economic change, while others point to omissions and errors of the past. Remaining obstacles include the shortage of real estate that is available for new plants or businesses. The relative weakness of small business and craft shops that might become suppliers for larger firms is also mentioned. Omissions and past errors include a degree of complacency among economic and political leaders who ignored the warning signs. The coal and steel industries themselves are guilty here; as large landowners, they often vetoed the settlement of new industries which were looking for suitable tracts of industrial real estate. The fear of new industries competing for scarce labor in the sixties and early seventies often motivated this "hoarding" of industrial real estate. The most shocking example involves the Ford car company which, in the late sixties, was forced to abandon plans for a large assembly plant in Dortmund and move to Belgium instead. Political leaders have also come in for their share of criticism for their alleged failures to "sell" the Ruhr aggressively to potential investors. Such remarks are often made by federal Christian Democratic and Christian Social leaders when they evaluate the performance of the Social Democratic government in Düsseldorf. Land governments in turn charge the Bonn government with "abandoning" the Ruhr after 1982. There is some truth to these charges and countercharges. But other issues are even more crucial. Questions are now raised about the inherent limitations of corporatist crises deals that have been the prevailing "solution" for the Ruhr's problems. The political basis of corporatist solutions has also become an issue. How long can labor support such solutions? And what incentives does business have to pay the costs of social peace in view of looming uncertainties on the international economic horizon? These questions will be addressed in the conclusion.

CONCLUSION

The steel crisis, combined with the continuing coal crisis, confronts all groups in the Ruhr Valley with difficult choices. Local governments experience an escalation of social costs along with the imperative of maintaining high levels of public investment to maintain infrastructures. Trade unions want internationally competitive industries that provide job security, but they do not want their members to bear the lion's share of the costs of economic adjustment. Business is also interested in competitiveness and cutting labor costs, but it does not want to endanger the cooperative relationship between labor and management. The state government faces the dilemma of choosing between maintaining a viable steel sector or reducing the region's dependence on steel. Should it pursue structural change, preservation of existing structures, or a mixture of both strategies? The federal government is torn between its preference for market-oriented solutions of the steel crisis and the impossibility of accepting the resulting economic devastation of an entire region. All groups are navigating more or less skillfully between these difficult choices, with the result that new corporatist deals are being struck to facilitate economic adjustments and to mitigate their human costs. Gourevitch correctly points out that West Germany's responses to the worldwide economic crisis of the eighties were characterized by greater continuity than British, American, or French responses.[5] But even in Germany the new deals are not simply continuations of previous responses to regional problems. Several departures from the earlier pattern stand out. First, adjustment pay for redundant steel workers is now lower and covers shorter time spans than earlier agreements. This suggests that in the future, union leaders will find it more difficult to control rank-and-file militance. Secondly, the regional economy's well-being takes second place after the steel industry's need to reduce costs to remain competitive. A regional Ruhr conference called by the Land government in 1979 and a Dortmund Conference convened by the city in 1980 demonstrated the capacity of political institutions to generate symbolic crisis-management outputs. But they also revealed their inability to achieve a dramatic breakthrough for the regional economy. Thirdly, industry has succeeded in gaining a freer hand in the management of painful adjustment processes, with the federal government showing greater reluctance in assuming a major share of the financial compensation for the victims of economic change. It took eight months—to mention just one example—before the federal government committed itself to a share of the social plan for steel workers who were made redundant in June of 1987.

Experts have calculated that forty-five billion deutsche marks have been spent on various Ruhr aid programs since the early sixties. What has this assistance produced? It is a sign of changing times that it has become fashionable in some political circles to raise this question. Some politicians from Southern Germany have begun to portray the Ruhr as a bottomless pit for aid. While this conclusion is not justified, it illustrates the difficulties facing Ruhr politicians who now find themselves in the position of seemingly permanent petitioners. Aid to the Ruhr has prevented the region from becoming a pocket of hopelessness and destitution—a fate that several other old industrial regions in Europe have not been able to avoid. And aid has helped maintain the social peace during hard times.

The fate of the Ruhr shows that West Germany's social consensus —a central feature of the paradigm of the social market economy— has not collapsed. But adjustment programs to needy regions and groups have become more stingy and will face increasingly close scrutiny as to their cost-effectiveness. This is not all bad. The new frugality might challenge the region's ingenuity. What is needed is a *new* approach to coping with structural economic change, an approach that goes beyond mere damage control. Is it totally unrealistic to hope that the region which created parity codetermination and social plans will pioneer yet another social policy breakthrough? There could hardly be a more significant contribution to strengthening the Federal Republic's social consensus on the eve of the twenty-first century.

NOTES

1. The following comprehensive studies of the Ruhr were helpful to the author: Werner Abelshauser, *Der Ruhrkohlenbergbau seit 1945* (Munich: Beck, 1984); Dietmar Petzina, "Industrieland im Wandel (1945–1980)," in Wilhelm Kohl, ed., *Westfälische Geschichte*, vol. 3 (Düsseldorf: Schwann, 1984), 439–531; Andreas Schlieper, *150 Jahre Ruhrgebiet* (Düsseldorf: Schwann, 1986).
2. Abraham Shuchman, *Codetermination: Labor's Middle Way in Germany* (Washington, D.C.: Public Affairs Press, 1957), 244.
3. Abelshauser, *Der Ruhrkohlenbergbau*, 175.
4. Martin Martiny, "Ist das Revier konservativ? Oder ist es heimlich radikal?" in Lutz Niethammer et al., eds., *Die Menschen machen ihre Gechichte nicht aus freien Stücken, aber sie machen sie selbst* (Berlin/Bonn: Dietz, 1984), 144.
5. Peter Gourevitch, *Politics in Hard Times* (Ithaca, N.Y.: Cornell University Press, 1986), 207.

10

ADENAUER'S LEGACIES: PARTY FINANCE AND THE DECLINE OF CHANCELLOR DEMOCRACY

Arnold J. Heidenheimer

What was it that produced Adenauer's "chancellor democracy" and how did it come to decline again? As someone who has been writing on German politics since the creation of the Federal Republic, I would like to reflect again on the first half of its existence, and juxtapose my analysis to interpretations made later by colleagues who have been closer observers during recent times. I particularly want to explore the relationship between the decline of the dominant chancellor and the "chancellor effect" and the regulation and subsidization of German party finance.

I was not present at the creation of the Federal Republic in the sense that Dean Acheson was. It was John Foster Dulles who first activated my interests when I and another reporter for the *Cornell Daily Sun* interviewed him in September 1949, during his reelection campaign. Talking with Dulles in an Ithaca hotel room, I asked him why both Democrats and Republicans had been so similar in their approval of the outcome of the first Federal German elections and the installation of Adenauer's right-of-center government. His response was: "Both major parties are in fundamental agreement on supporting free enterprise abroad. Truman just doesn't think it's a good policy at home," and then repeated the charge that President Truman's domestic Fair Deal proposals would "lead to socialism in this country."

I began to wonder just what politicians as diverse as Truman, Acheson, and Dulles liked about the new German chancellor, and why they preferred him so much to the SPD. I was writing an MA thesis on Schumacher's role in the SPD, and also analyzing policies that Adenauer was pursuing as chancellor in the early 1950s. Then as a graduate student at London, I undertook research on how and why Adenauer had managed to make himself leader of the CDU in the late 1940s and to develop the alliances which made possible his emergence as chancellor and the electoral victories of 1953 and 1957.

CHANCELLOR AND PARTY LEADER

What particularly intrigued me was that Adenauer seemed to have delayed his own election to the chairmanship of the CDU until a year *after* his election as chancellor in 1949. My research seemed to show that he succeeded in vanquishing his intraparty rivals like Andreas Hermes, Jakob Kaiser and Werner Hilpert by 1948, so that a bid for the party leadership before or during the meetings in 1948–1949 of the Parliamentary Council would, in all likelihood, have been successful.[1]

We can recall that Adenauer's primary emphasis on exercising his power through the chancellory led the CDU of the 1950s to be characterized as a "Chancellor party," or even as a *Kanzlerwahlverein*. It was a party of the *government*, rather than a *government party*. In keeping his relations to the party on a rather aloof basis, Adenauer displayed some commonality with his contemporaries, Presidents Eisenhower and de Gaulle. But unlike these two ex-generals, he found ways of more directly dominating the party which he had helped to shape. Rather than merging the government and party roles in the way that British leaders like Macmillan did, he played the two roles off against each other.[2] Thus, when challenged with regard to unworthy attacks on his political opponents, he repeatedly emphasized that he had been speaking not as chancellor but only as chairman of the CDU. "By encouraging the development of a 'Chancellor effect' as a substitute for more additive methods of eliciting party identification, Adenauer was able to attract voters who wanted to vote for 'National' goals while still indifferent or hostile to parties as such." By seeing to it that foreign policy issues dominated the party conflicts of the period he created a situation in which, for the bulk of relatively inexperienced CDU deputies, "who saw their own political futures increasingly tied to the public confidence in Adenauer, there was no alternative but to stand solidly behind the Chancellor."[3]

Adenauer's Successors

The leaders who succeeded Adenauer as chancellor or chancellor candidates in the FRG's second decade during the 1960s—Ludwig Erhard and Kurt Georg Kiesinger—can be grouped as less-dominant leaders within a system whose parties were themselves becoming more equal in electoral and other strengths.

With Adenauer remaining a highly critical kibitzer and CDU party chairman, Erhard's exploration of the chancellor's powers were wary and cautious. Far from laying down consistent "policy guidelines," he sought to delegate more authority to other ministers, and there were occasions when it was publicly announced that he had allowed his cabinet colleagues to outvote him. He made scarcely any attempt to use his powers of appointment to install men who were personally loyal to him.[4]

While the "normal" sequence in a parliamentary system is that of being elected party leader, then leading the party ticket to electoral victory, and then becoming government head, Erhard's career reversed that sequence. He led the CDU to another victory in 1965, but with both President Luebke and Adenauer pushing toward a Grand Coalition strategy, Erhard's electoral victory was a Pyrrhic one. He was named to the party chairmanship in a half-hearted and belated way in 1966, amid the party and coalition infighting which within another six months trailed inexorably to the collapse of his government coalition with the FDP.

That appointment was followed so quickly by embalming exemplified the predominantly draining rather than supportive effects which Erhard's roles of government and party heads had upon each other.

Kurt Georg Kiesinger, who became chancellor of the CDU-SPD coalition government in December 1966, was less inclined to distance himself from the party, for he had used it more than his predecessors in his political rise on both Land and federal levels. Unlike Erhard, he succeeded to the party chairmanship within a half year of becoming head of government. But the bargain through which the CDU got the chancellorship while letting the SPD fill the foreign affairs and economic ministries proved a dubious one, as the Social Democrats used these very visible offices to demonstrate their fitness to govern. The CDU was more equal than dominant within the coalition and that fact affected the importance of the "chancellor effect." Kiesinger's image as chancellor tended to fluctuate according to the impact and effectiveness of the coalition. Although like Erhard he enjoyed higher personal support than his party, the way in which the chancellor's role declined to that of a "walking mediation committee" between the parties diminished its stature. This paved the way for the CDU's relegation to an opposition role after twenty years of leading federal governments, and although Kiesinger was quickly relieved of the party chairmanship, his successors in that office could not use it effectively to regain government office. For almost two decades after 1963 the CDU failed to establish a viable ladder for converting the party chairmanship into the candidacy for chancellorship, as steps leading to electoral and coalition-building success.

When I met him in Washington in 1961, Adenauer referred to what I had published about the CDU's party finances.[5] Material from that article had been used in the 1958 Federal Constitutional Court decision, which invalidated the tax deductibility of party contributions, and pointed the way toward public party finance.

Part of the change that made the SPD more acceptable as a government party was the move away from the kind of socialist programs and rhetoric which had alarmed the American politicians. The Bad Godesberg conference and the introduction of German public finance of parties in 1959 occurred within a year of each other. The impact of the change in program is well known; that emanating from party finance changes has been more difficult to discern, perhaps because it has been difficult to see the woods for all the trees. But then a striking parallel developed between the SPD's amazingly consistent march *toward* the institutions of government, and the broadening of public finance support under varying parliamentary coalitions in 1962, 1964, and 1967. I argued that the two phenomena were not only simultaneous, but were mutually reinforcing.

This was borne out particularly by the change in the SPD's position after the Federal Constitutional Court decisions of 1959 and 1966, which had undermined especially the CDU's sources of party funds. The SPD had opposed the Adenauer coalition's introduction of federal public financing in 1959–1962, but it came to embrace public financing by the mid-1960s, and to collaborate in the development of a new system of public subsidies that would satisfy the Court's criteria and meet the pressing needs of the CDU especially. In preparation for the 1967 Parties Law passed by the Grand Coalition, the SPD accepted a "fantastically generous formula, which all but made a mockery of the disclosure provision, since just about none of the contributions of even the largest corporate donors would need to be publicized. Fifteen years earlier, the SPD had attacked and accused the CDU of being 'bought' by Big Business because it received large secret donations from firms: now it was helping the CDU to collect secretly whatever such donations might still be forthcoming. Earlier it had attacked the CDU for abusing its governmental power in order to utilize public funds on behalf of its campaign: now it was collaborating with the latter to institute a system of public subsidies which the CDU needed much more than it did."[6]

SPD Party Leaders and Chancellors

Where Adenauer had molded the CDU as a chancellor party, Brandt came to power as his party's chancellor. The SPD had retained him as party chairman despite the shortcomings he displayed in the election campaigns of 1961 and 1965, common experiences which built mutual acceptance and affection that none of the CDU chancellors had developed with their colleagues. The tested decisionmaking of the SPD and FDP eased the selection of Brandt's 1969 coalition cabinet, as the SPD managed to implement the chairman to chancellor sequence.

But whereas Brandt, on the one hand, led the SPD to achieve its unique election victory of 1972—the only time its votes exceeded those of the CDU/CSU—his was probably also the tenure during which the chancellor bonus or effect lost most of its inherent potential. Even as he bathed in public support for his Ostpolitik, stalemates in ambitious domestic policy reforms and lack of firm control of his cabinet coincided to diminish the impression that he was even attempting to set the "policy guidelines." The manner in which his party's Jusos tried to force policy further to the Left, as I observed at the 1973 SPD Convention, set up tensions with the rest of the coalition which Brandt could not handle well.

Significant in the eight years of social-liberal government under Helmut Schmidt's leadership is that Schmidt was the only government head who ever came close to fully exploiting the constitutional powers of the chancellorship in the manner for which Adenauer had set the original model. But we cannot classify him as a *government and party leader*, because of course he never inherited the party chairmanship, a position which Willy Brandt continued to hold until 1987. That throwback to Weimar separation of the two offices meant that Schmidt never approached the degree of control over his party which Adenauer had achieved in the 1950s.

Like Adenauer, Schmidt was respected by the Germans both for his accomplishments at home, and for the high esteem in which he was held by secondary constituencies abroad. He had demonstrated his managerial capacity by leading his cabinet with a strong hand, without relying on the issue of formal policy guidelines, and by avoiding intracabinet disputes of the kind experienced by his predecessors. His reputation abroad came to be based especially on economic and strategic expertise. During his period in office Adenauer traveled to Washington thirteen times to consult with American leaders, while American presidents visited him in Germany only twice toward the end of his term. In Schmidt's case, foreign government heads regularly came to Bonn to seek his advice.

THE GROWTH OF PARTY EXPENDITURES

Toward the end of the Adenauer period I had calculated that the United States and West Germany were somewhat similar in their levels of campaign expenditures, with both expanding close to the equivalent of an hour's wage of an industrial worker per vote in a national election year. Later the United States was slightly ahead, with an 1960 index of 1.12, compared to one of .95 for Germany in 1961.[7] But by the 1980s the German rate of political expenditure has been calculated to be considerably higher than the American one, perhaps even three times higher by some calculations. Over these decades the established political parties' incomes rose at a rate more than 50 percent greater than did government revenues. In good part this was due to the continued increase in various forms of public party and campaign subsidies, which came to account for about a third of annual budgets of more than DM 500 million.

Comparing German public subsidies with those in Austria, Sweden, and Italy, for the decade from 1975 to 1985, Nassmacher found the German ones were unique not only because they were higher on a per capita basis, but in that their rate of increase remained considerably above the rates of both GNP growth and inflation. With 1975 data equated to a standard of 100, German cost of living had risen to 144 by 1984, while party subsidies rose to an index of 259; in Sweden the comparable 1984 index figures were 236 and 216.[8] But the increase in party expenditures was even higher, resulting in increasing indebtedness, especially for the SPD, which had to take out loans of DM 150 million in the early 1980s. Its treasurer disguised the legally required information as to the sources of large private donations, leading to the scandalous situation in which "the parties circumvented and consciously violated the laws which they had themselves created."[9] By 1983 its debt burden made it subject to "political extortion," so that it had to agree to dubious changes to the parties law and to the abortive "amnesty" proposal for violations of that law.

In the 1950s, toleration of various backdoor methods of party financing by business could be rationalized in terms of preoccupation with the larger tasks of establishing the new state's international legitimacy. While the chancellorship gained in stature during this phase, it was the Bundestag and the Federal Constitutional Court which were better positioned to increase their stature in the 1960s and 1970s. But whereas these institutions routinized their interactions as regards most jurisdictional arenas, that of the rules affecting political parties proved a decided exception. Various versions of the Parties Law and related legislation became shuttlecocks in a continuing legalistic contest that helped to structure the perception of a "parties' cartel." In time this somewhat undermined the legitimacy of the party system in the form that it evolved during these decades. But how can the party finance processes be seen as influencing the shape of the party system and the continued decline of the chancellor effect during the 1980s?

Factions and Party Finance

By the time Helmut Kohl finally led the CDU to a comeback in Bonn, many of the distinctive aberrations of German politics during the 1950s from other Western democracies, had come to be diminished or even dismantled. The German deficit with regard to subjective and objective measures of political participation and a sense of political efficacy had been eliminated, as attested both by systematic surveys and the sprouting of structures like the civic action groups. The supraparty appeal of the chancellorship, which I had in the fifties identified with the existence of something like a hidden "chancellor party," was scarcely visible or measurable. Kohl may have benefited more from sympathy at having to cope with the sharp attacks of the likes of Strauss than from any particular admiration for his acumen in political leadership. Indeed, Kohl differed from most of his predecessors as chancellor in the fact that his general political popularity tended to lag rather than to lead that of his party, and in that this has not changed significantly during his incumbency.

In this light, and in view of the more public and continuous factional struggles of the CDU/CSU over the preceding period, it seems paradoxical that in the end it was the SPD rather than the CDU which was decisively undercut by the challenge of groups who had formerly been largely among its supporters. How important a role did the operation of German party finance techniques play in facilitating this outcome?

The comparison with Japan may be employed, as Frank Langdon and I did to probe relationships between government office, party leadership, party factionalism, and the flow of financial supports. During the Adenauer period, the Japanese Liberal Democrats were supported by big business financial fund-raisers which bore many resemblances to those functioning in the Federal Republic. But prime ministers like Nobusuke Kishi (1957–1960) could not build on this support to achieve anything like the kind of power that Adenauer then had by virtue of positions as chancellor and party chairman.

The main reason was the pervasive position of organized factions in the Liberal Democratic Party, which caused the prime minister to be only one of numerous powerful faction leaders, each with their own support and patronage systems. Even strong prime ministers like Kishi could not much alter the way in which the factions participated in the party's policy-making organs and the distribution of central party funds. Had a leader like Kishi tried to radically cut off their share of financial support and influence, thus forcing the factions to transform themselves into splinter parties, these "would have remained financially viable" "by reason of the personal supports of company and association heads who would have remained loyal to their friends."[10]

Insofar as the power of factions, the role of prime ministers, and the dominant position of the Liberal Democrats has remained fairly constant, it has continued to be accepted that prime ministers as faction heads have to have sources for "feeding" their factions. In this context it was not surprising that Prime Minister Tanaka received funds directly from companies like Lockheed; unusual only were the methods he employed. The Liberal Democrats continue to rule Japan, and factions continue to rule the Liberal Democrats, mainly because the opposition parties have never mounted a credible image as a potential government.

But Germany, unlike Japan, did develop a pattern of alternating party governments, and this causes us to puzzle over why the SPD in the 1980s was more severely hurt by desertion of portions of its membership and voters, and what party finance regulation had to do with it?

Party Leaders and Organizations

As the SPD gradually drew even with the CDU/CSU in electoral capacity, it lost several of its advantages over that party in terms of mobilization potential. Its control over the party press and related enterprises became an albatross, while its member/voter advantage over the CDU eroded as the latter concentrated under Kohl in the 1970s on building up the party organization at the local level.

The overall effect appears to have been that the SPD, which had both the aura of possessing the more powerful party organization and was able to manipulate the levers of power in the federal government, came in the course of the 1970s into greater financial difficulties than the CDU did. Not only did it become more dependent on the public subsidies, partly to liquidate its declining media empire,[11] but it evidently became partially dependent on the illegal means of backdoor financing (*Umwegfinanzierung*), which had originally been pioneered by the CDU.

The growing significance of public subsidies probably weakened the SPD in several ways. Given the equality-based jurisprudence of the Court, it made it possible for the Greens who have comparatively low party membership and contributions to become the first new party to use subsidies to gain entry into the Bundestag. Then too it led to intraparty discrepancies, under which the federal party organization became primarily dependent on public subsidies, while the local and Land organizations continued to finance themselves mainly from membership dues. This imbalance of resource controls may have accelerated its loss of local centers of power, as party factionalism led to loss of SPD control of many big cities. Thus it undermined its inherited capacity to handle intraparty struggles better than the CDU/CSU.

Factional rivalry within the CDU/CSU was also affected by differentials in financial resources. Donors could see to it that the more conservative party groupings benefited more from their largesse. It was no accident that whereas the federal CDU often ended the year with a deficit, the Bavarian CSU hardly ever did. This seems due to the way in which some German firms and banks chose to channel donations through their Munich branches, thus strengthening Franz Josef Strauss. Insofar as this encouraged Strauss to overreach himself by imposing his chancellorship candidature in 1980, it prolonged Schmidt's tenure in office. But with that exception, the CDU/CSU managed gradually to contain the damage of its factional struggles, partly due to the fact that the CSU was dissuaded from contesting elections outside of Bavaria.

Parties in power are generally subject to a certain amount of decay. But in the case of the SPD it appears that this process was permitted to go further than it might have due to the division of powers between Schmidt and Brandt. Renate Mayntz has questioned the assumption in my 1961 article, that in parliamentary systems operating with something approaching two-party or two-party bloc systems it was problematic to separate the roles of head government and head of party.[12] Writing in 1979, she cited the Brandt-Schmidt case as illustrating a beneficial instance of the separation of these two offices, at a time when Schmidt was near the zenith of his power and his relations with Brandt were relatively stable.

Shortly afterward there began to develop a more overt and eventually fatal hostility between the Schmidt and Brandt "camps." Brandt's tolerance or indirect support for SPD politicians who joined forces with the peace movement and the Greens was defended against the chancellor camp with the argument that the SPD should not become a *Kanzlerverein* as the CDU had been in the 1950s. That Chancellor Schmidt in 1980 had at his disposal a separate election fund raised from business may have fed tension. Schmidt asserted that chairman Brandt had become a representative of the party functionaries, and his friends circulated policy theses critical of the Brandt position. The party infighting led to a significant net loss of party membership, and considerable losses in popularity for both leaders as well as the party.[13] As the Greens flourished in the 1980s by drawing the bulk of their voters away from the SPD, the SPD also became the heaviest loser in party identification, especially compared to the CDU. Taken together these developments cast a rather morosely ironic light on Mayntz's suggestion that the separation of offices "shields the Chancellor from the direct impact of his party's opinion and opens up new possibilities for conflict management."[14]

THE CHANCELLOR DECLINE IN LIGHT OF THE FLICK AFFAIR

For Peter J. Katzenstein, the replacement of chancellor democracy by a system under which the chancellor "manages" rather than "sets" the guidelines of policy is a manifestation of what he preceives as a "decentralized state" dealing with a "centralized society." The ability of post-Adenauer chancellors to unify the decentralized political system is labeled as "small."

The German "chancellor effect" in a sense had to diminish, since no successor could have accumulated the combination of unique powers that Adenauer had drawn on. Not only did he supervise the recreation of the federal bureaucracy, and win majority electoral support, but in the 1950s the CDU everywhere won larger vote shares in the federal elections than it had in the preceding Land election. How the diminished power bases were reflected in changing the chancellor's powers to "determine" the guide-lines of policy, into one where he merely "manages" them, might need to be analyzed more by comparing the various post-Adenauer chancellors. If chancellors lost power it may have been because they underperformed in their attempts to impose policies on their parties, as in Erhard's case, or because they overperformed in this role, as is arguable in the case of Schmidt.

Katzenstein characterizes organized business, with an associational staff of over 50,000 and endowed with a "pervasive legitimizing myth," as enjoying a "prominent place in West Germany's political life." Regarding the funneling of business financial support to parties, he stresses that the West Germans were "dismayed" at how the "largest political corruption scandal in the Federal Republic's history" revealed how far business "had penetrated German political parties."[15]

Had these funds been distributed through the centralized conveyer organizations operated by the business associations, that might have supported the posited "centralized society" schema. But the reason why the Flick investigation constituted a scandal was that funds were given personally and in cash by Flick's representative, von Brauchitsch, to CDU leaders like Helmut Kohl. Among the quid pro quos for which donations were exchanged was Rainer Barzel's resignation as CDU parliamentary party chairman, which paved the way for Kohl's becoming chairman of the party organization in 1973, a full nine years before he finally became chancellor in 1982.

The key role played by funds from one company might not have aroused much surprise in Japan, where party leaders are perceived as having to "feed" their party factions, just like all the other factional leaders. But in the German setting the Flick transfusions might cast some doubt on the formulation of Katzenstein's central thesis. If society and business were so centralized, why did the money come from one firm rather than from a centralized business association? If politics is so decentralized, why were the funds received in cash not by some subordinate or Land party official, but rather by the top parliamentary leaders of the CDU?

It seems evident that the diminution of the chancellory's powers were reflected in the increase of the powers of the other governmental institutions—not only the parliaments, but also the courts. Since Germany introduced state subsidies to political parties, the great majority of other Western systems have followed suit, to some degree or other. But in no other country has the regulation and subsidization of political parties been the subject of such continuing and conflicting altercations as it has in Germany over the past three decades. Major participants in these altercations have been the institutions which have won influence at the expense of the chancellory —the parties and bureaucracies, the legislature and the Federal Constitutional Court.

Ever since Adenauer brought the Chancellor's powers to a peak in the late 1950s, provisions of the party and party finance laws have been knocked back and forth like shuttlecocks between Bonn and Karlsruhe. Consequently much of the parties legislation has been judge-made law, which in turn may have affected the nominations by the Bundestag parties of judges to the Federal Constitutional Court. That chancellors have not had good opportunities to participate in this game has contributed to eroding their "sovereignty" of the system. For the legalistic web generated by the ceaseless rule-amending process may have woven silken threads which have enervated chancellors' aloof standing. This was made apparent when the fourth, fifth, and sixth chancellors had to answer for their actions to the Flick investigating committee.

Financing, Party System, and Chancellor Powers

In comparing the German political configurations of the 1950s and sixties with those of the 1980s, one can identify two deeply imbedded systemic trends. One is that the incumbent chancellors lost potential for enhancing their parties' electoral fortunes through the "Chancellor effect." Schmidt was hurt by this indirectly, Kohl more directly, thus contributing to the CDU/CSU's 1987 vote share becoming its lowest in thirty-four years. In contrast to this discontinuity, we are witnessing that the continuity in the expansion of public financing of political parties had led the Federal Republic to outmatch most comparable countries in the level of direct subsidies to political parties. But it probably also set new *indirect* public support records through the extent and complexity of additional tax expenditures, as manifested in the tax deductibility of party contributions as well as compensations therefore. Features of the newest party finance legislation, such as the "opportunity equalization" provision, should enhance especially the resources of parties like the Greens, who may have become the biggest beneficiaries of public finance development.

In the process, the party system has been transformed from a two-and-a-half-party system, which makes strong chancellors in the Adenauer mold possible, to a four-party system, which makes their recurrence much less probable. Do party finance developments hinder or reinforce these trends? Surely they now tend to reinforce them, probably by helping to guarantee the viability of the third and fourth parties through either or both means of support from tax revenues. The diminished likelihood of any chancellor being able to make "lonely" or even "tête-à-tête" decisions is reinforced by a comet's trail of secondary byproducts. For the viability of the third and fourth parties is likely to continue to enhance the maintenance of more or less organized camps and factions within the two major parties. Recurrent emissions from this combustible mixture, especially when refracted against the mirror (i.e., *Spiegel*) of public opinion, are likely to lead to recurrent return visits to seek adjudication from the Federal Constitutional Court.

NOTES

1. Arnold Heidenheimer, *Adenauer and the CDU: The Rise of the Leader and the Integration of the Party*. The Hague: Nijhoff, 1960).
2. Arnold J. Heidenheimer, "Der Starke Regierungschef und das Parteiensystem," *Politische Vierteljahresschrift* 2 (September 1961): 242–62.
3. Arnold J. Heidenheimer, "Party Discipline and Foreign Policy in the CDU," *Parliamentary Affairs* 13, no. 1 (Winter 1959): 70–84.
4. Arnold J. Heidenheimer, "Succession and Party Politics in West Germany," *Journal of International Affairs* 18, no. 1 (1964): 32–42.
5. Arnold J. Heidenheimer, "German Party Finance: The CDU," *American Political Science Review* 51, no. 2 (June 1957): 369–85.
6. Arnold J. Heidenheimer and Frank C. Langdon, *Business Associations and the Financing of Political Parties: A Comparative Study of Germany, Norway and Japan* (The Hague: Nijhoff, 1968), 88.
7. Arnold J. Heidenheimer, "Comparative Political Finance: A Note on Practices and Toward a Theory," *Journal of Politics* 25, no. 3 (August 1963): 790–811.
8. Karl-Heinz Nassmacher, "Öffentliche Parteienfinanzierung in Westeuropa," *Politische Vierteljahresschrift* 28 (March 1987): 1, 101–25.
9. Peter Loesche, *Wovon Leben die Parteien? Über das Geld in der Politik* (Frankfurt: Fischer, 1984).
10. Heidenheimer and Langdon, *Business Associations*, 227.
11. Göttrik Wewer, *Sozialdemokratische Wirtschaftsbetriebe.* (Opladen: Westdeutscher Verlag, 1987).
12. Renate Mayntz, "Executive Leadership in Germany: Dispersion of Power or Kanzlerdemokratie?" in Richard Rose and Ezra Suleiman, eds., *Presidents and Prime Ministers* (Washington, D.C.: American Enterprise Institute, 1980), 139–70.
13. Wolfgang Jaeger and Werner Link, *Republik im Wandel 1974–82, Geschichte der Bundesrepublik Deutschland*, vol. 5 (Stuttgart: Europäische Verlagsanstalt, 1987), 2.
14. Mayntz, "Executive Leadership in Germany," 149.
15. Peter J. Katzenstein, *Policy and Politics in West Germany* (Philadelphia: Temple University Press, 1987).

11

THE FINANCING OF GERMAN POLITICAL PARTIES

Arthur B. Gunlicks

The private financing of political parties in all democracies has often been associated with influence-peddling and various forms of corruption. At least a perception of impropriety arises when large donations to parties and candidates from individuals, groups, and business interests are made known to the general public, whether by enterprising newspaper reporters, by angry or envious opponents, or by periodic reports required by law. Many Germans in particular remember that during the waning days of the Weimar Republic, the Nazis received secret financial support from business interests frightened of the Left and blind to the dangers from the Right. Article 21 of the Basic Law of the new Federal Republic reflects the determination of German democrats to prevent a recurrence of the past, by calling for public reports by the parties on the sources of their income. While the Bundestag did not pass a law in conformity with the above provision until 1967, efforts to provide some alternative to or at least to supplement traditional methods of campaign financing had been undertaken from the early 1950s. Indeed, the argument will be made in this chapter that one of the many achievements of the Federal Republic since 1949—in spite of some serious setbacks—is the lead it has assumed among Western democracies in innovative approaches to campaign and party finance.

In the United States, campaign finance reforms introduced in 1972 required candidates in national elections to reveal the names of all but their smallest contributors and generally eliminated large contributions by individual donors; however, great controversy continues to surround the donations made by various interest groups to individual candidates, even though these are limited to $5,000 per candidate. American elections are candidate-oriented, and the receipt of relatively modest yet important contributions from hundreds of interest groups or political action committees raises questions about the independence that elected officials retain in their political decisionmaking.

In Germany, donations are not given to individual candidates but rather to the parties that run the campaigns. The role of political parties in campaign financing is one of the reasons for the designation of the Federal Republic as a "party state." With the focus in financing on the party, rather than the candidate, the American problem of preserving the independence of the individual elected official vis-à-vis various interests is less severe in the Federal Republic. On the other hand, German parties have become increasingly dependent on the state for public financing, in spite of their eager solicitation in the 1970s of private donations outside the law. This has raised difficult legal, political and philosophical questions concerning the proper relationship between political parties and the state in West Germany.

PARTY FINANCING FROM 1949 TO THE 1967 PARTY LAW

Some Background

The 1949 West German Constitution, or Basic Law, was the first to give explicit recognition to political parties in its Article 21.[1] To foreigners, the best-known provisions of this article are probably those in Section 2 that forbid antidemocratic parties. Under these provisions a neo-Nazi party, the Socialist Reich Party, was ruled unconstitutional in 1952, and the old Communist Party of Germany (KPD) met a similar fate in 1956 (however, since 1968 a "new" German Communist Party [DKP] has operated freely and openly in the West German political system). The controversy over the exclusion of political extremists from the public service also involves this section of Article 21. Of equal or even greater importance, however, are the provisions of Section 1 of Article 21 that recognize political parties, require a democratic internal order, and require a public accounting of their sources of income. Article 21, Section 3, calls for the regulation of the details of these provisions by federal law.

From 1949 to 1967, however, no federal legislation was passed that met the provisions of Section 2 calling for the detailed regulation of the internal order and sources of financial support of the parties. Some first steps toward a party law were taken by the Federal Ministry of the Interior in the early 1950s, but there was little response from the cabinet or Parliament. In 1955 a commission of professors was appointed by the Ministry of the Interior to study the issues involved in a future party law, but its report in 1957 failed to move the government or Parliament to act. Efforts in the late 1950s and early 1960s to write draft legislation were more successful, but they suffered irreparably from parliamentary adjournments and party conflict.[2]

While efforts to pass a party law were unsuccessful, provisions were made in the tax laws permitting generous tax deductions for the promotion of political groups and activities. According to an income tax provision passed by the Christian Democratic parties (CDU/CSU) over the opposition of the Social Democrats (SPD) and implemented in 1955, up to 10 percent of income or 0.2 percent of total sales, wages, and salaries could be deducted for contributions to political parties represented in the Bundestag or in a Land parliament. In 1957 the Federal Constitutional Court overturned the requirement that parties must have at least one representative in the national or a Land parliament to qualify, and in 1958 it ruled that tax deductions for political parties, even if granted to the contributors of all parties, whether represented in the Parliament or not, are unconstitutional violations of the principle of equality of opportunity or equality of treatment (*Chancengleichheit*).[3] The Court argued that some parties, for example, pro-business middle-class parties and their higher income supporters, would benefit more from such tax provisions than would working-class parties and their lower income voters.[4] *Chancengleichheit* has remained a major principle in the Court's rulings on parties and campaign financing to this day.

The Court's ruling in 1958 did not suggest that all public support —direct or indirect—for the parties was unconstitutional, and in 1959 the Bundestag passed a law which authorized the payment of public funds from the Federal Treasury to the political parties represented in the Bundestag for the purpose of "political education." In 1959, the total payment to the CDU/CSU, FDP (Free Democrats), and SPD amounted to DM 5 million. In 1962 it was raised to DM 20 million, and in 1964 to DM 1 for each voter, or DM 38 million divided among the parties in proportion to the number of seats occupied in the Bundestag. *Land* and local governments soon followed in giving qualifying parties financial support.

In 1965 several small parties, as well as one SPD-controlled Land (Hesse), challenged the 1959 law before the Federal Constitutional Court on the grounds that the subsidies violated the principle of equal opportunity. In 1966 the Court ruled that funds from the Federal Treasury could not be used for subsidies to political parties for purposes other than waging election campaigns.[5]

The 1967 Party Law

The rulings of the Federal Constitutional Court, which created a kind of judge-made law, and increasing public pressure for a party law as called for by Article 21, finally led to the passage of a comprehensive party law in 1967. There are seven sections of this law, the first of which recognizes the parties as a "constitutionally necessary part of the free democratic basic order" and defines them in such a manner as to exclude "voter groups" that limit their activities to the local level. Section 2 regulates in detail the internal organization of the parties, and Section 3 requires a secret ballot for nominating candidates. Sections 4 and 5 are concerned with party finance and will be discussed below. Section 6 deals with parties declared to be unconstitutional, and Section 7 contains a number of concluding provisions.

Section 4 began with a provision that gave the parties DM 2.50 for each voter in national elections in compensation for the "necessary costs of an appropriate election campaign." Parties with 2.5 percent of the vote in a Land or, under certain circumstances, 10 percent of the vote in a district, were to be eligible for compensation. Payments were to be made over a four-year period, with no more than 10 percent of the reimbursement to be paid in the second year following the election, 15 percent the third year, and 35 percent during the election year.[6]

Section 5 met the constitutional requirement for an accounting of sources of party income. This requirement was designed to promote legislation that would discourage the parties from accepting financial support from sources desiring to influence party policies in an antidemocratic direction. But viewed in the context of Article 21 as a whole, it can be understood in the sense of contributing toward securing more equality of opportunity among the parties. The voter's decision should not be affected by the ability of one party to participate in an election campaign with the benefit of significant financial support from sources unknown to the general public.

Therefore, each party was required to submit to the president of the Bundestag by September 30 a report approved by a professional accountant listing the totals of all receipts during the previous year. Each report was to list income from membership dues; regular special contributions, that is, *Fraktionsbeiträge* (practically another form of dues) from elected members of Parliament; income from capital, printed material, and assemblies; donations; loans; public funds for reimbursement of election campaign costs; and "other." Donations exceeding DM 20,000 for individuals or DM 200,000 for corporations were to be listed separately with the names of the contributors. Section 7 contained a provision which changed the income tax law to include deductions for individuals contributing to a party up to 600 DM and for couples contributing up to DM 1,200. Corporations could also deduct up to DM 600.[7]

Several changes in the above law were made in 1969 in response to a 1968 ruling of the Federal Constitutional Court. The Court let stand most of the 1967 law, including the provisions for tax deductions for individuals and couples; however, it said that corporations as well as individuals would have to be listed in the annual party reports for donations of DM 20,000 or more. It ruled that the requirement that a party receive 2.5 percent of the total vote in a Land in order to qualify for reimbursement of campaign expenditures was too high, and it suggested 0.5 percent, which was followed by the Bundestag.[8] In 1974 the party law was revised again to raise the reimbursement per voter by DM 1 to 3.50.[9] In 1979 the same reimbursement was authorized for the European Parliament elections, and in 1980 the tax deductions for individuals and couples were raised to DM 1800/3600.

THE PARTY COMMISSION RECOMMENDATIONS OF 1983

In January 1982, at the height of a party financing scandal to be discussed below, the leaders of the Bundestag parties asked the president of the Bundestag to create a commission to study party finance in Germany and to make recommendations for reforms that would provide the parties with sufficient funding but also avoid the problems associated with a number of questionable and even illegal practices. In March 1982 a commission was formed consisting of five members prominent in political science, law, and public administration. The commission had a professional staff and met thirty-four times before submitting its very thorough report and recommendations in April 1983.[10]

We do not have the space in this chapter to review in any detail the twenty recommendations made by the commission, but we can describe briefly some of the major proposals. One was to require that the parties report their expenditures as well as the sources of their income. Another was to eliminate the "special contributions" virtually deducted from the salaries of elected officials. On the other hand, in order to encourage more and larger donations, it was suggested that parties should be made "charitable" organizations for tax purposes. The commission recommended that up to 5 percent of personal income should be tax deductible for party dues and donations. So that these would not result in a violation of the principle of equality of opportunity (*Chancengleichheit*), a process by which equality could still be achieved was proposed. Still another proposal was made to raise the reimbursement per voter for campaign expenditures from DM 3.50 to 5.00; however, it was recommended that the procedure for compensating the parties be changed in some rather complicated ways, including applying a formula that would consider the number of districts in which the parties had candidates and the number of enrolled party members. It was also suggested that reimbursement be based in part on a "citizen bonus" that would allow voters to direct a certain sum from the state to the party of their choice while casting a ballot in a federal or European election. Finally, one proposal urged the creation of a special fund in the office of the president of the Bundestag so that citizens could contribute money without having to reveal to the tax authorities which parties they were supporting. The latter three ideas were not incorporated in the legislative reforms that followed.

Between the time the expert commission was created in March 1982 and its report in April 1983, the SPD-FDP coalition government had fallen apart, a CDU/CSU-FDP coalition government had replaced it (August–September 1982), and new elections had been held (March 1983) that confirmed the change in government that had taken place previously as the result of a constructive vote of confidence. The new Bundestag included for the first time a Green delegation that had made party finance a major issue in the March elections. Past pressures, the Flick scandal (see below), declining donations from nonparty sources, the political uncertainties arising from the success of the supercritical Greens, and continuing financial need encouraged the major parties in the Bundestag to act quickly in passing a revised party law that would take account of the expert commission's recommendations and clear the air.

THE NEW PARTY FINANCE LAWS OF DECEMBER 1983 AND THE FEDERAL CONSTITUTIONAL COURT'S DECISION OF JULY 1986

A few months after the publication of the expert commission's report in April 1983, hearings were held in the Bundestag. In spite of reservations—which were shared by outside critics—about the constitutionality of a number of the commission's recommendations, a compromise was reached among the coalition parties in the fall of 1983 concerning the revisions of the tax laws and the party law.[11] The result of this compromise was a series of proposals that changed considerably the existing party finance legislation. The old party law was revised in several places, and one entirely new section was added; important changes were made also in the income tax and corporation tax laws. Many of the recommendations suggested by the expert commission were incorporated, but several key recommendations were ignored. The legislative reform package was passed on 22 December 1983 and went into effect on 1 January 1984. Key provisions of the new reforms were immediately challenged by many groups—including the Greens, and individuals (among them many constitutional law scholars)—on the grounds that the changes were either bad policy, unconstitutional, or both.

Important changes were made in the party law and in the tax laws, and, to the surprise of many, most of them stood the test before the Federal Constitutional Court in 1986. For our purposes the major changes in the party law were as follows:

1. The reimbursement per voter was increased to DM 5.00 for future elections, and it was raised retroactively to DM 4.50 for the 1983 election.
2. The parties must now report not only their income but also their expenditures and assets. Some of the income categories have been changed: special contributions from the salaries of legislators have been made illegal and eliminated as a reporting category and loans are now included in the "other income" category; income from assets and from assemblies, from the sale of printed matter and other activities have been separated into two categories where they were combined before; transfer payments from lower party organs to the national parties are to be listed separately; and income from the new equalization measures (*Chancenausgleich*) is a separate category. Since expenditures were not listed before, all seven items are new: personnel costs, routine organizational costs, expenditures for internal party committee work and information, expenditures for public information and elections, transfers to lower party organs, interest payments, and "other expenses." A rather detailed listing of assets is also required.
3. A completely revised section of the law deals with donations. Parties are explicitly authorized to accept donations, but there is a list of exclusions. These include donations from the party foundations, from exclusively charitable and religious organizations, from foreigners exceeding DM 1,000, from professional associations acting as channels for others, from anonymous contributors who give more than DM 1,000, and from any source that indicates expectations of political or economic favoritism. As before,

contributions from individuals of DM 20,000 or DM 200,000 from corporations are to be listed separately by name and address.

4. A new section of the party law provides for "opportunity equalization" (*Chancenausgleich*), in which all parties that receive 0.5 percent of the vote in the previous national election participate. All donations and party dues received by the parties for the year are multiplied by 40 percent, the result of which is assumed to be the value of the tax expenditure (the loss of tax revenue due to tax deductible expenditures) of the federal government. This sum is then divided by the number of votes received in the last national election. The party that has the highest index score becomes the standard against which the others are measured, and the "deficit" parties then receive equalization funds, thus following the constitutional principle of equality of opportunity among the parties.

5. The sum of the public election campaign reimbursement for any one year is not to exceed the total income from other sources. Reimbursements above this level for any year are to be deducted from the next year's payments.

6. A party that receives donations illegally or funds not expended in conformity with the law or not listed in the annual party report of DM 20,000 or more must forfeit double the amount from its campaign reimbursement claim and transfer the funds obtained illegally to the president of the Bundestag.[12]

In addition to the significant changes in the party law outlined above, the income tax and corporation tax laws were changed to encourage contributions to the parties by designating them as "charitable" for tax purposes. This had the effect of making contributions up to 5 percent of an individual's income and up to 2 percent of the total sum of wages, salaries, and sales of a business tax deductible. These provisions were subjected to especially severe criticism because of their apparent violation of the constitutional principle of equality of opportunity. Others argued, however, that this was the only way to block the temptation to engage in *Umwegfinanzierung*, or going around the law. (In other words, the critics said, what had been illegal through indirect means was now to become legal through direct giving.) It was also suggested that the opportunity equalization (*Chancenausgleich*) provisions of the party law would compensate for the inequalities that would result from such generous tax deductions for party donations. It is interesting to note, however, that the coalition's own ministers of justice and interior refused to accept any responsibility for the bill's constitutionality.

Many critics were therefore surprised when the Federal Constitutional Court finally announced its decision on 14 July 1986, regarding the party finance laws of December 1983.[13] The Court upheld almost all of the new provisions, and where it did rule against the laws as predicted, its judgment was far more generous than almost anyone had expected.

The most controversial provisions of the legislation of December 1983 were those contained in the income tax and corporation tax laws that designated the parties "charitable institutions" for tax purposes, therefore allowing deductions of up to 5 percent of income or 0.2 percent of total wages, salaries, and sales for contributions to parties. The example frequently cited by critics in newspaper and other commentaries about the law was that of a wealthy individual who has an income of DM 20 million, gives 1 million to a party, and receives DM 560,000 (56 percent) back in a tax deduction (it is interesting to note, however, that very few large contributions were in fact made after 1983 according to the published detailed financial reports of the parties).

The Court agreed that these provisions were in violation of the constitutional principle of equality of opportunity, but then it said that a maximum deduction of DM 100,000 would be permissible. This is considered highly excessive by critics, but it does reduce significantly the potential amount that could be deducted under the original formula, and it is difficult to see how DM 100,000 could influence a *party* in contrast to an individual politician as in the United States.

INDIRECT PUBLIC FINANCING OF THE PARTIES

In addition to the exceptionally generous public reimbursement of their election campaign expenditures at the European (as of 1979), national, and *Land* levels, the German parties enjoyed after 1967 the unique advantage of public financing for party-related foundations. These were created in part in response to the Federal Constitutional Court's decision in 1966 that parties could not be subsidized for purposes of "political education." Since the late 1960s the foundations have taken on wide-ranging responsibilities for political education, research (including polling), and other activities indirectly related to party concerns, including numerous projects in foreign countries. These foundations were and are still not part of the individual party organizations, and they do enjoy considerable autonomy—both legal and practical—from the parties; nevertheless, their activities have been an indisputable aid to the parties. In the mid-1980s the Friedrich Ebert Foundation (SPD) had a staff of 670, 100 of whom were in foreign countries. The Konrad Adenauer Foundation (CDU) employed 340 persons in Germany and 1,500 abroad. The Friedrich Naumann Foundation (FDP) had 139 and 56 employees in Germany and abroad, respectively, and the Hanns Seidel Foundation (CSU) had a staff of 557. In 1984 the Ebert Foundation had a budget of DM 136 million, the Adenauer Foundation 126 million, the Naumann Foundation 64.5 million, and the Seidel Foundation DM 45 million. More than 90 percent of these funds came from public sources.[14] Of the DM 83.3 million received by the four foundations from the Federal Treasury in 1983, the Ebert Foundation received 37 percent, the Adenauer Foundation 33 percent, and the Naumann and Seidel Foundations 15 percent each.[15]

The Greens had also challenged the law that provides funding for the party foundations for their "political education" activities, on the grounds that such funding was in effect party financing through the back door. The Federal Constitutional Court said in its 1986 decision that in spite of occasional abuses, the electioneering of the parties and the political education of the foundations could be separated and justified. The Greens have indicated that they now intend to establish a foundation of their own, but disagreements within the party over a variety of questions concerning a foundation have prevented a decision thus far.

Another indirect subsidy that is not a part of the public reimbursements for election campaigns is the payment received by all parliamentary parties or party groups (*Fraktionen*, which are equivalent, in the United States to party caucuses in the legislatures) at all levels of government. This money is used for secretarial assistance, office equipment and supplies, limited staff assistance, and so forth. Since the parliamentary parties are organs of the Parliaments, these *Fraktion* payments are not considered to be *party* subsidies, and they are not listed as income in the annual party finance reports; as a result, the extent of public payments to the *Fraktionen* is not well known. Yet in 1987 the Bundestag parties received more than DM 60 million from the Federal Treasury![16]

It has long been the practice in Germany, as in many other European countries, for legislators to give varying amounts of their public salaries to their parties (which is an indirect public subsidy) in addition to any party dues they may pay. For all of the parties, but for the SPD in particular, these payments were an important source of income. However, they have been made illegal in the 1983 reform legislation.

As noted above in the discussion of the tax provisions concerning deductions for party donations, the German federal government incurs considerable tax expenditures from deductions for party contributions for individuals, couples, and, of course, legal persons such as corporations. These tax expenditures will increase now that the reforms of 1983 have made parties "charitable" organizations for tax purposes.

German parties—like most of their European counterparts—also receive free radio and television time (for European, national, and Land, but not local elections), which is divided among the parties based on past election performance with minimum time allotments for new or previously unsuccessful parties. Additional time may not be purchased. Free poster board space for all elections is provided by local governments in key locations, for example, in front of railway stations and in town and city squares.

Taken as a whole, then, the various forms of direct and indirect public party financing in Germany both before and especially after 1967 serve as a model that contrasts sharply with American practices, even when the reforms passed by Congress since 1972 are taken into consideration. The tax reforms passed by Congress in 1986 eliminated the very modest tax credit or deduction for political donations, which makes the contrast even more striking. The German parties received *billions* of deutsche marks during the 1970s in direct and indirect subsidies, so that there is no question that public financing has become a major characteristic of the German party system.

Why, then, has there been so much critical discussion of party financing in Germany? How, with so much direct and indirect public financing, could there be so many allegations of corruption and scandal? What is the "Flick affair," for example, and how typical was it?

THE NEGATIVE SIDE OF GERMAN PARTY FINANCE

Umwegfinanzierung

In spite of the various forms of public support and the tripling of total party income from 1968 to 1981, the German parties seemed always to be short of funds. This was not due just to profligate spending, as claimed by some critics. Inflation, strong pressures for improved services and increased staff, skyrocketing personnel costs, and other factors led to dramatic increases in expenditures.

The parties, not unlike a public bureaucracy that demands ever more personnel and funds for its delivery of public services, were under great pressure in the 1970s to find additional sources of income. Of the three major sources available to them—own sources, for example, membership dues; public funds for the reimbursement of elections; and external donations—only the last is flexible and adjustable. The election reimbursements are set by law, and membership figures usually fluctuate only slightly from year to year, so that the parties are left with soliciting more donations or taking out loans (*Kredite*). Since businessmen are interested in ways to reduce their taxes, the parties turned to them for donations that they, in turn, could claim as tax deductions.[17]

The problem, of course, was that the 1967 party law, as revised in 1969 by order of the Federal Constitutional Court, provided for deductions on donations of no more than DM 600 for individuals, including legal persons. And large contributors of DM 20,000 and more had to be listed in the annual party financial reports. The parties were interested in donations of much more than DM 600, and the businessmen and corporations were not interested in being named in the reports. The solution was to "go around" the law, or, as the Germans call it, to engage in *Umwegfinanzierung*.

Given the mutual interests involved, instruments were soon devised by which both sides could be satisfied. In order to encourage donations that could be deducted from taxes, a number of paths could be taken. These included using as fronts for party donations certain charitable organizations that benefited from tax deductions, "laundering" money in foreign accounts, setting up consulting firms that would issue bogus reports to companies in return for payments used for party purposes, and publishing advertisements in party publications at highly inflated prices.[18]

In spite of the efforts by the parties to keep the various illegal or semilegal financing practices from public exposure, a considerable amount of suspicion as well as hard information existed by the late 1970s concerning illegal financing practices. In 1977 and 1978 charges were brought against 105 firms suspected of tax fraud in connection with donations to the CDU. Party contributions plummeted for all parties, with donations for the CDU dropping from about DM 12 million in 1977 to about DM 12,000 in 1978. By the end of that year the CDU faced bankruptcy, and it was forced to take out loans for DM 24 million, thus raising new questions about dependency on the banks. The SPD was in even greater financial difficulty and owed its creditors DM 51 million by 1980.[19]

In 1979 the party law was changed to reimburse the parties DM 3.50 per voter in the elections for the European Parliament, which amounted to a total reimbursement far in excess of actual campaign costs and, therefore, a most welcome addition to the party treasuries. In 1980 the tax deductible ceiling for contributions for individuals and couples was raised from DM 600/1,200 to DM 1,800/3,600. Nevertheless, the parties claimed still to be in need of more funding, and they were still concerned about their numerous former contributors who were in trouble with the law for their assistance which usually had been solicited by the parties. In 1981 another legislative attempt to revise the party finance laws failed to gain consensus in the Bundestag.[20]

In the early 1980s a major scandal broke in the Federal Republic over the so-called Flick affair. For many years the management of

Flick, a large personally owned holding company, gave about DM 1 million annually to a charity operated by Augustine monks at a monastery near Bonn. A total of DM 10 million was given, eight of which was returned to Flick in cash. In the meantime Flick received a tax deduction for about half of the contribution. In the end, the charity got two million and Flick had about thirteen million, eight of which was untraceable. In 1975 Flick sold Mercedes-Benz stock for two billion deutsche marks. In order to avoid paying taxes of about DM 850 million, the company sought relief in a provision of the income tax law that granted tax exemption for investments that are "especially worthy and appropriate for promotion" and in a provision of the foreign investment law that grants exemption for investments that promote technological exchange. A ruling by the Ministry of Economic Affairs cosigned by the Ministry of Finance is required for such exemptions, and during the time in question the ministers who had the economic affair portfolio were Hans Friderichs and Count Otto Lambsdorff, both from the FDP. In spite of strong evidence that the Flick investments did not meet the legal criteria, Flick received the tax exemption and for several years the FDP and apparently all other parties as well received large cash donations.[21] By 1984 there were over 700 cases of alleged illegal contributions pending, 22 involving the SPD, 170 the CDU, and 510 (!) the FDP. The Flick affair was merely the most sensational of these.[22] The Greens, who eagerly proclaim moral superiority over all opponents at home and abroad, had a field day for the next few years.

Given the Federal Constitutional Court's decision allowing deductions up to DM 100,000, the question was raised immediately as to the effect this would have on the prosecution of party financing tax fraud cases still pending, including the Friderichs and Lambsdorff cases, and on those who had already been penalized for having made illegal contributions. The opinions varied from predicting a virtual amnesty for all contributors of less than DM 100,000 from 1949 to the mid-1980s, to seeing no retreat on any prosecutions up to the implementation of the new laws in January 1984. What will happen in some cases remains to be seen, but by the end of 1987 it was clear that in a number of cases involving important contributors of the past the prosecuting attorneys and courts were willing to proceed with energy.[23]

Evidence supporting various predictions could be taken from the conclusion of the trial of Friderichs and Lambsdorff in February 1987. Both were convicted of income tax evasion and fined $34,000 and $100,000, respectively; former Flick executive Eberhard von Brauchitsch was fined $306,000 and given a suspended two-year jail sentence. On the other hand, the two former FDP economic affairs ministers were acquitted of charges of having accepted bribes for lack of evidence due to "bad memories" on the part of most of the 80 witnesses. Count Lambsdorff was reelected to the Bundestag in January 1987, where he continues his role as his party's spokesman on economic affairs.[24] While he and his parliamentary colleagues are now covered by a new code of conduct that requires limited disclosure of sources of income and of major political contributions by interest groups,[25] this code appears to be much less restrictive than the rules that apply to members of the U.S. Congress.

CONCLUSION

A good deal of controversy has surrounded German party finance during recent years. On the one hand, concern has been expressed that the parties are becoming too closely tied to the state through public financing, thus creating the impression that they are a part of the state and discouraging party members and sympathizers from making a sufficient effort to support party activities through their own time and money. On the other hand, recent scandals, the best known of which is the "Flick affair," have raised questions about the role of illegal donations to the parties in order to secure tax benefits and influence public policy.

While it is probably an illusion to believe that any system of party finance could eliminate completely all dependencies and all illegal, unethical, or questionable practices, the provisions of the reforms that went into effect in 1984 together with the requirements of past legislation demonstrate that West German politicians are very much aware of the many problems associated with party finance and that they have been willing to act to correct major abuses and still provide the parties with a level of public funding that is unmatched in any other democratic polity. Outside observers may join with some German critics in questioning certain practices of the past and present, but few, if any, other countries, with the possible exception of the United States, have engaged in so much debate, self-criticism, and legal regulation in an effort to promote a public accounting of the income and expenditures of candidates (United States) or political parties (West Germany). In addition, the Germans have sought to secure generous public funding that preserves to a very considerable extent the dignity and independence of action of the parties that are so crucial to the operation of the political institutions of the Federal Republic.

NOTES

Note: Some portions of this chapter are taken from my article in *The Review of Politics* 50, no. 1 (Winter 1988):30–48.

1. Hans Herbert von Arnim, *Parteienfinanzierung: Eine verfassungsrechtliche Untersuchung* (Wiesbaden: Karl-Bräuer-Institut des Bundes der Steuerzahler, 1982), 5 (Foreword).
2. *The Law on Political Parties, Documents on Politics and Society in the Federal Republic of Germany* (Bonn: Inter Nations, 1978), 6–7.
3. Sachverständigen-Kommission, *Bericht zur Neuordnung der Parteienfinanzierung* (Cologne: Bundesanzeiger Verlag, 1983), 35; Arthur B. Gunlicks, "Campaign and Party Finance at the State Level in Germany: The Case of Lower Saxony," *Comparative Politics* 12, no. 2 (January 1980): 213.
4. Peter Kulitz, *Unternehmensspenden an politischen Parteien* (Berlin: Duncker & Humblot, 1983), 126–30. See also *Entscheidungen des Bundesverfassungsgerichtes* (BVerfGE), vol. 6, 280 and vol. 8, 51 and 64–69.
5. Gunlicks, "Campaign Party Finance," 214.
6. *Gesetz über die politischen Parteien (Parteiengesetz) vom 24. Juli 1967*, Section 4, *Bundesgesetzblatt*, part 1, no. 44.

7. *Parteiengesetz vom 24. Juli 1967,* Paragraphs 5 and 7.
8. *Gesetz zur Änderung des Parteiengesetzes vom 22. Juli 1969, Bundesgesetzblatt,* part 1, no. 65.
9. *Gesetz zur Änderung des Parteiengesetzes vom 24. Juli 1974, Bundesgesetzblatt,* part 1, no. 79.
10. *Bericht,* 15–16.
11. Hans Herbert von Arnim, "Verfassungsfragen der Parteienfinanzierung —Teil 1," *Juristische Arbeitsblätter* 17, no. 3 (March 1985): 126.
12. *Parteiengesetz, Das Deutsche Bundesrecht,* 514th installment, February 1984.
13. For excerpts of the Court's decision, see *Das Parlament,* no. 31 (2 August 1986): 7.
14. Goettrik Wewer, "Fragen an die politischen Stiftungen," *Das Parlament* (Themenausgabe Parteiendemokratie), nos. 37–38 (13/20 September 1986): 18. For background, see Henning von Vieregge, *Gesellschaftspolitische Stiftungen in der Bundesrepublik Deutschland* (Baden-Baden: Nomos, 1980).
15. "Parteispenden: Überraschend hohe Grenze," *Das Parlament,* no. 31 (2 August 1986): 7.
16. von Arnim, "Verfassungsfragen," 123; for a more thorough and recent study of *Fraktion* financing, see the same author's *Staatliche Fraktionsfinanzierung ohne Kontrolle?* (Wiesbaden: Karl-Bräuer-Institut des Bundes der Steuerzahler, 1987).
17. Kulitz, *Unternehmerspenden,* 134–35.
18. See ibid., 141–43; *Bericht,* 13–15; and Peter Lösche, *Wovon leben die Parteien? Über das Geld in der Politik* (Frankfurt an Main: Fischer Taschenbuch, 1984), 20, 58–60.
19. Kulitz, *Unternehmerspenden,* 141–42.
20. *Bericht,* 14–15.
21. Lösche, *Parteien,* 58–60.
22. Ibid., 20.
23. *Der Spiegel,* no. 48 (23 November 1987), 52.
24. *The New York Times,* 17 February 1987, A 12, and *The German Tribune,* 1 March 1987, 3.
25. *The German Tribune,* 21 December 1986, 3.

III

THE EVOLUTION OF THE PARTY SYSTEM

12

THE "MODEL" WEST GERMAN PARTY SYSTEM

Gordon Smith

THE TWO REPUBLICS

Within the league of successful liberal democracies, the Federal
Republic has come to occupy a high place as an exemplary case of
political moderation and pragmatic outlook. Her stability is in total
contrast to the awful German *Schreckensbild* (image of horror) con-
jured up by mention of the Weimar Republic. It seems as if that
horror story of democratic weakness and collapse has had a permanent and salutary effect on West German parties, electorate, and
politicians alike for the whole era since 1945. The contrast between
the two republics is so profound that any one kind of explanation is
likely to prove deficient. At least as a point of reference, however,
the party systems of the two periods serve to highlight the cardinal
differences. The stability of West German politics is reflected in—
and in part stems from—the smooth functioning of the party system, whereas the nature of party interaction in the Weimar Republic
was a recipe for disaster.

Sartori's formulation of "polarised pluralism" finds its archetype
—its caricature even—in the Weimar party system.[1] The complete
syndrome was there: extreme party fragmentation; highly polarized,
centrifugal competition; and two major antisystem parties whose
combined vote toward the end exceeded that of all the others. In
those circumstances it was inevitable that the life of any government

would be precarious and short-lived. The parties were little inclined to make compromises, ideology flourished, and the "politics of outbidding" was the normal order of things.

Perhaps the only point of resemblance between the Weimar and Bonn republics is that, once they had acquired their primary characteristics, little of substance was to change thereafter. For the Federal Republic, it was the antecedent phase even, the years of occupation between 1945 and 1949, that established certain features in what was to become the general pattern. The peculiarity of those early years—the time of "democracy under licence"—was that party competition proceeded without the parties themselves having to bear the responsibility for the (nonexistent) state. Arguably, the progressively relaxing tutelage enforced by the Western occupying powers provided just the right environment in which the democratic forces in Western Germany could build up their self-confidence and authority. Is that too much to claim? The alternative of "Germans left to themselves" would at the very least have invited a multitude of competing claims and panaceas for the plight of the country—in all probability not too dissimilar to the situation at the beginning of the Weimar Republic.

It was not only the responsibility exercised by the Allies that proved to have a lasting influence on later political development. Their close involvement in all aspects of German life left a permanent imprint. Not least in importance was their tight control over political activity and, in particular, their regulation of the parties; by the time the Federal Republic came into being, the dangerous years faced by a new democracy had already passed: neither the extremes of Left nor Right were subsequently able to gain a foothold.

In its initial shape the West German party system contained two disparate elements. Thus in many respects the first Bundestag elected in 1949 appeared to be a reversion to an older type, for even though political extremism was only weakly represented, nonetheless—with no fewer than eleven parties—it was a kaleidoscopic multiparty system; depending on the course of events, it could also have become a strongly polarized one. Yet the other element present promised a quite different future. Despite the presence of several parties, the bulk of the vote went to the two largest parties, the CDU and the SPD. Nor was this outcome in 1949 an entirely new departure. Those two parties in the *Länder* elections held in previous years had already demonstrated their primacy, and their position has become the distinguishing hallmark, the core of the "model" party system.

DOMINATION BY THE CATCH-ALL PARTIES

More than anything else, it was the rapid rise of the CDU and the SPD to a position of unquestioned supremacy that served firmly to anchor the concept of "party democracy" in the West German political system. In the Weimar Republic the idea of the *Parteienstaat* had distinctly negative connotations, based not only on the inadequate performance of the parties but also on the older view that the parties and the state belonged in different realms—the intrusion of the parties into the domain of the state was unacceptable.

If a jostling multiparty system had become reestablished, the negative judgments might well have persisted. As it was, however, the 1950s brought about a swift concentration of electoral forces in a few parties, although in fact the party system passed through various stages before reaching an apparently completed form in the 1970s. At the outset, the underlying bipolarity between the CDU and the SPD was to an extent obscured by the presence of several other parties. This initial diffusion quickly gave way to the period of CDU dominance—the years of the Adenauer era—with the SPD trailing far behind. The marked imbalance in the party system effectively came to an end with the formation of the CDU-SPD Grand Coalition in 1966, for although the gap between the two parties was still wide, the fact that the SPD at last had the chance to share in government changed the whole perspective. That proved to be the case, since the transitional phase then led directly to what is best described as a "balanced" party system. First, the CDU was forced into opposition in 1969 and, second, as a result of the 1972 election the SPD emerged as the largest party. In other words, a balanced party system implies that there is a high potential for the major parties to alternate in government. This possibility did undoubtedly exist throughout the 1970s, although as it transpired the CDU proved unable to wrest power back from the SPD until 1982. The picture that emerges is one of an exceptionally slowly adjusting balance—bearing in mind the initial long period of CDU dominance was followed by some thirteen years for the party in opposition. For the SPD at the present time—after its election defeats both in 1983 and 1987—the scenario presented by this model offers only distant comfort.

That the West German party system has shown itself to be remarkably stable has been largely thanks to the authority wielded by the two large parties, as well as to the balancing of political forces and options that they represent—with neither being permanently excluded from government. Yet, of course, the strength of the catch-all party, or people's party (*Volkspartei*) over the longer term has to be seen in relation to its ability to make a successful appeal to wide sections of the electorate, rather than just to secure support from a few well-defined social categories. Very early on, the CDU managed to become a party of popular integration. As an entirely new party, it was not burdened by the trammels of ideology and tradition, and it had the advantage of establishing itself in the period of postwar social change and dislocation. In those circumstances the new CDU was able to fashion a loose unity under the broad banner of "Christian Democracy" and to overcome the historical fragmentation of the German "bourgeois" center-Right. The integrative power of the CDU was confirmed by its ability to mop up smaller competitors at the same time as offering a political home for all those who were uprooted and displaced in the postwar upheavals. For them, the identification of economic recovery and the regaining of national self-esteem with the CDU were decisive factors.

There was no one road to the *Volkspartei*, and the SPD found its task altogether more difficult. In the first place, unlike the CDU, the party had to contend with its own traditions, in particular of being explicitly an *Arbeiterpartei*, rooted firmly in the industrial working classes. This restriction on the SPD's voting potential was not formally lifted until the adoption of the Bad Godesberg Program of 1959, when the party proclaimed that it was no longer to be identified with any particular class interest. The second major difficulty faced by the SPD lay in the fact that it had to follow the lead given by the CDU if it was to achieve a competitive parity. This lead however did not just require an emulation of the CDU's successful electoral strategy, for it also meant that the SPD was forced to accept "the CDU state": the years of power for the CDU had set a particular stamp on the character of the Federal Republic, determining its economic and social evolution as well as its international position. The SPD felt it had no choice but to accommodate itself to these realities.

This sense of "coming from behind" and of being merely the "second" *Volkspartei* was overcome in the 1970s. The leadership of Willy Brandt, the high point of the party's vote in 1972, and the strong role as chancellor taken by Helmut Schmidt, combined with the SPD's long term in office, all led the party to see itself as the natural party of government. Since the debacle of 1982, with the toppling of Schmidt, the defeats of 1983 and 1987, and Brandt's subsequent resignation as party leader, however, the SPD became pessimistic about its future. Perhaps the party had been favored by luck for a while. The wide popularity of its leading figures, together with the general attraction of Brandt's Ostpolitik, gave the SPD access to new voting groups, but maybe that was a transient phenomenon. If so, the implication is that the coequality of the two *Volksparteien* on which the model of a balanced party system is posited is in doubt, and that accords with the view that the CDU still has a structural majority in West German society.

Both major parties have experienced a decline in electoral support since the early 1980s, and that is shown most clearly in the gradual fall in their aggregate share of the vote. Their combined total rose almost uninterruptedly throughout the first three decades of the republic, from 60 percent in 1949 to well over 90 percent in 1976, but in the 1980s there has been a progressive, if still slight, decline down to around 81 percent in 1987. Does this trend foreshadow that the long era of the dominant *Volksparteien* is coming to an end?

THE CENTRIPETAL BIND

If these electoral trends are taken at their face value—and extrapolated—then there is certainly a question mark to be placed over the future development of the party system. Yet such a conclusion leaves out of account several factors that have the effect of preserving the status quo. The concept of the *Volkspartei*, based on drawing support from as many sections of the electorate as possible, leads to centripetal party competition, since the major parties are necessarily forced to compete in many of the same areas of the electorate, and any attempt to polarize opinion in favor of the interests of one section places the support of larger groups in jeopardy. This basic pattern has dictated the course and strategy of both the CDU and SPD over many years, with only one ill-fated exception when Franz-Josef Strauss stood as the CDU/CSU chancellor candidate in 1980.

This mutual gravitational pull between the two *Volksparteien* has colored political competition for much of the life of the Federal Republic. Yet they have never had the field entirely to themselves, since the Free Democrats have not only survived when other smaller parties succumbed but have become of increasing importance in the formation of coalition governments. The FDP has often been described as a kind of "makeweight" in the party system, but this considerably underestimates its significance, since the party has, in effect, imposed a kind of centripetal bind on the major parties.

A three-party system has characteristics of both a two-party and of a multiparty system. On the one hand, electoral choice is not restricted as in a straight two-party system, nor is government formation quite on an either/or basis. On the other hand, the presence of a third party can facilitate the alternation of the major parties in government—possibly even more readily than in a two-party system, since for alternation to occur it is not necessary for a significant electoral shift to take place, but only for a change in coalition partners to come about.

These features have become entrenched in the West German party system. On two occasions the FDP has acted as a critical lever to effect a shift in political power. The party brought the SPD into office in 1969 at a time when the CDU was still the largest party. The long-lasting coalition came to an end in 1982 when the FDP finally decamped to link up with the CDU. Those two decisions—although of undoubted significance—may give the impression also of being just isolated events. Yet such an assessment would rather miss the point. The question is just as much about the *possibility* of the FDP making a change as the actual change itself. The potency of this threat to the senior party in government is matched by the implied promise to the other party in opposition. Intracoalition disputes focus on differences about particular government policies, and these can normally be resolved on an ad hoc basis, but there is always the danger of escalation into a full-blown coalition crisis. Repeated incidents sour relationships, so that over a period the possibility of an alternative lineup becomes increasingly more attractive.

These considerations apply with particular force to the role played by the FDP rather than to either of the larger parties. The feasibility of the larger parties forming a coalition has remained low ever since the unsatisfactory experience of the Grand Coalition. It was in those years in the late 1960s that political extremism received its largest boost with the successes of the right-wing National Democratic Party (NPD) and the destabilizing activities of the extraparliamentary opposition, in its turn spawning political terrorism in the Federal Republic. The lesson was drawn that it was preferable to maintain a distance between the CDU and the SPD if both were not to be outflanked on the Right and Left.

This restriction on the major parties is of enormous benefit to the FDP, but it does not mean that the party has an unrestricted ability to act arbitrarily or to indulge in blackmail tactics. With its very small electoral base, any sudden and repeated change of coalition partner runs the risk of alienating supporters. The FDP is likely to take several factors into account, one of the most important of which is its performance in Länder elections, since they act as a kind of running commentary on the party's federal standing. In addition, the "split" nature of the party system in a federal structure means that a shift in the coalition pattern on the part of the FDP in one or more of the Länder can be used by the party as a kite-flying exercise in advance of a federal change.

The FDP can be portrayed as the "power broker" of the West German party system. It has the ability to decide whether the CDU or the SPD will have the chancellorship, given that neither party has more than an outside chance of winning an absolute majority. In addition to its function of acting as an agent of power exchange, the FDP also acts as an agent of electoral exchange: the inability of the party to build up a sizable and permanent following over many years reflects its position as a transient haven for voters either disaffected temporarily with the CDU and SPD or else traveling between them.

One kind of judgment on the Free Democrats is to see the party as being solely concerned with a strategy of keeping itself in office—and as a matter of record the FDP has been in government far longer than the CDU or the SPD since 1949. Yet it would be misleading to assess the party only in this way. European liberalism generally, and German liberalism in particular, displays an "ambivalence" as between left and right.[2] At least in part, its apparent ambiguity has resulted from the overwhelming competitive pressures imposed by left- and right-wing ideologies, and the resulting left-right axis of European politics has served to obscure the existence of other dimensions. This is especially true in the West German case, and an alternative rendering in the form of a triangular relationship linking the CDU, SPD and FDP brings out the duality of the FDP's connections: the affinity with the CDU via the commitment to a market economy, and the attachment to the SPD through their common concern with individual/civic rights—to mention just two salient aspects.[3]

Political competition in the Federal Republic is largely governed by the two *Volksparteien*. Their structure and style has ineluctably drawn them closer together. This kind of effect is usual among liberal democracies, but it is powerfully reinforced in the Federal Republic because of the centripetal bind imposed both by the positioning and by the strategy of the FDP. The party's constraining influence is also made apparent within the SPD and the CDU-CSU: neither party can afford to let its more radical elements make the running for any length of time without risking an estrangement from the FDP and thus forfeiting the chance of forming a coalition. For the SPD this means having to check the party's left wing, and for the CDU the problem largely consists in having to control the CSU—in the eyes of the Free Democrats the CSU has come to represent the unacceptable face of Christian Democracy.

EFFECT OF THE ELECTORAL SYSTEM

There appears to be little doubt that the West German electoral system has supported the centre-leaning character of the party system. It is a somewhat paradoxical outcome, for at the very least proportional representation is associated with multipartism and hence with a permissive position with regard to centrifugal tendencies. Yet the Federal Republic has experienced a steady decline in the number of parties, and the format of the three-party system only changed with the success of the Greens in 1983.

The operation of the 5 percent threshold—a high barrier compared with other proportionally based systems—has had a restrictive result. Its general bias against smaller parties is allied to two specific effects. First, it acts to inhibit party splits, and on the occasions that breakaway parties have come into being, always affecting the smaller parties, the minority faction has disappeared without trace; this discouragement may have helped the *Volksparteien* to maintain their unity. Secondly, the 5 percent clause has helped to exclude marginal protest and extremist parties. The narrow failure of the right-wing NPD to win representation in 1969 is the most telling illustration, and the SPD benefited over many years from the absence in the Bundestag of the KPD and later the DKP. In other words, the two large parties have not been distracted by serious competition from their outer flanks. This advantage is still enjoyed by the CDU, but the Greens have come to be a worrying presence for the SPD—and the predicament of settling its own competitive stance underlines the nature of the problem that the major parties were spared for so long.

In the present circumstances the 5 percent requirement is possibly unduly restrictive, since all the very minor parties fall way below it, and they are lucky if they are able to score a single percentage point. Still, their weak showing is also related to a natural disinclination on the part of the electorate to waste votes, and a significantly lower barrier might alter electoral behavior. The Greens thus far have proved to be an isolated exception, and their success may be explained by the argument that no artificial electoral restriction can indefinitely halt the rise of a strong social movement. But it is also relevant to see how the Greens made their federal breakthrough: they first became a political force within individual Länder; having secured a footing at Land level, it proved easier to mount a federal campaign. If a reverse sequence had been adopted, the final result would probably have been different.

An additional special feature of the electoral system is the "two-vote" provision. In the present context, the key aspect is the option voters have to split their preferences as between their first and second votes. The chief beneficiary of such vote splitting has been the FDP. Whatever the effect this tactic has on the final count of party representation—and analyses agree that it is the FDP that has gained most—there is also the more diffuse influence to be reckoned with: the possibility of signifying approval of two parties at once, usually the two coalition partners, also leads to a "spreading" of loyalties. For the *Volksparteien* this has meant a seepage toward the Free Democrats and thus has led to a further centripetal pressure.

AN EXCURSION INTO THEORY

The postwar patterning of German politics and subsequent development may easily be interpreted solely as a response to the specifics of history: the new start and a reaction against the chaos of the Weimar Republic and the excesses of ideological politics—with the *Volkspartei* as a kind of all-purpose answer. A wider theoretical perspective was supplied by Otto Kirchheimer in seeing related tendencies in several West European societies. His observations led him to adduce a model of development which could account for the apparent "transformation" of West European party systems.[4]

The terms of Kirchheimer's thesis involved giving full weight to the substantial social changes brought about by the upheavals experienced by European countries as a consequence of the war period, and they were accelerated by the increasing affluence in the years thereafter. These changes had the effect of making old social cleavages weaken, but they also led to the redundancy of the old-style parties based upon them—along with their brand of ideological politics. The new type of catch-all party that would take their place was bound to be more successful, since—in appealing across the lines of social cleavage—it would have a much larger potential electorate. Once one such new party had made headway, other parties would be forced to follow its course. There was no alternative but to adopt the course of centripetal competition.

This bare framework of Kirchheimer's argument is sufficient to set alongside the course of development taken by the West German party system. In the broad thrust of what happened there is a remarkable correspondence: the CDU emerged as a highly successful new-type party, and the SPD, seeing itself operating at a competitive disadvantage throughout the 1950s, made the transfer as well. The virtual disappearance of small, ideological parties and the concentration of pragmatic competition in the two large ones was exactly in accord with the theory of transformation.

Compared with other West European countries, the West German party system went furthest in confirming the theory, and the fact that it proved to be a rather exceptional case naturally raises the question as to whether the dominance of the *Volkspartei* is to be explained completely in the way in which Kirchheimer saw it. It is anyway clear that the "mechanics" of the three-party system, and with it the centripetal bind operated by the FDP, acted both as a reinforcement of the prevailing trend as well as imposing a kind of inertia on the party system once the three-party pattern had become entrenched. As we have seen, too, certain features of the electoral system have further underpinned the static system.

One reason for querying the "transformation" argument as an entirely sufficient explanation is the manner in which the *Volkspartei* became so prominent early on. Its portrayal as a kind of nonideological sponge reveals only one side of the character of West German politics both in formative and later years. The other side shows the strength of the constraints suppressing ideological expressions on the left and the right of the party spectrum—neither of the extremes stood any chance of rehabilitation in the Federal Republic, although for quite different reasons. Although from one point of view it is correct to see the CDU and SPD as moderate and pragmatic parties, both adopted a sharp ideological *Abgrenzung* (demarcation) toward the extremes of right and left, respectively. This strict demarcation had the effect of limiting the ideological distance available. To put it another way: superimposed on the centripetal tendencies were others of a different order—amounting to an imposed "centrality" —and it was the combination of the two that gave the West German party system its particular character.[5]

The Greens: A Revival of Ideology

At least on the level of the party system, the political situation in West Germany proved to be remarkably stable until the early 1980s, but the ability of the Greens to disturb the party cartel in the intervening period points to the need to reconsider the factors at work. In the first place it shows that the assumption that there would be a steady attenuation of ideological politics in Western democracies generally was misplaced. But for the Federal Republic in addition, it seems that—as the legacy of the past has gradually waned—the constraints on expressions of party ideology have been loosened. But why should the Greens appear to have been especially favored in this respect?

What helped the Greens through the net of ideological restriction was that as the standard-bearers of the "new politics" they could not easily be categorized in the language of the conventional Right and Left where the ideological restriction was most apparent. Moreover, and as their title implies, the Greens seemed to be more like a single-issue ecological movement than representing a coherent ideological position.

It is still a matter for debate as to whether or not the Greens can sustain a coherent ideology, and critics incline to treat the party as a convenient gathering-ground for all kinds of minority causes, with the factional infighting taken as evidence of their incompatibility. Yet much of the Greens' incoherence stems not so much from disagreement about the goals of the movement as from the strategies to be adopted. Even though certain objectives appear to be unrealistic or utopian, the various strands relate to a postmaterialist framework. It would anyway be invidious to claim that other, established political traditions are "coherent," but deny that coherence to the Greens.

IMPACT ON THE PARTY SYSTEM

Even though a strong case can be made for regarding Green ideology as distinctive, the fact is that the party has developed as a new expression of the radical Left in West German politics. This shift can be explained on three main grounds. First, with the important exception of the attitudes toward the restructuring of the economy and the question of limiting economic growth, many of the aims of the Greens are compatible with ideas of "democratic socialism." Second, much of the initial impetus for the new party derived from a disaffection with the policies pursued by the SPD when in office: the "homeless Left" was given the opportunity to adapt the Greens as a new party of the Left. Finally, there were the pressures and exigencies of party competition. The fact that both parties appeal to similar sectors of the electorate, especially among young voters, has inevitably led to a competitive relationship developing which would not be the case if the new politics attracted support equally from left and right.

Thus the immediate impact of the Greens has been felt by the SPD rather than being transmitted throughout the party system, although how the SPD chooses to react will then have wider ramifications. There are various ways in which the choices facing the party can be presented, but they all revolve around the question of "competitive direction": the extent to which the SPD chooses a centripetal or a centrifugal course. In terms of its role in opposition, the SPD has to decide between offering a radical alternative or staying with its tried style of "political competition." This choice in turn has far-reaching implications for the party's policy program, as it does for the selection of its leadership cadre. Decisions about competitive direction can also be formulated in relation to alliance/coalition strategy: whether the SPD should look to a return to government with the help of the Free Democrats or whether it should risk making common cause with the Greens.

Behind all these considerations lie two opposing pictures of the future West German party system. One is predicated on the continuing survival of the three-party system, that is, based on the existing mechanics of party competition and government alternation. For this version to hold good it would not be necessary for the Greens to disappear, but simply that they should be "marginalized" in the party system. At the same time, perhaps, the Greens would continue to function as a useful safety valve for political protest—while kept away from governing power.

The alternative scenario offered is one based on the idea of two broad political blocs of left and right. The constellation of a two-bloc system—CDU + FDP versus SPD + Greens—invites a picture of a greater and more clear-cut polarization of political forces in the Federal Republic than has hitherto been the case. How convincing is it?

THE SURVIVAL OF THE "MODEL" SYSTEM

It may well be argued that the "large" questions about the future of a party system are likely to be resolved not so much by the parties individually making grand strategic choices as by the marginal losses and gains of one or the other. This line of thinking is persuasive if for no other reason than that the force of "coalition arithmetic" is frequently the decisive factor. If—as is a justifiable assumption for West Germany—all three established parties have an overwhelming desire to govern, then much else will be put on one side if the chance of participating is government is offered. For the SPD the opportunity would come through a majority with the help of the Free Democrats or the Greens, and it could not afford to spurn either party. Seen in this light, the future direction of the party system appears most to depend on which of the two smaller parties has the greater potential for growth, since the SPD, given its lagging performance in 1987, would require a prospective junior partner appreciably stronger than either the FDP or the Greens at the present time.

There are imponderables in using coalition arithmetic as a basis for forecasting future development. Seeking to assess the potential of parties draws in all kinds of contingent factors. For example, the possibility of the FDP increasing its vote is largely dependent on what happens to the CDU over the next few years. Again, if the

Greens were able substantially to grow in size, would not this inevitably mainly draw votes away from the SPD—with the possibility of a new majority on the left as elusive as ever? The hazards of speculation are considerable, and it is wiser to concentrate instead on the proven features of the party system. There is, after all, no real evidence that the CDU or the SPD would wish to forfeit its claim to be a *Volkspartei* in favour of a risky polarization. The centripetal bind operated by the FDP with careful finesse over the years is not a strategy that the party would willingly discard. Nor is the electoral system likely to lose its supporting role or even be subject to major revision. These constants all operate in the same direction and serve to make fundamental change remote.

This conclusion relegates the Greens to the role of permanent outsiders in the party system. As a channel for minority discontents, the Greens can be seen as a preferred alternative to an alienation from the political system that could once more take the road of extraparliamentary opposition. But in the longer term this instrumental, if not manipulative, attitude would fall short of providing for the assimilation of a new perspective on German politics. It remains to be seen whether the Greens will be able to act as a catalyst for change on a model system that may have become too static.

NOTES

1. G. Sartori, *Parties and Party Systems: A Framework for Analysis* (Cambridge: Cambridge University Press, 1976).
2. G. Smith, "Between Left and Right: The Ambivalence of European Liberalism," in E. Kirchner, ed., *Liberal Parties in Western Europe* (Cambridge: Cambridge University Press, 1988).
3. F. Pappi, "The West German Party System," *West European Politics* 7 (October 1984): 7–26.
4. O. Kirchheimer, "The Transformation of Western European Party Sys-

tems," in J. LaPalombara and M. Weiner, eds., *Political Parties and Political Development* (Princeton: Princeton University Press, 1966).
5. G. Smith, "The German Volkspartei and the Career of the Catch-All Concept," in H. Döring and G. Smith, eds., *Party Government and Political Culture in Western Germany* (London: Macmillan, 1982).

13

THE SOCIAL DEMOCRATIC PARTY: REFORMISM IN THEORY AND PRACTICE

Gerard Braunthal

The coming fortieth anniversary of the Federal Republic is a propitious time to take stock of a political party that can claim to be nearly three times as old. The Social Democratic Party (*Sozialdemokratische Partei Deutschlands*, SPD), founded in 1875 as an amalgamation of two major Marxist and non-Marxist groups, is proud of a heritage spanning the Empire era, when it was outlawed from 1878 to 1890; the Weimar era, when it headed coalition governments from 1919 to 1920 and 1928 to 1930; the Nazi era, when it was driven underground; and the Federal Republic era, when it has alternated as the major opposition party and the party in power.

An assessment of the SPD in the four decades of the Federal Republic must include its rise from the ashes of 1945, its role in opposition from 1949 to 1966 and from 1982 to the present, and its record as a governing party from 1966 to 1982. A balance sheet must also include its successes and failures; changes in its leadership, membership, voter support, and ideology; and predictions about its future.

REFLECTIONS ON THE PAST

Postwar Era

A number of SPD leaders, who during the Nazi era had taken part in the resistance, were imprisoned, or were forced into exile, lost no time in building up the party once Allied officials had given permission. In East Germany, under Soviet occupation, the leaders' efforts were short-lived in what was once their stronghold. Soon Soviet officials forced the SPD to merge with the Socialist Unity Party (SED)—the communist organization created to be the governing party. Since 1949, when the German Democratic Republic (GDR) was founded, the SED has maintained unchallenged control.

In West Germany and West Berlin, Kurt Schumacher, whom the Nazis had imprisoned for years, became SPD chairman at the first party convention in 1946. As in the period before 1933, when the SPD served as a model for other European socialist parties, the party created an impressive organization in the years following, consisting of a network of local, district, and regional branches and national policy-making bodies. It reestablished ancillary organizations, ranging from youth and women to sports, and launched a number of newspapers in major cities. By 1947, more than 875,000 members had joined, although three years later the figure had dropped to 683,000—still a respectable number given the lower membership of other postwar parties.

Schumacher and senior SPD officials set the ideological and programmatic tone. They called for transferring ownership of the major means of production to the public sector to assure democracy and prevent a repetition of giant firms supporting fascism. Although eschewing total nationalization, the party program still contained enough Marxist concepts to appeal to the older workers, the party's loyal supporters. Party officials did not neglect to emphasize foreign policy objectives, such as reunificiation of the divided country.

Once the Western occupation zones were merged and the Federal Republic was created in 1949, the party's subdued optimism of the immediate postwar years vanished when the returns of the first federal election on 14 August were tabulated. The Christian Democrats (CDU/CSU), led by Konrad Adenauer, outpolled the SPD by less than 2 percent (31 to 29.2). The SPD was unable to gain much additional support in the next four national elections (1953, 1957, 1961, 1965) and had to be satisfied with its role as the chief opposition party in the Bundestag. The continuing defeats were caused primarily by the successful economic revival credited to the CDU/CSU-led governments, Adenauer's unwavering anticommunist and pro-West stance, the SPD's loss of its bastion in the GDR, the voters' lack of enthusiasm for its neo-Marxist electoral rhetoric, and its inability to shed the image of being a class party based primarily on workers' interests.

Godesberg Program

To change this image and to emerge as the strongest party in national elections, delegates at the 1959 Bad Godesberg convention adopted a new reformist program, which marked a historic turn from a party mixing Marxist ideology with reformist practice to one committed to reformist ideology and practice. The program abandoned Marxist determinism and affirmed the religious and philosophical roots of democratic socialism. To erase its anticlerical image and to win over Catholics, it spoke of respect and cooperation with churches on the basis of a free partnership with them. It upheld the principles of freedom, justice, and solidarity in a parliamentary, democratic system. In a major shift, it no longer considered nationalization the major principle of a socialist economy, but only one of several, and then only the last, means of controlling and preventing economic concentration and power. The program called for competition whenever possible and planning whenever necessary, and for full employment on the basis of financial stability. In foreign policy, it committed the party to the defense of the country and support of the army. Finally, in an attempt to broaden the base of the party, it proclaimed: "From its beginnings as a party of the working class, the SPD has become a party of the whole people."

The 1959 Godesberg program reflected or paved the way for similar changes in programs of the Socialist International and socialist parties in Britain, Sweden, and Austria. Their leaders were becoming increasingly aware that an employment shift in their populations was decreasing the number of traditional socialist blue-collar workers and increasing the number of white-collar workers who were less sympathetic to neo-Marxist slogans and more attracted to a moderately left party that espoused a mix of public and private economies. The SPD and others shifted from being workers' to people's parties in the hope of capturing a wider segment of the electorate.

In the Federal Republic, the SPD hoped the voters would recognize that it was no longer a party of principled opposition to an array of the government's domestic and foreign policies, but that it was willing to support a number of them. It dropped its alternative proposals that had limited electoral appeal—for example, opposition to West European economic and military integration—and embarked on an "embracement" policy with the government coalition parties (CDU/CSU and FDP). The SPD's ingenious strategic mastermind, Herbert Wehner, discreetly explored the possibility of the SPD joining with the CDU/CSU in a Grand Coalition government in order to shed the popular image of the SPD being a perpetual political opponent not interested in supporting a liberal, pluralist democratic order based on a neocapitalist economy.

Junior Governing Party

Until 1966, Wehner's efforts failed, even though the party had nominated the charismatic Willy Brandt, mayor of West Berlin, as its chancellor candidate in 1961 and 1965. Brandt's support of reformism within the party and the Western alliance system, and his opposition to communism were well known among voters, but many still had doubts that the party had undergone a significant shift in policy. The SPD received more support from urban residents and young people in the two elections, but not enough to gain a plurality.

In 1966, the SPD seized the opportunity to share in governing the country upon CDU Chancellor Ludwig Erhard's sudden resignation when faced by a recession and financial and economic policy differences with France and the United States. The CDU/CSU nominated Kurt Georg Kiesinger, minister-president of Baden-Württemberg, as its candidate for chancellor. Unable to gain FDP support for a new cabinet, Kiesinger asked the SPD to join a Grand Coalition. The offer produced a heated debate within the SPD. Wehner and other proponents contended that this was a golden opportunity for the party to show its ability to govern the state. Opponents, including primarily the left wing, were wary of forming a governing alliance with a conservative party that had been a bitter foe since 1949; they feared a threat to democracy if only the FDP, with 8 percent of the seats, became the sole opposition party. The proponents won the debate; on 1 December, the SPD joined the government—the first time since 1930.

Ten CDU/CSU and nine SPD ministers were in the new cabinet that governed the nation from 1966 to 1969. SPD ministers were eager to transform their reformist aspirations into reality, but knew the CDU/CSU's reluctance to accept any sweeping proposals for change. Aware of economic difficulties facing the country, Minister of Economic Affairs Karl Schiller (SPD) launched Keynesian pump-priming programs, on the American New Deal model, to rescue the economy—rather than any socialist program of income redistribution or nationalization of industry. He also initiated a "concerted action" between the government, the business community, and the trade unions to produce social peace on the industrial front. As a result of Schiller's successful efforts, the economy moved ahead again and the SPD improved its image of economic competence and crisis management. Its support of the controversial emergency laws designed to let the government cope with a national crisis also showed voters the party's loyal support of the state. Foreign Minister Brandt began to initiate closer relations with Eastern bloc states, the harbinger of his Ostpolitik. Yet because the SPD's domestic and foreign policies had to be tailored to a programmatic accord concluded with the CDU/CSU at the time of the cabinet's formation, the SPD lost some flexibility as a result of being the junior coalition partner.

Senior Governing Party

In 1969 the Grand Coalition neared the end of the four-year parliamentary session. SPD leaders, unwilling to renew their uneasy alliance with the CDU/CSU, entered the electoral campaign on a platform that emphasized their differences with the conservative coalition partner. They reminded voters of their Keynesian economic policy that had generated a recovery and of their flexible policy toward communist countries. The SPD made gains at the polls, especially among middle-class voters and students, and was able to form a governing coalition with the FDP. After lengthy negotiations on a government program and the distribution of cabinet seats, SPD and

FDP leaders agreed on key aspects of domestic and foreign policies. At last the SPD had achieved its aim: to become the senior governing party and shape the nation's destiny, subject to FDP concurrence. The CDU/CSU finally had lost political power; its deputies had to sit on opposition benches until 1982.

Chancellor Brandt spoke of a policy of "continuity and renewal" in his government declaration, implying that no radical shifts in policy but rather modest reforms were to be made. Until 1972, some reforms, especially in social policy, were undertaken, but others relating to education, land law, and taxes did not get enacted, to the dismay of many SPD members, because of their complexity, a shortage of time, or FDP stonewalling. On the other hand, Brandt made great strides in his Ostpolitik, concluding treaties on a renunciation of force with the Soviet Union, Poland, and Czechoslovakia, for which he received the Nobel Peace Prize. Some conservative SPD and FDP deputies, who formerly had been refugee politicians, assailed the détente policy as a sellout to communism. When they defected to the CDU/CSU opposition benches, the SPD and FDP lost its parliamentary majority and had to call a premature election in 1972.

For the first time the SPD outpolled the CDU/CSU (by 1.1 percent) and the FDP gained significantly. The SPD's 45.8 percent of the vote, mustered by an influx of radical youth and a pragmatic-oriented middle class, was the highest it has received to date. As a result of the majority vote obtained by the SPD and FDP, Brandt formed a new cabinet committed to a speedup of domestic reforms. Yet the prospects of achieving them worsened in the face of adverse international economic conditions caused by the oil crisis and the difficulty of raising enough income to finance them. Brandt could only pursue a policy of "small steps" in domestic and foreign policies, including his Ostpolitik. In 1974, he faced further obstacles when public service workers went on strike; the radical Young Socialists (Jusos), in a minority, clashed with older, conservative members on a range of issues; and a spy scandal broke in the Chancellor's Office that led in turn to press revelations about Brandt's personal life. As a consequence he resigned the chancellorship in May, but kept his post as party chairman.

Schmidt's Chancellorship, 1974–1982

Helmut Schmidt, who had held a number of cabinet posts (defense, economics, finance) and had been a vice-chairman of the SPD since 1968, succeeded Brandt as chancellor. Relations between them were cool, partly because of ideological differences; Schmidt was a leader of the right wing and Brandt of the left-center wing. A number of new cabinet ministers, more technocratic and pragmatic than their predecessors, pursued policies that no longer had the reform impetus of earlier years.

In the 1976 election, the SPD and FDP won only a ten-seat majority as compared to a forty-six-seat majority in 1972. Continuing national economic problems, especially high unemployment and welfare expenditures; Juso attempts, mostly unsuccessful, at all levels of the SPD to obtain its endorsement of socialist rather than neocapitalist policies; and corruption scandals cost the governing parties many votes. The CDU/CSU once again captured a plurality of votes, but, unable to find a coalition partner, remained in opposition. Schmidt, reelected as chancellor, refrained from making promises of major, expensive reforms. Instead, he promised to restore full employment, reduce public borrowing, and put the health and old-age pension systems on a sound financial base. In 1977, skillful at crisis management, he authorized pump-priming public works programs to get the economy moving.

Schmidt's popularity within the SPD never matched that of Brandt; the new chancellor was criticized by the left wing for his stern and aloof leadership style and his unwillingness to accept a number of policy recommendations from the party. On the other hand, the center and right wings, especially in the *Fraktion*, maintained their loyal support for him. Schmidt's popularity as a national leader also remained high; indeed, the party gained some dividends from the prestige he enjoyed in the international community as a result of stimulating the economy and fighting terrorism. When, in addition, the ideological schisms in the party began to subside, the SPD fared well in most *Land* elections held from 1978 to 1980.

Yet the 1980 election results for the SPD showed the disillusionment among many voters with the government's record in the previous four-year parliamentary session. The party managed to score only slight gains over its 1976 vote, but was able to form another coalition with the FDP. The new Schmidt cabinet faced severe problems from the outset. Differences between the coalition partners over budgetary and economic policies surfaced during the negotiations over a new government program. The FDP, aided by the conservative businessmen and bankers who dominated Schmidt's inner circle of advisers, got many of its proposals accepted and was able to block SPD demands for more reforms.

From 1980 to 1982, the government met mounting difficulties. The economy stagnated; unemployment rose in 1982 to 1.7 million (7.4 percent), the highest in thirty years. The recession produced sharp differences among SPD and FDP ministers. The latter, in discussions over the budget, insisted on cuts in social programs and corporate taxes as a means of increasing business investments. The SPD ministers, on the defensive, tried in vain to prevent cuts in social programs, to increase funds for public works projects, and to raise taxes on high-income groups. Much of the party's rank and file was dissatisfied by SPD concessions to the FDP in the cabinet.

Schmidt's problems increased when the party split over two major policies that he strongly endorsed. Left-wing members protested the 1979 NATO decision to deploy medium-range missiles in West Europe, including West Germany. At regional party conventions in 1981, they introduced resolutions rejecting Schmidt's acceptance of the deployment of Cruise and Pershing II missiles on West German territory. The resolutions did not gain majority support, but they put Schmidt on guard, especially when ten SPD deputies abstained or voted against the deployment plan in a Bundestag debate in May 1981.

At the party's Munich convention in April 1982, the increased opposition to the NATO decision forced party leaders, aware of Schmidt's threat to resign as chancellor unless he received the party's backing, to work out a compromise resolution. It called on the United States and the Soviet Union to agree on arms controls at talks then being held in Geneva and recommended a moratorium on the production or deployment of missiles until the Geneva talks had concluded. After the Geneva talks deadlocked, sentiment in the party turned increasingly against missile deployment, as seen when an overwhelming majority of delegates at a special convention in November 1983 voted against deployment while Schmidt (no longer chancellor) and a few diehards voted in favor. By then, the position of the SPD, out of power, had little effect on defense policy.

Another internal policy debate that Schmidt confronted in his last years in power as chancellor concerned nuclear energy. Ever since 1976 the Jusos and ecologists in the SPD had opposed the construction of new nuclear plants and had favored instead the development of energy alternatives. They were opposed by SPD cabinet members and trade union leaders in the SPD who, fearful of increased unemployment, contended that nuclear energy was critical for domestic needs. In 1980, Jusos strongly opposed a plan approved by the SPD government of Hesse to construct a new nuclear plant or enlarge an existing one. In 1981, the left-leaning Mayor Hans-Ulrich Klose (SPD) of Hamburg resigned when a majority of party leaders in his city did not support him in his opposition to the continued construction of a nuclear plant in nearby Brokdorf. In 1982, one-third of the delegates at the SPD national convention voted against a resolution backed by Schmidt committing the party to further support of nuclear energy. The party's stance alienated an increasing number of youth who gravitated toward the Greens, whose opposition to nuclear power and nuclear missiles was a cornerstone of their program.

Loss of Power in Bonn

In its last two years in office, the Schmidt government had less public support. A number of the chancellor's critics within the SPD urged the party to end its coalition with the FDP, which had veered to the right in domestic policies. They preferred the SPD to go into opposition as a means of renewal and regeneration. Most SPD leaders, however, counseled Schmidt and other SPD ministers to continue the coalition, but not make any further concessions to the FDP on its economic demands. While discussions continued within the SPD on the best course of action, the four FDP ministers, eager to enter into a coalition with the CDU/CSU, announced their plan to resign from the cabinet. On 17 September 1982, Schmidt proclaimed the end of the coalition. He blamed the FDP ministers for wrecking the government's mandate to rule the nation for four years. In turn, Foreign Minister Genscher (FDP) blamed the SPD's abandonment of the coalition program and its adoption of left-leaning policies. The mutual recriminations were meant to put the blame for the crisis on the other party and gain electoral advantages whenever a new election was scheduled.

On October 4, CDU leader Helmut Kohl formed a CDU/CSU-FDP government. The new chancellor, intent on consolidating his own power in the CDU, did not schedule a new election until March 1983. SPD leaders chose Hans-Jochen Vogel as the party's candidate for chancellor. A former mayor of Munich and West Berlin, as well as housing and justice minister, Vogel initially had been a right-winger in the party, but had moved to the center in the early 1980s. In West Berlin, where he was sent to shore up the ailing SPD, he became tolerant of left-wing protest movements. During the campaign he attempted to wean potential voters away from the Greens by emphasizing the SPD's commitment to a sound environment. He hoped to prevent the Greens—and the FDP—from gaining the requisite 5 percent of the vote to qualify for Bundestag representation, and thereby give the SPD a chance to muster more than 50 percent of the national vote and form a government without a coalition partner. In such a case, the party would not need to dilute its program to accommodate its partner's policy demands.

In January 1983, the SPD adopted an electoral platform pledging that an SPD-led government would reduce unemployment through a 35-hour week and early retirement, launch a massive investment program, improve environmental protection and vocational training for youth, build more housing, and spur energy savings and local coal production rather than nuclear energy. In the realm of foreign affairs, the platform reaffirmed the party's commitment to NATO, but was ambiguous on the intermediate-range missiles issue.

The CDU/CSU assailed the SPD's ambiguous foreign policy position and accused it of following a neutralist course between East and West. The CDU/CSU accusation was based on the statements of some SPD leaders critical of aspects of American foreign policy. Despite a few policy differences between the major parties, the campaign did not arouse much excitement among the voting public. The results of the March 1983 election were disappointing to the

SPD. It won only 38.2 percent of the vote, a drop of nearly 5 percent from 1980. More than 1.5 million voters, including many workers who had cast their ballots for the party in 1980, switched to the CDU/CSU. They viewed the Kohl government, which remained in power, as more competent to deal with economic problems, including unemployment, than a potential SPD-led government. Another estimated 750,000 former SPD voters switched to the Greens, primarily because they supported the Greens' firm opposition to nuclear missiles and nuclear energy. Although the SPD picked up the votes of 700,000 former FDP voters disillusioned with their party's alignment with the CDU/CSU, the net loss of voters contributed to the malaise gripping the SPD.

One consequence was a change of leadership. Wehner, who had been a long-time chief of the SPD *Fraktion* (parliamentary group), retired; Vogel replaced him and also became one of the two vice-chairmen. Johannes Rau, minister-president of North Rhine-Westphalia, remained as the other vice-chairman. Brandt kept his post as party chairman while Schmidt gave up his posts. Thus the troika leadership of Brandt, Schmidt, and Wehner that, despite ideological and personal differences, had played such a powerful role during much of the SPD-governing period, was replaced by a new team of Brandt, Rau, and Vogel. It promised to work for greater unity within the party and to present constructive policy alternatives to the government.

After the 1983 election, party leaders, intent on developing a new electoral strategy, requested a group of party specialists to study the electorate and to identify groups of potential SPD voters. The specialists, in a report entitled "Planning Data for a Majority SPD," categorized voters not only by their occupations and socioeconomic status, but also by their social milieu, life-style, and psychological profile. They put emphasis on the SPD wooing the numerically growing group of the technical intelligentsia, which includes skilled workers and middle- to upper-level white-collar workers; the critical youth of the postmaterialist generation interested in quality-of-life issues; and the blue-collar workers.

In the legislative session from 1983 to 1987 the party introduced bills in the Bundestag designed to appeal to these three groups and to provide a convincing alternative to legislation introduced by the government. In support of the German Trade Union Federation (DGB), 90 percent of whose leaders and members were SPD members, the SPD drafted a bill calling for a 35-hour week to create more jobs. It also pushed bills on the humanization of work, the maintenance of the welfare system, the integration of foreign workers and their families into German society, protection of the environment, and the safeguarding of individuals against state surveillance. Needless to say, the party's proposals had little chance of enactment given its minority status in the Bundestag. The legislative activity was designed rather to provide an appealing profile to potential voters in the 1987 election. The party, maintaining its accommodationist position vis-à-vis the capitalist system, eschewed radical positions or participation in extraparliamentary activities other than supporting the peace movement. Its criticisms of government policies, such as Kohl's support of Reagan's Star Wars Program, were often sharp, but the substantive differences were less pronounced in many fields, including state intervention in the economy and the bulk of welfare policies.

On some issues, however, the SPD differed appreciably from the governing parties. On nuclear missile deployment, the party, as noted, shifted its position from its earlier unqualified support, to a conditional support, to outright opposition. On nuclear energy, the party, originally committed to a limited expansion, shifted its position after the Chernobyl accident and favored a phasing out over a ten-year period. This represented a compromise within the party between the trade union and environmental blocs.

These shifts in position reflected less an ideological commitment than a pragmatic, opportunistic course designed to maximize votes for the party in local, state, and national elections. The party was especially worried about its loss of power in cities (Berlin, Frankfurt, and Munich, among others) that had been its strongholds since the founding of the Federal Republic. One cause for the SPD plunge was the rise of the Greens. As a result of shifts in power, the two parties formed a few local coalitions whenever they could agree on common programs. But in the *Länder*, no coalition government emerged, except in Hesse from 1985 to 1987, partly because the right wing in the SPD and the "fundamental" wing in the Greens were both opposed.

SPD right-wing leaders, including some union chiefs, contended that the party must stop being a left protest party and become instead a centrist party giving priority to economic and social issues, on which elections are won or lost. They assailed coalitions with the Greens whose priority was ecology at the expense of economic growth; some preferred a grand coalition of SPD and CDU/CSU in Bonn following the 1987 election. But centrist and left-wing SPD leaders opposed a new governing alliance with an increasingly more conservative CDU/CSU in Bonn and the *Länder*.

The party nominated vice-chairman Johannes Rau as chancellor candidate for the January 1987 election. The popular minister-president of North Rhine-Westphalia, who was responsible for the SPD victory in the 1985 *Land* election with the help of strong union support, emphasized centrist issues during the campaign. He was a staunch opponent of a coalition with the Greens, whom he accused of not pursuing responsible policies. Rather, he insisted repeatedly that the SPD intended to win an absolute majority. Most observers viewed the statement as absurd and unrealizable, given the historical record of prior elections. The SPD has never been able to gain such a majority and the CDU/CSU only once. For the SPD or the CDU/CSU to gain more than 50 percent of the vote in the foreseeable future is extremely unlikely in a period when an increasing number of voters have given up their traditional support for the two major parties.

As public opinion surveys indicated, the SPD had little chance of becoming the strongest party in 1987. In an election characterized by a low voter turnout (84.4 percent), the SPD was able to capture only 37 percent of the vote, its worst showing since 1961. While the CDU also lost votes, the Greens and the FDP increased theirs when compared to the 1983 election results. Chancellor Kohl renewed his CDU/CSU-FDP government and the SPD and Greens remained in opposition.

In elections of the 1980s, the SPD has suffered from the continuing shifts in the socioeconomic profile of the voters. Although the party has received support from its core of loyal supporters among unionized, Protestant, blue-collar workers in urban areas, their number is shrinking decade after decade. An increasing number of the gainfully employed are civil servants and salaried employees, not necessarily unionized, whose voting preference for the SPD—or CDU/ CSU—is not assured. Indeed, their lack of party identification has produced may votes for the FDP or Greens instead. Thus, the SPD has lost votes to the Greens or other parties in medium-size and large cities in which the service and high-technology sectors have become more important. In addition, the SPD has found it difficult once again to attract the postmaterialist, left-alternative-oriented younger voters who have gravitated toward the Greens. The SPD has had more success in gaining the votes of left-liberal-oriented post-materialist voters, including a segment of the "yuppies" (the other segment being identified with the CDU/CSU).

REFLECTIONS ON THE FUTURE

In the forty years of the Federal Republic, the SPD's rise to power and fall from power in Bonn has been typical of other political parties. The SPD's sixteen years in government, both as junior and senior coalition partner, gave it a chance to shape domestic and foreign policies. Brandt's reign from 1969 to 1974 marked the party's success in making domestic reforms, producing détente through Ostpolitik, and being receptive to a new political culture marked by the rise of important social movements. Schmidt's reign from 1974 to 1982 was less innovative and more reactive to negative domestic and international developments. Yet many policy initiatives begun during the Brandt administration were continued by Schmidt and even by the Kohl governments since 1982. On the other hand, the SPD has suffered serious setbacks in recent years and finds itself lacking direction, self-confidence, and identity.

While it is difficult to assess the postwar historical record of the SPD, it is even more difficult to guess at future developments. The SPD's many problems and occasional successes as an opposition party provide some clues as to what may lie ahead. Whether the party can regain power in the next national elections in 1990 or 1994 will depend partly on its leadership, performance, member-ship configuration, coalition possibilities, and programmatic direc-tion.

New Leadership

The leaders' performance is as important at election time as between elections when policy questions, membership recruitment, and organizational cohesion are at stake. In March 1987, Brandt resigned suddenly as the patriarchal party chairman after twenty-three years in office. Although he had announced his intention to retire in 1988, his humiliating resignation was precipitated by a minor matter—his nomination of a press spokeswoman to whom many senior officials and rank and file objected. He had been the last of the Brandt-Schmidt-Wehner troika to resign or not stand for reelection, and many party chiefs wished he had resigned a year earlier when his prestige had not yet declined. Since then, however, the party has suffered serious setbacks in several *Länder* elections and in the 1987 national election. Brandt's opponents in the party, especially in the right wing, accused him of steering the party too far toward the left, of being too aloof, and of only half-heartedly supporting Rau during the election campaign. A bitter Brandt accused his critics of using the dispute over the press spokeswoman's nomination as a way to settle old accounts and of saddling him with responsibility for all of the party's recent setbacks. Despite the heated charges and counter-charges in the wake of Brandt's resignation, his impressive record as party chairman, Berlin mayor, chancellor, Socialist International chairman, and head of the North-South commission for development projects will have earned him a distinguished name in history.

At a special SPD convention in June 1987, Hans-Jochen Vogel, the party's Bundestag leader, was elected to succeed Brandt as chairman. In the party's political mainstream, Vogel is an able pragmatist and stern taskmaster, but does not have the charisma of his predecessor. He hopes to successfully integrate the party's warring left- and right-wing factions, and may succeed—based on his record as head of the Bundestag *Fraktion,* a post which he will keep. Respected by both factions, he was the most suitable and least controversial candidate the party could have chosen as its leader during the period of renewal.

Oskar Lafontaine, minister-president of the Saarland and an erstwhile young leader of the party's left wing, was elected a vice-chairman of the SPD; Rau, representing the center-right wing, remains another vice-chair. At the 1988 party convention, Herta Däubler -Gmelin, a leader of the parliamentary *Fraktion*, was selected as a third vice-chair, symbolizing the greater representation of women in the party. Lafontaine's selection, supported by Brandt, gives hope to the party's leftist and young voters that their goals will be taken into consideration in party policy. Lafontaine, a controversial figure, once had advocated that the Federal Republic should withdraw from the integrated NATO military command; he dropped that proposal when the senior SPD chiefs assailed it. He does want the party to move into an "ecosocialist" direction, in which traditional social issues important to workers and environmental issues important to the new politics voters are emphasized. The 43-year-old politician has been one of the few SPD leaders who has publicly supported a coalition with the Greens, should the need arise. To the discomfort of the party's right wingers, his name reappears in the press as the most likely SPD candidate for chancellor in the 1990 election. Although his dissident statements generate conflict within the party or with the unions, such as his 1988 proposal that unions should accept cuts in pay if they gain cuts in working hours, he is cautious or opportunistic enough to withdraw those that cannot command enough support.

It would not be surprising if Lafontaine moves closer to the political center should he be nominated as the party's next chancellor candidate. Rau has indicated that he may not want to run again, but Vogel, although bypassed as the candidate for the 1987 election, is viewed as a serious contender. Yet the unpredictability of politics can make short shrift of the likeliest scenario. The Vogel, Rau, and Lafontaine team, seen as a transitory one until the early 1990s, will need time to show its mettle. To the team must be added the right-leaning Anke Fuchs, a vice-chairperson of the Bundestag *Fraktion*, who in 1987 became party secretary; and Hans-Ulrich Klose, a former left-leaning Hamburg mayor, who became treasurer.

Waiting in the wings to move into top posts is the younger intellectual generation of Brandt's "nephews and nieces," former Juso leaders who have moved up into middle-level positions or are *Land* chairmen, such as Gerhard Schröder (Lower Saxony) and Björn Engholm (Schleswig-Holstein). They are likely to push the party into a slightly more left position, although some of them have become more conservative in middle age.

Membership Configuration

As a consequence of the party's loss of political power in Bonn, the continued infighting among its warring factions, and the rise of the Greens, SPD membership has declined about 10 percent from its peak at over one million in 1976 and 1977. Although blue-collar workers still join, their number in the labor force is steadily declining. Many have become disillusioned because in the party's local branches the professionals (teachers, social workers, etc.) are the activists who make policy not in consonance with their own more conservative cultural and political views.

The party also has had difficulty recruiting youth as members in the last decade, even though substantial numbers of young voters still cast their ballots for it. The idealists joined the Greens, the opportunists the CDU/CSU, and the apolitical no party. As the currently crisis-ridden Greens have seen their membership plummet, the SPD may have a chance to attract young members again into its Juso ranks. But the party will have to make intensive efforts to recruit new members, including women who constitute only about 25 percent of total membership, from an array of other age and socioeconomic groups. Once that goal is achieved, it will have to make major efforts to mobilize more of its members to participate actively in the party's organization and in election campaigns, in which bland slogans no longer will suffice to convince the uncommitted voters to cast their ballots for the SPD.

Coalition Possibilities

The party has been unable so far to reconcile the sharp schism in its ranks between the right wing, with continuing but reduced strength in the *Fraktion,* and the left wing, with strength in the local organizations and among Jusos. In recent years, the wings have been unable to agree on whether the party should move toward the left in order to capture potential Green votes or toward the center to gain workers' and middle class, including small entrepreneurs, votes. Right-wing leaders and theoreticians, such as Richard Loewenthal, contend that if the party moves to the left there will be continued erosion of the workers' vote in coming elections to the CDU/CSU. On ideological and pragmatic grounds, they strenuously oppose coalitions with the Greens, advocated by the Left, as suicidal for the SPD, especially given the conservative mood of the 1980s. A red-green coalition in Bonn or the *Länder,* they argue, will drive away the large number of moderate voters who want political stability and no experiments.

On the other hand, some left-wing leaders support coalitions with the Greens, but only if its moderate, "realist" wing gains the upper hand or if some of its extremist demands are dropped. They contend that there are enough commonalities between the two parties—the need for environmental safeguards, development of alternative technologies to nuclear power, protection of minorities, and nuclear-free zones in central Europe—to forge a winning alliance advocating an ecologically oriented industrialized society. (They also call on the SPD to work more closely with the peace and women's movements as a means of showing solidarity with their causes.) As a result of the breakdown of the Hesse red-green coalition and the current weak position of the realists in the Green Party who support alliances with the SPD, prospects for cooperation or coalition between the two parties in coming *Länder* elections and in the 1990 national election have dimmed considerably.

Yet if the SPD can repeat in coming *Länder* elections its 1987 victories, as in Bremen, or score major gains, as in Schleswig-Holstein, and if more voters support its domestic planks and foreign policy initiatives, the party's prospects will improve in 1990. While the domestic planks include calls for greater social justice, the foreign policy initiatives seek, among others, a rapprochement with the German Democratic Republic. The SPD, in pathbreaking moves, in recent years signed an accord with the GDR Socialist Unity Party calling on states to create nuclear- and chemical-free zones in Central Europe, and issued a joint document with the East German Academy of Social Sciences noting that the mixed economy and communist systems must give up the idea of triumphing over each other through force, and instead concentrate on overcoming their differences through mutual reforms.

Should a dynamic SPD, which has tried to shed its image of being primarily a party of blue-collar workers in decaying smokestack industries, gain a plurality in the 1990 election, it will need a coalition partner. As noted, few observers see a possibility of a coalition with the Greens as presently constituted. More observers predict a renewed alliance with a resurgent FDP, should the party remain liberal in foreign policy and become more liberal in domestic politics.

Although such a programmatic change and coalition may not take place until 1994, a more likely scenario in 1990 is that the CDU/CSU will gain a plurality and form a cabinet once again with an ideologically conservative FDP. If, however, in the meantime major crises erupt and substantial numbers of CDU/CSU and FDP voters lose confidence in the government's performance, especially in its economic and social policies, then the SPD may decide that its best tactic prior to the election is to keep the coalition question open, and during the campaign emphasize the government's inability, for instance, to solve mass unemployment or its continuation of tax policies favoring the rich.

A final coalition possibility, a grand coalition with the CDU/CSU, based on the 1966–1969 precedent, is unlikely, given the wide gap between both parties on a range of issues and given the antipathy among most SPD members toward the CDU/CSU. Yet such a coalition cannot be ruled out, especially if coalitions with the other parties currently represented in the Bundestag should fail.

Programmatic Direction

The well-publicized difficulties facing the SPD make observers forget the party's impressive achievements since the nineteenth century, including the creation of a welfare state (which other parties would not dare dismantle, except for cuts in costly programs) and the launching of a policy of détente with communist powers since the 1960s (which the CDU/CSU opposed initially and currently champions). As these achievements are currently taken for granted, the SPD searches for a distinctive profile.

In an era where interparty ideological confrontations, left-right schisms, and class conflicts have become less sharp, the hope among leftist voters that the SPD would become a true socialist party with a left orientation is gone. Most SPD leaders believe that the future of the party lies in a moderate left-center policy, because a majority of voters fails to back socialism and a radical course would be derailed by the country's dependence on the international economy.

As a consequence, the SPD, to regain political power and end its identity crisis, decided that it can only attract more members and voters if it complements short-range electoral platforms with a long-range nonideological program to replace the partly obsolete 1959 Godesberg program. In 1984, the SPD convention authorized a commission, consisting of members of the various party wings, to draft a new program. In 1986 the commission finished its first draft and submitted it for discussion to all organizations within the party. In 1989, a special convention is expected to approve a revised and shortened version to be prepared by a new commission to include representatives of the twenty-two party districts.

The program warns about the survival of mankind as long as nuclear bombs and arms races threaten the peace and as long as states lag in environmental protection. Unlike the Godesberg program's emphasis on unrestricted economic growth, the 1986 draft underlines the social and ecological priorities of an industrial society. The state will need to guide investments to promote a policy of selective growth. Qualitative rather than quantitative indicators will determine which economic sectors should grow or shrink. A strategy will need to be developed for retraining the unemployed, increasing overall employment, expanding codetermination, and humanizing the workplace.

The program warns about unrestricted technological changes. Nuclear energy plants must be phased out over time, environmental pollution must be minimized, data systems designed to gather maximum information about individuals must be curbed, and genetic technology must be controlled. Workers and employees should have the right to participate more in decisions concerning the introduction of new technologies. In the social sphere, the program endorses governmental responsibility for the general welfare and opposes any cuts in programs. To prevent a further bureaucratization in the administration of programs, guaranteed assistance for self-help projects should be promoted.

The program emphasizes the basic principles of democratic socialism—freedom, justice, and solidarity—and demands equality of women and men. In the party, women, who will gradually comprise 40 percent of all executive posts (according to a 1988 convention decision), must be given more opportunities to run for public office. In the nation, women must have equal job opportunities, equal pay, and must not be discriminated against in social and insurance legislation.

In foreign policy, the program calls for an end to reliance on nuclear weapons, an eventual liquidation of military blocs, and an expansion of atomic-free zones in order to create a peace-promoting partnership between East and West. Such proposals must be carried out on a multilateral rather than unilateral basis.

To conclude: the program attempts to synthesize the often conflicting traditional and alternative views of the right and left wings in the SPD. Although it succeeds in this integrative function, the two main subcultures in the party will continue to have ideological and tactical differences on ecology versus economy, qualitative economic growth, the role of the state in the economy, and national defense strategy. The program's architects, however, in their lengthy discussions learned to appreciate each other's different views. The program thus serves an important integrative function. Whether this consensual mood will last beyond the program's adoption in 1989 and how it is translated into policy demands remains to be seen. The pragmatic reform program, neither too radical nor too visionary, may provide a renewed identity to the party—a positive development in an era of uncertainty for all West German parties—and may enhance its chance of recapturing political power before the end of this century.

SELECT BIBLIOGRAPHY

Beyme, Klaus. *Political Parties in Western Democracies.* New York: St. Martin's Press, 1985.

Braunthal, Gerard. "Social Democratic-Green Coalitions in West Germany: Prospects for a New Alliance." *German Studies Review,* no. 3 (October 1986): 569–97.

———. "The Social Democratic Party." In *West German Politics in the Mid-Eighties: Crisis and Continuity,* edited by H. G. Peter Wallach and George K. Romoser. New York: Praeger, 1985.

———. *The West German Social Democrats, 1969–1982: Profile of a Party in Power.* Boulder, Color.: Westview, 1983.

Eppler, Erhard, ed. *Grundwerte für ein neues Godesberger Programm.* Hamburg: Rowohlt, 1984.

Lehnert, Detlef. *Sozialdemokratie zwischen Protestbewegung und Regierungspartei, 1948–1983.* Frankfurt am Main: Suhrkamp, 1983.

Miller, Susanne, and Heinrich Potthoff. *A History of German Social Democracy: From 1848 to the Present.* New York: Berg, 1986.

Padgett, Stephen. "The West German Social Democrats in Opposition 1982–86." *West European Politics* 10, no. 3 (1987): 339–56.

Padgett, Stephen, and Tony Burkett. *Political Parties and Elections in West Germany: The Search for a New Stability.* London: Hurst, 1986.

Paterson, William E. "The German Social Democratic Party." In *The Future of Social Democracy,* edited by William E. Paterson and Alastair H. Thomas. Oxford: Clarendon, 1986.

Reuter, Lutz R. "A New Socialist Schism? The West German Social Democrats Between Labor Unionism and Green Ideology." Paper read at the Sixth International Conference of Europeanists, Washington, D.C., October 30–November 1, 1987.

14

THE CHRISTIAN DEMOCRATS

William M. Chandler

No one would deny the centrality of the Christian Democrats for understanding postwar West German politics. Yet confusion abounds as to the true nature of this movement. Is it basically a conservative fortress against socialism at home and Soviet hegemony in Europe? Is it more accurately seen as a traditional "Christian" milieu party? Or is it neither of these but instead a complex amalgam of both progressive and conservative inclinations? The difficulty in finding consensus answers to such questions is twofold. On the one hand, Christian Democratic movements generally do not fit easily within the traditional ideological families of left and right. Nor have they provided organizational types that match up accurately with cadre/mass or representation/integration models of party structure. On the other hand, and certainly in the West German case, Christian Democrats have been treated with a degree of benign neglect that does not conform to their crucial importance as the Federal Republic's largest and most successful electoral alliance. The task of the discussion which follows is to provide an impression and interpretation of this political force that since 1949 has played a unique and often dominating role in shaping postwar German democracy.

THE HERITAGE OF CHRISTIAN DEMOCRACY IN GERMANY

The 1933 Nazi *Machtergreifung* terminated Weimar's fragmented party system. Twelve years later military defeat led to the cautious reestablishment of democratic party competition under conditions set by the occupying powers. Of the four parties first licensed, only two, the Social Democrats and Communists, were direct recreations of their pre-1933 antecedents. By contrast, Christian Democracy represented an essentially new postwar phenomenon—although it, too, had significant Weimar ties, primarily to the Catholic *Zentrum*. Any interpretation of modern German conservatism requires an appreciation of this past.

Under the *Kaiserreich*, the Zentrum constituted the political expression of Germany's Catholic minority, and as such served as a party of integration, mobilizing and defending this confessional milieu. It was primarily concerned with defense of Church interests and developed as a classic "pillar" party. Within the Bismarckian regime, the Zentrum shared with the SPD the status of an excluded force and was the target of the *Kulturkampf*. Its formative experience was therefore one of opposition rather than governing (and, thus, quite opposite to that of the CDU/CSU after 1949).

However, the parliamentary politics of Weimar suddenly transformed the role of the Zentrum by making it a party crucial to coalition building in the newly formed democratic order. True to its centrist label, this party shared power, starting with the Scheidemann government of February 1919 through the Brüning government that collapsed in May 1932, in twelve Weimar coalitions. Of these, the Zentrum provided the chancellor for five. In other words, the Weimar Zentrum took on the role of "pivot party" essential to building majorities, a role that the FDP would cultivate in the Federal Republic post-1949.

The transition from opposition force to mainstay of the parliamentary system did not, however, produce any internal restructuring of the party. Organizational and value change became significant only in the postwar context. Even so, by virtue of its confessional base, the Zentrum constituted an interclass party as well as a milieu party, and therefore may be viewed as a forerunner of the catch-all conservatism that would emerge within the CDU/CSU after 1945.

Beyond the traumatic experience of recurrent governing crises, the most significant electoral feature of the Zentrum was its "social insulation." The party vote did decline slightly over the course of the Weimar years (17.8 percent in 1920, compared with 14.8 percent in November 1932) but held relatively firm in the crisis atmosphere prevailing in the last Weimar elections.[1] The Zentrum "pillar" minimized the volatility of a Catholic "floating" vote and therefore provided limited opportunity for Nazi inroads into its electoral core. This stability stood in sharp contrast to the electoral decimation of other nonconfessional middle-class parties, and at war's end may have contributed to the legitimacy of Christian Democracy as resistant to fascism. However, the Zentrum's own reputation as a party of Weimar (and as a party that had voted for Hitler's enabling law in 1933) compromised its chances of providing a convincing postwar alternative.

POSTWAR REBUILDING OF THE PARTY SYSTEM

After some forty years, it is easy to forget the multiple unknowns and uncertainties that pervaded the rebuilding of German society, economy, and politics. With the end of hostilities in 1945, three and then four zones of occupation replaced the defunct German state. Beyond the most basic issues of how and under what conditions a new political order would be established, there also existed uncertainty about the shape of the postwar party system, including the status and character of individual parties. Such concerns were naturally more relevant to the newly established CDU than to the SPD whose cadres, organizational structures, and ideological traditions were recovered more or less intact.

Two crucial factors in the early development of this new party concerned ideological underpinnings and confessional ties. With regard to the latter, there existed the possibility of reestablishing a Catholic milieu party along the lines of the Zentrum. Certainly one of the key achievements in the immediate postwar climate was to straddle the historic religious division and to establish a commitment to an interconfessional alliance. Importantly, this reconciliation of Catholics and Protestants permitted the CDU to become the natural representation for many in those support groups who, prior to the rise of the National Socialist German Workers or Nazi Party (NSDAP), had voted for the three Protestant liberal-center parties or the rightist German Nationalist People's Party (DNVP), also a largely Protestant party. With this decision, the door was open, first, to building a credible alternative to the SPD and various liberal and regional formations in Protestant areas and, second, to attracting support from among the large numbers of expellees and refugees flowing in from the East.

Because parties were reestablished first at the local and then regional levels, that is, from the grass roots, confessional and social diversity were to a degree established without a plan or conscious choice. Indeed, for the CDU with only a loose confederal organization, no centrally planned strategy was even remotely conceivable. It nevertheless remains true that Adenauer and other party leaders were very influential in insuring an interconfessional course for the party. The political wisdom of rejecting a confessional strategy was to be confirmed by postwar secularizing trends in society, which also allowed the post-Godesberg SPD to attract an increasing portion of the nominally Catholic electorate.

The ideological character and direction of the new party was also undetermined. In most of Western Europe, immediate postwar elections indicated a clear swing to the left, with communist, socialist, and Christian Democratic parties being the principal beneficiaries. Although the first Bundestag election would not be held until 1949, signs of the same trend were to be found in the reconstituted parties. Within the formative CDU in the British zone, a Christian Socialist alternative advocating a mixed economy was formulated in the Ahlen program, but this was quickly rendered obsolete by the ascendancy and organizational victory of Adenauer over the more progressive Berlin party led by Jakob Kaiser. Any real prospects for this reformist bent were firmly quashed by the overnight success of Erhard's 1948 currency reform that set in motion the economic miracle and cemented a commitment to a free-market economic order. In addition, growing cold war tensions were beginning to isolate and marginalize the CDU in the Soviet zone from the rest of the party in the Western zones. This facilitated Adenauer's primacy and bolstered his conservative inclinations. Thus the combination of Adenauer's filling a political vacuum on the center-right and Erhard's success in economic policy set the CDU on a course of pragmatism that over the years has been reinforced by the diversity of the CDU/CSU electorate and its support groups.[2]

Ideological Bases

Although Christian Democracy does not refer to any single ideological position or coherent doctrine, certain core ideas within the spirit of Catholic social thought can be said to have been prevalent within postwar European Christian Democracy. These involve a common commitment to a middle way, to accommodative solutions to conflict with social values based on subsidiarity and solidarity rather than class warfare. In the context of a posttotalitarian, morally bankrupt society, the churches remained the only institutions relatively untainted by nazism and the only agents for reestablishing a new ethical order.

The stress on democracy in the self-definition of the CDU reflected a conscious attempt to distinguish postwar Christian Democracy from the often antidemocratic and antiliberal political Catholicism of the nineteenth and early twentieth centuries. In addition, a strong commitment to Europeanism provided the party with a value goal to replace discredited nationalism.

However, Catholic thought has never produced unambiguous directives for policy action. Thus comparatively and within any given Christian Democratic movement, one is likely to find ideological diversity and flexibility. It is generally true that the immediate electoral success of many of these parties, when combined with their frequent, and in some cases permanent, governing role during the reconstruction of Europe after the war, made the attempt at coherent doctrine unnecessary and undesirable.

Given this, it is not surprising that Christian Democracy in West Germany lacks a strong tradition of internal programmatic debate. It is true that in the formative period the Ahlen program did articulate a possible model for the coming economic order and that various party congresses also addressed value questions and policy directions, but the early history is largely devoid of comprehensive efforts to delineate basic values or ideology. As with important transformations in party organization and membership (discussed below), it is only with the experience of political opposition starting in 1969, reinforced by defeat in 1972, that we can observe a systematic effort to elaborate a statement of basic values. One of the first significant steps in this direction was the establishment of a Commission on Basic Values in 1971. The leadership change from Barzel to Kohl after 1972, plus Biedenkopf's arrival as general secretary, also prompted a new look at programmatic matters. Between 1973 and 1978 these issues drew increasing attention and critical discussion in various party meetings, culminating in the adoption of a set of basic principles (*Grundsatzprogramm*) at the 1978 Ludwigshaven party congress.

This 1978 program defines basic goals such as freedom, solidarity, and justice. It also confirms the social market economy as the guiding model for social and economic policy directions and addresses the so-called new social questions, particularly those dealing with elements in society not protected by established networks of organized interests. There are some parallels in this document to the famous SPD Godesberg program of 1959. Both were constructed as a foundation for reconquering power. Both sought to provide a programmatic alternative to the ruling coalition, and both took approximately ten years in opposition before coming to fruition. The biggest difference is, of course, that unlike the Godesberg program, the 1978 CDU program does not signify any radical turning point in party positions. It served rather to articulate basic core elements within the CDU governing tradition and therefore confirmed the party's political continuity.[3]

A Party of Government

Two facts are crucial to understanding the organizational character and ideological fluidity of German Christian Democracy. One is certainly the immediate assumption of power by Adenauer in 1949, for this meant that chancellorship preceded party leadership. Governing also predated the existence of a national party apparatus. The occupation of state power gave to the CDU/CSU the special task of supporting the chancellor in office. Decisions concerning party policy and strategy were set by the chancellor, the federal government or the CDU/CSU parliamentary group, that is, within state institutions by official holders of state authority. The legitimacy and autonomy of party officials (whom Adenauer generally prohibited from simultaneously holding public office) remained limited. Thus the party developed very much as a government party. It also meant that the CDU in particular did not need to mobilize for the conquering of power. The organizational traits of the party in the formative postwar years were, as a consequence, stabilized within a decentralized and relatively underdeveloped organization. The workability of this organizational model that typifies the Adenauer years depended on the blending of an organization composed of political notables with the status of government party, a combination that demanded rather little of the party executive.

This was less true in those *Länder* where the CDU or CSU faced early challenges or experienced intervals of opposition. In Bavaria, the licensing of minor parties forced the CSU after 1948–1949 to respond to the sudden and unexpected popularity of the regionalist appeals of the Bavarian Party (BP). In the Landtag election of 1950, the BP won 17.9 percent and cut into much of the CSU's support, which fell from 52.3 (1946) to 27.4 percent. Although by 1954 support for the BP was on the wane, a four-party coalition blocked the CSU from power. Without the advantages of state office, the CSU was forced to develop its own organizational capacity, so that from a party of notables the CSU emerged as a strong organization with both a mass membership and the ability to integrate all major social sectors.[4]

The second important fact to note is the early and unexpected electoral success of the CDU at a time when its organizational capacity was rudimentary at best. In the formative 1945–1949 period, the CDU and CSU were no doubt aided by the relative prestige of the churches whose Christian values they could claim to share. They were also helped by the division of Germany that chopped off traditional conservative Protestant bastions in the Eastern territories and rebalanced the Catholic-Protestant split to relative equality. In addition, Allied licensing prohibited the formation of regional parties until the Christian Democrats were already well entrenched locally and regionally. There was as well a general sympathy for the CDU and CSU shown by the American occupation authorities.[5] In the Bundestag election, the Christian Democrats outpolled the organizationally superior SPD, 31.0 to 29.2 percent, and by 1953 advanced to 45.2 percent. These victories confirmed a broad and socially diverse nonsocialist electorate that had quickly coalesced around the CDU/CSU. They also meant that the party was one of voters rather than of members or of effective organizational machinery.

The 1953 election witnessed a sharp increase in turnout, and the Union parties established undisputed preeminence by increasing their popular support by some five million votes while the SPD slid backward. This permitted Adenauer to pursue an alliance strategy based on consolidating segments of the minor parties—the FDP, Federation of Expellees and Dispossessed (BHE), and German Party (DP). He did this by first incorporating these parties into the coalition and then by coopting their ministers and some Bundestag members into the CDU. By 1956 the coalition consisted of the Christian Democrats and the DP. The DP only survived the 1957 election by virtue of CDU support for some of its direct seat candidates. The 1957 landslide victory produced the only single party absolute majority in the history of the Federal Republic and confirmed the CDU/CSU as a hegemonic governing party. However, it did not mean the end of coalition politics.

Dispersion of Power in a Federalized Party

Where federalism is concerned, the CDU/CSU certainly helped to shape the constitutional order, but it is also true that Germany's federal structures have themselves reinforced the decentralized character of the party. Because postwar parties were reconstituted first at the local and regional levels, Adenauer, in consolidating his own leadership, inherited a collection of autonomous organizations operating under a common Christian Democratic umbrella. In this setting the chancellor became something of a feudal monarch presiding over various regional barons, each of whom remained autonomous within his own fiefdom.[6]

CDU *Land* parties (*Landesverbände*) were well established and in control of organizational functions and resources several years prior to the formal establishment of a federal party in 1950. As a consequence, *Land* organizations controlled candidate selection and party finances, powers they were unlikely to concede to a weak central organization. Their organizational strength was effectively entrenched through federalism, with the Bundesrat providing a prestigious federal arena and status for *Land*-based political elites. All of this fostered a stable system of political bastions dominated by regional power barons, typically *Land* minister-presidents.

However, the control of state office in Bonn provided an effective counterweight against this decentralized pattern. As Adenauer's political machine expanded its influence, it created a centripetal pull by attracting regional elites toward the center.

Not surprisingly, the interaction of federalism and party organization has also accented the importance of elite recruitment from *Land* capitals to Bonn and vice versa. The career of Helmut Kohl from municipal and *Land* to federal politics is typical. Generally, *Land* party leaders have provided a reservoir of potential chancellor candidates. Occasionally, senior ministers in Bonn may hold concurrently *Land* leadership positions (for example, Norbert Blüm, federal minister of labour and social affairs, who in 1987 also assumed the chairmanship of the North Rhine-Westphalian *Land* organization). The career of Gerhard Stoltenberg illustrates the possibility of moving in both directions. In the 1950s, he served in the Schleswig-Holstein Landtag but from 1957 to 1971 was a member of the Bundestag, and from 1965 to 1969 a federal minister. He went back to Kiel to become minister-president, with his eventual return to Bonn to become federal minister of finance in 1982 (retaining control over the CDU in Schleswig-Holstein as *Land* chairman). Also moving both up and down has been Walter Wallmann, a member of the Hessian Landtag in the 1960s, the Bundestag in the 1970s, then mayor of Frankfurt and Hessian party leader. He became federal minister of the environment in the wake of Chernobyl and in preparation for the 1987 Bundestag election. Shortly thereafter, he returned to Wiesbaden to lead the CDU to power in Hesse. Of course, the best example of a regional potentate operating at both levels was Franz Josef Strauss, the "prince of Bavaria" whose enduring influence was unrivaled in the postwar era. In all these cases, *Land* influence (through Bundestag, intergovernmental relations, and internal party representation) has blended with Christian Democratic endurance as a "state-party" in most Länder to give political vitality to postwar German federalism.

Essential to understanding the federalized character of German Christian Democracy are the special relations that link the CDU and

CSU. Major parties inevitably include distinct ideological currents, client groups, and factions; but only West Germany's Christian Democrats have uniquely institutionalized such divergences within a two-party structure. Formed separately, the CDU and CSU have never constituted a single party but joined forces in 1947 in the British-American zone and then in the Parliamentary Council of 1948–1949. This parliamentary alliance has persisted throughout every Bundestag since 1949. During the Adenauer years, the CSU's effective alliance partner can be said to have been the chancellor himself rather than the CDU.

In 1961 Franz Josef Strauss became chairman of the CSU. Starting with the 1962 *Spiegel* affair, followed by intrigues during the Erhard period, relations between the two parties became increasingly conflictual. These tensions surfaced most publicly following the 1976 election, when the CSU acted on its long-standing implicit threat to terminate the alliance and constitute a fourth federal party, a move that was blocked by the CDU's counterthreat to field candidates in Bavaria. Despite recurrent tensions, the CDU and CSU have remained in permanent alliance for contesting Bundestag elections and have remained united at the top in a single parliamentary group. This special relationship originated in postwar circumstances and was reinforced by the strident defence of a separate Bavarian identity on the part of the CSU. What might appear as an awkward arrangement has proved to be particularly advantageous to the CSU, which has maximized its share of power through skillful bargaining with the much larger CDU. Certainly, the preeminence of Franz Josef Strauss firmly cemented this organizational dualism, for he was able to serve simultaneously as political ally, rival, and king-maker for CDU elites. On questions of policy and strategy, Strauss often found support among the more conservative, "Stahlhelm" elements within the CDU. His successors in Bavaria appear to be notably less conservative.

The tensions built into the relationship between these two parties are basic to appreciating the character of German Christian Democracy as a whole. They are, of course, in part a function of distinctive ideological leanings and policy preferences found within the two parties. More basic, however, than policy disagreements, have been the tensions between the two sister parties evident in the leadership rivalries and strategic debates that have permeated party life over the past several decades.

Within the CDU, the internal distribution of power in favor of the *Land* party organization began to shift with the organizational modernization of the party as a whole. The establishment of a general secretary in 1967 followed by the consolidation of party administration in Bonn were essential preconditions, but the most significant increase in authority of the national party did not occur until the Christian Democrats had to adapt to the realities of opposition and until a new reform-minded leadership took office in 1973. It can be plausibly argued that the transition from a weak confederation of autonomous *Land*-based organizations to a federal structure having the capacity to set national party priorities and design campaign strategies ranks among the most significant transformations in internal party life. The CDU's central organization of the 1980s has become an integrative and integrating political force. In this regard, there is little chance of mistaking it for its organizational ancestor of one generation ago. Although *Land* party leaders still constitute significant centers of influence, they no longer dominate organizational activity. Today, influence is structurally concentrated in an institutional triangle comprising the Konrad Adenauerhaus, the parliamentary group (*Fraktion*), and the regional (*Bezirk*) organizations.[7]

Leadership Dilemmas

The history of German Christian Democracy is marked by the frequent recurrence of leadership crises. Adenauer's personal dominance made the CDU an instrument for embedding "chancellor democracy," but paradoxically, in the post-Adenauer era leadership became a preoccupying problem for the Union parties. Chancellor domination allowed the survival of an organizationally weak and underdeveloped party apparatus in which power was decentralized and factional interests institutionalized.

The 1959 selection of a presidential candidate to succeed Theodor Heuss exposed a bitter feud between Adenauer and Erhard and initiated a long period of leadership turmoil within the party. Adenauer's attempt to push Erhard into the presidency in order to deny him the chancellorship, followed by his own abortive candidacy, aroused disquiet within Christian Democratic ranks and marked the beginning of the end of the Adenauer era. Within this context and starting with Erhard's chancellorship, leadership surfaced as a troubling problem. It has plagued all party chairmen and Chancellor candidates since Adenauer and has remained an undercurrent even with the return of the CDU/CSU to power in 1982.

Erhard's chancellorship in 1963 brought a new atmosphere of enthusiasm within party ranks. Erhard was seen as the electoral locomotive that could restore vitality and lead the CDU/CSU on to victory in the 1965 election. Such optimism was reinforced by Landtag election victories in Lower Saxony and Baden-Württemberg in 1964. However, Erhard never effectively secured his own leadership at the top, in large part by refusing to become party chairman. Internal disagreements over both domestic and foreign policy unsettled the party and fostered a climate of tension within the coalition. A bitter split began to emerge, especially in the wake of the 1963 Franco-German treaty, between "Atlanticists" and "Gaullists." Chancellor Erhard and his foreign minister, Schroeder, were clearly identified as Atlanticists, while Struss surfaced as the most vocal Gaullist alongside Adenauer, whose criticisms kept pressure on Erhard. This division served to strain relations between the CDU and CSU, between Protestants and Catholics, as well as between the chancellor and the parliamentary party.

Perhaps most importantly, Erhard's own style of leadership contained a fatal flaw. He sought to be a "peoples' chancellor" above party, neglecting the reality that he had to govern within a party state. Thus he never succeeded in establishing his undisputed authority, and given this, his political survival depended almost entirely on his standing in public opinion. Electoral victory in the 1965 Bundestag election, rather than solidifying his authority, disguised his vulnerability. A stunning political setback for the CDU in the 1966 Landtag election in North Rhine-Westphalia was enough to destroy Erhard's one trump card of popularity.

The ensuing leadership vacuum was filled when the parliamentary party chose a dark horse, Kurt Georg Kiesinger, who appeared acceptable to both the Gaullist and Atlanticist wings of the party. His selection ushered in the Grand Coalition and a new era in postwar German politics. By sharing power on relatively equal terms with the SPD, the Christian Democrats were obliged to adjust their ingrained political habits that had been learned through uninterrupted governing hegemony. Although Kiesinger was a popular chancellor, his function in the coalition was that of balance rather than dominant force. Within the party, he provided a pause in leadership wrangles and internal disputes. The beginnings of an organizational revival were further prompted by the evident popularity of the SPD ministers, Brandt and Schiller, and by signs of growing neo-Nazi NPD support to the right of the CDU/CSU.[8]

The end of the Grand Coalition in 1969 ushered in a difficult interregnum for the Christian Democrats. The party was without a chancellor but with two leaders, Kiesinger and Barzel, neither of whom had undisputed claim to preeminence. By 1971 this tenuous relationship was apparently settled in favor of Barzel, but the ambiguous position of the party and uncertainty about its own self-definition prevented any effective consolidation of power. The debate over leadership was crucially linked at this stage to the dispute over whether party strategy should be aimed at an immediate reconquering of power or a long-term rebuilding. The first of these options was plausible primarily because of the frailty of the very narrow SPD-FDP majority.

Decisive defeat in the 1972 election left the Christian Democrats in a state of pessimistic gloom. It also served to erase any illusions about the CDU/CSU's role as a party of opposition, for there could be no early return to power. Barzel's departure from his several leadership positions made possible substantial leadership changes. The new approach to leadership divided positions of power, with Kohl as party chairman, Carstens as parliamentary leader, and Biedenkopf as general secretary. This signified a temporary truce in the leadership battles and opened the way to organizational renewal. Of course, the question of picking a chancellor candidate for 1976 inevitably brought the issue of leadership back to the surface. This time, there were several credible potential candidates, but in the end the choice was between Kohl, with his organizational edge as CDU chairman, and Strauss, with his seniority and solid base of support among hard-line conservatives in both the CSU and CDU.[9]

1976 restored to the CDU/CSU its status as Germany's strongest party, but it also unleashed a direct challenge to Kohl's leadership. In addition to the CSU's threat to end the common parliamentary caucus with the CDU and to compete nationwide as a fourth party, Kohl's headaches were further intensified by the resignation of Kurt Biedenkopf as general secretary, who then quickly joined in the mounting criticism of Kohl's leadership performance. For the CDU/CSU as a whole, the post-1976 period can be characterized as one of recurrent internal squabbling and jostling for advantage. Thus the near-victory of 1976, in which the CDU/CSU polled its highest vote share since 1957, also led directly into a new period of feuding at the top and set in place a rivalry between Kohl and Strauss that permeated party affairs until Strauss's death in 1988.[10]

The 1980 Strauss candidacy did have a cleansing effect on the CDU/CSU, which in the aftermath of electoral defeat appeared once again unified. Kohl was reelected Bundestag leader, and Strauss declined his seat in Bonn to return to Munich as minister-president. This turned out to be a temporary lull rather than a permanent settlement of tensions, for new threats and challenges would soon emanate from Bavaria. For the moment, however, the Union parties enjoyed a newfound confidence that was sustained by the sinking popularity of the social-liberal coalition in the face of worsening economic indicators during the 1980–1982 period. Importantly, the Kohl-Strauss relationship dramatically changed, compared to the 1976–1980 period, in the politically crucial 1982–1983 transition. Kohl successfully pursued his alliance strategy with the FDP and excluded Strauss from determining the direction of the party. Strauss was blocked in his desire to return to Bonn as foreign minister, and the CSU, although it claimed five cabinet seats, could capture only one ministry of first rank (Interior). 1983 brought electoral rewards of unanticipated magnitude to the Christian Democrats and seemed to confirm Helmut Kohl's preeminence. However, his chancellorship from 1983 to 1987 produced neither a strong leadership image nor an electoral bonus in the subsequent election. Indeed, 1987 witnessed a substantial erosion of support for Christian Democracy and predictably spawned another round of internal debate about leadership qualities and style.

Political Strategy

Related to the conflict over leadership in the post-Adenauer party is an often intense controversy about the optimal political strategy the party should pursue. Threats of secession on the part of the CSU in the late 1970s constitute the most serious episodes in this debate, but it is correct to say that such issues have provided an undercurrent of discontent that has never been laid to rest.

Two strategic alternatives have tended to define these tensions. One may be labeled a "southern" strategy in which Christian Democratic ascendancy is maximized through the mobilization of a Christian-bourgeois popular base. It presumes an underlying conservative majority with the Union parties' southern bastions as crucial. The second, or "northern," strategy conceives of a Christian-liberal alliance as the preferred means for mobilizing a viable majority. From this perspective the attraction of nonsouthern, middle-class, and often Protestant, voters is essential. Within this disagreement over political strategies alternative relationships with the FDP are, of course, fundamental. Strauss, who had a long-standing feud with the FDP, saw the liberals normally as the allies of the SPD. This view also presumed a natural competition between two political camps, in which the CDU/CSU could effectively cultivate a conservative majority and in which the FDP's role was to be minimized, even eliminated, if possible. The contending interpretation, as advanced by party moderates like Kohl and Geissler, is a strategy of competing for the middle of the political spectrum, in which the FDP is a desirable ally and in which a three-party system is taken as the norm. In the wake of the 1976 election defeat, the CSU, in its Kreuth manifesto, proposed a "fourth party strategy" according to which it would become a national party competing against, or alongside, the CDU outside Bavaria. This challenged the understanding that the two Union parties would never compete within the same territory. It also challenged Kohl's attempt to build a new alliance with the FDP. A counterthreat by the CDU to field candidates in Bavaria put an end to this maneuver, and Strauss's nomination as chancellor candidate in 1980 appeared to settle the matter permanently. But it is notable that the same strategic debate quickly reemerged in the recriminations over the massive CDU/CSU loss of votes in the 1987 Bundestag election.[11]

Internal Revival

The organizational bases of the CDU/CSU have evolved in important ways over forty years. Certainly one very basic change has involved the transition from a relatively primitive machine for reelecting the chancellor into a modern mass party. Symptomatic of this has been the growth of party membership. For the first twenty years of the Federal Republic, during which the Christian Democrats maintained their role as a state party, the old-fashioned cadre style, based on a combination of powerful regional notables plus monopolization of the chancellorship in Bonn, required no serious modification. Correspondingly, party membership, especially in the CDU, stagnated during this period. Figures for 1954 indicate a total CDU membership of 215,000, which by 1968 had inched up to just 286,541. The combined CDU/CSU membership in that year (1968) corresponded to 49 percent of SPD members, whereas by 1985 the Christian Democratic total equalled 99 percent of the SPD's.

From the early years of the Federal Republic, a large and diverse electorate had coalesced under the Christian Democratic umbrella, making the CDU/CSU Germany's first true catch-all party. Inside the CDU, however, there was little organizational strengthening corresponding to this success. Membership stagnated and infrequent organizational modifications signified only marginal adjustments. During the 1960s there was growing recognition of the need to adapt, but as Schönbohm notes, efforts at reform tended to be "half-hearted and too late." It was instead the shock of opposition after 1969 that prompted the Christian Democrats into a conscious process of organizational renewal.[12]

The early 1970s were years of sharpened polarization along relatively new lines. Brandt's Ostpolitik opened an intense debate on foreign policy and German-German relations. These were also times of concern over educational reform and recently politicized moral issues like divorce and abortion. Such new policy challenges provoked the CDU/CSU to adapt to the unaccustomed role of opposition and encouraged a revitalization of party membership.

CDU membership traditionally had included a low proportion of women, of industrial workers, of youth, and of Protestants. Occupationally, the self-employed (including a significant proportion of farmers), white-collar and public servant categories tended to be overrepresented. By the end of the 1960s, certain patterns of malrepresentation were changing. The party was getting younger, and the proportion of the self-employed was falling. However, the percentage of women had not increased and the extreme imbalance between confessional groups remained unchanged. Generally, party membership through the 1960s remained predominantly Catholic, male, middle-aged, and bourgeois but tilted in favour of the old middle class.

Normally, party membership structures are not subject to sudden transformations, but over the course of one decade, we observe quite dramatic changes in the CDU. A total membership of about 300,000 in 1969 exploded to just under 700,000 by 1980, and this quantitative leap forward provided room for change in the structure of membership as well. Among the underrepresented groups, two changes are especially notable. Women increased from 13 to 21 percent of members, and for the first time the enormous confessional disproportion was narrowed. By 1980 the Catholic-Protestant imbalance had declined from an approximate ratio of 76-24 to one of 65-35 percent of members.

In occupational terms, the self-employed and the older middle class, who previously were sharply overrepresented (especially in farming regions like Schleswig-Holstein and Lower Saxony) have shrunk noticeably. On the rise have been the white-collar groups—public servants and salaried employees. As a consequence, the CDU/CSU achieved by the 1980s a membership that is considerably more representative of the population than was earlier the case. This broadening of social bases (especially for women and Protestants) has increased the degree to which the party mirrors the diverse social bases of its own electorate. It is, of course, only a distorted mirror, for enduring patterns of underrepresentation, although ameliorated, remain in place.[13]

Networks of Affiliated Organizations

Clues to the nature of a party are often found not only in its popular support but also in its organizational bonds. Like all successful parties, the Christian Democrats have well-established connections to particular social sectors, and correspondingly certain groups have special ties to the Union parties. Of greatest interest in this regard are the major organizations of business, labour, agriculture, and the churches.

In confessional terms, military defeat and division cut off from the Western zones much of Protestant Germany and made the emerging Federal Republic more Catholic. This meant that Protestants were especially concerned with the question of reunification, while for many Catholics, Adenauer's Western tilt was regarded positively. However, the interconfessional stance of the CDU created a certain distance between Church and party, even if the CDU depended heavily on its inheritance of Zentrum support in the Rhine/Ruhr region. The success of the catch-all strategy depended in an important sense on bridging the confessional divide. With the secularization of West German society in the postwar era, any thought of a close confessional bond became inconceivable. Nevertheless, there has always existed a broad, if ill-defined, affinity between the Catholic church and the Christian political alternative, and practicing Catholics have provided the most loyal core of support. The link between the Protestant church and the Union parties is less obvious, but the practice of proportional quotas in all offices *(Proporz)* has guaranteed a strong Protestant elite voice. The Protestant Work Group (EAK) represents the most direct organized input.

Major economic interest groups must maintain contacts with all parties having the potential to occupy power, but business group ties have always been stronger with the CDU/CSU than with the SPD. There is, for example, considerable overlap among the directors of the Christian Democratic Economic Council *(Wirtschaftsrat)* and positions in major peak business associations like the Federation of German Industry (BDI), the Federation of German Employers Associations (BDA), and the German Industry and Trade Association (DIHT). Similarly, the well-organized Federation of German Farmers has very close ties to the CDU and CSU. However, as both parties discovered in 1987, this may not always preclude farmers from withholding their support over federal and European Community agricultural policy.

After the war, labour unions were reestablished on the basis of industry, preventing a return to ideological, fragmented, and partisan unions. However, the natural common interests between the DGB and SPD quickly became evident, and throughout the history of the Federal Republic, a close relationship, including extensive overlap in membership, offices, and parliamentary mandates has existed between them. But there also remains a "Christian-social" minority within the DGB and a corresponding voice for labor inside the CDU best seen in the role of the Social Committees (CDA). In addition, white-collar and public servant unions—(DAG) the German Employees Union and the German Civil Servants Federation (DBB)—often identify closely with CDU/CSU views.[14]

An important part of the linkage between Christian Democracy and organized interests is to be understood in the existence and role of auxiliary associations. Like many mass parties, the CDU/CSU has a built-in organizational density that lends to it modes of operation that do not conform to the stereotype of traditional cadre party politics. This is nowhere more evident than in the network of affiliated organizations that support internal party life and give to the CDU/CSU a hybrid organizational quality. By assuring the representation of diverse social interests within the party structure, these auxiliaries reinforce the catch-all pluralism found in the electorate and allow for a limited degree of integration between party and society.

What is less clear about this array of support groups is the extent of their influence in determining party priorities. Although some operate as client groups in policy debates and programmatic formulation, it would be inaccurate to view these affiliates simply as lobbyists, for all are, in essence, party organs rather than interest groups. Their functions are therefore structures in terms of communication, mobilization, and recruitment of activists and future leaders.

By party statute the CDU has established a set of such associations (*Vereinigungen*) having official links and overlapping memberships. These include a youth organization (*die Junge Union or JU*), a womens' association (*Frauenvereinigung*), an employees' group with strong ties to Catholic trade unionists (*Sozialausschüsse der Christlich-Demokratischen Arbeitnehmerschaft*), a local government association (*Kommunalpolitische Vereinigung der CDU und CSU*), two groups to represent business/employer interests (*Mittelstandsvereinigung* and *Wirtschaftsvereinigung*), and an organization representing refugees and expellees (*Union der Vertriebenen und Flüchtlinge/Ost- und Mitteldeutsche Vereinigung*). Various other groups have less formal connections to the CDU and CSU, for example, Christian Democratic Students (RCDS) and a Secondary School Union (SU) affiliated with the JU, an Economic Council (*Wirtschaftsrat*), the Protestant Work Group (EAK), and several Catholic lay organizations.[15]

Where recruitment of party elites is concerned, the Junge Union has tended to have a particularly significant function. For example, much of the top party leadership in the 1980s had, during the 1950s or sixties, held executive positions in the JU. Of the 1987 Kohl cabinet, one-third established early political credentials within this organization.

Electoral Trends

The Federal Republic's first Bundestag election in 1949 has been called the "last election of the Weimar Republic" because it at first appeared to have set the stage for a return to Weimar-style polarization.[16] However, this outcome was prevented both by the catch-all strategy of Adenauer's party and by the enactment prior to the 1953 election of the 5 percent national minimum for the proportional sharing of seats. These two factors opened the door to building new partisan loyalties, and early electoral trends undoubtedly worked to the advantage of the Union parties. By 1953 the CDU/CSU's broad appeals of recovery, prosperity, and anticommunism had effectively united much of the nonsocialist electorate.

With the 1953 election, an emergent pattern of party competition was already evident. The party system was in the process of being simplified, and an unbalanced struggle between the two "giants," CDU/CSU and SPD, had been set in place. Although the Social Democrats eventually came to recognize the need to imitate the

CDU/CSU's catch-all strategy, their electoral progress was delayed and gradual. From the late 1950s on, the gap between the two progressively narrowed, and with Willy Brandt's victory in 1972 the SPD could claim the largest block of votes, although this turned out to be but a momentary superiority. Of course, from the Christian Democratic perspective, 1972 represented a psychological low point. Informed observers talked of the ghettoization of the party into its most traditional socioeconomic enclaves. Others spoke of a long-term realignment in patterns of competition. However, the 1976 Bundestag election demonstrated the capacity of conservative forces to regroup. In this they were no doubt aided by the erosion of Social Democratic cohesion and by the declining popularity of the governing coalition, signs of which were evident in preceding Landtag elections. In any case, the CDU/CSU led by a new chancellor candidate, Helmut Kohl, reclaimed much of the electorate lost in 1969 and 1972, increasing its level of support from 44.9 to 48.6 percent (the party's best performance since 1957).[17] The general impression emerging from the 1976 election is of a return to normal. In 1969 the Brandt-led SPD had captured a wave of new support, including many traditional Union party voters. By 1976 many of these prodigals apparently returned to their traditional ways. In this light the Brandt phenomenon evokes the model of deviating elections, with 1976 constituting a restoration of earlier divisions in partisan loyalty.

With the Franz Josef Strauss candidacy four years later, the CDU/CSU, still in opposition, discovered its electoral dilemma to be quite unlike that of 1976. In 1980 the party was faced with the prospect of new defections. Disenchantment with Strauss was most prevalent in Protestant regions and among moderate Christian Democrats. The primary beneficiary of this ambivalence was the FDP which, with strong gains in the north, secured its highest share of the vote (10.6 percent) since 1961. Because many supporters had foreseen electoral defeat in the Schmidt-Strauss confrontation, the worst CDU/CSU result in thirty years (44.6 percent) did not have the negative impact one might have expected. The Union parties did remain the single largest bloc, and even more importantly, the election in Christian Democratic eyes could be taken as a crucial juncture that finally had been passed. The contest had not been the rout it might have been; the SPD had failed to capitalize; and the Union parties had been purified of the perennial, Strauss-inspired threat of schism. As a result, and in contrast to a growing malaise within the Schmidt coalition, the 1980 election opened the door to CDU/CSU revitalization.

The 1982 collapse of the Schmidt government and the election of Helmut Kohl as federal chancellor according to the procedures of the constructive vote of no confidence set the stage for early elections in March 1983. Polls prior to this election consistently showed the CDU/CSU ahead of the SPD by at least 5 percentage points. As the FDP became sure of gaining at least 5 percent, the outcome appeared increasingly certain. What was surprising was the solidity of the Christian Democratic victory (48.8 percent) and the resounding quality of SPD defeat (38.2 percent). The 1983 election confirmed the Christian-liberal coalition and established a new electoral imbalance of over 10 percent between the two major parties. Although aggregate results demonstrated substantial electoral movement in 1983, this change may be partially misleading because, to a considerable extent, what happened in 1983 was (like 1976) a return of wayward conservatives to the Christian Democratic fold.

The 1987 Bundestag election was characterized neither by grand issues nor by dominant personalities. Political intensity was lacking and sentiments appeared unpolarized, an atmosphere reinforced by the growing belief, as the campaign dragged on, that the Christian Democratic-Liberal majority would be reconfirmed in office. Even so, voters did produce some unanticipated results. The biggest surprise in 1987 was reserved for the CDU/CSU, which polled its weakest share of the popular vote since 1949 (44.3 percent). In general, the dominant pattern of electoral mobility was one of shifts within the Left and Right rather than between them. Especially disturbing to Christian Democratic strategists were signs of disaffection within certain core support groups, notably farmers in many traditional CDU or CSU bastions and middle-class voters in major urban centers.

Despite these losses, four decades of voting trends attest to the extraordinary stability and loyalty of Christian Democratic support. Since 1953 the range of fluctuation in levels of support has been less than 7 percent. Moreover, this base has, with the exception of 1972, allowed Christian Democracy to retain its status as West Germany's most popular political force. Of course, given the coalitional character of governing majorities, vote totals have not been accurate predictors of government-opposition relationships. As a general rule elections have not been mechanisms for ousting one set of leaders and replacing them with another. More typically, new coalitions have been formed through a process of elite bargaining, which may subsequently (as in 1983) be confirmed at the polls.

THE RETURN TO POWER: CHRISTIAN DEMOCRACY IN THE 1980s

After thirteen years in the wilderness of opposition, the CDU/CSU was offered the golden opportunity of reclaiming power as the Social-Liberal coalition disintegrated. Thus the immediate cause of the return of Christian Democracy to power cannot be found in its own renewal but instead in the tormented reversal of the Free Democrats, who adjusted their alliance strategies in the face of a worsening economic climate and drooping popularity. As in 1969, it was West Germany's pivot party that brought about a fundamental change in governing majority.

For the Christian Democrats this change meant a reinstatement of their traditional governing vocation. The reuniting of the office of chancellor with the party chairmanship inevitably altered the power dynamics reflected in the controversies over leadership and alliance/electoral strategy referred to earlier. The persistence of such disputes demonstrates how deeply ingrained they are within the Christian Democratic family. They cannot be explained solely as artifacts of the years in opposition.

In terms of organizational change, the 1980s look considerably calmer than the 1970s. Following the influx of new members and a corresponding generational renewal, the party's established elites have reasserted their internal preeminence. Even if organizational innovation has lost momentum, its effects on Christian Democracy have been lasting. It is furthermore essential to recognize the extent of qualitative and quantitative development that characterizes the first four decades of this party's existence. In the early years of the

Federal Republic, the CDU/CSU became a *Volkspartei*, but only in terms of its popular support. Organizationally, it started off as a party of notables and in this regard remained underdeveloped until challenged to adapt by the loss of power. Since then, a modern party apparatus has been constructed, complemented by a mass membership. These modernizing trends evident within the Union parties are largely irreversible. This means that the return to power federally, with the inevitable overlapping of state and party offices, cannot lead to any reversion to the chancellor-party formula of the Adenauer era.

Christian Democracy entering the 1990s is once again ensconced as a state party. Any attempt to define the policy directions or ideological leanings of this complex and amorphous alliance is made extremely difficult by the impossibility of disentangling party from government objectives. Within major policy concerns such as economic performance and international relations, what stands out most prominently are the strong elements of continuity with the past.

In the 1983 campaign, the Christian Democrats stressed their strategy for economic recovery (the much-vaunted *Wende*). But this was never translated into a dramatic set of policy changes nor any systematic attempt to redefine the relationship between state and economy—as occurred in Great Britain and the United States through Thatcherite neoconservatism and Reaganomics. Of course, the improving world economy after 1983 made it relatively easy for Chancellor Kohl and his government to claim success within the established policy consensus (despite the acknowledged failure to significantly reduce unemployment).

In foreign affairs one observes a parallel pattern of continuity. Willy Brandt's Ostpolitik had provoked strong opposition within Christian Democracy in the early seventies, but by the 1980s much of this polarization had subsided. The record of the Kohl government is essentially one of the extension of a consensus on Ostpolitik, as evident in the 1987 "working" visit of Honecker to the Federal Republic and Kohl's 1988 visit to Czechoslovakia. In effect, while insisting that the German question remains open and that reunification remains an ultimate goal, actual policy has stressed regular contacts within a normal and pragmatic working relationship. The political thrust of the Geissler Commission in addressing the question of reunification represented an effort to put dreams aside in favor of a pragmatic Deutschlandpolitik compatible with the strategy of competing for centrist voters.

West Germany's Christian Democrats can lay claim to being the party par excellence of the postwar consensus. They, more than any other party, defined their meaning through the social market economy and the integration of West Germany into the Western alliance and the European Community. Over time that consensus has been challenged, and its substance in terms of specific issues and problems has been modified. But in broad terms, it has not been broken down or fundamentally redefined. The Christian Democratic return to power in the 1980s has reinforced the party's traditional inclination to defend that consensus through a politics of the middle way.

NOTES

1. Gordon Smith, *Democracy in Western Germany*, 3d edition (New York: Holmes and Meier, 1986), 22–23. Figures include support for the BVP, the Bavarian affiliate.

2. Klaus von Beyme, *Political Parties in Western Democracies* (Aldershot: Gower, 1985), 81–98; Peter H. Merkl, *The Origins of the West German Republic* (New York: Oxford, 1963); Herbert Kühr, ed., *Vom Milieu zur Volkspartei* (Konigstein/Taunus: Hain, 1979); Arnold Heidenheimer, *Adenauer and the CDU: the Rise of the Leader and the Integration of the Party* (The Hague: Nihoff, 1960); and Ute Schmidt, "Die Christlich Demokratische Union Deutschlands," in Richard Stöss, ed., *Parteien-Handbuch* (Opladen: Westdeutscher Verlag, 1983), 490–660.

3. Ulrich Sarcinelli, "Das Grundsatzprogramm der CDU, Selbstverständnis, Aussagen und Parteitagsdiskussion," in Heino Kaack and Reinhold Roth, eds., *Handbuch des deutschen Parteiensystems* (Opladen: Leske, 1980), vol. 2, 76–78; and Wulf Schönbohm, *Die CDU wird moderne Volkspartei. Selbstverständnis, Mitglieder, Organisation und Apparat, 1950–1980* (Stuttgart: Klett-Cotta, 1985), 138–48.

4. Alf Mintzel, "The Christian Social Union in Bavaria," in Max Kaase

and Klaus von Beyme, eds., *Elections and Parties* (London: Sage, 1978), 201–4.

5. William E. Paterson, "The Christian Union Parties," in H. G. Peter Wallach and George K. Romoser, eds., *West German Politics in the Mid-Eighties* (New York: Praeger, 1985), 61; and Peter Merkl, "Allied Strategies of Effecting Political Change and Their Reception in Occupied Germany," *Public Policy* 17 (1968): 75, quoted in Paterson, "The Christian Union Parties."

6. Smith, *Democracy in West Germany*, 95.

7. Paterson, "The Christian Union Parties," 72; Stephen Padgett and Tony Burkett, *Political Parties and Elections in West Germany* (London: Hurst, 1986), 114.

8. Geoffrey Pridham, *Christian Democracy in Western Germany* (New York: St. Martin's Press, 1977), 144–75, provides a valuable analysis of the leadership problems in the 1960s.

9. Pridham, *Christian Democracy*, 207–22.

10. Peter Merkl, "Adenauer's Heirs Reclaim Power: the CDU and CSU in 1980/1983," in Karl Cerny, ed., *Germany at the Polls* (Washington, D.C.: American Enterprise Institute, forthcoming); and Reinhold Roth, "Der Konflikt um die Strategie und den Kanzlerkandidaten in der CDU/CSU," in Kaack and Roth, *Handbuch*, vol. 2, 119–46.

11. Merkl, "Adenauer's Heirs"; Paterson, "The Christian Union Parties," 73.

12. Schönbohm, *Die CDU*, 4–8, 160–90; and Eva Kolinsky, *Parties, Opposition and Society in West Germany* (London: Croom Helm, 1984), 132–37.

13. Schönbohm, *Die CDU*, 160–212.

14. Peter Haungs, "Die Christlich Demokratische Union Deutschlands (CDU) und die Christlich Soziale Union in Bayern (CSU)," in Hans-Joachim Veen, ed., *Christlich-demokratische und konservative Parteien in Westeuropa*, (Paderborn: Schoningh, 1983), vol. 1, 130–42.

15. Haungs, "Die Christlich Demokratische Union Deutschlands," 51–64; Wolfram Höfling, "Die Vereinigungen der CDU," in Kaack and Roth, *Handbuch*, vol. 1, 125–45.

16. Jürgen W. Falter, "Kontinuität und Neubeginn, die Bundestagswahl 1949 zwischen Weimar und Bonn," *Politische Vierteljahresschrift* 22, no. 3 (September 1981): 236–63.

17. Werner Kaltefleiter, *Parteien im Umbruch* (Düsseldorf: Econ Verlag, 1984), 43–112.

15

"NOT WITHOUT US!" THE FDP's SURVIVAL, POSITION, AND INFLUENCE

Christian Søe

The liberal Free Democratic Party has long been one of the most significant and endangered of all established small parties in Western Europe.[1] Its importance derives primarily from the process of West German coalition politics, where the FDP occupies a strategic position in the delicate balance of power. The Free Democrats were able to exercise pivotal influence as majority-maker even at the time of the Bizonal Economic Council, before the formation of the Federal Republic of Germany. In the new state they joined the slender bourgeois coalition that, by the narrowest of margins, elected Konrad Adenauer to be founding chancellor in 1949. Since then the FDP has been a member of different government coalitions in Bonn for almost four-fifths of the time—considerably longer than either of the *Volksparteien*.

The last of the FDP's two relatively short stints in opposition, from 1966 to 1969, ended before the youngest of today's voters were born. Thereafter, the small party shifted coalition course on two occasions, making possible the major transfers of power that produced first a center-left era of West German government and then, in 1982, the present center-right one. Each of these political realignments came very close to destroying the small party, but they underscored its continuing ability to tip the scales of power. When the Greens entered the Bundestag in 1983, the FDP lost its exclusive hold on the parliamentary balance between the Christian and Social Democrats, but it remained a necessary building block for any majority coalition that did not include both of these catch-all parties. If anything, the principled aversion of many Greens to the politics of accommodation and compromise has made the FDP appear even more important for the governability of the Federal Republic.

The political clout of the small party has been displayed most dramatically by its considerable role in the making and deposing of West German heads of government. Each of the first six chancellors, from Adenauer to Kohl, has had his term in office decisively affected by the crucial support offered, withdrawn, or (in the case of Kiesinger, in 1969) refused by the Free Democrats. However, it would be easy to overstate the FDP's power, as though its strategic advantage had turned it into the mighty midget of West German politics, free of the normal restraints affecting other actors in Bonn. In reality, the tiny FDP is severely limited in its political maneuverability.

The possibilities and limits of the FDP's role in West German politics are drawn to a large degree by the small party's peculiar combination of positional influence and political vulnerability. If the FDP uses its leverage in what appears to be a willful manner, it may invite retributions by the large parties or the electorate that would destroy it. A change of coalition course, as in 1969 and 1982, can only be a last resort, since it is a mortally dangerous undertaking for the FDP. At the same time, the perennial role as junior coalition partner entails the danger of becoming overshadowed by the larger ally. To establish its autonomous identity without losing its attractiveness as coalition party, the FDP must therefore perform a careful balancing act between cooperation and conflict with its cabinet partner, avoiding extremes of harmony or disharmony. In policy matters, the FDP can serve as an element of both continuity and innovation in Bonn's changing coalitions, but it normally is not able to determine the agenda of a government headed by a much larger party. To be sure, strong FDP ministers have at times appeared to set the directions in foreign affairs and economic matters, but it is more common for the party to serve as a moderating or quickening rather than a determining force in governmental policy.

A LIBERAL COALITION PARTY

As a member of government, the FDP has been adept at advancing its own interests and those of its largely middle-class clientele. Even sympathetic observers have seen its politics as motivated in large part by what Rudolf Wildenmann has aptly called a "structural opportunism," built into the small party's dogged struggle for parliamentary survival and political influence through a place in government. Conceivably, the party's theoreticians could retort by drawing on the classical liberal and pluralist argument that rationally pursued self-interest in an orderly and competitive setting often has socially beneficial consequences. Instead, they have developed a more political case for what is presented as their party's contributions to public life in the Federal Republic. They no longer draw upon the hardly disguised elitist argument that the FDP represents "quality over quantity," as Karl-Hermann Flach once suggested, but they present a slightly more subtle version of the assertion to be "klein aber fein" by lovingly distinguishing their party of individualist Liberals from the populist mass parties of Christian and Social Democrats. Their basic theoretical case for the FDP usually rests on the party's twin claims of representing "organized political liberalism" and making some crucial "functional" contributions to the West German system of coalition government. These recurrent arguments will be personalized whenever possible by references to Liberal political leaders, such as Theodor Heuss, Thomas Dehler, Walter Scheel, or Hans-Dietrich Genscher, but it has become increasingly difficult to make credible the traditional assertion that liberalism is unusually rich in outstanding personalities.

The party's attempt to develop a liberal profile runs into a familiar combination of obstacles. These include the difficulty of staking an exclusive claim to represent political liberalism in a bourgeois society where the established parliamentary parties all show unmistakably liberal, democratic traits. Given the broadly centrist positions of the mainstream in the CDU/CSU and SPD, the FDP simply cannot present a convincing case that these parties represent the traditions of political conservatism (or clericalism) and socialism respectively.

The Free Democrats face an additional problem in ideological positioning because the classical left-right differences with political liberalism continue to be echoed (often without the participants' full awareness) in the party's own internal differences over policy and strategy. Some recent controversies in the FDP, to be discussed briefly later in this chapter, give ample testimony that Free Democrats are not in agreement over the kind of liberalism they want their party to pursue. (On one major issue, however, there has been an ideological simplification: The traditional "national-liberal" tendency, which was well represented in some of the FDP's state organizations during the first decade of the Federal Republic's existence, has long since disappeared from a party which served as an early promoter of the new Deutschland- and Ostpolitik of the 1970s and which now likes to emphasize its "European" outlook.) Finally, of course, it cannot be overlooked that the FDP is not a *Weltanschauungspartei* in the classical sense. Many of its supporters and members are motivated politically by some very pragmatic reasons that have precious little to do with liberal principles. Their politics are often more easily understood as the instrumental pursuit of special interests, just as many party leaders and activists will define the FDP's best strategy in terms of the organizational goals of survival and influence.

But Free Democrats have also developed a more "functional" argument for their party's indispensability. Already in the 1950s, Karl-Hermann Flach gave a classical formulation to this idea, when he suggested that Germany needed the FDP as a dynamic "third force" that would offset the tendencies toward both inertia and power abuse in single party rule by one of the two mass parties— or, even worse, in a grand alliance of both *à l'Autriche*. Equally to be avoided was the alternation in government of two adversary parties pursuing sharply disparate goals and hence forcing abrupt policy changes whenever one replaced the other. Instead, the FDP would serve as a coalition partner of one or the other major parties in government, acting at times as a brake and at other times as a dynamic force that would provide the necessary balance of continuity and change in West German politics.[2]

At a time when the Westminster model of representative government by a single majority party served as kind of role model for many West German political reformers (as well as some less disinterested party politicians in the CDU/CSU), Flach's argument against the monopoly of either major party represented an intellectually grounded partisan argument appealing to a perceived *horror majoritatis* among West German middle-class voters. The FDP has returned to this functional argument repeatedly, especially when its political extinction seemed near at hand. Then it falls back on some version of the slogans "Against rule by a single party (*Alleinherrschaft*)" and "Germany needs the Liberals." In a more recent adaptation, the FDP has responded to the appearance of the new "third" party of Greens by stressing its own availability for a coalition and warning of the ungovernable "red-green chaos" to be expected from a political alliance of the SPD and the ecologists.

Without subscribing uncritically to the FDP's self-presentation, one may agree that its absence from the Bonn cabinet would indeed have a noticeable impact upon the performance of government and the direction of policy in the Federal Republic. There is by now some evidence that the Greens, with their strong inclination toward a politics governed by an "ethics of conviction," or *Gesinnungsethik*, cannot become a functional substitute for the FDP in coalition cabinets. But what would single-party government by one of the *Volksparteien* in Bonn be like? The records of such administrations by the CDU, CSU, or SPD at the state level vary considerably and may have limited relevance for conclusions about the federal arena. A simple "thought experiment" suggests that one should expect not only some policy shifts of emphasis in foreign affairs, economic matters, civil rights, or social policy. Changes would also be likely in the prevailing style of governance, where movements between limited confrontation followed by compromise seem endemic to West German coalition politics. Party alternations in power would probably become even more infrequent than now—and perhaps result in greater discontinuities between governments of the right and left of center. A statist-conservative tendency could assert itself more freely in governments by a CDU/CSU majority, while the socialist wing of the SPD would have a stronger hand if the Left came to power alone. Under either of these dispensations, the missing liberal additive also might result in a greater corporatist emphasis in the economic and social policy-making process of the Federal Republic.

THE THREAT OF POLITICAL EXTINCTION

Such speculation is not wholly pointless, for the history of the Free Democratic Party is strewn with reminders of mortality. Its share of the second vote, which determines party strength in the Bundestag, is normally less than 10 percent and sometimes dangerously close to the 5-percent minimum required for parliamentary representation. During the consolidation of the West German party system in the late 1950s, the FDP managed to survive a widely perceived "inexorable trend toward a two-party system." It was able to repeat this feat of survival under even more difficult circumstances in the early 1970s. A few years earlier, the Free Democrats had eluded another kind of fatal danger when the SPD, for reasons of its own, halted the Grand Coalition's plan to abandon proportional representation and produce by electoral engineering what the voters had failed to create with their ballots: rule by a single majority party along the lines of the Westminster model of parliamentary government.

During the past decade, the FDP has been hounded by the most severe and enduring challenge to its continued parliamentary existence. The present problems can be traced back to the late 1970s when, after appearing to have recuperated fairly well from setbacks that followed the switch of 1969, the Liberals again began to show signs of internal disunity and loss of electoral support. This gradual weakening of the party was offset only temporarily by the spectacular victory in the Schmidt-Strauss election of 1980, where the FDP for the first time in nearly two decades received more than 10 percent of the West German vote. The transient resurgence was possible only because the party capitalized on a political situation that permitted it to appeal simultaneously to CDU/CSU-oriented voters, who were uncomfortable with the chancellor candidate of the Union parties, and to supporters of Chancellor Schmidt, who wanted to curb the left wing of his SPD.

The FDP itself had become divided between left and right tendencies over social and economic policy as the postwar economic boom petered out in the 1970s. Simply put, the Free Democrats were in disagreement over whether to continue on the reform path of "social liberalism," with its commitment to "more democracy" and a "reform of capitalism," or to return to a less interventionist economic liberalism that more closely reflected the market ideology and business interests associated with the FDP in the founding years of the republic. The division crystallized around specific issues of policy and coalition strategy. Seen in historical perspective, however, it reflected a long-standing if often dormant tension within political liberalism between "emancipatory" or "progressive" supporters of a more activist, socially transformatory politics, and "moderate" or "neoconservative" advocates of a reduced role of the state and politics in societal life. The two orientations overlap, and their differences are not always sharply formulated. It is nevertheless possible to distinguish corresponding left and right tendencies or wings in the party.

With only a tiny core of loyal voters and an ambiguous political identity, the FDP was in a poor position to fend off losses that resulted from a combination of adversary developments for both it and the SPD-FDP coalition government. In a confusing political landscape that simultaneously registered an apparent dampening of the country's earlier reform mood (*Tendenzwende*) and the rise of new, change-oriented social movements, each of the FDP's wings could point to evidence that seemed to promise political success if its views became the basis of party strategy. The emergence of the Greens as an alternative "third" party presented a dilemma for the Free Democrats, whose left wing wanted to promote its own version of participatory and ecological values. In the end, however, this new postmaterial party on the left served to bolster the FDP's rightward shift—just as the more transient success of the ultraright National Democrats had been a supplementary factor in the liberal "opening to the left" in the late 1960s.

THE COALITION CHANGE OF 1982

When this combination of electoral considerations and growing policy differences with an increasingly leftward-oriented SPD convinced the FDP leadership to change coalition partners in the fall of 1982, popular support for the small party plummeted to the lowest point ever. It must be stressed, however, that much of the disapproval centered on the manner in which the FDP abandoned Chancellor Helmut Schmidt rather than the policy implications of the move. Until a few weeks before the Bundestag election of March 1983, called after an early parliamentary dissolution to legitimate Chancellor Helmut Kohl's new center-right government, it was widely doubted that the FDP would be able to haul itself across the 5-percent threshold. Once again, though, political obituaries on the Liberals turned out to be premature. The party returned to the Bundestag with a reduced but fairly comfortable share of 7.0 percent of the vote.

But this victory against heavy odds had ominous Pyrrhic qualities. Assessments written after the 1983 election, also by myself, generally concluded that the new lease on life provided no long-term guarantee of survival and influence for the FDP. To be sure, the left-right tensions abated once more, as the remaining party members accepted the new coalition course, but the FDP seemed unable to overcome a pervasive organizational and political anemia. Unlike the earlier leftward shift, the move to the right failed to inspire Free Democrats or attract enthusiastic recruits to offset the losses in membership and morale that had accompanied the realignment. It did not help matters that the FDP suffered disproportionately from the political fallout of some dubious party financing practices, highlighted by the Flick affair, that came to light at this time. In 1984 one of the FDP's two most prominent cabinet members, Economics Minister Otto von Lambsdorff, gave up his government post after he was indicted for illegalities in channeling business contributions into party coffers while serving as treasurer for the FDP in North Rhine Westphalia during the 1970s. But Lambsdorff kept his Bundestag seat and remained the FDP's foremost authority on economic policy. Over three years later, he was convicted and fined for aiding and abetting tax evasion by financial supporters of the FDP. Both the Christian and Social Democratic parties had indulged in creative financing similar to Lambsdorff's, and tax officials had long turned a blind eye to some questionable practices such as using charitable "front" organizations as conduits for political contributions. Once official tolerance ceased, however, the involvement of the former economics minister as well as his Liberal predecessor in the cabinet, Hans Friderichs, put the FDP in the public spotlight for a while. To top it all, West German's Liberals were disoriented about their own role in the four-party system that had emerged with the parliamentary breakthrough of the Greens. Having lost the pivotal position between the two large parties, they were running into the danger of becoming identified as a dependent and ultimately dispensable junior member of a "bourgeois bloc" in the West German party system.

The political nightmare of Free Democrats became partial reality between 1982 and 1984. In some places below the federal level, a new three-party system emerged as the ecologists not only surpassed the Liberals in strength but at times even replaced them as sole "third" party. The low point was reached in the European elections of 1984, when the Free Democrats received only 4.8 percent of the vote and for the first time ever sank under the 5-percent mark in the country as a whole. Their place as third West German party in Strasbourg was taken by the Greens, who won 8.2 percent of the vote.

My own evaluation made at that time may serve as a convenient benchmark for a new attempt to take stock of the FDP's position in the late 1980s. It concluded that the FDP seemed, at best, to be headed for some more lean years, in which its fortunes would depend in large part on developments in the political system that were beyond its immediate control:

Its energies will be largely consumed by the exigencies of daily politics, including the tasks of co-governing in Bonn and preparing for the never-ending electoral bouts at the state and local level, staggered between the Bundestag contests. Under these difficult circumstances, the party motor will probably be kept running through "patch-up" repairs rather than a major overhaul. It will be a major accomplishment if the FDP can perform somewhere between its minimum organizational goal of political survival —or resurrection, in many places—and its maximum goal of political stabilization and increased influence at all levels of local, state and federal government.[3]

YET ANOTHER POLITICAL REVIVAL?

As if to belie even such cautious assessments, the FDP began in the following year to resume its performance as the *Steh-auf-Männchen* (stand-up doll; a doll that gets up again after being knocked down because it is weighted at the bottom) of West German party politics. In 1985 it elected a new leadership, adopted the Liberal Manifesto as party program, began a return to several state parliaments and cabinets from which it had been expelled, and gained fairly consistently in poll standings. One need not agree with Martin Bangemann, party leader and federal minister of economics between 1985 and 1988, who joined other professional optimists in detecting a "political renaissance of liberalism" in West Germany,[4] to recognize that the FDP was in far better shape by this time. More than anyone else, the small party's leading politician and former chairman, Hans-Dietrich Genscher, personified the turnabout in political fortunes. After leaving the party leadership and concentrating upon his role as foreign minister, Genscher climbed from the bottom rank on the popularity scale of West German politicians, where he had landed after the coalition change, to the very top place. After almost two decades as cabinet minister, Genscher appeared to symbolize much less the heralded turnabout (*Wende*) of 1982–1983 than political continuity and stability in Bonn. As the *Neue Zürcher Zeitung* pointed out in March of 1988, some of the very press organs that five years earlier had attacked Genscher and his party for their "treason" against Chancellor Helmut Schmidt now treated the foreign minister and vice-chancellor with solicitous respect for his "professionalism" and "tactical finesse."[5]

In the late 1980s, there appeared to be a revived electoral appreciation of the FDP's functional roles as balancer and corrective in the party system. Polls indicated that many supporters of the SPD had put aside their morally charged contempt for the faithless erstwhile partner. They now again preferred, in impressive numbers, a coalition with the FDP to one with the Greens.[6] By the fall of 1988, the FDP was a coalition partner in five of the eleven state governments (Hamburg, Hesse, Lower Saxony, the Rhineland-Palatinate, and West Berlin), where it had been present in only one (the Saar) at the time of the coalition change in 1982. It was represented in all but two of the eleven state parliaments (the exceptions being Bavaria and Schleswig-Holstein), where it had been absent from six legislatures during the fracas of the early 1980s. In short, the joke which translated the small party initials as "Fast Drei Prozent" or "almost three percent," had not only become somewhat stale—it would appear to have been rendered meaningless by the FDP's electoral revival. In this sense, the FDP's capture of 9.1 percent of the vote in the Bundestag election of 1987 confirmed a turnabout that had been detectable in polls and state contests over the previous two years.

The FDP's political recuperation was remarkable, but it was offset by stubborn evidence that the party had not yet overcome the structural problems that make it peculiarly vulnerable. Such a conclusion was supported by the party's shockingly poor performance in the March 1988 election of the Landtag in Baden-Württemberg. In this traditional liberal stronghold, the FDP had hoped to break the CDU's parliamentary majority and enter a sixth state government as junior coalition partner. Instead, the southwestern Liberals recorded their lowest result in the entire postwar period. With only 5.9 percent of the vote, they barely secured their return to Parliament in a state where they once used to garner impressive double-digit results. The setback of 1988 can in large part be explained in terms of local and transient factors, such as Minister-President Späth's astute campaign to win many voters back to the CDU or the FDP's own unattractively presented bid for a share of power. But the defeat was also a reminder that, for the Free Democrats, electoral bouts would continue to be struggles for survival even more than for influence.

The party's continuing frailty was underscored two months later, when Schleswig-Holstein held an early Landtag election in the wake of a political scandal that had shocked the northern state. The "Waterkantgate," as it was dubbed by the West German press, resulted from some unsavory tactics used by the recent CDU minister-president, Uwe Barschel, against his SPD opponent in the regular election of the preceding year, 1987. Having only recently disavowed its "social-liberal" orientation in Schleswig-Holstein, the FDP was somewhat slow to join the Social Democrats in taking a strong stand against the ruling Christian Democrats, with whom it had hoped to cogovern. Such tactical ambivalence did not help the Liberals. In the ensuing state election of May 1988, they received only 4.6 percent of the vote and thus failed to enter both Parliament and cabinet —their minimum and maximum strategic goals respectively.

A new assessment of the FDP's efforts to strengthen its position in West German party politics requires an examination of (1) its continuing electoral weakness, (2) its fragile membership structure, (3) its organizational underdevelopment, (4) its leadership changes, and (5) its programmatic renewals.

1. The Imperative of Electoral Survival

The most basic problem of the FDP remains its inability to secure a broader and more solid electoral base. Its core of loyal supporters has been less than 5 percent since the leftward realignment in the late 1960s, and this makes the party chronically dependent on capturing itinerant voters who will boost it over the electoral threshold. Such "floating" voters are notoriously unreliable, and the FDP must forever seek to attract new ones to replace the ones who move on at each election. Neither the SPD nor the CDU/CSU, each with broad electoral strongholds that are rooted in social structures, has a comparably high rate of turnover among its supporters despite a recent loosening of such traditional ties to the *Volksparteien*.

In terms of social composition, not surprisingly, the small party's electorate in recent years shows a return toward a more traditional *Mittelstand* clientele. In itself, this shift reflects the change of coalition course and need not weaken the party, if only it were able to attract substantial numbers of such voters with some regularity. However, the FDP's share of both the "old" and "new" middle-class vote, while considerably above its overall average, is neither very large in absolute terms nor very dependable. This share may well be increased, but there are at best great risks as well as opportunities in the FDP's growing identification with occupational groups whose members tend to be governed by tactical, situational considerations in their electoral choices. As internal party studies indicate, such voters often develop a short-term instrumental identification with the FDP, but this must not be confused with the long-term affective or structurally rooted support of a loyal electoral base that alone can guarantee a greater degree of stability.

It has been recognized by the small party's strategists for decades that the long-term solution of the electoral problem requires building such a loyal base or *Stammwählerschaft*. Over the years, the party headquarters has produced or commissioned a long stream of studies and strategic recommendations on this subject. They predictably conclude that the "potential" electorate of the FDP lies in the solid double-digit range and that it is composed primarily of members of the growing "new" middle class. But they fail with equal predictability to establish a practical way of attracting the members of this supposed "liberal potential," who are in any case courted just as eagerly by the Christian and Social Democrats. As long as this is the case, the FDP is doomed to muddle on with its never-ending appeals to voters who for one reason or another are reluctant to back either of the established major parties or opt for the alternative Greens.

The FDP's main gambit is to present itself as a coalition party, sometimes only in *spe*, using the triple-pronged "functional" argument that the Free Democrats are needed to promote a certain policy, build a working government majority, or prevent the alleged dangers endemic in *Alleinherrschaft*. The message is aimed primarily at so-called "coalition supporters," for whom the FDP represents a necessary or desirable addition to a cabinet headed by its larger coalition partner. Such voters may decide to support the FDP because they identify with one or more of the small party's distinctive positions (for example, Genscher's foreign policy, Lambsdorff's economic orientation, or Baum and Hirsch's civil rights positions). More fundamentally, they may agree with the FDP's argument against government by a single party and support the Free Democrats as a kind of check against political excess. Or they may simply vote for the FDP as a way to ensure that there will be a governmental majority headed by the larger coalition party, in the belief that the latter cannot win such a majority on its own. In any case, the FDP's freedom as majority-maker is severely restricted by the convention, based on perceived voter expectations, that it must make known its coalition commitment or preference in advance of the election.

To a much greater degree than previously, the FDP now resorts to a ticket-splitting strategy aimed at capturing the crucial "second" vote in West Germany's two-ballot system. Since 1953, the FDP has always received more second than first votes, and in only two of the last six Bundestag elections has it topped 5 percent of the first vote (in 1976 and 1980). In the two most recent Bundestag elections, 1983 and 1987, the FDP's total first vote has been only two-fifths and one-half of its total second vote respectively—even less than in the classic year of ticket-splitting, 1972, when the ratio plummeted to three-fifths (57 percent) from the previous low of fourth-fifths (83 percent in 1969).

It was in 1972 that the FDP for the first time resorted to a determined "second vote" strategy, directed at supporters of the embattled SPD-FDP coalition under Chancellor Brandt. At the time, FDP leaders and strategists regarded the move as something of an embarrassing and temporary expedient justified by the electoral crisis facing the small party after the recent coalition switch. In the wake of the coalition government's victory, the FDP announced that it would return to the traditional strategy of seeking *both* votes as part of its renewed attempt to build a dependable electoral base. This approach dominated the election of 1976, but since then expediency has become the norm: The Liberals now regularly campaign in federal elections with the slogan second ballot for the FDP, *"Zweitstimme F.D.P."* The gap between the results on the two votes has grown accordingly.

In the last few years, the small party has gone even further and sought to create the conditions for a similar ticket-splitting strategy in state politics. It has prevailed upon its coalition partners in West Berlin and Lower Saxony to introduce the two-ballot system for Land elections, and it is pursuing the same goal in Rhineland-Palatinate and Hesse. It remains to be seen if and how much the ticket-splitting made possible by a two-ballot system will strengthen the FDP at the state level, but party strategists are understandably hopeful. They like to remember the historically unique opportunity for ticket-splitting in the Rhineland-Palatinate in 1983, when the Landtag election was coterminous with the Bundestag contest. In this state, the FDP received 7.0 percent of the second vote for the Bundestag (the same as its overall result in the Federal Republic) but only 3.5 percent of the one-vote ballot for the Landtag on the same day. It is not implausible to assume that the small party would have done considerably better in the state election if there had been a two-vote ballot here as well.

In another attempt to change the rules in its own favor, the FDP has promoted the Niemayer system of proportional voting in local, state, and federal elections. Unlike the d'Hondt system, which was used in Bundestag elections before 1987, the Niemayer system does not give a slight advantage to the bigger parties in the distribution of parliamentary seats. While this can have only a very small if any impact on large representative bodies, such as the Bundestag or some of the Landtage, it can make a considerable overall difference in the numerous but much smaller elected bodies of local government, where the FDP's presence in recent years has been relatively weak. According to one FDP estimate, the Niemayer system would have given the Liberals a total of several hundred additional council seats in the last local elections of a big state like Lower Saxony. The effect in any given community would be marginal at best, but the electoral change could at least help to shore up the FDP's eroding position in local government.

Upon forming a coalition government with the CDU in Lower Saxony in 1986, the FDP insisted upon the adoption (in this case, reintroduction) of the Niemayer system for state and local elections. Similar demands have been made upon the coalition partner in the Rhineland-Palatinate and Hesse. They can be expected wherever the FDP enters a state government in a Land that still uses the d'Hondt system. In view of past attempts by the *Volksparteien* to use electoral engineering against the FDP, it is ironic but hardly surprising that the small party now advocates its own self-serving changes in the rules of the game. It need hardly be added that the Greens, who would also fare better under the Niemayer system, support its adoption as well.

2. A Frail Membership Party

The FDP's membership has never been very high as compared with the Christian and Social Democrats. Even the CSU is able to attract between two and three times as many members in its home state of Bavaria as the FDP can muster in the entire Federal Republic. For many years, the Free Democrats also have had an unusually high rate of turnover. During the 1970s, all the established parties showed a considerable growth in membership that has since come to a standstill and in some cases given way to a slow erosion, but the FDP's present stagnation only set in after a sharp drop that the others appear to have been spared.

A comparison of the membership development after the FDP's two political realignments underlines the peculiar nature of the party's current problem in retaining old members and attracting new ones. Both events resulted in heavy losses among supporters of the abandoned coalition course, but whereas the FDP recovered fairly rapidly in the early 1970s, it has been unable to do so in the 1980s. Between the beginning of 1969 and the end of 1972, there was a slight *net* gain in the FDP's membership, with the *total* losses and gains almost equalling each other (29 and 30 percent, respectively), followed by a period of rapid growth from almost 57,000 in 1972 to almost 87,000 in 1981. By contrast, the FDP had a *net* loss of about 25 percent of its membership in a comparable four-year period at the time of its second realignment (end of 1981 to end of 1985): The *total* losses were considerably higher but the party has never released the full statistics that would document the enormous turnover. Since the mid-eighties, the membership figures have practically stagnated at just above 65,000, again in contrast to the rapid upswing that took place in the 1970s. Even if one grants the party's argument that many of the losses were of nominal members, who were dropped with the introduction of a stricter system of collecting party dues introduced after 1983, there can be no doubt that the FDP's second realignment has been accompanied by an even greater and more lasting bloodletting than the first. It is generally acknowledged among Free Democrats that the defections of the early 1980s were especially heavy among the more active members, whereas the much smaller number of newcomers to the party have tended to be people who are less involved in party affairs.

The overall effect of the membership losses has been to shift the political center of gravity rightward, but the remaining left Liberals sometimes make up in energy and talent for what they lack in numbers. Their presence in the party is still very much felt. As a membership party, the FDP is too weak and unmotivated to become engaged significantly in electoral campaigning. In matters of policy and strategy, the party leadership usually calls the shots. But it would be a mistake to overlook the occasional surges of participatory energy that arouse a part of the membership to demand a say in such matters. In some cases, this has led to significant challenges to the party leadership on questions of both policy and personnel, as in the issues of amnesty for illegal party financing (1984), several leadership changes (1984, 1985, and 1988), and the rights of political demonstrators (1987).

3. Organizational Anemia

After the long history of organizational and ideological division within political liberalism in Germany, the founding of the FDP as a unified liberal party in 1948 was a remarkable political accomplishment. However, this postwar merger of remnant liberals was also a *sine qua non* of political survival after the emergence of the CDU/CSU as catch-all parties outside the socialist camp. From the beginning, the FDP was decentralized and loosely organized at all levels. Over the years, party strategists have complained repeatedly about the lack of both material resources and political will to establish a stronger party organization. It is difficult to compare the present situation with the earlier years of the Federal Republic, but the party's own studies suggest that its "organizational deficit" is now an even greater problem than in the previous decade. In the early 1980s, heavy campaign debts forced a pruning of the already meager staff in the party headquarters. The Thomas Dehler House now employs a staff that is about one-tenth as large as those found in the Erich Ollenhauer or Konrad Adenauer houses respectively, and the party's overall personnel costs stand in a similar proportion to those of the large parties. While the state organizations have maintained a comparably small core staff, the party can afford only a patchy organizational network at the local level in many parts of the Federal Republic.

The resource problem was aggravated until recently by the fact that private contributions to the FDP, its most important source of funding, slowed to a trickle in the wake of judicial investigations of tax evasions in connection with the dubious financing practices of the 1970s and early 1980s. As already noted, the CDU/CSU and SPD were also affected by this development, but they have always been relatively less dependent upon large private *Spenden*. Legal and political changes appear to have brought some relief, for the most recent party finance reports, covering 1986, indicate that the FDP is once again attracting over two-fifths of its income from private contributions. The improved electoral results in recent years have also strengthened the FDP's financial position by bringing an increase in the public reimbursement of its campaign costs. However, none of this makes it likely that the skeletal organization will soon take on enough flesh and muscle to make a significant difference in the small party's competitive position.

4. Leadership Changes

The realignment of 1982 led to an extensive turnover at the top of the party's state and local organizations, prompting Genscher and others to speak of a new generation of vigorous leadership in the party. But there are at least two structural reasons for doubting that the party will so easily overcome its problems in this area. First, even after its recent strengthening in state and federal politics, the FDP is no longer a dependably short route to public office at any level of government for pragmatic and ambitious young politicians. Second, the small party's image has become too undistinctive or ambiguous to attract the more conviction-oriented kind of personality upon which Liberal parties have often prided themselves in the past. The result is an embarrassing lack of qualified personnel when party or government positions do open up. The FDP's apparent inability to find impressive and qualified people to fill some of its ministries in Bonn and the state capitals is an embarrassing and highly visible illustration of the problem.

Nor should one overlook the dearth of intellectual energy in a party that once prided itself on such names as Karl-Hermann Flach, Werner Maihofer, and Rolf Schroers. The recent decision of Ralf Dahrendorf to leave the FDP (reportedly to join the Social and Liberal Democrats in Britain) deprives it of the last well-known member of a group of theoreticians that not long ago gave political liberalism some substantial meaning in party debates. There are potential replacements with the FDP, or close to it, but their voices are not often heard in party councils. A reinvigoration of the journal *liberal*, once a disorganized but lively monthly forum of liberal debate and now a more pretentious but uninspiring quarterly, might help to reawaken intraparty discussion.

In retrospect, it is clear that Genscher gained in political stature by giving up the party leadership in 1985 and concentrating on his post as foreign minister: He remained the party's leading figure without the encumbrances of the formal leadership role. His transitional successor, Martin Bangemann, opted already in 1988 for a resettlement in Brussels as EC commissioner. As party chairman and minister of economics, Bangemann was frequently criticized for lacking some of Genscher's tactical ability or Lambsdorff's grasp of policy, but he could claim to have presided over the reintegration of the party after the batterings of the early 1980s. Neither he nor anyone else could hope to exorcise the structural problems that continue to haunt the small party.

In October of 1988, a party convention in Wiesbaden chose between two prominent candidates for the FDP leadership: Otto von Lambsdorff and Irmgard Adam-Schwaetzer. The two represented different generations (she was forty-six to his sixty-one), leadership styles and, somewhat less clearly, strategic orientations. Lambsdorff, who had declared his candidacy early, was known as a hardworking, eloquent, and somewhat abrasive politician. He had long been closely identified with business interests and a neoliberal market ideology. In 1982, he was the party's most outspoken advocate of the coalition change, which he justified in terms of economic and social reforms that the SPD would not support. His backers underlined his political experience that would serve the party well also in coalition negotiations with the CDU/CSU. Unlike his rival, Lambsdorff made it clear that he did not want a seat in the cabinet which he had left when indicted in connection with the Flick affair. The party continued to express solidarity with him during his trial for the financing practices from which it had benefited, but his conviction for aiding and abetting tax evasion in this matter was a lingering embarrassment that undoubtedly cost him the votes of some fastidious delegates. Despite his long-standing support of civil libertarian positions, some Liberals also found Lambsdorff to be too closely identified with the party's right wing. He countered this impression by expressing interest in such matters as environmental protection and developing more contacts with people on the center-left in West German politics, including the leading Social Democrat, Oskar Lafontaine. His most important symbolic initiative was perhaps to nominate Cornelia Schmalz-Jacobsen as his candidate for general secretary of the party well in advance of the convention. She was clearly identified with the FDP's left wing and would replace Helmut Haussmann in the leading party position when he moved into the cabinet chair left vacant by Bangemann.

Irmgard Adam-Schwaetzer was also located somewhat to the left of Lambsdorff, but she was not a "social liberal," having been the only one of eight women in the parliamentary party to support the coalition switch in 1982. Thereafter she had served first as the FDP's general secretary and then as party treasurer before becoming junior minister (*Staatsministerin*) at the Foreign Office under Genscher. She was thought to be more accessible and consensual in style than Lambsdorff, but some missed in her the veteran's skill and experience. Her supporters suggested that the FDP should take the risk of turning to a new and younger leader. They also emphasized that the FDP would become more visible and attractive to many voters by being the first of the established parties to be chaired by a woman.

In the end, Lambsdorff was elected in a relatively close race (he won 211 votes to his rival's 187). He immediately nominated Adam-Schwaetzer as his first deputy, and she received the overwhelming endorsement of the convention (355 votes). Schmalz-Jacobsen was duly elected general secretary and there were additional changes in the party's presidium and national executive that represented its whole left-right spectrum. The FDP was clearly determined to appear united behind its new leadership before facing several difficult electoral tests in 1989.

5. Programmatic Renewals and Ambiguities

Within two years after joining Willy Brandt's SPD in the reform coalition of 1969, the FDP announced its commitment to social liberalism in the Freiburg Theses. Although the programmatic statement had little policy import, it filled a symbolic need by giving the FDP a progressive image that in turn attracted new members and supporters. It is hardly surprising that the party sought to mend its battered profile after the second coalition change by once again casting about for a programmatic vision.

There has been no paucity of advice on where the party should position itself. One well-meaning suggestion argues that the FDP should abandon all pretense of becoming a programmatic party and accept instead its proper role as "safety valve" (*Ventil*) in the political system. As such, it would continue to provide an important outlet for voters who become disenchanted with one of the major parties without wanting to support the other. Carried to its logical extreme, such a strategy would result in the FDP becoming primarily a stopover for electoral migrants. Even though the party in some ways resembles a kind of institutionalized "floating vote," it is not likely to accept the *Ventil* function as its raison d'être. If nothing else, such an openly mercantile relationship to the voters could invite electoral disaster. Indeed, it can be argued that the party's problems stem in large part from having too little of a recognizable and dependable political position over and above its coalition commitment.

Whereas the "safety valve" function would apparently require the FDP to shift orientation to accommodate changing groups of political itinerants, another suggestion recommends that the party should finally accept its political future as that of an "economic party" (*Wirtschaftspartei*), as in the Weimar Republic, representing business and industrial interests. This is how the FDP was widely perceived until its opening to the left in the 1960s, and it is a role that would require abandoning any dabbling with the kind of mild social reforms that are still dear to its left wing. Some proponents of the business course suggest that the FDP is only harming itself by continuing to become entangled with social causes or concerns about civil rights for minorities that have little attraction for most of its potential old middle class (*Mittelstand*) clientele.

But the role of *Wirtschaftspartei*, while undoubtedly an important policy function of the FDP, is not going to suffice for the small party's self-image. Despite considerable changes in the social and political composition of the FDP, it is remarkable how a civil libertarian tendency has been able to maintain itself in the more active and leading elements of West Germany's Liberals. Throughout the party one still encounters many members who have been attracted to the FDP, and stayed with it, because they continue to view it as a needed "progressive" or "emancipatory" force in West German politics. As the coalition change ceased to be a topic of dispute, the party has become more tolerant of the remaining adherents of left liberal positions. Lambsdorff is in agreement with other party leaders and members that the FDP must have broader and more appealing image than that of a political action committee on behalf of the material interests of the *Mittelstand*. So the party continues to espouse some decidedly postmaterial concerns as well, although an outsider is struck by the tendency to paper over their potential conflict with the productivity orientation of the economic wing. But political programs are rarely marked by a willingness to recognize that desirable goals may be mutually incompatible or at least involve difficult trade-offs.

In recent years, Liberal party conferences have polished up the FDP's liberal credentials on civil rights matters, such as the laws on demonstrations, political asylum, the residence rights of foreign workers, the right to choice on abortion, and so on. These are issues on which the FDP also makes its voice heard in the cabinet, where it counteracts the statist-conservative positions of the CDU/CSU's right wing. In foreign affairs, Hans-Dietrich Genscher represents continuity in the policy of détente and concern for third world development. Conservative attacks on him by sometime "hardliners" in the CSU seem only to have increased his popularity. They also serve the unintended consequence of giving the FDP some needed publicity by reminding voters of its claim to be the "liberal corrective" in government. The death in October 1988 of Franz Josef

Strauss, the controversial leader of the CSU, deprived the Free Democrats of an opponent whose spirited denunciations probably helped far more than harmed the Liberals. The CSU can be counted upon to bring forth other vituperative critics of the Liberals, but none is likely to command the rhetorical powers of this remarkable Bavarian politician whose problems with the FDP dated back a quarter of a century, to the *Spiegel* affair of 1962.

THE LIBERAL MANIFESTO

In February 1985, a little over two years after the latest coalition change, the FDP adopted a new program that presents the party as a future-oriented and problem-solving force on behalf of individualism in an increasing technical and bureaucratic society. The Liberal Manifesto addresses "a society in transition (*Umbruch*)." It announces that the country stands before great challenges, created by a "third industrial revolution that opens the way into the information society of the future." Postindustrial visions abound, both as a promise for expanded choice and freedom for the individual, and as a potential threat if the individual should be subordinated to the new technical and organizational powers. Written at a time when West Germany was passing through a widely reported mood of *angst* of the future, the program presented the Liberal position as optimistic and progressive, based upon trust in the ability and willingness of human beings to build a "free, peaceful and socially just world."

The Liberal Manifesto refers approvingly to the Freiburg Theses by way of a special insertion added to the ratifying party conference. But it is hardly a continuation of the concerns expressed in the program of "social liberalism" only fourteen years earlier. Indeed, the program could be said to reflect a frequently heard view that echoes Ralf Dahrendorf's proclamation of "the end of the social democratic century." If the Freiburg Theses had been the party's latter-day link to such a century, then the Liberal Manifesto could be seen as a quick shortcut for the Free Democrats into the next one. But that would ascribe far too much policy importance to each of the two programs, whose main functions were to provide a symbol of political reintegration in the small party after the disarray that accompanied each of the coalition changes.

All the same, the language of the Liberal Manifesto provides an instructive contrast to the Freiburg Theses. The latter essentially subscribed to a "positive" conception of liberty in a party that had previously been associated with considerable passivity on societal questions. They emphasized the social character of the individual and envisioned an important role for politics and the state in creating a free, democratic, and just society. In particular, the Theses addressed the need to create the economic preconditions for individual freedom and to curb undue exercises of private economic power. The Liberal Manifesto, on the other hand, is concerned primarily with "negative" liberty, that is, the need to defend the individual's "freedom from" enslavement by such forces as bureaucratization, regimentation, paternalism, and social prejudices. It explicitly confronts a politics that seeks "salvation only through the state," whether it takes the form of "conservative, socialist, or green" promotions of order and planning.

But the Liberal Manifesto is not a libertarian tract. Apart from the prefunctory nod to the social concerns of Freiburg Theses, it picks up a number of issues that require some kind of creative social intervention: For example, the need for societal and environmental protection from irresponsible economic development, the desirability of increased opportunities for shared deliberation and decision-making (*Mitsprache und Mitwirkung*), the possibility of promoting bureaucratic dismantlement through initiatives for decentralization, and the need to create opportunities for the individual's development of meaningful social ties in a world dominated by large and anonymous organizations. It is striking, however, that the Liberal Manifesto presents the competitive private market economy, properly contained, as a source of solutions. In the Freiburg Theses, the emphasis was on the social costs of such an economy's recognized capacity to produce efficiently.

The changed political metaphors in socioeconomic questions do reflect important policy shifts in the FDP. More than any other parliamentary party, the FDP promotes the market economy and the ideal of a social order based on individual achievement. There is inevitably a conflict with organized labor in many policy areas, such as the party's opposition to a shortened workweek without paycuts or its advocacy of more flexible wage rates and the loosening of the restrictive store-closing hours in West Germany. The self-achievement values spill over into other policy areas as well. In school and university policy, for example, the FDP used to be in the vanguard of the progressive reforms made in the name of equal opportunity during the 1960s and early 1970s. Today, FDP leaders are again in the forefront of a reform movement, but now it is one that advocates both private and elitist alternatives in higher education. They argue in favor of institutional reforms that would be designed to identify and give advanced technical or scientific training to outstanding students in order to fill the country's growing needs in this area, where some perceive a creeping technological gap.

CONCLUSION

The left wing of the FDP would like their party to be a source of "creative unrest" in a changing society, distinguishing it from the social inertia and bureaucratic proclivities associated with the Christian and Social Democrats, respectively. Its pendant on the right focuses more on the economic priorities associated with modern capitalism. There is good reason to believe that the small party can continue to hold both tendencies together, despite their intermittent conflicts over strategy and policy priorities. Lambsdorff's first moves as new party leader were designed to placate Liberals who suspected him of being too exclusively identified with the business wing of the party.

The FDP's self-presentation as representative of "organized political liberalism" is clearly an idealized view of reality which ignores the considerable "structural opportunism" that has always been an important component of the party's political behavior. However, it can be plausibly argued that its "corrective" function, primarily within the government but occasionally also in the opposition, has served repeatedly to promote essentially liberal goals and values in a society that historically has placed relatively little value on individualism, spontaneity, choice, and the effective control of governmental power. Here, it would appear, the FDP has made its most important liberal contributions to West German politics.

It is still true that the FDP lives dangerously and cannot expect to overhaul itself as a political party in the near-future. Most of its meager resources will continue to be committed to the ongoing "holding operation" that has become a way of political survival for Liberals. It is possible that the FDP, under a determined direction by Lambsdorff, may develop more distinctive positions and insist on greater autonomy as a cabinet member than previous leaders have thought advisable. Such a course would carry with it considerable risks but also some opportunities. Should the Liberals ever fail the electoral test for the Bundestag, despite some recent years of improved standing in the polls and the resort to such survival devices as the second-vote strategy, they may yet join the other now largely forgotten parties that once had their chance to "strut and fret" upon the political stage in West Germany.

Yet the FDP has always been different from such "splinter paraties," and its disappearance would have significant consequences for both the balance of power and the direction of policy in Bonn. If history is any guide, it would be premature to write an obituary on this vulnerable but strategically placed "third" force. While it is also too early to expect yet another transfer of power engineered by the FDP, the small party no longer seems locked into the "bourgeois camp" that for a short while after the coalition switch in 1982 seemed to have become its final political address. The reach of the FDP's positional influence will continue to be governed by political circumstances it normally cannot control. At this point, for example, the possibility of another coalition realignment in Bonn would seem to depend far more on changes in the SPD than in the FDP. But whatever form the next *Machtwechsel* takes and however it comes about, it does not seem unlikely that the Free Democrats will continue "hanging on" and "muddling through" in a way that, on the whole, contributes to the remarkable stability, moderation, and dynamism that characterizes government and politics in the Federal Republic.

NOTES

1. An earlier and much shorter version of this article appeared in *German Politics and Society*, no. 14 (June 1988): 19 ff.
2. The argument predates Karl-Hermann Flach, but he gave it a fuller and more sophisticated development than anyone before him. For an early exposition, see Flach's pamphlet, *Dritte Kraft. Der Kampf gegen Macht-missbrauch in der Demokratie* (Bonn: FDP, 1957). An updated version of the thesis is found in *Liberale Standpunkte 1978*, pt. 2, "Die Rolle der Liberalen," reprinted in Günter Verheugen, ed., *Das Programm der Liberalen* (Baden-Baden: Nomos, 1979).
3. Christian Søe, "The Free Democratic Party," in H. G. Peter Wallach and George K. Romoser, eds., *West German Politics in the Mid-Eighties* (New York: Praeger, 1985), 161. The article was completed right after the FDP's defeat in the elections to the European Parliament in June 1984.
4. See the first chapter in Hans Vorländer, ed., *Verfall oder Renaissance des Liberalismus?* (Munich: Olzog Verlag, 1987), 9–11.
5. R.M., "Genscher—Garant eines Kurses der Mitte," in *Neue Zürcher Zeitung*, 5 March 1988, 5. A similar conclusion is drawn by Elizabeth Pond, "Genscher—Hero or Villain?," in *The Christian Science Monitor*, 1 April 1988.
6. See the EMNID polls reported by *Der Spiegel*, 25 April 1988, 29, according to which just over 50 percent of the supporters of the SPD in April 1988 preferred an alliance with the FDP as compared with 26 percent who would rather have the SPD enter a coalition with the Greens.

16

THE GREENS: FROM YESTERDAY
TO TOMORROW

William E. Paterson

Since their formation in 1980, the Greens have been and remain an unpredictable element in the political and social life of the Federal Republic. There has been a very heated academic and political controversy on both the emergence and future prospects of the Greens. Within the Greens themselves there are deep divisions on the future goals of the party. This debate is at its most intense in discussion of the desirability or not of coalition with the SPD, the major left-wing party in the Federal Republic and a party of which most leading Greens were at one time members.

This chapter will focus on three main areas. In the first section six explanations of the Greens' emergence and their implications for the Greens' survivability will be analyzed. This is followed by a detailed analysis of the theory and practice of Green ideas on party democracy, while the final section will look at the impact of the Greens on the West German political system.

THE FORMATION OF THE GREENS

The decision to found the Green Party in January 1980 was the culmination of years of extraparliamentary activity by a whole range of groups articulating the various issues that together make up "the new policies."[1]

The major breakthrough at the federal level had taken place in 1979. The pool of potential support had been greatly increased by the dramatic growth in the peace movement attendant upon the adoption by NATO of the dual track resolution which envisaged the large-scale stationing on German soil of Cruise and Pershing missiles should the Soviets fail to withdraw their SS20s from Eastern Europe. A more immediate incentive was provided by the imminence of the first direct election to the European Parliament in 1979. Participation in the election held out the promise of enough financial support to maintain a permanent organizational infrastructure, since any party competing in the election would receive DM 3.50 from state subsidies for every vote it gained. A federal congress of the Greens was held in Frankfurt in March 1979 at which it was agreed to launch a protoparty, the "Sonstige Politische Vereinigung; Die Grünen." In order to conform with West German electoral law the party elected an executive committee, but no agreement was reached on an electoral program or a formal organizational framework.

The SPV achieved 3.2 percent in the European election and at a conference in Karlsruhe in January 1980 a decision to form a Green Party was taken by over 90 percent of the delegates, though it took a further conference at Saarbrücken in March 1980 to adopt an agreed formula. During these discussions the Left, who argued in favor of a party that was both ecological and adopted a generally left-wing stance on other issues, triumphed and the final program clearly placed the Greens to the left of the SPD on the party spectrum. This outcome made the position of conservative environmentalists like Herbert Gruhl, an ex-CDU MdB who had been joint chairman of the SPV executive, impossible and they withdrew. Henceforward the Greens were a party to the left of the SPD, both in their own perceptions and those of the West German electorate in general (see Table 16.1).

Electoral Consolidation

The CDU/CSU's choice of Franz Josef Strauss as chancellor candidate in the Green's first federal election in 1980 squeezed the Green vote as many potential Green voters switched their support to the SPD to help prevent a victory for Strauss. By 1983 the Greens had secured representation in a number of Länder and in the federal election they polled 5.6 percent of the votes which gave them 27

Table 16.1

Ideological Self-Assessment of Supporters of the Greens and the
Established Parties (in percent)

	CDU/CSU	SPD	FDP	Greens
Left	0.2	4.3	1.2	8.8
Center-left	3.5	30.9	11.6	37.9
Center	35.5	49.1	61.2	38.3
Center-right	42.8	11.8	17.3	11.4
Right	18.0	3.9	8.7	3.6
Total	100	100	100	100

Source: *Der Spiegel,* no. 45, 1984.

seats in the Bundestag. In 1987 the Greens were able to increase
their share of the vote to 8.3 percent and secure 42 seats in the
Bundestag.

In attaining these results the Greens have had the support of a
relatively stable electorate. Its major features are its generational
character (under thirty-five), high level of formal education, predominantly urban location, and relatively weak integration into the
rest of society. Its hard-core electorate of consistent voters is estimated to be 6 percent and in common with other highly educated
sections of the population their turnout is normally very high.

Explanations

The formation and electoral consolidation of the Greens has been
the subject of a great deal of academic attention and six broad
explanations have been advanced.

Explanation 1: Historical German Idealization of Nature. A first
explanation which has been especially influential at the level of
serious journalism is to point to historical continuity. A rejection of
industrial and materialist values and practice and an idealization of
natural values has been an important feature of German life since
the advent of the romantic movement. It has made an especial
appeal to youth, whether in the ideas of the Wandervögel (German
youth movement) or of the early supporters of the NSDAP. In this
argument, it is the apparent unequivocal triumph of materialist

values in the Federal Republic that looks unusual and a reversion at some point was only to be expected.

Explanation 2: Alienation of Young SPD Left. A second explanation relates the emergence of the Greens to the reduced integrative capacity of the SPD after Schmidt took over from Brandt as chancellor in May 1974.[2] Many members of the APO (Extraparliamentary Opposition) had been attracted into the SPD after 1969 by Willy Brandt's program of "daring more democracy." Brandt had made a conscious effort to respond to their participatory drive in the various attempts at writing a party program for the eighties, but they were immediately alienated by three aspects of Schmidt's chancellorship. Under Schmidt's leadership, the federal government launched a massive program for the construction of nuclear power plants in order to make West Germany less dependent on external energy sources, where cost had risen very steeply during the oil price shock of 1973. In mobilizing opposition to the construction of these plants the Left, inside and outside the SPD, found that they could attract much wider strata of the electorate in affected areas than they had been able to do on previous issues.

The experience and ideas of the student movement had imbued many younger members of the SPD after 1969 with the wish to move the SPD in a more participatory direction. Their attempts to transform this intention into practice met with very limited success. The chief instrument they envisaged was the so-called imperative mandate by which parliamentary representatives would be bound by the instructions they were given by their local party institutions. This view ran into very strong opposition from the parliamentary elite who successfully appealed to the presumptions in favor of the representative principle contained in the Basic Law.

During this period the JSOs or Young Socialists, the party youth section, acted as a focus for these demands. After Helmut Schmidt's advent to power they suffered a double loss of influence. Schmidt was much less prepared than Brandt to take account of party opinion in the formulation of his policies and he was least inclined to take account of the dimension of party opinion represented by the Young Socialists. His primary orientation was toward maintaining West Germany's economic competitiveness and in SPD terms this implied an accommodation with the trade unionists rather than the Young Socialist wings of the party.

A final reason for the alienation of the younger left-wing members of the SPD during the early years of the Schmidt chancellorship was the failure of the government to accept the real importance of ecological issues. There were three principal reasons for this. First, the junior coalition partner, the FDP, has always seen itself as the most "industry-friendly" party. The FDP held the two most important ministries in relation to environmental policy, those of economics and the interior. The desire of Gerhart Baum, the interior minister, whose ministry was responsible for nearly all environmental regulation, and some of his leading civil servants to institute ambitious reforms was checked by the Economics Ministry which sees itself as an attorney for German industry. Helmut Schmidt, the federal chancellor from 1974 to 1982, was as close to industry as is possible for an SPD chancellor. His preferences, whether in relation to expansion of the provision of nuclear energy or environmental regulation of industry, were determined by considerations of economic rationality rather than by a desire to improve the quality of life in a wider sense. This position was buttressed by a close relationship with the trade union movement expressed inter alia in a record number of leading trade unionists holding ministerial portfolios in the first Schmidt cabinet. Although relations with the trade union leadership soured as unemployment climbed, they remained allies in opposition to any environmental measures which would seriously affect the competitiveness of German industry. In a recent interview, Albrecht Müller, one of Schmidt's closest confidants and former head of the planning division in the Chancellor's Office, said Schmidt's opposition to environmental regulation of the chemical industry rested on his talks with top management and senior union men at Bayer.[3]

Explanation 3: The New Social Movements. The alienation of many of the younger members of the SPD Left interacted with an explosive expansion of citizen action and new social movements in the seventies. Most of the initial groups were devoted to environmental issues and by 1980 over a thousand such groups were registered with the Umweltbundesamt (Federal Environmental Office) in Ber-

Table 16.2
Involvement of Different Party Supporters in the New Social
Movements

	CDU/CSU	SPD	FDP	Greens
Ecology movement:				
Active supporters	12	22	21	68
Opponents	50	31	43	7
Antinuclear movement:				
Active supporters	11	24	18	64
Opponents	56	31	43	7
Peace movement				
Active supporters	26	42	30	62
Opponents	35	21	31	5

Source: Ferdinand Müller-Rommel, "Die Grünen im Lichte von neuesten Ergebnissen der Wahl-
forschung," in T. Kluge, ed., *Grüne Politik* (Frankfurt am Main: Fischer, 1984), 135.

lin. The environmental groups were joined later by feminist groups
and other groups. After 1978 there was also a massive expansion in
the peace movement which became the largest single group. Some
of these groups were organized at federal level but most were locally
based.

These new groups reflected a disenchantment with established
political parties, especially the SPD, and their capacity to articulate
these issues. However, by the late seventies doubts about the ability
of these movements to change the political agenda without electoral
participation were strong enough to lead to the formation of the
protoparty, but there was an equally strong insistence that this implied no diminution in the role of extraparliamentary opposition
and the new social movements. The Greens were simply to be another leg of the new social movements. Tensions have sometimes
arisen between the new social movements and the Greens' *Fraktion*
on one issue or another, for example the peace movement has never
accepted the sole prerogative of the Greens to speak for it in the
Bundestag, but the overlap between movements and party is very
high (see Table 16.2).

Explanation 4: Value Shift. An important explanation locates the
emergence of the Greens in differences in values between political

generation and the adoption by the third postwar generation of new values. Ronald Inglehart suggested in his influential book, *The Silent Revolution*,[4] that younger electors in Western societies were, as a result of long periods of prosperity and greater access to higher education, increasingly likely to be moved by postmaterial and quality-of-life issues. Baker, Dalton, and Hildebrandt in *Germany Transformed* wrote of a "new politics" dimension based on Inglehart's postmaterialist index.[5] This concern for quality-of-life issues was buttressed by a high level of distrust in established parties and some degree of distance to established social institutions. These insights have been exhaustively discussed by younger German political scientists, notably Wilhelm Bürklin and Ferdinand Müller-Rommel.[6]

Explanation 5: Changes in the Labor Market. The labor market explanation concentrates not on the prosperity of the Federal Republic as is implied in the new politics/sunshine politics approach, but on the impact of developments in the labor market on the younger, academically educated generation. Until the late seventies, over 80 percent of university graduates went into the public service but

By the end of the 1970s, this situation has drastically changed.—First, the two oil-price crises of 1974 and 1979 as well as the concomitant economic decline destroyed the financial basis for the social-liberal reform policy. The consequence was severe cuts in the civil service. No new job opportunities were forthcoming in the civil service and industry/commerce did not increase their share of university graduates.

The commerce graduate employment situation was worsened by generally higher unemployment rates. Decreased job opportunities for academic jobseekers were reinforced in the late seventies by two factors:

a) as a consequence of the educational reforms drastically increasing numbers of each age studied at university;
b) in the 1970s, the post-war baby boom generations went to the universities and onto the labor market.

Politically, the worsened economic situation was paralleled by a withdrawal from the cost intensive social-liberal reforms. This change from idealistic to pragmatically-oriented policies was reflected in the change in the chancellorship from Willy Brandt to Helmut Schmidt.[7]

These changed conditions weakened the trust of those in the affected generational groups in the established system and moved them to support those new political aims and values, which were at odds with the established economic and pragmatic ideology.

Explanation 6: System-Structural Explanations. The emergence and consolidation of the Greens as a political party were also aided by two features of the electoral arrangements. The relatively low threshold of representation (5 percent) and the proportional basis of the West German electoral system make the successful representation of a small party much easier than in a first-past-the-post system like Britain's, where the costs of entry are very daunting indeed.

More importantly, the state subsidies for political parties which are extended in the interests of equity to parties which fail to surmount the 5-percent threshold, constitute a very important incentive to enter the electoral game. These subsidies (now DM 5 per voter) make it possible not only to found and maintain a party like the Greens but also to contribute toward the maintenance of extra-parliamentary activities.

Are the Greens Here to Stay?

It is extremely difficult to assign precise weightings to each of these explanations and they are clearly to quite a large extent complementary. However, they do tend to give different answers to the question of the long-term survival of the Greens.

The historical parallels (Wandervögel and so forth) are too imprecise and the fit of circumstances is not close enough to allow us to draw any very useful inferences about the survivability of the Greens. The second explanation, which relates the emergence of the Greens to the unresponsiveness of the SPD to new issues and Schmidt's backing for the expansion of a nuclear power program and the modernisation of theater nuclear weapons, would suggest that the Greens are not here to stay. In recent years, especially since it entered opposition in 1982, the SPD has reversed its policies on theater nuclear weapons and, since Chernobyl, on nuclear energy. On many other environmental issues it now takes a position much closer to that of the Greens than to its own previous policies, a development known as *Themenklau* (issue theft). In any case the saliency of the missiles issue has been much reduced by the INF

Treaty, though its importance would be revived by a modernization of battlefield nuclear weapons. "The shorter the range the deader the German," remarked Volker Rühe, a leading member of the younger Christian Democrats. The manifold links between the Greens and the new social movements mean that the declining vitality of the new social movements also weakens the Greens.

The labor market argument would also seem to raise questions about the long-term role of the Greens. The changing demographic character of the population of the Federal Republic is expected to greatly improve the prospects, especially for new entrants, in the labor market in the 1990s. This will probably still leave the case of those who were excluded from public service jobs in the seventies and eighties but, other things being equal, it implies a relatively undynamic future for the Greens.

The value change shift is central to the concept of political generations. The key question here is whether the change is of a long-term secular character or whether it is an epiphenomenon found in one generation. Available evidence on this dimension appears not unfavorable to the Greens. The salience of environmental issues remained very high in the 1987 election. The Greens also managed in 1987 to increase their level of support among first-time voters (13.9 percent in 1983; 15.5 percent in 1987).

H.-J. Veen has recently suggested that a key element in sustaining the Greens electorally is the degree to which the Greens have become a milieu party.[8] In that sense the Greens are a reversion to the style of party politics very familiar in Germany before the dominance of the *Volkspartei* (catch-all) model. The two most successful democratic parties in the Imperial regime and in the Weimar, the Catholic Center Party and the German Social Democratic Party, were both "milieux" parties, that is, they represented and were sustained by the particular milieux of the Catholic church and the labour movement. Clearly, the milieu which supports the Greens lacks, except in some university cities, the dense, geographically concentrated character of the traditional milieux like the Ruhr for the SPD and some Catholic areas for the CDU/CSU, but nevertheless the existence of a network of alternative social and economic institutions does seem to help sustain the Greens electorally and in a wider sense to "negatively integrate" into West German society.

The balance of the above explanations would seem to indicate a relatively secure electoral niche for the Greens and the widely aired doubts about the future of the Greens in recent months relate less to its electoral future and more to the incessant clash between the "Realos," the pragmatic wing of the Greens and the "Fundis" or fundamentalists.

The conflicts between these wings reflect opposing orientations toward political activity and the party political system. The realists, whilst not denying the importance of extraparliamentary activity, accord a much higher place to parliamentary activity. They are interested, where possible, in cooperation with the SPD to achieve the adoption of their political goals and do not exclude the possibility of coalition with the SPD, at least at Land level.

The fundamentalists are much less reconciled to the importance of the parliamentary level. They argue that the real centers of power in the Federal Republic lie outside the Bundestag and the Länder parliaments in the centers of economic power and the bureaucracy. Accordingly, compromises to achieve parliamentary victories should be avoided since they rest on the illusion that Parliament itself is the site of the decisive encounters in an advanced industrial society. The fundamentalists are opposed to any arrangement with the SPD, arguing that since the SPD's long-term strategy must be to absorb the Greens (drain the Green marshes), the Greens should not help the SPD to achieve this aim.

The boundary between these positions is not fixed and immutable and individuals can move from one position to another. The open nature of Green decision-making bodies moreover often means that participation in conferences and meetings changes fairly frequently. This results, not surprisingly, in the balance between the two positions changing from conference to conference.

The majority of party members have normally been Realos. The Realos have also normally been strong in the *Bundestagsfraktion*. The Fundis have predominated in areas such as Hamburg and in the fundamentalist executive. The tensions between the federal executive and the *Bundestagsfraktion* and between the Realos and the Fundis, which had been a feature of the 1983–1987 legislative period, have grown much more intense since the election success of 1987. The federal executive has become even more identified with the "Fundi" position. Jutta Ditfurth, Regina Michalik, and Christian Schmidt, who were elected as spokespersons for the federal executive in May 1987, are all well-known Fundis.

The new *Bundestagsfraktion* is much more evenly balanced. The Realo position is well represented. Not surprisingly, it contains many more members who place a great deal of emphasis on the parliamentary dimension. One-quarter (11/44) of its members are serving for the second time. They include Otto Schily, the most articulate and best-known Realo.

Relations between the two wings started to decline quite sharply in the spring of 1987. Two explanations suggest themselves. The first relates to the Fundis and their increased involvement in party life. This reflects at least in part the decline of the new social movements, especially the peace movement, once the missiles had actually been installed. On the other hand, the Realos were even keener to work with the SPD who were in a chastened mood after the Green's electoral success and who were in any case now much closer to the Greens on many issues than they had been at any point in the past.

Relations between the two wings deteriorated sharply in the autumn of 1987. The federal executive issued a bitter condemnation of statements inaccurately attributed to Otto Schily, Waltraud Schoppe, and Dietrich Wetzel on a visit to Israel at the end of October 1987. More significantly, Jutta Ditfurth's ambivalent response to the murder by demonstrators of two policemen at a demonstration in Frankfurt in November alarmed the Realos.

Throughout November and December a war of press interviews took place between the two wings, with a group around Antje Vollmer representing some kind of median position. Despite dire predictions of imminent collapse, and a contentious basic resolution of the *Fraktion* on 9 December excluding cooperation with the most militant groups, a truce was agreed at a joint meeting of the *Fraktion* and federal executive on 12 December 1987.

It seems fairly likely that this truce will hold. If the party divided, it is quite unlikely that either of the two new parties would surmount the 5-percent threshold. This would be a clear loss to the Realos since they believe that something can be achieved at a parliamentary level. The financial dependence of the Greens on state electoral subsidies and the contributions of MdBs to Ecofunds for ecological activism by citizen initiative groups, mean that the Fundis also have an important stake in parliamentary representation.

The real danger for the Greens is not so much a dramatic split as a deadening combination of inconsistency and immobilism. The changing composition of party meetings leads to inconsistent positions and over time to immobilism as a victory for the Fundis is quickly counterbalanced by one for the Realos and vice versa. In the long run there is always the danger that this immobilism will lead to the desertion to the SPD of some leading Realos like Otto Schily and the onset of a downward electoral spiral.

THE ATTEMPT TO REALIZE PARTY DEMOCRACY

Their enthusiasm for participation and the negative experience of many of the founder members in the SPD meant that the Greens were determined to replace the pyramidal top-down, Bonn-centred model characteristic of the established political parties by structures based on the rights of ordinary local party members at the party base (*Basisdemokratie*). They were also concerned to assert the legitimacy of extraparliamentary activity, an aim which seems to the established parties to represent a failure to learn from the collapse of Weimar.

The structures devised by the Greens are novel and were constructed to realize three aims: of preventing the emergence of a professional class of politicians and functionaries, of encouraging participation, and of drastically reducing the autonomy of the parliamentary elite. The desire to inhibit the emergence of a class of professional politicians is reflected in a number of provisions. Office holding in the party is unpaid beneath the federal level. Parliamentary representatives were expected only to draw the salary of a skilled worker, with the considerable residue to be paid into party funds during their tenure of office. They were also expected to "rotate" and make way for a designated successor (*Nachrücker*) at the midway point in a legislative session.

Participation was to be encouraged by very loose membership structures. All meetings were in principle open and all party members could participate in party conferences. The holding of multiple party office, which is very widespread in other parties, was expressly forbidden.

The autonomy of the parliamentary elite was to be constrained in a number of ways. Rotation was designed to permanently refresh the parliamentary elite from the party base and the new social movements. The key concept, designed to reduce the autonomy of the parliamentary elite, was the imperative mandate, a favorite idea of the Left in the SPD in the 1970s, which envisaged that MdBs should be bound by instruction from the local party that had sent them to the legislature.

The Practice

The Greens' organizational principles represent a very optimistic reading of human nature and putting them into practice has proved problematic. Rotation, which was the principal device to prevent the emergence of a class of professional politicians, proved extremely problematic. It proved to be extremely controversial, though all but Petra Kelly and Gert Bastian, who resigned and rejoined the Greens, were eventually rotated in the Bundestag session 1983–1987. The experience of the Greens was, however, that once rotated MdBs rarely rejoined the extraparliamentary struggle but remained active, awaiting the chance to return to the parliamentary stage, for example Joschka Fischer, a notably reluctant rotatee, became a driving force to form a coalition between the Greens and the SPD in Hessen. The practice of both members and their designated successors in the *Fraktion* simultaneously was not a happy one and led to intense rivalries.

Rotation has now been dropped at the federal level, although there is an expectation that members will not serve more than one term without a break. Eleven of the forty-four members in 1987 were former members of the Bundestag. In some areas like Frankfurt rotation is still encouraged, in others it is ignored. Perhaps even more revealingly, the Greens in North Rhine-Westphalia adopted the principle of paying some members of the Green executive in summer 1987.

Participation is not strikingly higher in the Greens. The loose

Table 16.3
Degree of Organization of Parties in West Germany

In the country as a whole: Party	Voters	Members	Ratio	%
Greens	2,167,431	25,000	87:1	1.2
SPD	14,865,807	950,000	16:1	6.4
CDU	14,857,680	734,082	20:1	4.9
CSU	4,140,865	182,665	23:1	4.4
FDP	2,706,942	78,763	34:1	2.9
Greens in the individual states: State	Voters	Members	Ratio	%
Schleswig-Holstein	91,098	1,200	76:1	1.3
Hamburg	90,174	780	116:1	0.9
Lower Saxony	278,587	3,600	77:1	1.3
Bremen	44,576	273	163:1	0.6
North Rhine-Westphalia	581,350	5,700	102:1	1.0
Hessen	218,898	2,800	78:1	1.3
Rheinland-Pfalz	113,185	1,300	87:1	1.1
Baden-Württemberg	389,863	4,500	87:1	1.2
Bavaria	323,901	5,400	60:1	1.7
Saarland	35,789	500	72:1	1.4
West Berlin	90,653	2,800	32:1	3.1

Source: Helmut Fogt, "Basisdemokratie oder Herrschaft der Aktivisten," *Politische Vierteljahresschrift* 1 (1985): 105.
Note: Figures are based on second votes in the 1983 federal election and the West Berlin election of May 1981. Membership figures for the Greens are according to Green Party statistics for April–September 1983.

structures place little premium on joining and the membership ratio is by far the lowest of the parties represented in the Bundestag (see table 16.3). Surveys also indicate that the active membership is not significantly higher than in other parties. The problem of apathy in the participatory party is illustrated by Kolinsky. In 1982, the Hesse Land Congress to formulate the election program was attended by only 80 of the 2,500 members; moreover ten of those were members of the Land executive.[9] The major success of the Greens in terms of participation is the much higher participation by women in the Greens at all levels including the *Bundestagsfraktion.*

For the second half of the 1983–1987 legislative session the Bun-

destagsfraktion was run by six women—the so-called *Feminat*. In the present Fraktion leadership (1988) women hold two-thirds of the positions. In December 1986 the Hamburg Greens were conspicuously successful in the Land election with an all-female slate.

The attempt to reduce the autonomy of the parliamentary elite has largely failed. The imperative mandate was soon ignored, because, while apparently binding MdBs to instructions from the local level, it was quickly perceived that the heterogeneous nature of the Greens would mean that the instructions would conflict and that the *Fraktion* would then be either *handlungsunfähig* (unable to act) or it would simply ignore them. In any case the very loose conditions for party membership inevitably means that the party base of activists is subject to very large fluctuations which clearly militate against its pursuing a consistent policy of imposing its wishes on its parliamentary representatives. The federal executive has been in fairly consistent conflict with the *Fraktion* but has little or no success in curbing the autonomy of the *Fraktion*. If anything, the autonomy and weight of the *Fraktion* has actually increased over the period since it came into being. Of course, this is partly simply what one would expect in a party in which resources and paid jobs are concentrated at the parliamentary level, but it also reflects the declining vitality of the new social movements. At both local and federal level the assumption was that representatives of these movements would help the *Fraktion* under considerable pressure and indeed through the rotation mechanism that there would be a continuous interchange of personnel. The new social movements, especially the peace movement, have lost a great deal of dynamism and they no longer put the continuous pressure on the *Fraktion* they once did. Moreover, although "rotation" did in fact take place in 1985, it did not achieve the intended effect which was that the "rotatees" would return to the extraparliamentary struggle and utilize their parliamentary experience to aid the party base of activists in keeping the *Fraktion* up to the mark. Nearly all the "rotatees" simply hung around waiting to get back into the Bundestag. One could in any case argue that there was an inherent tension between the principle of rotation and the desire to make the parliamentary elite more responsive. The fact that an MdB knew that, as a matter of principle, he or she would be rotated halfway through the legislative period, was likely to make him or her less and not more responsive to the grass roots.

Since their electoral success in January 1987 the Greens are showing some signs of moving closer in organizational form to the established parties. The most important manifestation of this is their intention to establish a parallel political foundation to the party. Such a foundation would correspond to the Friedrich Ebert Stiftung (SPD), Konrad Adenauer Stiftung (CDU), Hanns Seidel Stiftung (CSU), and Friedrich Naumann Stiftung (FDP). It would also be a radical break for the Greens who have consistently attacked the corruption they associate with the established political foundations. Otto Schily, in particular, during the hearings on the Flick scandal, was held by opinion well beyond the Greens to have made a number of very solid criticisms of the practices of the foundations. This decision was no doubt prompted by the unexpectedly lenient attitude of the Federal Constitutional Court toward the practices of the foundations (especially in relation to tax matters) in its 1986 ruling on party finance, but it does represent a major accommodation with one of the central elements of "the system."

The working practices of the *Fraktion* between 1983 and 1987 had shown similar signs of accommodation. The Greens had originally, like the nineteenth-century SPD, been against specialization because it would lead to a hierarchy and the consolidation of professional politicians, but, within the *Bundestagsfraktion*, a division of labor evolved, with MdBs being allocated responsibilities for specific areas. There were also indications of the emergence of a clientelistic relationship between the Greens in the Bundestag and Länder Parliaments and their constituencies, such as teachers and alternative economy projects.

Non-Greens have also derived a great deal of wry satisfaction, not to say *Schadenfreude* (glee) from continual reports that the Greens, like the conventional parties before them, are now experiencing considerable problems with their rebellious youth sections.

THE WIDER IMPACT OF THE GREENS IN GERMAN POLITICS

Despite being a minor party with a very low chance of participation in government, the impact of the Greens has been very considerable in terms of issues, practices and the party system.

Issues

The emergence and electoral consolidation of the Greens has had a major impact in the way in which the West German political system responds to environmental issues and to women's issues. The Greens clearly owed part of their electoral success to West German perceptions of environmental threat. Without the Greens, it is likely that the fit between this widespread concern on environmental questions and policy output would have been much looser, since all the other parties, including the SPD, would have continued to accept the priority of economic competitiveness on world markets. The success of the Greens in 1983 had a major impact on SPD policies in these areas between 1983 and 1987, since the SPD felt it had to compete for postmaterially minded voters.

The effects of this adaptation were most marked in SPD policy on chemicals and in the SPD's post-Chernobyl resolution to support phasing out nuclear power within ten years. Both these decisions were taken against considerable opposition from the affected union interests which solidarized with their respective industries. The ecological disasters of Chernobyl and the series of chemical spillages into the Rhine in late 1986 made support of the status quo by the federal government untenable. They are now proceeding extremely cautiously on nuclear energy and are processing a number of new and to the chemical industry very unwelcome restrictions on the production of chemicals.[10]

Women's Issues

Another central area of concern to the Greens has been women's issues.[11] This concern has been reflected in a number of different ways, beginning with the issue of participation of women in the party itself. Green candidates' lists for party and public office are ideally put together on the zip principle, that is, alternating female and male candidates and this was made official party policy at their party conference in May 1986. This policy has certainly increased the representation of women and women's representation increased from 35.7 percent of the 1983 *Bundestagsfraktion* to 57 percent after the 1987 federal election. This quota has sometimes been exceeded, as in the 1986 Hamburg elections where all the Green candidates were women.

In the membership as a whole every third member is female as compared with one in four in the established parties. The difference then lies less in the participation rate in the membership as a whole but in the inversion of the normal rule of West German politics that female participation decreases as one ascends the party pyramid toward Bonn. Female membership in the *Bundestagsfraktion* is strikingly higher than in the party as a whole and between 1985 and 1987 women held all the leadership positions in the *Fraktion* and at present occupy two-thirds of them.

This successful representation of women is all the more striking since the almost complete absence of paid posts, apart from the *Fraktion*, means participation is a very costly activity and this is generally held to affect women more adversely since they are more likely to have to pay the costs of looking after children while they involve themselves politically.

The striking success in terms of representation is less apparent as an electoral effect. Paradoxically the FDP, which made no concessions towards women's representation and the CDU/CSU which made minimal concessions, attracted more female than male voters whilst the SPD, who made considerable efforts to increase female representation and the Greens who made it a central organizational principle, both attracted more male than federal voters in the 1987 election. However, the Greens did make significant gains in a key target group of women between twenty-five and forty-five, with an unprecedented gain of 7 percent among thirty-five- to forty-five-year-old women. A potentially hopeful development for the Greens was the high degree of abstention of eighteen- to twenty-four-year-old women, based to some extent on distrust of the established system. This could well be a platform for Green gains among the succeeding generation of women voters.

Despite the very considerable representational advances and the more modest electoral advances on women's issues, the Greens have been much less successful in this area than in the environmental issue area in transforming the agenda of West German politics. There are two principal reasons for this relative lack of progress. Feminist issues have been much less electorally salient than environmental issues in the Federal Republic and this clearly means that there is much less of an incentive for *Themenklau* by the established parties in this area. There is also no real feminist equivalent in terms of size or organization to the peace and environmental movements which had a considerable impact not only on the Greens but on the SPD as well. The women's movement by contrast is fragmented, though its central pole is the magazine *Emma*, 80 percent of whose supporters in a public opinion survey supported the Greens.

Women's issues occupy a fairly prominent role in the activities of the *Bundestagsfraktion* and in the party outside Parliament where they are aggregated by the *Bundesarbeitsgemeinschaft—B.A.G. Frauen*. The parliamentary and nonparliamentary levels in the party have worked together fairly harmoniously and in 1986 produced a draft antidiscrimination law which, however, failed to attract much support from the established political parties. Paradoxically, the increased representation of women in the new *Fraktion* seems to have weakened the Greens' capacity to articulate women's issues by introducing a new disunity over the abortion issue. In the new *Fraktion* several members now oppose abortion and want to emphasize the role of mothers rather than the independent women as a role model. Tensions remain within the extraparliamentary movement, and the Greens and *Emma* were unable to combine in campaign against the restrictions on abortion placed by Article 218 of the German Criminal Code.

The Impact on the Party System

The major impact of the Greens on the West German party system has been to weaken the SPD. The degree to which the Greens would weaken the SPD was initially disguised by the selection by the CDU/CSU of Franz Josef Strauss as its chancellor candidate in 1980. This resulted in a very polarized electoral contest and the squeezing of the Green vote. However, in 1981 and 1982 the Greens advanced electorally largely at the expense of the SPD. This advance and the consequent electoral decline of the SPD strengthened the view of those in the FDP who had begun to think of bringing the coalition with the SPD to an end. It thus played a not insignificant role in the breakup of the SPD/FDP coalition in September–October 1982. In opposition since 1982 and under the constraint of electoral competition with the Greens, the SPD has moved its position leftward, especially on environmental and defense questions. The result is a reversion to a party system of two blocs and the disappearance of the readiness of all parties to enter coalitions with each other which characterized the West German party system between Bad Godesberg (1959) and 1982. The resulting blocs are of unequal strength since the CDU/CSU is clearly the strongest party and the favored coalition partner of the FDP.

The left bloc suffers from a double disadvantage. The SPD is perceptibly weaker than the CDU/CSU and the question of coalition or even tolerance arrangements between the SPD and the Greens has proved very contentious. Coalition with the SPD has been a major cause of division between the Realos and the Fundis in the Greens, but surveys consistently show that it is supported by a very clear majority of ordinary members of the Greens. The SPD position is also ambiguous. The SPD leadership has been split on this issue. Willy Brandt as party chairman talked of a "majority left of the center" after the Hessian election of September 1982 and appeared at various points to be advocating coalition. Moreover, the Greens and the SPD participated in the coalition in Hesse between December 1985 and spring 1987. However, in the two federal elections of March 1983 and January 1987 the chancellor candidates, Hans-Jochen Vogel and Johannes Rau, were at pains to play it down as an option. The conflicting statements of the SPD leadership on coalition reflect the diverging attitudes of party members. In a survey taken just before the federal election in 1987, 43 percent of SPD supporters favored coalition with the CDU/CSU while 43 percent favored coalition with the Greens.

This division of opinion in the SPD on the desirability of coalition with the Greens neatly reflects the divisions within the SPD between the postmaterialist perceptions of many younger members and the more traditional views of those members still connected through trade union membership with the productive economy.

The success of the Greens in the 1987 elections strengthened opinion in the SPD in favor of some accommodations with the Greens. Oskar Lafontaine, the minister-president of the Saar, criticized Rau's rejection of coalition with the Greens on the day after the election and in April 1987 after Brandt's premature retirement as party chairman and his replacement by Hans-Jochen Vogel. Lafontaine took Vogel's place as vice-chairman. The first draft of the SPD's new basic program indicated some greening of the SPD, but uncertainty persists as it has now been dropped.

Considerable problems remain in the way of a united Left. The Greens' rejection of NATO membership would make a federal coalition a very risky enterprise for the SPD. The collapse of the coalition in Hessen on the issue of the licensing of nuclear plants, despite the fact that the decision to license the plants was constitutionally a matter for the federal government, strengthened the convictions of those in the SPD who were skeptical about the possibilities of coalition. Lafontaine and others appear in early 1988 to be exploring the possibilities of future coalition with the FDP rather than the Greens.

CONCLUSION

The major conclusion of this chapter has been that the Greens are here to stay, at least in the medium-term. There now appears to be a reasonably secure electoral niche for the Greens in the Federal Republic and, despite intense dissention about orientations between the "fundamentalists" and the "realists," it has been our argument that a split in the foreseeable future looks unlikely.

Whilst the electoral achievement of the Greens was both undeniable and largely unforeseen, its status as an alternative model of political action to the established political parties and its continued ability to alter the agenda of West German politics looks much more questionable. The major elements in the alternative model have been analyzed in the section on party democracy. With the exception of the gender issue, the picture has been largely one of disappointment. The open participatory structures of the Greens have failed to significantly increase participation at the grass roots level, and the lack of formal chains of representation and authority and the concentration of resources at the parliamentary level have in practice concentrated participation and effective decisionmaking in the public sphere. Green party politics is dominated by a group of *Profis* (professionals) or "political entrepreneurs" who can mobilize the greatest personal resources in terms of acquisition of information, intellectual abilities, and rhetorical skills.[12] Clearly this professionalization of the Greens would be strengthened and its status as an alternative model reduced if they go ahead and establish a party foundation on the model of the other parties.

The argument of this chapter has been that Green innovations to institute party democracy, such as the imperative mandate and rotation, have in general not achieved the intended results and the parliamentary party has, as in other parties, continued to play the dominant role and in practice formulates day-to-day policy. The open participatory structures do continue to play a role, however. Macro political questions such as future coalition strategy and the programmatic orientation of the party are not, and cannot be, concentrated in the same way at the parliamentary level, given Green structures and philosophy. The open nature of the structures and the fluctuating nature of participation at party conferences means that any rational strategy to realize the policy goals of the new politics on the basis of continuity is ruled out. This must reduce the potential impact of the Greens.

If the Greens are here to stay and if, as we have argued, the parliamentary orientation (*Spielbein*, or mobile leg) has become more important, the Greens can plausibly be presented as strengthening West German democracy by integrating a section of West German society, otherwise alienated from the basic concensus, into the parliamentary game. That they are "negatively integrated" in the sense that they continue to oppose many of the dominant values of the system, is neither novel nor contradictory since it was on this basis of negative integration in the late nineteenth century that the SPD began its political journey to its present position as one of the three established parties of the Federal Republic.

NOTES

1. See S. Padgett and T. Burkett, *Political Parties and Elections in West Germany* (London: Hurst, 1986), 171–98.
2. See W. E. Paterson, "The German Social Democratic Party," in W. E. Paterson and A. Thomas, eds. *The Future of Social Democracy* (Oxford: Clarendon Press, 1986), 127–52.
3. Cited in W. Grant, W. E. Paterson, and C. Whitston, *Government and the Chemical Industry: A Comparative Study of Britain and West Germany* (Oxford: Clarendon Press, 1988).
4. R. Inglehart, *The Silent Revolution* (Princeton: Princeton University Press, 1977).
5. K. Baker, R. Dalton, and K. Hildebrandt, *Germany Transformed. Political Culture and the New Politics* (Cambridge, Mass.: Harvard University Press, 1977).
6. W. Bürklin, "The German Greens. The Post Industrial, Non-Established and the Party System," *International Political Science Review* 6, no. 4 (October 1985): 463–81, and F. Müller-Rommel, "Social Movements and the Greens," *European Journal of Political Research* 13 (1985): 53–67.
7. W. Bürklin, "The Future of the West German Green Party," *ASGP Journal* 14 (1987): 1–17 at 3–4.
8. H.-J. Veen, "Die Anhänger der Grünen—Ausprägungen einer neuen linken Milieupartei," in M. Langer, ed., *Die Grünen auf dem Prüfstand* (Bergisch Gladbach; Lübbe, 1987), 60–128.
9. E. Kolinsky, *Parties, Opposition and Society* (London: Croom Helm, 1984), 310.

10. For exhaustive detail, see Grant, Paterson, and Whitston, *Government and the Chemical Industry.*
11. This section relies heavily on E. Kolinsky, "The German Greens: A Women's Party," *Parliamentary Affairs* 41, no. 1 (1988): 129–48.
12. H. Kitschelt, "Organization and Strategy of Belgian and West German Ecology Parties," *Comparative Politics* 20, no. 2 (1988): 127–54 at 13.

IV
THE INTERNATIONAL ENVIRONMENT

17

THE FEDERAL REPUBLIC OF GERMANY, THE UNITED STATES, AND THE ATLANTIC ECONOMY

James Clyde Sperling

When the Federal Republic of Germany was created out of the French, British, and American zones of occupation in 1949, it emerged as little more than an American protectorate with limited sovereignty. Today it is one of the three leading economic powers of the capitalist world economy and America's most important military partner on the European continent. Over the course of the postwar period, the foreign economic policies of the United States and the Federal Republic have generally promoted the global multilateralization of trade and payments. But this common ground obscures disparate geopolitical and geoeconomic interests and perceptions. It also deflects attention away from important and divisive differences in the objectives and styles of domestic economic management which have had a significant impact on the postwar development of German-American economic relations.

This chapter will investigate these and other sources of discord and collaboration in the domestic and foreign economic policies of the Federal Republic and the United States.

THE BALANCES OF POWER AND GERMAN-AMERICAN ECONOMIC RELATIONS

The current economic and military balances of power no longer resemble the balances of the immediate postwar period: there has been a relative decline of American economic power, a concomitant rise in the economic power of Europe and Japan, and the transformation of America's military-strategic superiority vis-à-vis the Soviet Union into a condition of parity. This evolutionary change in the international system has altered the context of West German (and American) foreign policy calculations: as the West Germans were progressively freed from American domination, they were enabled to fashion policies more congruent with German interests and to resist American policies inimical to those interests. It also pushed to the surface inherent geopolitical tensions between the United States and the Federal Republic that had been represented by America's unquestionable economic and military-strategic hegemony in the early decades of the postwar period.

The American efforts to reconstruct postwar Europe reflected the belief that economic prosperity would remove the temptations of communism in France, Italy, and elsewhere, that it would facilitate the political and economic integration of Europe, and that it would nurture a community of states capable of resisting Soviet expansion. The keystone of American reconstruction efforts was the European Recovery Program (ERP). ERP funds eased imports from the dollar area and provided an additional source of investment capital for a prostrate Europe. The United States linked the disbursement of these funds to the liberalization of inter-European trade and payments and to the extension of most-favored-nation status to West Germany. The United States also supported the European Payments Union (EPU) and the European Coal and Steel Community (ECSC). Both institutionalized European discrimination against American goods, but served the political objective of integrating the West German and European economies: the EPU multilateralized payments within Europe and eased the access of West German goods to the European market; and the ECSC Treaty formed the basis for the requisite Franco-German political rapprochement by crafting an acceptable solution to the knotty problem posed by the International Ruhr Authority.

American foreign economic policy in the 1950s established the preconditions for European embrace of the dollar-dominated Bretton Woods fixed exchange rate monetary system and the GATT trade system based on the principles of nondiscrimination and reciprocity. Bretton Woods and the GATT represented the institutional manifestations of America's economic hegemony, served America's foreign policy objectives, represented the externalization of American economic interests and economic values, and were sustained by American power. But despite the convertibility of the major European currencies in 1958, discrimination against American goods continued with the erection of the European Economic Community (EEC). Moreover, the convertibility of the European currencies sounded the knell for the dollar-exchange standard and an important source of American power; and the high level of economic growth in Europe in the 1950s and 1960s led inexorably to the relative diminution of American power.

By the mid-1960s, increased European economic and monetary power was enhanced by the inability of the United States to resist the temptations and indulgences of informal empire—the New Frontier, the Great Society Programs, and the Vietnam War. The demise of American hegemony precipitated a redefinition of American interests and a retrenchment of American commitments by the Nixon administration. When the Nixon administration entered office, it sought an orderly retreat from empire. The Nixon foreign policy signified a subtle change in the American attitude toward its obligations to the Europeans and the Nixon Doctrine represented an effort to force the Europeans to assume a greater responsibility for their own military and economic security, to pay a higher price for the changed and hedged American security guarantee, and to retain the benefits of hegemony.[1] The marked shift in American priorities and preferences outlined by the Nixon administration has been enduring and has revealed geopolitical tensions between the regional economic and security concerns of West Germany and the global economic and security concerns of the United States.

The change in the economic and diplomatic balances of power within the Atlantic economy created the context and the opportunity for open and acrimonious debates on a broad range of economic questions; economic questions mooted by the previous two decades of unquestioned American economic and military-strategic dominance. Yet the departure of Richard Nixon, the need for cooperation on macro-economic management of the major economies after the oil price rise in 1973–1974, and the close relations and similarity of outlook shared by Chancellor Schmidt, President Ford, and President Giscard d'Estaing produced a remarkable period of cooperation in Atlantic economic affairs that promptly evaporated with the election of James Earl Carter as president of the United States. German-American relations hit a postwar nadir during the Carter administration, owing to palpable conflicts of interest compounded by the mutual personal antipathy of Carter and Schmidt. The Germans were disturbed not only by Carter's management of the dollar and assertive trade policies, but by Carter's preoccupation with human rights. Chancellor Schmidt perceived the Carter administration's departure from the rhetoric of realpolitik as a threat to West Germany's economic and political interests in Central and Eastern Europe.

The Reagan administration's reassertion of American military power shifted the diplomatic terms of trade in favor of the United States. Yet differences of opinion over the virtues of détente with the Soviet Union and the inability of the United States successfully to impose an oil pipeline embargo on the Soviet Union in 1982 illustrate the divergence of interests and changed balance of power within the Alliance. The Kohl-Genscher government has also remained unremittingly independent on issues of economic policy and has resisted American entreaties and pressures to abandon either fiscal prudence or floating exchange rates.

The increased West German independence on economic and diplomatic issues since the mid-1970s reflects changes that took place in the military and economic balances of power in the late 1960s, changes occasioned partly by the self-inflicted squandering of American economic and human capital, and partly by the diligent efforts of the West Germans, Japanese, and others.

THE COSTS OF CONTAINMENT: A SOURCE OF ATLANTIC DISCONTENT

An important source of West German discontent with the United States is located in the interdependence between American domestic economic policy, the containment of the Soviet Union, and its ramifications for the West German economy. American security policy over the past forty years has fluctuated between what John Lewis Gaddis has called the symmetrical and asymmetrical strategies of containment.[2] The strategy of containment chosen by each new American administration has mirrored the then current perception of America's economic capacity, the limitations of American power, and the severity of threat posed by the Soviet Union. The symmetrical containment of the Soviet Union is characterized by excessive optimism about American power and economic potential combined with undue pessimism about the danger the Soviet Union poses to the United States, while the asymmetrical containment of the Soviet Union reflects a sober view of the limits to American power and economic potential combined with a more relaxed attitude about the requirements of American security. The swings in American foreign policy ambitions and perceptions have created cyclical complications in German-American economic relations: American efforts to enlist German support in the symmetrical containment of the Soviet Union have been frustrated by the West German preoccupation with price stability, the concomitant commitment to fiscal rectitude, and the predilection to protect the competitiveness of West German exports with an undervalued Deutschmark (DM).

Periods of stress in German-American relations were introduced by the symmetrical containment of the Soviet Union, the hallmark of the Kennedy-Johnson and Reagan administrations' foreign policies. Each administration cut taxes to stimulate economic growth, increased defense expenditures, and engaged in military adventurism. In each case, the consequences were unsustainable budget deficits, an exhaustion of the American economy, an overextension of American power, a retrenchment of American commitments, and the bankruptcy of America's claim to leadership.

The Kennedy-Johnson administration financed containment with the manufacture of dollars whose value was guaranteed by the Bretton Woods fixed exchange rate system. A system of floating exchange rates forced the Reagan administration, on the other hand, to finance containment with foreign savings drawn by high real interest rates. On both occasions, American economic policy confronted the West Germans with the herculean task of resisting unwanted economic impulses emanating from an unapologetic and unrepentent United States.

Western Europeans viewed the inflationary domestic economic policies of the Kennedy and Johnson administrations as an "imperial tax" levied by the United States on its economic partners to defray the costs of containment. This imperial tax was unwelcome in the Federal Republic, because it threatened the continuation of the Bretton Woods fixed exchange rate system, domestic price stability, and an undervalued DM supplying a competitive edge to West German exports. As American economic policy became increasingly inconsistent with the demands of the fixed exchange rate system, upward pressures on the DM became increasingly irresistible. By 1968, a strong export performance by the Germans, de Gaulle's refusal to devalue a weak franc, and a battered pound sterling and dollar created considerable diplomatic pressures for a DM revaluation. The Germans refused the invitation, but effected a quasirevaluation of the DM with a combination of export surcharges and import rebates in November. Nonetheless, pressures on the DM continued and in October 1969 the new Brandt-Genscher government revalued the DM by 8.5 percent. The Germans attributed incessant pressures on the DM, the ever-present threat of imported inflation in the 1960s, and the eventual collapse of the Bretton Woods monetary system in 1973 to the American subordination of economic prudence to foreign policy folly in Vietnam.

Ronald Reagan, preoccupied with the threat of communism and the Soviet Union, entered office determined to revitalize the containment of the Soviet Union and to restore America's economic strength.[3] Tax cuts, the reduction of social welfare expenditures, and a contractionary monetary policy were expected to increase economic growth, lower unemployment, and reduce the debilitating rate of inflation inherited from the Carter administration. This economic strategy, in turn, would provide the wherewithal to pay for the Reagan administration's desire to achieve military-strategic superiority vis-à-vis the Soviet Union. But the Reagan administration's strategy was doubly flawed: the goal of military superiority was purchased at the price of economic competitiveness; and the policies of economic renewal precluded the coordination of macroeconomic policy and the convergence of economic performance in the Atlantic economy. It also resembled the Kennedy-Johnson strategy in one important respect: the costs of containment were involuntarily financed by America's military and economic partners in Europe.

The Reagan era ushered in a period of rancor in Atlantic economic relations, fed by high real interest rates, budget deficits, distorted exchange rates, and massive trade deficits: the real discount rate went from an average of −0.87 percent between 1976 and 1980 to an average of 5.8 percent between 1981 and 1987, while the real prime lending rate skyrocketed from 1.77 percent in 1980 to 12.86 percent in 1982;[4] American budget deficits rose from 2.68 percent of GDP in 1981 to 6.19 percent of GDP in 1983[5]—the semblance of fiscal propriety only being achieved by the legislative fiat of the Gramm-Rudman-Hollings Act and by the "budget summit" precipitated by the October 1987 stock-market crash; the DM depreciated by 48 percent against the dollar between late 1980 and February 1985, and then appreciated by almost 105 percent against the dollar by January 1988; and the cumulative American trade deficit between 1980 and 1987 was just under $700 billion.[6]

The United States has placed pressure on the West Germans to implement expansionary economic policies to offset any American effort to put its own house in order. The West Germans have reduced the discount rate from 4 percent in 1985 to a postwar low of 2.5 percent in December 1987 in an effort to stabilize the dollar, but have steadfastly refused to violate their sense of fiscal propriety or reverse their successful reduction of the budget deficit from 2.33 percent of GDP in 1981 to a low of 0.71 percent of GDP in 1986. Tax cuts in 1988 and scheduled for 1990 amounting to $26.5 billion should spur West German aggregate demand, but the West Germans refuse to jeopardize domestic economic objectives to compensate for earlier American excess.

The 1987 stock-market crash, the growing domestic concern over the size of the federal budget deficit, and a renewed consideration of the external consequences of domestic economic policy mark the end of the Reagan cycle of American overconsumption and self-absorption. A declining trade deficit in early 1988, the bipartisan effort to reduce the budget deficit beyond the level of cuts called for by Gramm-Rudman-Hollings, the recent success of the INF agreement, and the push for a significant cut in the superpowers' strategic nuclear weapons arsenals signal a more sober view of American power, of American economic capacity, and of the requirements of containment. This change in perceptions, if carried over into the next administration, portends a return to a policy of the asymmetrical containment of the Soviet Union; and it may also provide the basis for the coordination of German and American economic policies on terms acceptable to both parties.

THE AMERICAN SECURITY GUARANTEE: THE TIE THAT BINDS

The Federal Republic was the creature of American security policy and the onset of the cold war. The United States desired a strong West German ally, both militarily and economically. After the outbreak of the Korean War, Chancellor Adenauer skillfully exploited the military and economic potential of West Germany to achieve the interrelated objectives of rearmament, reunification, and full sovereignty.[7] The successful West German linkage of security and economic affairs in German-American relations in the 1950s slowly became a source of American leverage with the West Germans. As the dollar became strained by chronic payments deficits and the German payments position moved into chronic surplus, successive administrations yielded to the temptation of linking West German financial support of the dollar to the American security guarantee.

The Anderson mission in 1960 represented the first formal and explicit linkage between American payments difficulties and the stationing of American troops in Europe. The Eisenhower administration encouraged Chancellor Adenauer to offset the German trade surpluses with increased capital outflows. The Kennedy and Johnson administrations extracted, in exchange for a continuing (and steadily discounted) American security guarantee, various ad hoc support measures for the dollar—Roosa bonds, prepayment of ERP loans, induced capital outflows, the Blessing Letter promising to support the dollar, and a series of offset agreements. Direct financial support of the dollar and the German promise to refrain from converting excessive dollar balances into gold eased the international strain on the dollar which was created by domestic economic policies incompatible with external equilibrium and by the overextension of American power, most notably in Vietnam.

The fairly smooth cooperation between the United States and the Federal Republic of economic issues in the 1950s and early 1960s reinforced the mutually acknowledged linkage between economics and security. Overlapping economic interests and the Federal Republic's security dependence on the United States made the Federal Republic eager to accede to American demands for West German financial and monetary support of the dollar in exchange for military security and diplomatic support on the issue of reunification. But the progressive decline in the dollar's real value and the increasingly prohibitive costs of supporting it threatened the West Germans' ability to conduct a domestic economic policy consistent with the quasi-constitutional principles of fiscal prudence and price stability. As the American payments deteriorated, as the real value of the dollar (and consequently the real value of the Europeans' currency reserves) declined, and as U.S. domestic economic policy remained unmindful of its external consequences, frictions arose between the United States and the West Germans that were played out in tedious negotiations over burden sharing in the Alliance and Congressional threats to reduce unilaterally American troops stationed in Europe.

The payment of occupation and stationing costs between 1945 and 1960 and a series of offset agreements between 1961 and 1976 represented a formal and explicit connection between the American security guarantee and West German financial support of America's global economic and military pretensions. But the American failure to link the resolution of outstanding economic problems with security disputes during the "Year of Europe" in 1973 and the European success in compartmentalizing security issues in NATO and economic issues in the IMF, GATT, and OECD rather than the EEC, effectively severed the political-diplomatic connection between the American security guarantee to Europe and European support of American economic hegemony. The Germans also argued that the introduction of floating exchange rates in 1973 eradicated the rationale for and undermined the logic of continued offset payments. The United States accepted German reasoning in 1976 when the last offset agreement was signed by President Ford and Chancellor

Schmidt. Since that time, the Reagan administration extracted West German financial support for the forward stationing and operating costs of American military materiel with the 1982 Wartime Host Nation Security Agreement; and the West Germans assumed a large proportion of the costs associated with the 1985–1990 NATO infrastructure program.[8]

The unsuccessful 1984 Nunn amendment, which linked greater defense spending by the Europeans to American troop strength in Europe, is unlike its predecessors, the Mansfield amendments of the late 1960s and early 1970s. Senate support for the various Mansfield amendments was driven by a diverse set of emotions and calculations, running from efforts to extract greater financial support of the dollar to isolationism and populist pique in response to European criticism of America's participation in the Vietnam War. The Nunn amendment reflected the military-strategic calculation of enhancing European conventional defense capabilities and has used the threatened withdrawal of American troops to achieve that objective. Despite the Reagan administration's efforts to resurrect the burden-sharing issue in early 1988, it has kept security and economic issues on separate, albeit parallel, tracks. This cisatlantic reorientation has reduced the American temptation to confound military-strategic issues with economic concerns and has thus removed an important source of irritation in German-American economic relations. This development and the mutual security dependence of the United States and West Germany have worked to reverse the centrifugal forces of economic conflict in the Atlantic economy.

GEOECONOMIC TENSIONS: THE EMS, THE DOLLAR, AND GERMAN COMMERCIAL DOMINANCE IN EUROPE

The German economy enjoyed domestic economic balance and an external economic complementarity prior to the Second World War. Domestically, the western portion of the country had supplied industrial goods to the eastern portion in exchange for agricultural goods; and externally, Germany provided industrial goods to the nations of Eastern and Southern Europe in exchange for raw materials and agricultural products. The postwar settlement in Europe and the cold war forced the West Germans to seek an integration of the West German and Western European economies. Both the United States and West Germany dedicated their energies to the integration of the European economy. Both nations hoped for the political and economic unification of Europe: it served the United States' interest of containing the Soviet Union and the Federal Republic's interest in restoring economic prosperity and enhancing its economic security.

Toward these ends, the West Germans pushed for the acceleration of trade liberalization within Europe during the 1950s and for the convertibility of the European currencies, in accordance with American preferences and West Germany's interests as an exporting nation. These foreign economic policies accelerated the multilateralization of world trade and promised an end to the discrimination against dollar-area goods—outcomes not unwelcomed by the United States. But the convergent trade and monetary interests of the Federal Republic and the United States in the 1950s have diverged steadily after the establishment of the EEC and the convertibility of the major European currencies in 1958.

The Bretton Woods monetary system lent the United States an ability to finance its payments deficit with its own liabilities. The West Germans initially supported this system, because it coincided with their security and economic interests in Europe; and because the Eisenhower administration conducted a domestic economic policy consonant with the requirements of a stable dollar and a fixed exchange rate system. Moreover, the deflationary bias of West German economic management, combined with an undervalued DM, gave the West Germans a comparative advantage in the production of industrial goods and offered the West Germans the prospect of commercial dominance in Europe. The West German export sector benefited from continued support of the dollar-dominated Bretton Woods system so long as the United States maintained a low rate of inflation and modest payments deficits.

American economic policy went seriously awry in the 1960s, however. Neither monetary nor fiscal policy was consistent with internal or external balance. The demands of the Vietnam War and the Great Society Program strained industrial capacity, created overemployment, and generated global inflation. As the dollar's real value steadily deteriorated, the DM became an object of speculation. Incompatible economic developments in the United States and the Federal Republic intensified pressures on the DM: while the dollar was weakened by chronic payments deficits, a declining trade surplus, rising capital exports, and inflationary fiscal and monetary policies, the DM was strengthened by chronic payments surpluses and contractionary fiscal and monetary policies. West German resistance to meaningful changes in the value of the DM and an unwillingness to accommodate inflation left the federal government and the Bundesbank in a bind that could only be resolved by changes in American economic policy—changes that were not forthcoming.

The inability of the Nixon administration to quickly wind down the war in Vietnam and continuing downward pressures on the dollar forced the West Germans to float the DM unilaterally in May 1971 after its European partners refused the invitation to float jointly against the dollar. A joint float would have had the twin virtues of spreading to West Germany's partners the risk of absorbing massive dollar inflows and of protecting the price competitiveness of German exporters in their most important markets by leaving intact the cross rates between the European currencies. The unilateral float of the DM relieved West Germany of the obligation to purchase dollars at a fixed rate of exchange and the associated pressures on the domestic price level. It also reflected an emergent geoeconomic tension between the West German commercial interest in preserving a regional, German-dominated European trading bloc and the internationalization of the DM which posed an additional threat to West German monetary autonomy.

Unrelenting upward pressures on the DM—reinforced by the reserve role thrust upon it after March 1973—confronted West German exporters with the unpleasant prospect of having their goods priced out of the European market unless the DM could be tied to the currencies of its European trading partners. The federal government was faced with the difficult task of contracting the DM's growing role in the international economy to support its regional trading interests. The chosen instrument for effecting the realignment of West Germany's commercial and monetary interests was a regional fixed exchange rate system. After the realignment of the major currencies at the Smithsonian Agreement in December 1971, the Europeans took a tentative step toward tightening the bond between their economies with the "snake-in-the-tunnel" arrangement in March 1972. The EEC currency snake, which narrowed the permissible band of fluctuation between the member-state currencies, was intended to create a "zone of stable exchange rates" in Europe. But by 1976, the snake had contracted to a DM-dominated currency bloc embracing Central and Nordic Europe. This hard currency bloc performed the triple trick of buffering the DM and the German economy from gyrations of the dollar, of preserving the price competitiveness of West German goods with its major European trading partners, and of allowing West Germans to export their deflationary bias in macroeconomic policy to their weaker and dependent European neighbors.

The Carter administration's hapless stewardship of the American economy and a return to the "benign neglect" of the dollar reinforced the German view that a consolidation of its commercial and monetary interests was essential if Germany were to escape the twin dangers of imported inflation and an appreciating DM. A growing sense of urgency in Europe created the context for Franco-German monetary cooperation and produced the agreement at the 1978 Bremen Summit to create the European Monetary System (EMS). Despite the close cooperation of Chancellor Schmidt and President Giscard d'Estaing, the EMS represented a German-led declaration of monetary independence from the United States and the dollar. The EMS constructed an elaborate fixed exchange rate system between the EC currencies (minus the United Kingdom) and established the institutional mechanisms that could eventually lead to monetary union. It was designed to protect Europe from the gyrations of the dollar and the mismanagement of the American economy; to create a "zone of stability" in Europe shielded from a dollar-dominated world.

Although the Carter administration introduced a package of measures to arrest the dollar's decline in November 1978, the foreign exchange markets promptly returned to disarray after 1981. The extreme exchange rate volatility of the Reagan era has produced pressures for the adoption of target zones for the values of the DM, yen, and dollar. Although the Japanese and Americans have warmed to the idea of a target zone arrangement, the West Germans remain devotees of floating exchange rates. They reject a target zone proposal for a number of reasons: it would establish rates of exchange independent of their proper economic value and subject those rates to political compromise; the politicization of exchange rates would further aggravate trade disputes; target exchange rates would subordinate German economic policy to an exchange rate *diktat* and consequently American economic policy; and finally, the West Germans argue that no one nation commands an accepted and respected leadership role required for a workable target zone arrangement— erratic (and wrong-headed) American economic policies have disqualified the United States from playing that role and the Germans only feel qualified to play a regional role within the EMS.

The EMS has been, from a German perspective, a qualified success. There has been a convergence of economic performance in Europe—inflation rate differentials have narrowed, domestic credit has expanded at similar rates, interest rates have moved in the same direction, and growth rate differentials have narrowed.[9] The convergence in economic performance has been matched by a convergence in economic objectives of a distinctly Germanic cast. The EMS has also fostered greater exchange rate stability within Europe and has protected German exports by minimizing fluctuations in the cross rates of European currencies. The geoeconomic tension between West Germany's monetary and commercial interests in Europe may be resolved with the steady development of a European monetary personality encompassing a European economic area. The resolution of that tension, however, may also prove to be the source of Euro-American commercial and monetary conflicts well into the 1990s.

ECONOMIC OPENNESS, ECONOMIC CULTURE, AND ECONOMIC CONFLICT IN THE ATLANTIC ECONOMY

Economic openness and the pattern of convergence and divergence in the West German and American economic cultures points to important sources of cooperation and intractable sources of conflict in the Atlantic economy.[10] The West German economy is an open one: the federal government and the Bundesbank have had limited success in insulating the German economy from global economic developments; and the level of German interest rates, the rate of inflation, and the value of the DM have been extremely sensitive to American fiscal and monetary policies.

Economic culture identifies the noninstitutional proscriptions and imperatives facing national authorities in the formulation and execution of economic policy; it defines the minimum tasks and responsibilities of the state and sets the boundaries of legitimate state activity. Disjunctions between national economic cultures limit the potential for the coordination of macroeconomic policies of the coordination of exchange rate intervention. The disjunction between the West German and American economic cultures reflects the different historical lessons drawn from the calamities of the interwar period and the Great Depression: for Americans, political instability has become generally associated with high unemployment; whereas for Germans, the political collapse of the Weimar Republic and the rise of national socialism are attributed almost universally to a middle-class ruined by hyperinflation. Consequently, the American economic culture forgives fiscal extravagance and prefers an inflationary macroeconomic policy ensuring full employment, while the West German economic culture demands fiscal rectitude and a deflationary macroeconomic policy targeting price stability.

West German–American conflicts over the shape of the international monetary system, the management of the dollar, and trade relations within the Atlantic economy have reflected a clash of economic cultures as well as of economic interests. Tensions in German-American relations, therefore, have been located not only in disparate interests, which are in principle subject to compromise, but also in conflicts of values, which usually are not.

The clash of these nations' economic cultures only became troublesome after the convertibility of currencies in 1958. Convertibility transformed desirable and necessary American payments deficits into a source of West German displeasure; and it raised the specter of a perpetual fight against "imported inflation." Until the generalized float of the dollar in 1973, the West Germans faced the dilemma of revaluing the DM, which would reduce the competitiveness of German exports, or of accommodating imported inflation. The West

Germans counteracted inflationary impulses from without with contractionary monetary and fiscal policies and assuaged pressures on the DM by propping up the dollar. These policies, however, only exacerbated domestic inflationary pressures in Germany and upward pressures on the DM; and they removed any incentive for the Americans to defend the dollar by reversing their policies of fiscal profligacy and monetary laxity.

The DM's strength and the dollar's weakness became a persistent source of discord between the United States and West Germany. The West Germans believed that revaluations of the DM in 1961 and 1969, along with the quasirevaluation in 1968, were unjust rewards for their economic propriety and America's economic dissoluteness. Mutual dissatisfactions on monetary issues were reflected in the debates over the reform of the international monetary system in the 1960s and 1970s. Both nations pushed for greater symmetry in the adjustment mechanism, but the Americans desired an adjustment mechanism that encouraged surplus nations to adopt inflationary domestic economic policies, while the West Germans preferred an adjustment mechanism that forced the deficit nations to adopt deflationary economic policies. The Americans wanted an adjustment mechanism that forced surplus nations to correct their external imbalance without jeopardizing economic growth and full employment in the deficit nations, while the West Germans demanded an adjustment mechanism that restored external balance in deficit nations without jeopardizing price stability in the surplus nations. These positions reflected disparate domestic economic concerns embedded in their economic cultures.[11]

The difficulties confronting the effective coordination of West German and American monetary and fiscal policies were pushed to the surface by the stagflation that plagued the Atlantic economy for the last half of the 1970s. The Americans pressured and cajoled the West Germans to reflate, but the West Germans dismissed the American argument that they were capable of fulfilling the role of "a locomotive" that pulls the Atlantic economy; and they even remained skeptical of the more modest proposal of the Carter administration, a "modified convoy" strategy. The West Germans suspected that such strategies would inevitably sacrifice the German virtue of price stability on the Anglo-Saxon altar of full employment and economic growth.

The election of Ronald Reagan promised conservative economic policies and the wringing out of inflation in America. The Reagan promise of economic orthodoxy was quickly transmogrified into the Reagan nightmare of supply-side economics and military Keynesianism. The Reagan economic strategy produced the deepest recession of the postwar period, massive budget deficits financed by foreign savings drawn by high real interest rates, a ballooning of the national debt from $1 trillion to almost $3 trillion, and growing trade deficits driven by overconsumption and an overvalued dollar.

The fiscal recklessness and monetary astringency of the Reagan administration quickly became the focus of West German criticisms. West German entreaties to cut budget deficits and reduce high real interest rates fell on deaf ears in Washington. The Reagan administration denied any connection between high real interest rates and the need to finance budget deficits; and between high real interest rates, an overvalued dollar, and massive American trade deficits. Moreover, different political and economic priorities at each end of Pennsylvania Avenue ruled out any significant reduction of the budget deficit and consequently of interest rates, of the dollar's value, or of the American trade deficit. Once the Reagan administration turned to the West Germans and Japanese to reverse the dollar's climb in September 1985, the Americans found a reluctant and suspicious economic partner in the Federal Republic.

In September 1985, the finance ministers of the G-5 nations (Britain, France, Japan, the United States, and West Germany) met at the Plaza Hotel in New York. They agreed to effect an orderly appreciation of their currencies against the dollar with the coordinated intervention by their monetary authorities in the foreign exchange markets. Although the Plaza Agreement helped correct the overvaluation of the dollar and paved the way for a coordinated interest rate reduction in 1986, it left the West Germans unhappy: an agreement to narrow the interest rate differentials between the American and European capital markets was not forthcoming nor was agreement on the expected equilibrium value of the dollar established. Moreover, the West Germans resisted American pressures to adopt more expansionary economic policies until the United States made serious cuts in the budget deficit.

Renewed turbulence in the foreign exchange markets in early 1987 and the failure of the Baker-Miyazawa accord to stabilize the dollar-yen rate produced the Louvre Accord in February 1987. At the Louvre meeting, the major industrial nations agreed to stabilize exchange rates at the existing levels and to intervene in the exchange markets toward that end. But over the course of 1987, the Germans voiced their concern that the United States would rely upon a depreciating dollar rather than corrective domestic economic policies to reverse the American trade deficit. After the October 1987 stock-market crash, the G-7 (the G-5 nations plus Canada and Italy) met in late December and reaffirmed the objectives of the Louvre Accord. The communiqué committed the United States to significant cuts in the budget deficit, the Japanese to expansionary economic policies consistent with a reduction of the trade surplus, and the Germans to tax cuts and an interest rate reduction.

Trade policy has also been a source of discord and collaboration between West Germany and the United States. The American policy of the global open door, which emphasized the consumption benefits of free trade, has reflected the Manchesterian conviction that free trade and the integration of national economies would ensure global peace and prosperity. The West Germans, enamored by the production benefits of global free trade, have nonetheless retained a strong preference for a protected regional trading arrangement; a preference corresponding to the German historical experience, economic necessity, and the desire for European political integration. The West German dedication to the liberalization of trade outside Europe has reflected a combination of theoretical conviction, the political accommodation of the United States, and the West German interest in opening and securing new markets for German manufactures and in gaining assured access to raw materials.

West German fidelity to the discriminatory trade policies of the EC did not preclude German-American cooperation at the Kennedy and Tokyo rounds of trade negotiations however. Both nations pushed for the reduction of tariff and nontariff barriers to trade, with the notable exception of agricultural trade.[12] This pattern continues within the context of GATT today. In the present Uruguay round, both the United States and the Federal Republic seek rules protecting intellectual property rights, the removal of restrictions on direct foreign investment, and the development of rules governing trade in the service sector. Furthermore, the deterioration of America's export performance and the congressional fixation with America's bilateral trade deficits with the nations of the Pacific rim have created a fragile community of interest between the United States and the Federal Republic. The West Germans, fearing an indiscriminate closure of the American market and retaliation against the EC, have increasingly labeled Japan, South Korea, Taiwan, Hong Kong, and Singapore as the primary sources of disequilibrium in world trade. But the growing protectionist sentiment of the Congress, the creeping bilateralization of trade by the United States, and America's propensity to live beyond its collective means have remained targets of West German concerns and criticisms.

If the decline in the American current account deficit in early 1988 does not persist and if bilateral trade agreements continue to proliferate, then the progress made at the Tokyo round will be undone, the outcome of the Uruguay round will be largely irrelevant, and the progressive liberalization of global markets set in motion with the 1949 Annecy trade negotiations will be reversed.

CONCLUSION

The INF Treaty, the stark implications of the remaining short-range nuclear weapons stationed in West Germany, a conventional imbalance in Central Europe, and the prospect of deep cuts in strategic nuclear weapons have renewed West German skepticism about the credibility and nature of the American security guarantee. German distrust of American intentions are reciprocated by Americans who point to the pending institutional regionalization of trade promised by the EC decision to create a single "internal market" by 1992 and the EC-EFTA[13] Luxembourg Declaration of 1984 to develop a European economic area. Moreover, the January 1988 Franco-German agreements to strengthen defense and economic cooperation hold out the promise of a credible Franco-German directorate of Europe; of an independent Europe supported by West Germany's economic power and protected by France's independent nuclear deterrent. Thus, German doubts about the American security guarantee, German dissatisfactions with American domestic economic policy, and American suspicions of European integration may combine to fracture the Atlantic world into two antagonistic monetary and trade blocs. But the future direction of Atlantic economic relations depends largely upon domestic political and economic developments in the United States.

The Reagan presidential bequest will confront the Bush administration with the unenviable task of reducing the elephantine budget and trade deficits of the past eight years, while sustaining economic growth, high employment, and reasonable price stability. One of two likely policy options will be adopted by the next administration: it can cut government expenditure and increase taxes to reduce the budget deficit and the consumption of foreign goods; or it can reduce the trade deficit with an undervalued dollar and continue to finance federal budget deficits with world savings. If the former strategy of domestic readjustment prevails, a credible basis for German-American cooperation will be established. If the latter course is chosen, however, the German-American disagreements of today only foreshadow a permanent rift in the Atlantic economy tomorrow.

The Atlantic Alliance and the Atlantic economy cannot withstand the stress of an American security policy that periodically casts its security guarantee to Europe into doubt or an American domestic economic policy that is conducted with an indifferent eye to its external consequences. Nor can it withstand a West Germany that makes conformity to West German economic preferences a prerequisite for Atlantic cooperation or a West Germany that treats price stability as a categorical imperative. Unless the United States and West Germany accommodate one another in an effort to cope with the economic consequences of Ronald Reagan, the West Germans and Americans will work at cross-purposes in their efforts to manage the Atlantic economy.

NOTES

1. On the economic implications of the Nixon Doctrine, see James Clyde Sperling, "Three-Way Stretch: The Federal Republic of Germany in the Atlantic Economy, 1969–1976," Ph.D. dissertation, University of California, Santa Barbara, 1986. For excellent treatments of the military and diplomatic consequences of the Nixon Doctrine, see Christian Hacke, *Die Aera Nixon-Kissinger 1969–1974. Konservative Reform der Weltpolitik* (Stuttgart: Klett-Cotta, 1983) and Robert Litwak, *Detente and the Nixon Doctrine: American Foreign Policy and the Pursuit of Stability, 1969–1976* (Cambridge: Cambridge University Press, 1984).

2. John Lewis Gaddis, *Strategies of Containment: A Critical Appraisal of Postwar American National Security Policy* (Oxford: Oxford University Press, 1982). See also David P. Calleo, *Beyond American Hegemony: The Future of the Western Alliance* (New York: Basic Books, 1987).

3. For a discussion of the initial Reagan strategy, see Robert E. Osgood, "The Revitalization of Containment," *Foreign Affairs* 61, no. 3 (America and the World) (1982): 465–502.

4. High real interest rates were necessary to reduce the high level of inflation inherited from the Carter administration, but even after inflation was reduced to 3.3 percent in 1983 from 13.5 percent in 1980, the real discount and prime lending rates remained above their historical average. The prime lending rate differential between the German and American capital markets after 1981 consistently favored the United States (with the exception of 1986), was supported by the monetary policies of the Federal Reserve, and contributed to the overvaluation of the dollar.

   Tables 17.1–17.3 list the real discount and real prime lending rates in the United States and the Federal Republic. They were derived by subtracting the rate of inflation (based on the producer price index) from the nominal interest rate.

5. The 1987 American budget deficit should decline to about 3.56 percent of GDP. The discrepancy between German and American fiscal policies after 1981 is apparent from an examination of table 17.4.

6. This compares with an aggregate West German trade surplus of $248.18 billion and a Japanese trade surplus of $361.09 billion between 1980 and 1987 (see table 17.5).

7. This argument is developed in Wolfram F. Hanrieder, *West German Foreign Policy, 1949–1963: International Pressure and Domestic Response* (Stanford: Stanford University Press, 1967).

8. The cost of the 1985–1990 infrastructure program is $13.17 billion at current exchange rates ($1 = DM 1.67). The West Germans' contribution

Table 17.1
Real Discount Rates, 1978–1987 (in percent)

	1978	1979	1980	1981	1982	1983	1984	1985	1986	1987
FRG	0.3	1.83	2.1	−0.3	3.0	2.75	2.1	4.43	6.45	−1.4
U.S.	1.9	0.77	−0.5	2.9	6.5	7.25	5.6	7.93	8.45	2.1

Table 17.2
Real Prime Lending Rates, 1978–1987 (in percent)

	1978	1979	1980	1981	1982	1983	1984	1985	1986	1987
FRG	4.63	4.46	6.64	6.89	11.5	9.25	7.42	9.96	11.7	4.44
U.S.	1.46	1.44	1.77	9.77	12.86	9.54	9.64	10.36	11.3	4.88

Table 17.3
Real Interest Rate Differentials, 1978–1987 (in percent) (+ in favor of United States)

	1978	1979	1980	1981	1982	1983	1984	1985	1986	1987
Discount Rate:	1.9	0.77	−0.5	2.6	3.5	4.5	3.5	3.5	2.0	3.5
Prime Rate:	1.6	−1.6	−2.6	2.88	1.36	0.29	2.22	0.4	−0.4	0.44

Sources: International Financial Statistics Yearbook, 1986 (Washington, D.C.: International Monetary Fund, 1986), 346–47, 468–69; and International Financial Statistics 41, no. 2 (February 1988): 228–29, 522–23.

Table 17.4
Budget Deficits as a Percentage of GDP, 1978–1987

	1978	1979	1980	1981	1982	1983	1984	1985	1986	1987
FRG	2.06	1.98	1.82	2.33	2.0	1.97	1.84	1.11	0.71	1.26
U.S.	2.75	1.49	2.91	2.68	4.07	6.19	4.89	5.44	5.13	3.56

Source: IMF Survey, 25 January 1988, 28; figure for Federal Republic in 1987 calculated from International Financial Statistics 41, no. 8 (August 1988): 242–43.

Table 17.5
Trade Balance, 1980–1987 (+ surplus/ – deficit) (in billions of dollars)

	1980	1981	1982	1983	1984	1985	1986	1987
FRG	8.72	16.46	25.03	21.37	21.94	28.55	55.95	70.16
Japan	2.13	19.96	18.08	31.46	44.26	55.99	92.82	96.39
U.S.	−25.50	−27.97	−36.45	−67.08	−112.51	−122.15	−144.34	−160.28

Source: For 1980–1986, *International Financial Statistics* 41, no. 1 (January 1988): 226–27, 296–97, 520–21; for 1987, *International Financial Statistics* 41, no. 8 (August 1988): 242, 312, 538.

Table 17.6
NATO-Member Shares of 1985–1990 Infrastructure
Program (in percent)

United States:	27.8	Belgium:	4.6
Federal Republic:	26.8	Norway:	0.8
United Kingdom:	12.2	Turkey:	0.8
Italy:	8.1	Greece:	0.8
Canada:	6.4	Luxembourg:	0.2
Netherlands:	4.6	Portugal:	0.2

Source: The Federal Ministry of Defence, *White Paper 1985: The Situation and the Development of the Federal Armed Forces* (Bonn: 1985), 102.

of 26.8 percent of the total costs was only second to the American contribution of 27.8 percent. See table 17.6 for the other NATO members' contributions.

9. See Horst Ungerer, Owen Evans, Thomas Mayer, and Philip Young, *The European Monetary System: Recent Developments*, Occasional Paper No. 48 (Washington, D.C.: International Monetary Fund, December 1986), chapter 5.

10. The interrelationship between economic culture and economic management in advanced capitalist states is treated in James Clyde Sperling, "Economic Culture and Economic Management in an Open Economy: A Conceptual Analysis," Michigan State University, March 1987, mimeographs.

11. The American position resembled, ironically, the proposals of John Maynard Keynes for the reform of the international monetary system that were rejected by Harry Dexter White in the 1940s. As it was expected that the United States would enjoy chronic surpluses, the Americans wanted to ensure that the burden of adjustment would be placed on deficit nations. Once the United States suffered chronic

deficits, however, it adopted a Keynes-like position. But the forces driving the different American positions were quite dissimilar: in 1944, the United States feared that a "lenient" adjustment mechanism would obligate the United States to finance the expected deficits of Britain and other nations, while in the 1960s and 1970s, it was expected that without such an adjustment mechanism, the United States would be forced to adopt unwanted deflationary economic policies.

12. The West Germans, despite their considerable dissatisfactions with the Common Agricultural Policy (CAP), have generally resisted American demands for the wholesale opening of the European market to American agricultural products. Such demands are viewed as threats to both the CAP and the EC, and thus resisting them forms an important component of West Germany's foreign policy.

13. EFTA stands for European Free Trade Association. EFTA was formed in 1959 by nine non-EC states, such as Scandinavia, the British Isles, Austria, and Switzerland as a free trade area of those excluded from EC.

18

THE ROLE OF THE FEDERAL REPUBLIC OF GERMANY IN NATO

Werner J. Feld

The Federal Republic of Germany (FRG) became a member of NATO on 5 May 1955, through the institutional device of the Western European Union. In order to make the participation of German military units in NATO acceptable to France, the old Western Union Defense Organization of the Brussels Treaty was revised, linked into NATO, and expanded to include Germany and Italy in a Western European Union. WEU was empowered to fix the maximum force levels of its members. Moreover, the FRG made a unilateral declaration not to manufacture atomic, chemical, or biological weapons and to refrain from producing guided missiles, magnetic mines, warships, and long-range bombers, except on the request of NATO's Supreme Allied Commander in Europe (*SACEUR*) and approved by a two-thirds majority of the WEU Council. In return, the FRG gained the full authority of a sovereign state over its internal and external affairs, a national military establishment, and a position of international influence. The French National Assembly approved these arrangements—the so-called Paris Agreements—on 28 December 1955, albeit with a narrow margin of 287 to 260.

This chapter will trace the development of FRG policies toward NATO, evaluate the degree of support given to NATO strategies, assess possible conflicts between FRG/NATO interests and its Ostpolitik aspirations, and analyze West German interests in nuclear as well as conventional arms reduction efforts. We will also touch on West German public opinion with respect to NATO and inquire whether other security options and strategies for the FRG may be preferable.

THE MLF ISSUE

Control over nuclear weapons is a highly sensitive matter in a military alliance such as NATO. Despite West Germany's formal declaration not to manufacture nuclear weapons, the Federal Republic considered it essential in 1962 to receive information about the kind and location of American nuclear weapons in Europe, to be given a guarantee that those weapons could not be withdrawn against the will of the countries where they were deployed, and to have a voice, either positive or negative, about the utilization of nuclear weapons stationed on its own soil. During the NATO Council meeting of May 1962, Washington agreed with part of these demands and was prepared to "consult" the allies, but not to share the decision for utilization.

In order to offer tangible evidence of nuclear weapons cooperation among the NATO allies, the U.S. government attempted to implement a plan developed under the Eisenhower presidency which envisaged a multilateral naval force consisting of twenty-five surface vessels and submarines, each equipped with Polaris missiles, and manned as well as commanded by nationals of different allied countries. The missiles were to be used only with the consent of all participating governments, including that of the United States.

Initially, both Bonn and Washington were enthusiastic about the concept of the Multilateral Force (MLF), and it was anticipated that Britain would form one of the pillars of the MLF, but other European allies, especially France, had serious reservations. West Germany may have hoped to obtain a finger on the nuclear trigger through this arrangement, but French and British objections to such a development were intense in spite of the conclusion of the Franco--German Friendship Treaty in 1963. Indeed, General de Gaulle opposed adamantly German participation in nuclear decisionmaking because it would tie the FRG more closely to Washington.

Since most NATO members had not shown much interest in MLF and the Soviet Union placed Washington before an undesirable choice of either the continuation of MLF or the prospect of a nuclear nonproliferation treaty, the Johnson administration scrapped the MLF policy. The FRG, suspicious about a forthcoming deal between the superpowers at the expense of the NATO allies, was greatly displeased about this development which caused Chancellor Ludwig Erhard much embarrassment.

West Germany's concern to become a participant in nuclear weapon decisionmaking was at least partially satisfied when the FRG became a member of the Nuclear Planning Working Group (NPWG), a part of the Defense Planning Group. The NPWG had the important task of introducing the nonnuclear member NATO partners to the problems of nuclear policy. The NPWG was dissolved a year later and replaced by a permanent National Defense Planning Committee and a permanent Nuclear Planning Group (NPG). The FRG, the United States, Britain, and Italy became the four standing members of the NPG which provided a forum for Bonn to share information and participate in nuclear planning and decisionmaking.

The NPG has developed into one of the most important organs of NATO. It has elaborated guidelines for the deployment of nuclear weapons, developed procedures for consultation, and evaluated the required modernization of existing weapons systems. While the federal government values its work with the NPG very highly, Bonn does not regard its participation in this Group as a substitute for a German role in a possible European nuclear force.

DÉTENTE AND ARMS CONTROL

The Grand Coalition between the CDU and SPD, formed in December 1966, ushered in a new era for West German security and for NATO. As for the latter, Council meetings in December 1967 and June 1968 set two important goals: (1) The establishment of a more stable international relationship essential for a just and lasting peaceful order in Europe, and (2) efforts to bring about mutual and balanced force reductions (MBFR) among the NATO allies and the members of the Warsaw Pact. Bonn was interested in the force reductions as they would strengthen a climate of détente which, in turn, might promote the long-range (though perhaps unrealistic) goal of reunification between West and East Germany.

While German-American cooperation inside and outside NATO remained the backbone of Bonn's foreign policy, Willy Brandt sought a closer relationship with the Soviet Union, Eastern Europe, and the German Democratic Republic; and for that purpose he was prepared to accept the territorial status quo in Europe which, however, was likely to undermine any West German claims for reunification. The largely successful Ostpolitik was basically completed in 1974, but its effects continue. Unfortunately, MBFR, whose progress originally was tied by Washington to the convening of the European Security Conference in Helsinki, so far has not shown any success.

Although Ostpolitik aroused the suspicions of many Americans about West Germany's continuing and sincere support of NATO, or that the FRG was beginning to follow a more neutralistic path, the federal government rejected these accusations. It pointed out that Ostpolitik strengthened the goal of stability and reconciliation in Europe, reduced Soviet incentives for military action outside the Warsaw Pact area, and thereby helped to solve German military security problems at their political roots.

As preparations were made for the 1975 Conference on Security and Cooperation in Europe (CSCE), NATO committees held weekly meetings to coordinate ideas and positions. The FRG played an important role in these consultations and also strengthened its NATO burden-sharing contribution.

As for détente in general, a high-water mark was the American-Soviet summit in May 1972 between President Nixon and General Secretary Brezhnev which resulted in SALT I and the ABM Treaty. A year later, during Brezhnev's visit to Washington, an Agreement on the Prevention of Nuclear War was signed and in November 1974, President Ford and the Soviet leader concluded an accord in Vladivostok setting quantitative and qualitative limitations on strategic nuclear weapons. The SALT II agreements, signed in Vienna in 1979, imposed slightly lower limits for strategic nuclear weapons beginning January 1981, and also restricted modernization of these weapons and prohibited mobile ICBMs. All these bilateral arrangements caused apprehension in Bonn because there was fear that they may have been made, at least in part, at the expense of European NATO members. This fear was deepened by the strong minority support in the U.S. Senate given to the Mansfield resolution for the withdrawal of American forces from Europe, reflecting U.S. unhappiness that the Europeans were not carrying their fair share of the common burden. This raised the specter of the United States decoupling itself from Western Europe to which the Germans were especially sensitive. Moreover, the FRG was quite ambivalent about the objectives of MBFR unless the result would be militarily equitable and politically advantageous for the Europeans, and especially for West Germany. Otherwise, Bonn was concerned that, in view of the Soviet military buildup in Eastern Europe, NATO's response to either military aggression or political pressure would be weakened.

Despite these concerns, the federal government was pleased to see the two superpowers reaching a rough consensus regarding parity of their nuclear arsenals and giving up, seemingly, aspirations for superiority. This appeared to be a significant factor for stabilization and a decisive contribution to détente. Yet, there remained the creeping suspicion that the Soviet Union was gaining a first-strike capability which could be exploited politically, if for one reason or another the utilization of nuclear weapons by the United States would lose credibility.

THE DOUBLE-TRACK DECISION AND INF ELIMINATION

Beginning in 1977, several allied leaders had become increasingly concerned with growing Soviet theater nuclear force capabilities, especially the deployment of a new intermediate-range mobile missile, the SS-20. Chancellor Helmut Schmidt demanded in October of that year dismantlement of these weapons because they represented a regional disparity in favor of the Soviet Union seriously disturbing the attempt of SALT I and the Vladivostok agreement to attain strategic parity.

Fear was also expressed in NATO circles that the increasing deployment of SS-20s could impair the effectiveness of the strategy of forward defense and flexible response on which the Alliance's policy of deterrence was based. Hence, a task force was established to examine NATO's future requirements for modernized theater nuclear forces. The NPG was entrusted with this task and concluded that an arms control effort was needed to help achieve the basic Alliance goal of a more stable balance at lower levels of nuclear weapons. The consequence of these deliberations, in which the FRG played a significant role, was the NATO double-track decision on 12 December 1979. This decision aimed at (1) the construction and deployment in Europe of 572 new U.S. ground-launched nuclear theater systems with 107 Pershing II missiles stationed in the FRG and 464 cruise missiles deployed elsewhere in Western Europe, and (2) parallel and complementary negotiations regarding the elimination of Soviet intermediate-range nuclear forces. At the same time, NATO ministers were urged to increase their defense budgets by 3 percent, for which the FRG became one of the strongest advocates.

General Secretary Brezhnev had declared already before the NATO double-track decision was taken that the Soviet Union was ready to engage in negotiations on the reduction of SS-20 missiles, and in addition was ready to reduce the Soviet forces stationed in the GDR by 20,000 men and 1,000 tanks. When the NATO double-track decision was announced, Moscow reacted against the plans of deploying American theater nuclear weapons in Western Europe with severe political threats directed primarily against the FRG and showing clearly that, for West Germany, security and détente were difficult to bring on a common denominator. On the other hand, the NATO decision confirmed two pillars of West German security policy: preparedness for defense and willingness to negotiate.

The negotiations on intermediate-range nuclear forces (INF), began in October 1980. There was some doubt as to how much Washington was truly interested in complete INF arms reduction. For political reasons (that is, to strengthen its hold on the European allies), U.S. missiles were to be deployed under any circumstances because it was considered unwise to have the arms control track overtake entirely the deployment track. But for the Kremlin, the basic objective for negotiations was to freeze nuclear weapons and, therefore, to compel NATO to forgo the deployment of Pershing II and cruise missiles.

The Reagan administration took over in 1981, and the president announced on 18 November of that year that the United States was prepared to cancel its deployment of Pershing IIs and cruise missiles if the Soviets would dismantle their SS-20, SS-4, and SS-5 missiles. This announcement reflected the acceptance by Reagan of the Pentagon's view to aim at a "zero only" goal in contrast to the State Department's position of a "zero plus" objective which implied the negotiability of weapons quantity. But in March 1982, after consultation with the NATO allies, the United States expressed a willingness to accept an interim solution of equal levels of warheads on U.S. and Soviet longer-range missiles. Indeed, during recurring conversations in Geneva held exclusively between the American and Soviet chief negotiators, Paul Nitze and Yuli Kvitsinski, in restaurants or "walks in the woods," a solution was agreed upon that included the abandonment of the Pershing II deployment and reduction of the SS-20 missiles. But this solution was rejected by the governments of both superpowers, although the newly installed FRG chancellor, Helmut Kohl, would have preferred a more forthcoming U.S. attitude.

In November 1983, the Soviet Union broke off the INF talks and in December of that year NATO's INF forces were beginning to be deployed in the FRG, Italy, and Great Britain.

With the deployment of the Pershing IIs the Soviets may have sensed an increasing threat to their security, since the flight time of these missiles to hit Russian territory was very short and their target accuracy very high. In turn, this may have tempted Moscow to engage in a preemptive SS-20 strike against Western Europe, a set of circumstances representing a significant destabilizing factor in East-West relations. On the other hand, the FRG, by insisting on the principle of "nonsingularity" and thereby on the stationing of the new American nuclear weapons in the territories of other European allies besides itself, managed to share risks and costs among the NATO countries. This, in turn, strengthened the transatlantic "coupling" process.

Although many observers in the fall of 1984 doubted that the Soviet Union would return to the Geneva arms control negotiations with the United States, Moscow agreed to revive the talks in March 1985. Three sets of negotiations were begun—on strategic, INF, and space weapons—each with a separate chief negotiator in charge. While the ultimate U.S. objective from the outset was and remained a zero-zero outcome for INF, Moscow's initial centerpiece for these negotiations was a moratorium on further deployment of INF missiles. This position was abandoned by the Soviet Union when, on 16 January 1986, General Secretary Mikhail Gorbachev called for the complete elimination of INF weapons, both ballistic and cruise missiles. This proposed elimination did not touch British and French nuclear forces which the Soviet Union earlier wanted to be included in any count of INF weapons, but on which it gave up during the Reykjavik "presummit" meeting on 16 and 17 October 1986.

While it appeared that after Reykjavik the problems of long-range and INF missiles, and verification were being resolved, shorter-range missile systems (300–600 miles) were still to be covered. Agreement was reached to include the latter in the elimination of INF and the only major obstacle to a final INF accord was the 72 Pershing I-A missiles owned by West Germany, but whose warheads are controlled by the United States. The Soviet Union had declared that these warheads had to be part of any pact and it was up to the FRG to resolve this growing obstacle to a first major arms reduction arrangement. Chancellor Kohl met this challenge and promised to scrap the Pershing I-As in the event that the INF talks were success-fully concluded.

Kohl's statesmanlike action in support of a gradual denucleariza-tion process of Europe must be highly appreciated, considering the fact that the land-based nuclear missiles remaining in Europe with a range of 300 miles or less would most likely be targeted on West Germany. Moreover, the conventional superiority of Warsaw Pact forces would be further enhanced by the elimination of INF and would give Moscow greater leverage over Western Europe. At the same time, gaining public support for expanded budgets to pay for larger conventional forces in the European NATO member states may be difficult to obtain.

Meanwhile, the INF agreements were signed during a summit meeting of President Reagan and General Secretary Gorbachev on 8 December 1987. Ratified in 1988 by the U.S. Senate, this complete elimination of a whole category of weapons has been an enormous step forward in East-West arms control and may be followed by agreements on strategic weapons and conventional forces, highly critical to the security of the FRG and to the continuity of an effec-tive NATO.

THE FRENCH CONNECTION AND NATO

In early 1963, the FRG and France signed the Franco-German friendship treaty which called for regular meetings between German and French officials. For Chancellor Adenauer, always a dedicated Francophile, this was a very important policy development. When Ludwig Erhard followed Adenauer as FRG chancellor in the fall of 1963, differences between the two governments began to arise, as the new chancellor was not as sympathetic to various French policy projects as had been his predecessor. Nevertheless, for the first time in its history as a nation, Germany had a friendly country as a neighbor to the West. This provided the Germans with a diplomatic advantage reinforced by a psychological need.

When early in 1966 General de Gaulle announced that France would withdraw from NATO's command structure and that NATO bases and command facilities would have to be removed from French territory, it was feared in Bonn that the FRG's security would become undermined. Moreover, this development raised difficult legal and political questions as to how the French troops could remain on West German territory once they were withdrawn from NATO and returned to retain these forces on German soil. Eventually this issue was resolved when Bonn consented to the continuing presence of French troops in their country on French terms. These were trying times for Bonn but, in spite of recurring security concerns, the FRG remained basically committed to the NATO alliance.

West German–French relations during the last twenty years have had their ups and downs as far as regional economics and politics were concerned but, in the military sector, German and French troops found various aspects of cooperation, such as combined maneuvers, enjoyable and productive. Moving gradually away from de Gaulle's go-it-alone and independent security policy, French military doctrine rejected the notion of France being an "absolute sanctuary" as being unrealistic. Instead, it was suggested in 1976 by General Guy Mery, chief of staff of the armed forces, that although French forces would not participate in NATO's forward defense preparations in times of peace, France would be willing to take part in a forward "first" battle and French tactical nuclear weapons would have to be employed to affect the outcome of such an engagement. Hence, French forces would participate in the NATO defense of West Germany, including tactical nuclear weapons utilization close to the French border with strategic nuclear arms serving as the ultimate backup in the defense of French territory. The consequence would be the concept of an "enlarged sanctuary," as it was impossible to separate the defense of France from that of Central and Western Europe.

Calls on France can now also be heard to abandon its concept of national independence in order to make a decisive contribution to the construction of a united political Europe. Within such an effort, Franco-German military cooperation could be seen as the broadening nucleus of "European" security that would be based on adequate and increasingly comprehensive defense collaboration among West European states. However, this does not imply abandonment of the NATO alliance; indeed, President Mitterand has been quoted as saying, "The worst danger for us would be that Americans move away from the shores of our continent."

Franco-German military cooperation was intensified in the summer of 1987 when a 4,200-man joint brigade of German and French troops was established. Initially commanded by a French officer, its command would later alternate with German officers. Although a specific mission for the brigade had not been defined immediately, the French and German defense ministers stated: "In the event of crisis, it will fight alongside the other European and Atlantic forces, but it won't be part of NATO's integrated command." General Bernard B. Roger, who was being relieved at that time from his position as NATO's Supreme Allied Commander in Europe (*SACEUR*), insisted that the brigade remain under the command of his successor, General John R. Gavin, because the latter could not "afford to lose a brigade." However, Bonn acquiesced to the French position that the brigade should stay outside NATO's integrated structure like the rest of France's armed forces. While this may not be a German attitude that pleases Washington, and especially the Pentagon, it should be kept in mind that the peacetime strength of the German armed forces amounting to 495,000 men represents 50 percent of the NATO land forces in Central Europe and more than 60 percent of

NATO's main battle tanks. The 2,100 German members of the joint brigade, therefore, should matter very little.

In September 1987, the joint brigade conducted maneuvers, named "Bold Sparrow," which were commanded by a German officer and designed to demonstrate the commonality of the Franco-German security area. This was followed by a Mitterand proposal for setting up a Franco-German Defense Council which was fully accepted by the Kohl government and was seen as a "great step closer to a German-French as well as a European security community." The Bonn government stressed in connection with the establishment of the defense council that it, as well as the brigade, would strengthen the "European pillar of the Atlantic Alliance."

For many Germans, the Franco-German Friendship Treaty provides a significant basis for European security policy, although a strong majority wants to continue in the NATO alliance. For France, which is no longer a frontline state, the Federal Republic is the strategic forefield. For Germany, France is the indispensable supplementary element for the forward defense. Through this strategy, the French sanctuary is extended from the Rhine to the Elbe. The increasingly close Franco-German cooperation could induce other West European countries to collaborate in their security policies through either WEU or the European Community.

But, as Hans-Gert Poettering points out, there are also limits to Franco-German cooperation.

1. The French strategy of massive retaliation is incompatible with NATO's strategy of flexible response;
2. France is striving for dominance in the arms policy sector;
3. The "onus" of the Federal Republic of Germany is to work for reunification; and
4. Germany has limited scope for action due to its dependence on the United States.

It is interesting to note that, according to a 1985 poll conducted by *Le Monde*, 57 percent of the French favor France's assisting West Germany in case of war, and 40 percent seem to approve the extension of the French nuclear shield to the Federal Republic.

In summary, while the French connection has become increasingly important for the security and defense strategies of the Federal Republic and should be intensified, NATO and the United States remain the ultimate security backbone for the German people in the foreseeable future. This does not include cooperative defense enterprises among the European allies which, in fact, are highly desirable for both Western Europe and the United States, as they are likely to strengthen the alliance's defensive capabilities and may reduce tensions. The more self-confidence the individual NATO member states can gain through participation in and consultation regarding the common task, the more harmonious will be the necessary interactions within the organization and the easier it may be to reach a gradually improved East-West relationship.

GERMANY'S SECURITY AND U.S. STRATEGIC NUCLEAR WEAPONS

If, as appears likely, the recently signed INF agreement between the United States and the Soviet Union is ratified and implemented over a few years, the FRG's security will become ultimately dependent on U.S. strategic nuclear weapons. The number of these weapons may also be reduced in future arms control negotiations between the superpowers, a step which undoubtedly will be welcomed not only by Bonn but by the other NATO allies as well. For all of the European NATO allies, the objective during 1985 and 1986 was to persuade the Reagan administration to continue compliance with the SALT II Treaty. There was also widespread disappointment among them, including the FRG, when Reagan announced the abandonment of the SALT II obligations in the fall of 1986.

What the impact of the American Strategic Defense Initiative (SDI) will be on NATO and FRG security is difficult to predict and a matter of considerable speculation. Would it strengthen or undermine the "coupling" process between the United States and Western Europe? Would it provide an impetus to a realistic "European" defense system? These are issues that need to be pondered not only by Bonn, which participates in SDI research, but also by the other NATO allies. No definite answers may be available until a clearer picture emerges about this issue between Washington and Moscow.

Table 18.1
West German Assessment of NATO

A. Support for NATO Membership				
	1966	1980	1985	1986
In favor of:				
Remaining in NATO without change	82%	85%	87%	88%
Leaving NATO	3	1	7	8
No response	15	4	5	4

B. Significance of U.S. Troops in FRG				
	1970	1980	1985	1986
Essential	72%	81%	76%	77%
Unimportant	11	11	12	12
Damaging	7	5	12	11
No response	15	4	5	4

C. Degree of Threat Perception				
	1962	1980	1985	1986
High	63%	48%	37%	35%
Not serious	22	48	61	64
No response	5	3	1	1

D. Strength of NATO Defense				
	1962	1980	1985	1986
NATO strong enough to hold WTO force aggression	31%	51%	50%	58%
WTO force will overrun NATO defenses	44	47	40	
No response	21	2	2	

Source: Adapted from *Bundeswehr Aktuell,* 29 October 1986, Poll 11b.

VIEWS OF THE WEST GERMAN PUBLIC

With the circumstances surrounding the West German security situation being somewhat uncertain and the East-West relationship moving through a period of change, it may be interesting to look at some selected public opinion data.

As already briefly mentioned, a strong majority of Germans want the FRG to remain a member of NATO. Indeed, the number of those

Table 18.2
European Assessments of Defense

	Type of Alliances			
	Germany	France	Britain	Italy
Links with U.S. and NATO	54%	26%	41%	19%
Common European Defense	19	35	23	38
Own defense	25	20	26	31
No response	2	20	10	12

	Eurodefense: Nuclear or Conventional?			
	Germany	France	Britain	Italy
Nuclear, Franco-Britain	12%	6%	13%	3%
Nuclear, all countries	14	35	35	14
Conventional	29	25	35	70
None of these	44	13	4	6
No response	2	15	13	7

Source: Adapted from the Guardian, 19 February 1987.

in favor has increased since 1966 as seen in table 18.1. Even the age group from sixteen to twenty-four shows 81 percent of the respondents in support. At the same time, a substantial majority of West Germans considers the presence of U.S. troops in the FRG as very important. In 1987, a poll conducted by the magazine Stern indicated that 51 percent of the respondents would regret it if American forces were withdrawn from Europe. As for the threat perception of the West Germans with respect to aggression by Warsaw Treaty Forces (WTO), the concerns of the respondents as seen in part C of table 18.1 have declined markedly. During the same period (1962–1986), an increasing number of respondents considered NATO sufficiently powerful to stop an attack by WTO forces and prevent Western Europe from being overrun.

In polls conducted by the Guardian in West Germany, France, Britain, and Italy and reported on 16 February 1987, some questions similar to those discussed in table 18.1 were posed. Should the alliance be continued with NATO and the United States or should the four countries establish a common European defense, or perhaps only their own national defense? If a common defense, should it be

Table 18.3
European Assessments of SDI

SDI: More Peace or More War?				
	Germany	*France*	*Britain*	*Italy*
Increase chances of peace	23%	23%	28%	17%
Increase risk of war	40	21	30	42
No effect either way	35	34	38	22
No response	2	21	4	19
Participation in SDI?				
	Germany	*France*	*Britain*	*Italy*
Participate in SDI	22%	19%	27%	20%
Develop own system	19	25	20	19
Not get involved at all	58	35	48	46
No response	2	21	5	15

Source: Adapted from the *Guardian*, 19 February 1987. Polls took place between November 1986 and January 1987.

"nuclear, Franco-British based," nuclear, all countries involved, or only conventional? In Germany, 54 percent opted for links with NATO and the United States (see table 18.2), while a strong plurality of Germans (44 percent) were opposed to any kind of Eurodefense.

Finally, it is interesting to note German opinions on SDI, especially as compared with those in other European NATO countries. In terms of increasing the chances of peace or the risks of war, table 18.3 suggests that 40 percent of German respondents consider it as increasing war risks. Indeed, 58 percent of the Germans do not want to get involved at all in SDI, compared to 22 percent who are interested in participating in SDI. It is noteworthy that, for whatever reason, 21 percent of the French respondents have no response to either question.

In summary, then, the data in all tables provide persuasive evidence that the Germans constitute very loyal allies of NATO and the United States in general. They may not have been persuaded by the possible benefits of SDI, but quite a few Americans, perhaps more than half, have not become convinced either.

MUTUAL BENEFITS AND CONCERNS

In reviewing the period from 1955 to 1988, during which the FRG has been a member of NATO, we can identify significant mutual benefits flowing from Bonn's NATO strategies for both entities, but must also recognize various concerns which have occasionally marred a basically quite harmonious relationship.

1. West Germany's security has been safeguarded since the end of World War II through NATO's deterrent powers consisting of nuclear weapons, mostly those of the United States, and strong conventional forces in which the *Bundeswehr* and American troops have played major roles.
2. The complete elimination of INF nuclear weapons has been accepted by Bonn, including the scrapping of the FRG-owned Pershing I-A launchers, an act of political wisdom by the Kohl government. Reductions in strategic offensive nuclear weapons by the superpowers are likely and will be supported by NATO and the FRG.
3. Nuclear deterrence in the future will depend mostly on U.S. strategic missiles located in America or on submarines. This set of circumstances, combined with the possibility of a successful SDI, could lead to a gradual "decoupling" of the defenses on the two sides of the Atlantic and could result in a reduction of the FRG's security.
4. The Franco-German military cooperation is apt to be intensified, strengthening conventional military and perhaps limited nuclear capabilities in Europe, but this will not reduce the FRG contribution to NATO and may, in fact, enhance it.
5. German concerns about full participation in decisionmaking regarding the deployment of nuclear weapons have been assuaged by the FRG's permanent membership in NATO's Nuclear Planning Group.
6. Bonn's discomfort and fears that superpower agreements on arms control may be made at the expense of European NATO allies have been lessened, while German freedom to pursue selected aspects of Ostpolitik and détente is recognized by the NATO

partners, with the goal of reunification, however, remaining questionable.
7. American desires for greater burden sharing by the FRG remain alive, but muted.

To eliminate existing and future potential tensions within NATO and maintain an effective defense system, some of Henry Kissinger's suggestions made in late 1987 should be adopted:

- Europe-bashing on burden sharing should end, especially since agreement is lacking on precisely what burden is to be shared.
- Defense policy must be related to arms control policy and this must take into consideration the geographic realities, especially as far as the reduction of conventional forces is concerned.
- Allied strategic doctrine should be reviewed and hopefully the threshold raised at which nuclear weapons would have to be used.
- A greater European sense of identity in defense matters within NATO should be encouraged which could include eventually the utilization of British and French nuclear forces. As Kissinger states: "Allowing Europe to assume greater responsibility for its own defense will in the long run strengthen Atlantic ties and help Germany overcome its sense of isolation." In this connection, it is noteworthy that FRG defense minister Manfred Woerner was chosen on 11 December 1987, as secretary general of NATO. He assumed his new post on 1 July 1988.

19

THE WEST GERMAN SOCIAL DEMOCRATS' SECOND PHASE OF OSTPOLITIK IN HISTORICAL PERSPECTIVE

Ann L. Phillips

The depth of West German commitment to liberal democracy and to the Western alliance remains an underlying concern to some American and West European leaders forty years after the end of World War II. The historical antagonism of German intellectual circles toward the limited vision offered by liberal democracy and the painful memory of the fate of Weimar form the basis of that concern. Ralf Dahrendorf, an eminent West German sociologist, provided a richly detailed analysis of the roots and weaknesses of liberal democracy in Germany in his classic *Gesellschaft und Demokratie in Deutschland* which first appeared in 1965. Periodic academic conferences and analytical writings attempt to assess the stability and health of the political system fashioned by the Western powers in the Federal Republic of Germany (FRG) after World War II.

A resurgence of uncertainty concerning West German commitment to the West and its liberal democratic values has been generated by the Social Democratic Party (SPD) in recent years. Washington has become worried that the SPD, the largest, oldest, and presently chief opposition party in Germany, has become increasingly soft on security policy and ambivalent about its orientation in the East-West conflict since Helmut Schmidt's demise as chancellor in 1982. Alarm was reflected and created by articles such as one in the *Wall Street Journal* in December 1986 which asserted, "The SPD makes itself at home in a role it has been moving toward for years— accomplice to Moscow." More scholarly analyses of the SPD's Second Phase of Ostpolitik by some U.S. observers reveal similar suspicions.[1] The charge is serious and reflects deep-seated fears of any West German tendency toward neutralism in the East-West contest. In order to assess the validity of this change, it is necessary to first examine the substance of the SPD's Second Phase of Ostpolitik which has stirred all the controversy.

THE SECOND PHASE OF OSTPOLITIK

The Second Phase of Ostpolitik is presented by the SPD as the consolidation, continuation, and development of the Ostpolitik since the late 1960s, but under changed conditions. That period, now characterized as the First Phase, marked the beginning of a normalization of West German relations with its neighbors to the East. Treaties with Moscow and Warsaw in 1970 explicitly accepted the political and territorial boundaries which emerged after World War II and committed the signatories to a mutual renunciation of force. Subsequent negotiations between the two Germanies led to the Basic Treaty (December 1972) in which Bonn gave up its claim to represent all Germans and accorded de facto recognition to the German Democratic Republic (GDR). By 1973 the FRG had established diplomatic relations with all members of the Warsaw Pact. The Eastern treaties provided the foundation for the Ostpolitik strategy of *Wandel durch Annäherung* (change through rapprochement) which required a climate of stability and security in Europe.

The first or political phase of the Ostpolitik is today largely considered an unqualified success among all major parties in the FRG. The conservative CDU/CSU-FDP coalition which came to power in October 1982 for the first time in thirteen years pledged not only to abide by the Eastern Treaties (*Pacta sunt servanda*) but also to build upon those accomplishments. Particularly strong support exists across the political spectrum for the continuation of Deutschlandpolitik along the lines begun by the SPD. Ostpolitik did not always enjoy such acclaim. In the early 1970s, vocal elements of the opposition CDU/CSU denounced the SPD and their then coalition partners, the Free Democrats, for their policies of rapprochement with the East. They accused the Brandt government of selling out German interests and likened the Eastern treaties to a second Versailles. Thus, the most convincing evidence of the success of Ostpolitik is the gradual and sometimes grudging support it has won from the opposition.

Given then that a broad consensus has developed in the FRG in support of Ostpolitik and all sides have pledged to continue it, why has the SPD's Second Phase policy stirred so much controversy? Concern has developed in two arenas emanating from different premises. First, the United States found continuation of Ostpolitik, at a time when it had abandoned détente, suspect at best. Second, within the FRG, widespread support for continuation of Ostpolitik did not translate into agreement on what that meant in substance.

Some members of the SPD began calling for a Second Phase in the late 1970s while the party was still in power, although the phrase and the concept gained wider currency after the change in government in 1982. The SPD wanted to renew the impetus and vitality of Ostpolitik in the face of deteriorating U.S.-Soviet relations. A fresh point of departure was deemed necessary in light of the superpowers' differing and incompatible interpretations of détente and the recognition that political agreements would not automatically lead to disarmament—a fundamental assumption of the early 1970s. As a result, issues which were not central to the First Phase of Ostpolitik, such as disarmament and environmental issues, have become the centerpiece of the Second Phase of Ostpolitik. The SPD's initiatives on security matters have become the focal point of controversy both within NATO and within the FRG.

Security Policy

A key concept of the SPD's security policy is *security partnership*, best translated according to SPD members as mutual security. Mutual security denotes the condition created by nuclear forces which requires for the first time that one's own security is predicated on the security of one's adversary. Former chancellor Helmut Schmidt developed the concept of security partnership and first used it at the United Nations in 1978 although antecedents are present in the mutual renunciation of force clauses in the Eastern treaties.[2] Security partnership dictates the search for a more stable relationship between the two blocs through greater efforts for nuclear disarmament and agreements on substantial and verifiable confidence-building measures. Security partnership underlines the conviction that there is no military solution to the East-West conflict, rather there is only a political solution to what has become a military problem. The common feeling of being threatened, which is both cause and effect of the arms race, can only be overcome through a policy of mutual security between the blocs, according to the SPD's party platform on security adopted at the Party Congress in Nuremberg in August 1986.

A prerequisite for this process is stability in Europe which requires respect for the integrity and sovereignty of all European states within their current borders. This is a fundamental principle of both Ostpolitik and its Second Phase. The SPD cites NATO's Harmel Report, adopted in 1967, which outlined military security and détente as the two complementary pillars of NATO strategy in support of its position. On these grounds, the SPD has asserted that its call for renewed focus on détente does not deviate from alliance policy but promotes it.

The party does not accept the division of Europe into two opposing alliances as a long-term solution to the problem of European security, but it does recognize the importance of the alliances for stability in the foreseeable future. The SPD again cites the Harmel Report which looks to a European settlement to overcome the barriers between East and West in support of its own long-term goal of overcoming the division of Europe.

Not surprisingly, such assurances have not assuaged concerns about current SPD thinking on national security matters. Unease has been heightened by the most critical SPD writings on NATO strategy: Oskar Lafontaine's book *Angst vor den Freunden* (afraid of our friends) and the von Bülow paper.[3] Written in the early 1980s, both analyze the failure of NATO and Warsaw Pact strategy to make progress toward alleviating the East-West conflict. Both reflect frustration with European dependence upon the superpowers for security and survival and impatience with the inability or unwillingness of the superpowers to move ahead on substantive arms reduction at that time. And both reflect deep-seated opposition to U.S. deployment of intermediate-range nuclear missiles—a symbol of bankrupt NATO strategy in the East-West competition. Although the Warsaw

Pact and the Soviet Union were harshly criticized by the authors, the fact that NATO and the United States were castigated in similar terms elicited outrage within the FRG and the Western alliance. At the same time, Lafontaine's call for West German partial withdrawal from NATO à la France further contributed to the rising specter of a neutralized FRG.

Although SPD foreign policy specialists largely discount the more radical proposals of Lafontaine and von Bülow and understand the concern they generated in Washington, they agree that changes in NATO are necessary. The SPD's governing program for 1987–1990 emphasizes the need for NATO to take into account the interests of all of its members and calls for a reform in NATO strategy to reflect readiness for détente as well as an adequate defense capability. Both NATO and the WTO are admonished to develop structures and weapons useful only for defense (*strukturelle Nichtangriffsfähigkeit*). At the same time, the party rejects the argument that the Strategic Defense Initiative could contribute to the defensive restructuring of military forces.[4]

The SPD's position on the role for nuclear weapons and deterrence strategy in maintaining peace remains unclear. The party applauds the Intermediate-range Nuclear Forces (INF) Treaty signed by President Reagan and General Secretary Gorbachev in November 1987 and supports deep cuts in strategic nuclear weapons as a logical next step. This does not, however, necessarily translate into support for the elimination of nuclear weapons from Europe. Bernhard Zepter, SPD *Fraktion* specialist for national security policy, has argued that the whole concept of security partnership is predicated on the existence of nuclear weapons. Therefore, deterrence remains fundamental to European security. But the concept of sufficiency should replace the arms race or pursuit of the chimera of complete disarmament as the basis for security, he argues. Thinking should be reoriented toward establishing the minimum number of nuclear weapons necessary to maintain deterrence. Zepter calculates that 90 percent of nuclear weapons in Europe are superfluous.[5]

Others in the party reject any long-term compatibility of deterrence and lasting peace. They cite the historical failure of deterrence to prevent war, decoupling the strategy of deterrence from nuclear capability, and argue that nuclear weapons have only heightened the imperative to overcome deterrence. This line of reasoning is elaborated in the SPD-Socialist Unity Party (SED) paper, "Conflicting Ideologies and Common Security," discussed in the next section.

SPD Initiatives in the East

The SPD defines its vision of progress on East-West relations primarily as a constructive alternative to the policies of confrontation. Building upon contacts, understanding, and goodwill established by the SPD's Ostpolitik, the party created working groups with the CPSU and several of the governing parties of East Europe to discuss and resolve specific problems in East-West relations. The motive for establishing the working groups was to test the concept of security partnership between antagonistic state systems in a concrete way.[6]

The SPD-CPSU working group has focused on the diversion of resources from efforts to combat third world underdevelopment by the arms race. Other working group topics include: environmental issues and pollution control (SPD and Communist Party of Czechoslovakia); expanding economic cooperation (SPD and Hungarian Socialist Workers Party); and confidence-building measures (SPD and Polish Communist Party).

SPD discussions with the Socialist Unity Party (SED) of the GDR have been the most fruitful and the most controversial. The centerpiece of those discussions is the document "Conflicting Ideologies and Common Security," jointly presented by the Basic Values Commission of the SPD and the Academy for Social Sciences of the SED Central Committee on 27 August 1987. A product of three years' work, the document sets forth a framework for survival and development of competing systems in the nuclear age. Central to that framework is acceptance of the concept of mutual security by both sides. This, in turn, necessitated fundamental revision of the concept of peaceful coexistence: each accepts the long-term right of the other system to exist, each regards the other for the first time as capable of reform and capable of peace (*reformfähig und friedensfähig*). This provides the theoretical foundation for overcoming deterrence as the basis for East-West relations and moving toward a positive competition between systems as well as cooperation on global problems such as the environment and underdevelopment.

Proposals for the elimination of chemical and nuclear weapons from Central Europe prepared by special working groups of the SPD and SED in 1986 are presented as concrete examples of mutual security and of the potential for more comprehensive agreements between opposing systems under such a framework. The arms control proposals were offered as models for agreements between the governments in power in Bonn and East Berlin. Further arms control discussions on conventional military strength and strategic nuclear weapons began in April 1988. A proposal detailing recommendations for the creation of a "Zone of Trust and Security in Central Europe" was presented by the working group as an interim agreement in July 1988.

A heated dispute arose concerning the significance of these model agreements. The position of each side, however, was bedeviled by inconsistencies. Those who traditionally assume the tightest control by the Soviet Union over the policies of East Europe have been the first to discount any connection between the agreements and the potential for similar agreements with the USSR—this, despite Gorbachev's endorsement of all SED–SPD efforts to date. The SPD, on the other hand, touts the SED as an independent negotiating partner, while promoting the proposals as pilot projects which test possibilities for general East-West agreements based on an assumption of ultimate Soviet authority over SED initiatives.

Much as the SPD seeks cooperation with the Soviet Union and the East, the ideological confrontation between Marxism-Leninism and democratic socialism is also very much a part of the Second Phase of Ostpolitik. The SPD-SED paper underscores the fundamental disagreement between the parties: SPD adherence to the pluralist values of liberal democracy is juxtaposed against SED commitment to the principles of Marxism-Leninism. SPD members who have participated in the working groups with Soviet and East European counterparts are quick to point to the bitter history of social democratic-communist relations to underscore their vigilance in any dealings with communists. Older party members vividly recall the suffering of Social Democrats in the Soviet occupation zone at the end of World War II and instill this memory in younger members.

The SPD has been careful not to establish official party relations with any governing Communist party, with the exception of the Communist League of Yugoslavia. The working groups have been organized and authorized by the *Fraktion*, not the party as a whole. The distinction is perhaps more significant to the Communist parties because of the importance signified by party ties over state-to-state relations, although SPD officials underline the difference as well.

Internal and External

In the Federal Republic, the SPD's Second Phase of Ostpolitik has been subject to severe criticism from both the Right and the Left, from within the party as well as outside. Among the latter critics, charges range from just short of treason on the right, to selling out on the left. During the 1986–1987 election campaign, the CDU/CSU took the SPD to task for being too harsh on the United States and NATO and too soft on the U.S.S.R. They accused the SPD of undermining the West German consensus on foreign policy in effect since 1959 by rejecting the double-track policy on deployment of inter-mediate-range nuclear weapons first proposed by Helmut Schmidt and then adopted by NATO. The FDP was more muted in its criticism because it remains a strong supporter of détente, but did join in the accusations that the SPD was conducting its own "shadow" foreign policy by concluding specific agreements with the SED. In private, foreign policy specialists of the governing parties agreed that much of the criticism of the SPD was preelection rhetoric and none disapproved of SPD efforts to maintain and pursue contacts with the CPSU or other governing parties of East Europe. They did, however, agree that the model agreements with the SED overstepped acceptable bounds. The consensus among the governing parties is that arms control agreements are the domain of the two super-powers and that West Germans have no basis upon which to initiate bilateral discussion on the subject.

The United States weighed in with the argument that NATO needs a united front in order to deal effectively with the Soviet Union. The fear also lurks in the background that the FRG may be lured away from the Western alliance by an offer from Moscow for a new association between the two Germanies. The SPD rejects neutrality as a viable policy option. West German withdrawal from NATO, they argue, would undermine not only European stability but also German influence on the superpowers. Furthermore, SPD leaders insist that German interests can only be asserted in concert with neighbors both East and West, not against them. They add that many of their criticisms of Reagan administration policy on East-West relations are shared by the opposition in Washington.

The SPD itself has not been united behind its foreign policy program. The small conservative wing led by Helmut Schmidt opposed the party's repudiation of the earlier decision to deploy Pershing IIs and cruise missiles in Europe. It tried, unsuccessfully, to equate support for the double-track decision of NATO with support for Western freedom. It also took the party leadership to task for downplaying the ideological differences with the communists and for being too critical of the United States.[7] This wing of the party has been weakened considerably by the retirement of its leading figure, Helmut Schmidt. It should be noted, however, that even Schmidt supports the need for greater European assertiveness, due to a perceived proclivity of each superpower to discount the interests of its allies. But he promotes West German cooperation with France as the key to that self-assertion and, therefore, the proper focus of Bonn's foreign policy rather than the party's emphasis on revitalizing contacts with the East.[8]

Criticism from the Left is probably the most painful for the SPD. The party seems caught in a no-win situation—the center Right denounces the Social Democrats for their swing to the left while the Left derides the SPD for its establishment politics. Much of the strong leftist constituency which traditionally supported the SPD has abandoned the party for the Greens. At the same time the Greens, along with opposition groups in East Europe, condemn the SPD's Second Phase of Ostpolitik for seeking stability in East-West relations at the expense of the East European people.[9] SPD policy is criticized on two levels: first, the SPD seeks good relations with the Soviet Union at the expense of East Europe; and second, it pursues relations with the East European establishment at the expense of the people. The issue is one of détente from above or below. Both the Greens and groups such as Poland's Solidarity support the latter.

SPD leaders counter that while they have full sympathy for the goals of such groups as Solidarity, history and political reality demonstrate that support for opposition movements in the USSR and East Europe—détente from below—is ultimately counterproductive. They are convinced, based on substantial changes in the Soviet bloc since Stalin's death and their own experience since 1970, that progress can be made in overcoming the East-West divide and in opening up East Europe and the Soviet Union by working within, not against, the established order. SPD policymakers remind critics of the significant progress made in East-West relations during détente. Travel, family visits, exchange of information, scholars, artists, family reunifications, emigration, and so forth—all increased markedly in the 1970s. By contrast, these measures showed a significant decline when confrontation replaced détente between the superpowers at the end of the decade. Thus, the SPD does not demand system change within the Soviet Union and East Europe as a precondition for cooperation, thereby putting it at odds with many on the left and right. The Social Democrats' expectation is that creation of a system of peace (*Friedensordnung*) in Europe is the most effective way to encourage change.

Swing to the Left?

Does the Second Phase of Ostpolitik represent a sharp swing to the left in SPD policy as many West German and U.S. critics have charged? Labels of left and right seem to obscure rather than clarify the question. Is a policy premised on European stability leftist? Stability and order are traditionally provinces of conservatives. At the same time, endorsement of European stability does not translate into SPD support for the status quo. Stability is regarded as the prerequisite for change. The difficulty in trying to accurately label such positions as left or right is further underscored by the apparent convergence of the Left and the Right in support of policies to destabilize East Europe and eradicate the postwar order, albeit with very different visions of a desirable replacement. Where does this leave SPD policy in terms of a left-right spectrum? The real issue is whether this policy represents a major departure for the SPD. For this, one needs a broader, historical perspective in order to judge.

The Second Phase of Ostpolitik is built upon the same philosophical orientation which gave rise to the Ostpolitik of the 1960s, but it does embrace new areas—the most controversial being defense and national security policies. The U.S. abandonment of détente in the late 1970s also contributed substantially to the perception of an SPD swing to the left. Both the Carter administration in its last years and the Reagan administration adopted military buildup and confrontation as the basic principles of East-West relations. The INF Treaty signed by President Reagan and General Secretary Gorbachev is presented by the U.S. administration as the fruit of its hard-line policy. U.S. policy toward the Soviet Union has ranged widely between cold war and détente in the postwar period. As such, U.S. policy provides a faulty point of reference from which to assess the constancy of SPD policy.

Another factor which contributes to the imagery of an SPD shift to the left was Helmut Schmidt's increasing isolation in the party during his last years as chancellor and the party's repudiation of his commitment to deploy the missiles shortly after he stepped down as chancellor. But the praise Schmidt's policies enjoy from members of the CDU/CSU gives rise to the possibility that Helmut Schmidt represented a swing to the right, so that the party's reassertion of traditional values and policy direction appears at first glance to mark a radicalization of the SPD. The argument that Schmidt diverged from the party mainstream would also explain, in part, the alienation of the SPD's traditional leftist constituency in recent years.

The case can also be made that the Second Phase of Ostpolitik represents continuity not only with Ostpolitik but also with the initial postwar orientation of the party. Early postwar writings of Kurt Schumacher, the party's first chairman, support this argument. Although many SPD members profess no affinity for Schumacher—in part because the conservative wing of the party claimed his mantle—one finds fundamental values in Schumacher's early postwar writings that consciously or unconsciously seem to orient the party today, despite the change in time and circumstances. Contemporary admirers and detractors of Schumacher in the SPD emphasize his anticommunism to such an extent that its place in his body of thought is distorted. Granted, Schumacher was outspoken in his denunciation of bolshevism as early as 1928, reacted strongly against the fusion of the German Communist Party and the Social Democratic Party in the Soviet occupation zone in 1946, and condemned every suggestion of a similar fusion in the Western zones. It is often forgotten, however, that Schumacher was also extremely critical of German cooperation with the Western occupying powers.[10] He opposed the imposition of an American political and economic system in the Western zones, much as he opposed the creation of a Soviet style system in the Eastern zone. Schumacher found both the American and Soviet systems flawed, writing that there can be no socialism without democracy and no democracy without socialism.[11]

Despite his fundamental differences with the Soviets, Schumacher insisted that a modus vivendi with the U.S.S.R. could and must be found. He premised a modus vivendi with the U.S.S.R. on accepting the Soviet Union as it is; change in the Soviet system was not a precondition for reaching an agreement. The recent SPD-SED paper applies this basic premise more broadly to relations between competing systems. Schumacher saw the solution to the German question in the establishment of an international community of peace (*Friedensgemeinschaft*) in which the U.S.S.R. would play a key role. Echoes of these thoughts are clearly present in the SPD's current formulation of a system of peace in Europe, even though the envisaged solution to the German Question has acquired new form. Schumacher argued for Europe to assert its own interests and held out great hopes for European cooperation, much as the SPD does today. The SPD continues to share Schumacher's commitment to overcome the division of Europe as well as his confidence in the attraction of social democracy for the East.

Another sort of continuity lies in Washington's and the CDU/CSU's perceptions of SPD policy toward the East. Both were as concerned about an SPD shift to the East in 1970 as they are today. By the same token, the SPD cited allied indifference to FRG interests as an impetus to party initiatives toward the East both in the 1970s and in the Second Phase.

To note these continuities is not to suggest that the SPD's Eastern policy has been static or that international conditions have not changed. Specific elements of the Second Phase reflect changes in both. More importantly, Adenauer's focus on cementing the FRG's commitment to the West provided both security and limitations which the SPD recognizes as the foundation for its initiatives to the East. Furthermore, the party itself underwent fundamental change when it abandoned its adherence to Marxist principles in the Godesberg Program of 1959 and accepted FRG alignment with the West in NATO the following year. Because these changes were in large part due to Soviet policy in the GDR, it is surprising, not that SPD policy has changed, but that Schumacher's immediate postwar vision for Europe and Germany bears such striking resemblance to the European peace system which the SPD promotes in the 1980s. On balance, then, it seems that SPD policy toward the East has maintained a fairly steady course, while the swings in U.S. foreign policy contribute as much as anything to the appearance of a major shift in SPD policy.

FUTURE PROSPECTS AND IMPLICATIONS

International conditions were in some ways more propitious for the Brandt government's Ostpolitik than those which exist for the SPD's Second Phase and, in some ways, they were less. During the Brandt initiative, both the United States and the Soviet Union were interested in détente, albeit for different reasons. Some disagreements over the pace and coordination of rapprochement with the East surfaced between Washington and Bonn, but by the late 1960s, the two governments' interests in improving East-West relations coincided. In the 1980s, by contrast, SPD leaders have found little support in Washington for their foreign policy interests, despite some modification in the Reagan administration's posture toward Moscow in its last year.

At the same time, favorable conditions for a new initiative in Ostpolitik—far more advantageous than any presented heretofore—have been created by the reform-minded leadership in the Soviet Union. During détente of the 1970s, Brezhnev sought economic exchanges with the West to gain access to Western technology in order to preserve the structure of the Soviet system. By contrast, Gorbachev seeks a resumption of détente as an integral part of structural reform of that system. The changes in climate underscore the extent to which the success of Ostpolitik is dependent upon superpower interest.

Traditionally, the West, and especially the United States, has sought to bring about changes in the U.S.S.R. through political, military, and/or economic pressure. The Soviet system and society have undergone significant changes since the early 1920s, but their resiliency in the face of an almost unprecedented combination of internal and external strains has defied expectation. Thus, the opportunity presented by the strong impulse for reform within the Soviet Union is not that the West can mold the direction and content of reform, but rather that it can contribute to an international climate which is favorable to indigenous forces of reform whose success is by no means certain.

Debate over the nature of the Soviet system and its potential for reform lies at the heart of the controversy over the Second Phase of Ostpolitik. The positions are so well known that they need not be repeated here. A related question, whether a revitalized Soviet Union is in the interests of the West, is also central to the reaction evoked by the SPD policy. The U.S. position is ambivalent. Although Washington has long professed a strong interest in the well-being of the Soviet peoples, it has also taken some comfort in the stagnating Soviet economy which undermines the Soviet claim to superpower status in all but military terms. An economically strong Soviet Union would be a more effective competitor in the international arena. Not only would Moscow be able to use the economic instrument in foreign policy more widely and effectively, some luster might also be restored to the Soviet system as an attractive model for others to emulate.

The SPD's response to the prospect of a rejuvenated Soviet Union is unequivocally positive. The Kohl government seems to have embraced this position as well. Hans-Dietrich Genscher provides a critical element of continuity in FRG foreign policy, having served as foreign minister and key supporter of Ostpolitik in both the Schmidt and Kohl governments. Since the Bundestag elections in January 1987 in which the FDP made a strong showing, Genscher has guided FRG foreign policy more firmly in the direction of the SPD's Second Phase of Ostpolitik. He has taken the lead among West Europeans in support of Gorbachev's reform program. He urged the West to "initiate a comprehensive process of disarmament and set up cooperative security structures; launch large-scale economic cooperation to help the Soviet Union modernize; and take up a concept of a 'common European edifice' where the divisions between East and West are overcome."

The poor showing of the CDU in the January 1987 elections was attributed to a significant degree to the hard line Chancellor Kohl adopted toward the GDR and East Europe during the campaign. The chastening effect of the electorate, plus public opinion polls in the FRG in 1987 which showed that Gorbachev inspired more confidence than Reagan among West German citizens, strengthened moderate voices within the party. In September 1987 Chancellor Kohl supported the U.S.-Soviet INF Treaty by agreeing to the relinquishment of West Germany's Pershing I-A missiles, the same month that Erich Honecker was welcomed in Bonn. Kohl has since postponed the question of modernization of battlefield-range nuclear weapons desired by NATO and pushed for further arms reduction negotiations between the superpowers. The CDU adopted a document at the Thirty-Sixth Party Congress in June 1988 on FRG-GDR relations which redefines the party's commitment to German reunification by predicating it upon the "understanding and support of our neighbors and friends."[12] The tone and content of government policy have become more compatible with SPD policy.

Although a marked convergence of government and SPD positions on Ostpolitik has taken place since January 1987, important policy differences continue to exist. The government emphasizes economic cooperation with the Soviet Union and East Europe and arms control, while the SPD has developed a much more comprehensive security component of its Ostpolitik. The government clearly does not place the same emphasis on improving relations between East and West that the SPD does. This is due not only to close ties with Washington, but also to the diversity of opinion within the ruling coalition in Bonn. Some CSU and CDU members are most reticent about expanding Ostpolitik.

Nonetheless, a new consensus within the FRG seems to be developing along the general lines of SPD policy in support of a revitalized Ostpolitik. Thus, rather than the SPD undermining the basic consensus on FRG foreign policy and national security in place since the late 1950s, as critics have charged, it appears to be contributing to a different one.

The implications of this new consensus for U.S.-FRG relations are uncertain. Periodic changes in the international environment put the relatively consistent SPD Eastern policy in and out of sync with U.S. policy. Cycles of agreement and divergence between the United States and the FRG reflect inevitable differences between a global and a regional power. Policy interests and alternatives for the United States are much broader than those of the FRG. As the Soviet Union has come to be regarded by many West Germans as a status quo power in Europe, the interests between the FRG and the United States have diverged. The SPD sees the Soviet-West German relationship removed from the global rivalry which characterizes U.S.-Soviet relations. Indications are that the Kohl government essentially agrees with this. Soviet actions outside of Europe are not of major concern. Thus, West Germans posit the divisibility of détente while the United States asserts its indivisibility. Washington does not accept this limited vision of German interests and emphasizes common values as the basis for concerted action in the international arena.[13] But as Eugen Selbmann, key architect of SPD Ostpolitik, prophetically observed, alliances have never survived on common values, only on common interests. The success or failure of Soviet reform will exert strong influence on future U.S.-FRG relations. It remains to be seen whether Gorbachev's new ideas about common security and peaceful coexistence will strengthen or undermine those common interests upon which the U.S.-FRG alliance has been based.

NOTES

1. Ronald D. Asmus, "The SPD's Second Ostpolitik with Perspectives from the USA," *Aussenpolitik* 1 (1987): 40–55.
2. Hans-Jochen Vogel, "Für eine neue Entspannung: Die Position der Sozialdemokraten," in *Zwanzig Jahre Ostpolitik: Bilanz und Perspek-*

tiven, ed. Horst Ehmke, Harlheinz Koppe, and Herbert Wehner (Bonn: Verlag Neue Gesellshaft, 1986), 362.

3. Oskar Lafontaine, *Angst vor den Freunden: Die Atomwaffen-Strategie der Supermächte. Zerstört die Bündnisse* (Hamburg: Verlag Rohwohlt, 1983). Andreas von Bülow, "Das Bülow-Papier: Strategie vertrauenschaffender Sicherheitsstrukturen in Europa: Wege zur Sicherheitspartnerschaft," (Frankfurt am Main: Eichborn Verlag, 1985).

4. *Regierungsprogram 1987–1990 der SPD: Beschluss des Parteivorstandes,* 22 September 1986, 58–60.

5. Bernhard Zepter, "Abrüstung und Rüstungskontrolle—Ausweg aus der Krise durch 'Suffizienz' und Vertrauensbildung?" *Die Neue Gesellschaft/Frankfurter Hefte* 2 (February 1985): 148–50.

6. Wilfried von Bredow and Rudolf Horst Brocke, *Das deutschlandpolitische Konzept der SPD: Darstellung, Hintergründe und Problembereiche der Deutschlandpolitik der SPD Mitte der achtziger Jahre* (Erlangen: Deutsche Gesellschaft für zeitgeschichtliche Fragen, 1986), 33.

7. Gesine Schwan, "Die SPD und die westliche Freiheit," *Die Neue Gesellschaft/Frankfurter Hefte* 10 (October 1983): 929–35; Jürgen Mahrung and Manfred Wilke, eds., *Wohin Treibt die SPD?* (Munich: Verlag Olzog, 1984).

8. Helmut Schmidt, "Europa Muss Sich Selbst Behaupten," *Die Zeit* 48 (21 November 1986), 3.

9. "Entspannungspolitik—in einer anderen Sicht: eine Antwort von einem Vertreter Solidarnosc," *Die Neue Gesellschaft/Frankfurter Hefte* 6 (June 1986): 548–52.

10. Kurt Schumacher, "Konsequenzen deutscher Politik: Aufruf Sommer 1945," in *Reden und Schriften,* ed. Arno Scholz and Walther G. Oschilewski (Berlin: Arani Verlag, 1953), 33–34.

11. Ulrich Buczylowski, *Kurt Schumacher und die deutsche Frage* (Stuttgart: Seewald Verlag, 1973), 34–35.

12. "Unsere Verantwortung in der Welt," Beschluss des 36. Bundesparteitages der CDU, *CDU Dokumentation* 19 (1988), 5.

13. Richard Burt, "Ein Loblied auf die Differenzen," *Die Zeit* 50 (5 December 1986), 9–10.

20

THE FEDERAL REPUBLIC OF GERMANY
IN THE EUROPEAN COMMUNITY

Emil J. Kirchner

The Federal Republic of Germany (FRG) and the European Community (EC) are of special significance to each other. To a large extent, FRG membership is the raison d'être of the EC whose main aim is to provide peaceful cooperation among its members. In the formative years of the FRG, the EC represented a lifeline for gaining equal status among the family of nations, for pursuing economic recovery, and for establishing internal and external stability.

Thirty years after the establishment of the EC, which today comprises twelve members, 320 million people, and the world's largest trading block, is West Germany now more or less inclined to foster the process of West European unification? Is the EC seen primarily as a means for enhancing national economic interest rather than as an entity which would replace national sovereignty? Is the process of West European unification incompatible with the aims of German reunification?

THE ESSENCE OF MEMBERSHIP

Due to Germany's past history, the importance of international organizations for security, German reunification, and economic development is recognized in the Basic Law of 1949. Its preamble calls for the pursuit of world peace in a united Europe and for the achievement, through self-determination, of German unity and freedom. Contained in these calls are both a rejection of nationalism and a commitment to reconciliation with the neighboring states.

Right from the start, therefore, the FRG has keenly sought and strongly supported attempts for European unification, including foundation of the Council of Europe, or the establishment of the Organization for European Economic Cooperation (OEEC) since renamed OECD. The formation of the European Coal and Steel Community in 1951 and the Common Market (EEC) and (EURATOM) in 1957 were seen as crucially important for the rehabilitation, confidence, and security of the Federal Republic. There were, however, some objections to membership in these organizations. The SPD feared that the ECSC and European Defense Community (EDC) would be impediments to German reunification.[1] The FDP expressed this concern with regard to the EEC, which it also saw as a threat to its anticlerical stand and to its free market commitments. The latter worry was shared by the economics minister, Ludwig Erhard, who also foresaw negative consequences for German farmers. In the end there was widespread support at elite and mass level for membership in these organizations. Not only was Chancellor Adenauer fully committed to these efforts, but the expected gains in political, economic, and security terms were considered as greatly outweighing potential disadvantages. Politically, membership in these organizations enabled the FRG to regain equal status in the family of nations. Economically, it represented a stimulant to economic recovery (promoting cross-border trade and stimulating economies of scale), and, as far as the EEC is concerned, a fair compromise between French agricultural interests and West German industrial ones. In security terms, these organizations strengthened the resolve against a potential Soviet expansion. In addition, there was a strong belief by Adenauer and the Christian Democrats that the success of these organizations would help to achieve German reunification.

As argued by Hrbek and Wessels (1984) the EC served as a framework for problem solving and as an overall frame for value reference. Through the former, the FRG could realize many of its national economic interests without undue sacrifice. Through the latter, values held by the EC, regarding basic human rights, democracy, and social justice, would be effectively internalized.

While a direct correlation between FRG economic strength and EC membership is difficult to establish, there is little doubt that this membership has helped to make it the strongest national economy in the EC and the world's largest exporter. Its EC trade in 1986 was 50.8 percent of total export and 52.2 percent of total import. Thirty percent of the FRG GNP is derived from exports; and 17 percent of GNP from EC exports.

But economic success has mixed blessings. It creates export dependency; involves financial transfers to less developed regions; provokes envy from EC partners; mounts pressure for a leadership role; and, paradoxically, may detract from the long-term goal of European unification. It is the latter aspect to which we will turn next.

THE FRG'S POSITION ON POLITICAL INTEGRATION

In the Adenauer era supranationalism was a main focus of the Federal Republic and nationalism was de-emphasized. However, already during that period some West German elites found the ECSC excessively supranational and felt that the Federal Republic was entitled to a dominant economic position (Haas 1958).

The commitment to supranationalism was also questioned when the FRG did not put up more of a fight over de Gaulle's veto to British membership in 1963 and over his "empty chair" policy— meaning the British chair at the EEC—in 1965. Of course, given that the Franco-German Friendship Treaty had just come into being, and that the Federal Republic had purposely refused to play a political role, it helps to explain why modest, rather than heavy, pressure was brought to bear. Nonetheless, by the time Brandt became chancellor, a more realistic approach toward the long-term goal of political unification seemed to prevail. For him, there was no automatic development from economic integration to political unification. Rather, European unification was a dynamic development process which must be a continuing object of political discussion among the participants (Feld 1981: 57). Whether this was a reflection of his own approach or a reaction to the 1965–1966 crisis is difficult to establish. Undoubtedly, the lack of solidarity with regard to oil supplies by Britain and France in 1973, infuriated and disillusioned Brandt, and left its mark on his successor, Helmut Schmidt. Schmidt's qualities as a crisis manager elevated the Federal Republic to a model position (*Modell Deutschland*) whose trademarks were economic efficiency and tight monetary policy. Other Community countries and the Commission had begun to emulate this model by the late seventies but were also judged, sometimes harshly, by the Federal Republic on this model. This instilled an element of arrogance (*Lehrmeister*) on the part of the Federal Republic, and provoked further envy from other member states. Some of the envy, however, turned to anger when the Schmidt administration excessively stressed its role as "paymaster" of the Community budget and attacked the Commission as inefficient.

In support of Schmidt it can be said that he had an excellent rapport with Giscard d' Estaing, and the two together established an exchange rate mechanism known as the European Monetary System (EMS) in 1979, which strengthened economic integration. Moreover, the grand principles toward the professed goal of Western European unification were upheld throughout the Schmidt period. In 1985, however, under the Kohl administration the Federal Republic made use, for the first time, of the infamous national veto, paradoxically because Kohl had adopted Adenauer's European policy as a model.

The eighties have witnessed much ambiguity in the Federal Republic's position toward political unification. On the one hand, Foreign Minister Genscher, together with his Italian counterpart, launched a plan for European union in 1981, which resulted in the Stuttgart Solemn Declaration on Political Union in 1983. On the other hand, there was more stress than usual on German reunification in the 1983 general election and the FRG's veto over cereal prices in 1985. Chancellor Kohl's position on the EC, in spite of being instrumental in the conclusion of the Single European Act in 1986, has often lacked clarity or drive. As a consequence, in 1987 Romain Leick, the EC correspondent of *Der Spiegel* noted that the old enthusiasm for Europe no longer prevailed among the German leadership.

What explains this waning of West German support? Has the EC outlived its usefulness for the FRG, or has the emphasis changed?

A number of plausible arguments can be considered for explaining a change in the FRG's attitude and position. These involve a benign neglect of or disillusionment with the EC, a growing national confidence, and structural factors and policy-making styles. Unfortunately space does not permit a detailed treatment of these arguments, and only some general consideration can be provided.

Benign Neglect and Disillusionment

Three different attitudes toward the EC warrant discussion: complacency, disillusion, and arrogance.

Economic success is often cited as a cause for West Germany's lack of drive for unification, implying that it has bred complacency and contentedness (*Europamüdigkeit*). Opinion polls, though not the most reliable indicators, seem to concur with this description. Their evidence seems to suggest that there has been a drop in the saliency of the European issue and that a noncommital attitude on EC issues prevails (Feld 1981: 92). Relatively low West German turnouts in 1979 and 1984 direct elections to the European Parliament, and a drop between 1979 and 1984, underscore still further the nature of the problem.

There could, however, also be a historical determinant. Past experience has made West Germany overly cautious and careful; emphasizing the present rather than the future, the safeguarding rather than the experimenting, and the economic rather than the political. This may help to explain the apparent FRG reluctance to act as a "locomotive" in stimulating economic growth, either within the EC or in the wider international context.

Another argument much in vogue since the mid-1970s is that the Federal Republic is too preoccupied with budgetary contributions and accounting exercises. It has thus lost sight of the long-term goals. The Federal Republic is accused of changing its tune once it realized that large financial transfers to less developed regions of the EC were necessary; and of treating the aspect of solidarity with contempt and the transfers as a nuisance and a liability, while still reaping large commercial and economic benefits from trading with EC countries. These critics point to the fact that for most of the past thirty years the Federal Republic has run a trade surplus with its EC partners, amounting to around $35 billion in 1987. The Community generates only 50 percent of West Germany's export trade but 85 percent of its trading profit. Finally, the argument is that even German farmers have turned the CAP to their advantage.

In fairness it can be said that West Germany has provided extra money over a long period of time and, in the main, willingly and without pressing for the kind of rebate which Mrs. Thatcher has demanded for Britain. Nonetheless, whether by Thatcher's campaign of wanting "my money back" or by the growing net contribution, critical voices within West Germany are increasing and affecting prointegrationist sentiments.

A third argument sees policy attempts for European unification eroded by the arrival of and insistence on the "German model" (*Modell Deutschland*). This model, a creation of the Schmidt era representing economic efficiency, reinstated confidence in the national solution. In addition, with the arrival of a new generation in West Germany a more critical attitude emerged within the FRG about economic performances in other EC member states and about the Commission's work. Disagreements with the French over the Economic and Monetary Union (EMU) in the 1970s (Was economic stability a prerequisite to EMU or a fallout of EMU?) were symptomatic of a growing self-confidence. Subsequently, no longer is there a belief that "what is good for the EC is good for the FRG." Rather, EC solidarity is often seen as impeding the dynamic force of West German economic and technological development (Leick 1987: 59).

In addition, the Commission is increasingly seen as wasteful and largely inefficient. This could be due to an element of competition, if not jealousy, between bureaucratic competences in Bonn and Brussels. In any case, unlike other member states, no politician of great stature has ever been nominated for either of the two top Commission positions available to West Germany. One German newspaper summed up this situation in 1985 by stating that "an able politician does not go to Brussels and indeed cannot afford to" (Erdmann 1986: 102).

INCONGRUENCE BETWEEN FRG AND EC POLICIES

While so far the arguments have assumed neglect or disillusion in West Germany's stand on political unification, another explanation refers to a conscious detachment from these aims. Detracting, if not counteracting, policy aims are associated with the FRG's Ostpolitik,

West Germany's global trade role, and an allegedly FRG hegemonic economic interest.

In the Adenauer years European unification was seen as a prerequisite for German reunification. In the sixties, the key to a solution of the German question was sought in the United States, but in the 1970s and 1980s the U.S.S.R. had also become an important focus of attention. The German question relates to the right of self-determination and how to overcome the present division between the two Germanies by peaceful means.

Ever since Brandt's introduction of Ostpolitik in 1970, there have been concerns voiced by EC members, notably France, that the forging of closer ties with Eastern Europe could push the FRG into neutralism, detract from its commitment to the EC and NATO, and allow the Soviet Union to drive a wedge between the United States and its European allies. These concerns were heightened when Chancellor Kohl stressed that the new generation of the Federal Republic had a right to a solution of the German question and when the GDR leader Erich Honecker visited the FRG in 1987. This caused particular consternation among certain French elites, like Michel Jobert, who saw signs of West Germany wanting to go its own way (*Sonderweg*) in Central Europe and make a deal with the U.S.S.R. about German reunification.

EC unification has not progressed sufficiently to judge whether or not it will achieve, or help to achieve, German reunification. Nor can it be sufficiently determined whether the 1987 INF Treaty between the United States and the U.S.S.R. will have fundamental implications for U.S. defense commitments in Western Europe or for Western European defense cooperation. So far, inspite of rhetoric to the contrary, there has been an overwhelming awareness among West Germans, both masses and elites,[2] that the path to European unification is the most sensible and promising one for reaching German reunification. Leicht of *Die Zeit* put this very cogently when he wrote "Europe is always more important than the German nation and there can be no progress for Germany at Europe's expense." But whether he stated this primarily for domestic consumption (and possibly addressing certain elites within the West German political system) or whether it was directed toward the EC and NATO partners, is unclear. No doubt as long as the German question remains open there will be uncertainties, especially from its partners, about the FRG's future and commitment to the EC.

Adding to these uncertainties is West Germany's global trade policy behavior. As the third-largest industrial nation and the world's leading exporter, it has economic interests going beyond those of the Community. As a matter of fact the Federal Republic's global interests do not always coincide with the EC's interests, as differences over trade liberalization have shown. There can also be significant cross-pressures for the Federal Republic. For example, the West Germans came under pressure in 1987–1988 to contribute to global economic growth. The envisaged tax cuts by the FRG were seen as moving in this direction. However, higher EC budget expenditures for 1988 curtailed the tax exercise and thus the growth potential.

There are also claims that partnership with weaker economies of the EC has, in fact, damaged the wider international competitiveness of German industry. Thus contradictory pressures come to bear on the FRG.

There is a question whether the foregoing point can be taken a step further; that the Federal Republic uses the EC as an instrument of national foreign policy rather than as an undertaking for European political unification. While it has become conventional wisdom by now that member states forgo certain national prerogatives, they effectively employ the EC in the armory of national policymaking. The extent to which this can be done varies from country to country and is at times difficult to pin down. For example, did the Federal Republic use the EC as an instrument in its pursuit of Ostpolitik, or were other member states fully supporting such undertakings? Similarly, the motives for Community actions are not always clearly discernible. Was Schmidt's concern over the EMS primarily domestically motivated (stability for the DM) or were solidarity principles with other member states foremost in his mind? There is also the question of usefulness. For example, to what extent can European political cooperation be effectively employed in West German foreign policy, given that its security is dependent on the United States?

The latter issue, though from a different angle, is taken up by Lankowski (1982b). To him the Federal Republic attempts to use the

EC as an instrument for economic hegemonic ambitions and as a substitute for political inferiority in world political affairs. Bulmer and Paterson (1987: 4) refute this argument by pointing out that there are both domestic and external constraints to such an approach. The federal structure, the independence of the Bundesbank, and policy styles are seen as such constraints. To them the FRG has neither a clear framework of action reflecting national interest nor demonstrated leadership. Rather, when taking initiatives, as on the creation of the EMS, it does so in tandem with France. Externally, it is believed that Britain and France would not allow a clear West German leadership role.

Policy Constraints

The federal structure, the independence of the Bundesbank, and the policy machinery impose constraints on the formulation of a coherent European policy. Drawbacks of the decentralized West German system became particularly visible during the ratification of the Single European Act in 1986. Complaining that they were to lose authority (notably over environmental policy) to the EC without any compensating participation in European policy formulation by the federal government, the Länder in the Bundesrat refused to ratify. The subsequent granting of participation may well delay in the future the Federal Republic's European policy formulation process, or make it more difficult to coordinate. Similar symptoms and obstructions emanate from the Bundesbank, which jealously guards its independence with respect to potential EC encroachments and only reluctantly supports efforts to strengthen the EMS or the use of the European Currency Units (ECUs).

A further main element affecting the coherence of the FRG's European policy relates to policy styles. As Bulmer and Paterson (1988: 232) point out, during the 1970s the FRG's European policy became increasingly sectorized or dominated by individual ministries.

This can lead to problems of coordination and, at worst, can produce incompatibility among conflicting "house" policies. However, it does facilitate ministries carrying out low-level policies. Ministerial autonomy and the element of competition foster the formation of alliances with interest groups, which suppresses the influence of the Foreign Office and promotes economic rather than political aspects of West German European policy. The consequences, as Feld (1981: 73) remarks, is that the pursuit of Western European unification is weakened in order to satisfy important national constituencies, replacing, in part, the original incentives for joining the Community.

Thus we find a routinized decision process, the absence of "active" policy, and the coordination of policy at a late stage. The upshot is that there is a wide gap between the rhetoric of integration and the nature of the policy process.

While none of the aforementioned factors account in themselves for a waning of support for political unification, a combination of these might. On the other hand there are also countervailing forces at work. The export dependency on EC trade, representing 17 percent of West German GNP and accounting for 20 percent of its workplaces, sets limits on the extent to which benign neglect can be practiced. The "paymaster" role can be seen more as a bargaining chip for securing advantages in economic and political fields generally (including security arrangements in Mediterranean countries) rather than as a significant obstacle to the West German position in political unification. A more assertive new generation of West German leaders will emphasize the German model, but will increasingly be confronted by the "give-and-take" syndrome expected from the implementation of the Single European Act. The FRG will continue to seek solutions to the German question, and Ostpolitik will continue to provoke suspicions from its partners, but there is no substantial evidence to suggest that Ostpolitik will be pursued as an alternative to European unification efforts. As Chancellor Kohl explained in an interview with the *Frankfurter Allgemeine Zeitung* (30 November 1987), "the West integration of the FRG is part of our raison d'état." Western European unification will continue to be an essential precondition for German reunification. Global trade interests will, of course, be a factor for the FRG, given its role as the world's leading exporter, but as the EC internal market becomes a reality, and especially if Austria, Norway, and Sweden should be part of it, the FRG trade interests with the Community will be strengthened at the expense of its global involvement. Even if attempted, which so far has not been the case, internal and especially external constraints (Britain and France) will not allow the FRG a hegemonic role. By design, and to some extent by default, the FRG has not played a leading role in the process of European integration. On the contrary, there are criticisms that West Germany is too passive or lacks a coherent European policy. Critics argue that the future of European unification depends on a more active and coherent FRG European policy role. The question is, can West Germany break with its self-assumed role pattern, its insecurities, and traditions?

FUTURE RELATIONS BETWEEN THE EC AND THE FRG

Both defense and the completion of the internal market will feature prominently in future EC-FRG relations. As the West Europeans feel increasingly exposed to U.S.-Soviet agreements on defense in Western Europe, and as implementation of the Single European Act proceeds, the political (and security) dimension could gain in importance and the member states could be forced to concede their sovereignty rather than strengthen it. The successful outcome of this seems to depend on a tricky exercise. It would require that member states, especially the bigger ones, consider it to be in their interests to enhance cooperation in the political and security fields, since this is the motivating force behind integration rather than, as earlier assumed, the logic of sectoral spillovers. Yet, by doing so they would be practicing self-deception, namely, that instead of safeguarding their national interests their growing cooperation would take them over the famous threshold where a reversal to national options is no longer a viable alternative, or where some member states cannot afford to move along with the pacemakers. Increasing competences and powers would have to accrue to EC institutions in this process, especially to the European Parliament (EP).

Given the FRG's export dependency, it can be expected that West Germany will benefit from a larger and more liberal market. But, equally predictably, not all promises of such a market are beneficial; some entail considerable hardship, at least in institutional and psychological terms. Much of the net transfers to poorer regions of the EC will have to come from countries like West Germany, thus increasing the financial burden of the FRG. This comes at a time when the FRG economic fortunes seem to be diminishing rather than growing, with the FRG growth rates below the OECD average, a depreciating U.S. dollar causing loss of export and corporate tax earnings, and increasing unemployment, requiring higher social security payments. Moreover, certain hitherto protected industries, like insurance, telecommunications, electricity, and road haulage, would face stiff competition. In some sectors, such as insurance, it will also entail a breakup of existing cartels. Other concessions would have to come on fiscal harmonization (VAT rates), on monetary compensatory amounts in the agricultural sector, and on border controls (detection of terrorists). Two aspects appear particularly crucial. One concerns the constitutionally stipulated independent role of the Bundesbank, the other the highly regarded West German industrial norms/standards. While the Bundesbank is reluctant to forgo its independence to a European authority and therefore gives a low priority to a strengthening of the EMS, West German industrialists view with horror the possibility of having to compromise on what they consider to be vastly superior industrial norms (about 20,000 in existence).

Whilst no quick strengthening of the EMS can be expected, the October 1987 stock market crash and the continuing slide of the U.S. dollar have even made the Bundesbank realize that the EMS helped to provide shelter against adverse conditions and, if strengthened, could not only meet further pressures more successfully but also provide additional bargaining power in monetary negotiations with the United States and Japan. There was also pressure from the French in early 1988 for the establishment of a European Central Bank. However, Chancellor Kohl indicated that this will only happen by the beginning of the next century. The chancellor insisted on certain prerequisites, such as the completion of the internal market, prior economic convergence, and harmonization of the tax systems.

On the question of West German defense, there have been increasing doubts, even in Bonn, concerning the dependability of American protection. The unease after Reykjavik and the INF Treaty have put defense and security high on the agenda in meetings among Western European leaders, especially in Franco-German gatherings.

On the occasion of the twenty-fifth anniversary of the Franco-German Friendship Treaty in January 1988, both countries agreed to set up a Security Defense Council and a joint Franco-German brigade. The Council will provide a forum for improving cooperation in military strategy, troop deployment, and arms procurement. The joint brigade will consist of 4,200 soldiers and function outside the NATO military structure. Whether France will actually commit itself to participate automatically in the frontline defense of West Germany is the crucial question. In theory French leaders speak of such a defense but in practice it is difficult to imagine, given French insistence on independence and West Germany's close ties to NATO's military command structure. How can France and Germany agree on common strategic concepts? If they do, will this, as feared for example by the Dutch, negatively affect NATO? The American defense secretary, Frank Carlucci, has welcomed Franco-German collaborative efforts in this field, but it wold be difficult to imagine that a separate strategic concept could be tolerated by the United States or NATO as long as America maintains the responsibility for defending West Germany.

Should the EC one day agree on a common defense, or, what is more likely, should Franco-German security efforts come to fruition, this could revive the lost enthusiasm for West European unification in EC countries generally and in West Germany in particular. It would demonstrate to the FRG that the EC has a political perspective. It could also be an essential reinforcing element for economic integration. As argued by Padoa-Schioppa (1987), an EC defense framework could considerably ease the acute problem within the EC of having to strictly balance costs and benefits devoid of any defense and security implications. That such a link was emerging could be seen when in January 1988 West Germany agreed to meet the cost of keeping in Europe the American F-16 fighters that Spain had insisted should leave its territory within three years.

Progress in the defense area could change the dictum that "the EC preserves the nation-states far more than it forces them to wither away." Meanwhile, the EC will continue to coexist with the nation-states and the clash between national governments and integration will increase rather than diminish. For the time being there are no clear indications that either the EC will supersede the nation-state or that the nation-state will outlive the EC. What appears reasonably certain is that the EC will edge forward incrementally and pragmatically rather than in big bangs. The initial enthusiasm for Western European unification has waned, but the belief still prevails among elites that European solidarity in numbers and in supranational sovereignty is crucial to survival.

CONCLUSION

There can be no doubt that the FRG has done well out of EC membership for its internal and external policies. If initially the Germans had feared the specter of French dominance, it is West German dominance, some even claim hegemony, which prevails. Though the EC has benefited the FRG disproportionately, the existence of the EC has contributed to stability and prosperity in the region generally. The EC, together with a favorable climate both within the FRG and in the international system, offered West Germans a chance to rehabilitate themselves as a people and as a state within the European scheme. The ideal of European unity was a rallying point for West Germans, but a combination of complacency, self-confidence, rising nationalism elsewhere, technical and bureaucratic details within the EC, and growing financial burdens have made the EC less attractive.

The FRG, unlike many other member states, has successfully incorporated the European dimension into its own policymaking but it has failed to provide effective leadership principles in return. This has to do with its decentralized decisionmaking both in style (sectorization) and in structure (federal system), although its security dependence on the United States, its concern with the German question, its global trade role, and its self-imposed reluctance to assume leadership have at times exacerbated the problems of sectorization and decentralization. An anomaly thus exists whereby the country with the central currency in the EC, nearly one-third of the EC GNP, and one-fourth of intra-Community trade, plays a reactive rather than an active role. Partly because of its economic strength, partly because of its past history, and partly because there is an urgent need to move the EC out of its technocratic, CAP-dominated and highly nationalistic impasse, the FRG, more than any other member state, should provide elements for a coherent EC policy, a vision for the future, and commitment for the long-term EC goal. Instead, however, we witness a lack of coherence on a European policy, a protracted attitude toward agricultural and monetary reforms, and a reluctance to accept the principle of solidarity.

Unlike the past, however, when economic success prevailed and a bi-polar world kept the German question largely concealed, the situation is substantially changing. Subsequently, partly for economic reasons (rising unemployment, falling growth rates, and increasing social security burdens) and partly due to repercussions of the INF Treaty, the FRG might be forced to seek a more active foreign policy role. Such a role will have to relate to three aspects: the German question, European defense, and the integration of the EC. The German question will continue in the future and the FRG will attempt to seek further solutions, but there are limits to how far bilateral contacts between the two Germanys can proceed. Clearly the German question has been internationalized and solutions must be sought in various arenas. Therefore the FRG would do well not to succumb to the wrong choice between the realities of Western Europe and unclarified ideas of a mythical Central Europe. The FRG's security is still dependent on the United States and the only viable alternative is a Western European security arrangement in which France would have to take a major lead and make large concessions on its independence. For the FRG, whether under continued U.S. protection or an alternative Western European one, greater financial contributions will probably have to be made; its actual per capita defense expenditure has so far been less than that of either Britain or France.

Whilst there are limits on the extent to which the FRG can influence the outcome of either the German question or the make-up of Western European defense arrangements, it can act effectively on the issue of EC integration by providing leadership and commitment to its cause and thereby hope that a positive contribution will be made toward the first two aspects.

A lot will need to be done by the FRG during the next four years to achieve a more active and coherent EC policy and to help in the completion of the internal market. It has a long way to go to become

once again the model child of integration (*Musterknabe*) and to lose
the image of the scapegoat (*Prügelknabe*) for the lack of EC progress.

NOTES

1. Interestingly, the SPD changed its position between 1951 and 1957 in
   that by 1957 it found FRG membership in the EEC to be compatible
   with attempts to bring about German reunification.
2. Fifty-nine percent find the German people's desire for reunification
   perfectly legitimate and only 28 percent see it as a danger for Europe.
   Quoted by Jean François-Poncet in *Time Magazine*, 7 September 1987.

BIBLIOGRAPHY

Bulmer, S., and W. Paterson (1987). *The Federal Republic of Germany and
the European Community.* London: Allen & Unwin.

Bulmer, S., and W. Paterson (1988). "European Policy-Making in the Fed-
eral Republic—Internal and External Limits to leadership." In W. Ews-
sels and E. Regelsberger, eds., *The Federal Republic of Germany and the
European Community: The Presidency and Beyond.* Bonn: Europa Union
Verlag, 231–65. Published as no. 2 of the series *Analyses of European
Policies* by the Institut für Europäische Politik.

Calleo, D. (1980). *The German Problem Reconsidered. German and the
World Order, 1870 to the Present.* Cambridge: Cambridge University Press.

Ehrhardt, C. A. (1987). "Europe Between National Sovereignty and Integration." *Aussen Politik* 38, no. 2 (2d quarter 1987): 103–19.

Erdmann, V. (1986). "The German Press (*Der Spiegel, Die Zeit*) on European
Matters during the Election Year of 1984." In P. M. Lutzeler, ed, *Western
Europe in Transition: West Germany's Role in the European Community.*
Baden-Baden: Nomos Verlagsgesellschaft, 99–107.

Feld, W. J. (1981). *West Germany and the European Community. Changing
Interests and Competing Policy Objectives.* New York: Praeger.

Frankfurter Allgemeine Zeitung (Interview by Johann G. Reismüller with Chancellor Kohl), 30 November 1987.

Haas, E. B. (1958). *The Uniting of Europe: Political, Social and Economic Forces, 1950–1957.* Stanford: Stanford University Press.

Heck, B. (1984). "Europe and the German Question. A Dominant Issue in East-West Relations." Reprinted from *German Comments* 3 (April 1984).

Hrbek, R. (1986). "German Politics and the European Community." in P. M. Lutzeler ed., *Western Europe in Transition: West Germanys Role in the European Community.* Baden-Baden: Nomos Verlagsgesellschaft, 19–44.

Hrbek, R. (1987). "The German Länder and the European Community." In *Aussen Politik* 38, no. 2, (2nd quarter 1987): 120–33.

Hrbek, R., and W. Wessels (1984). "Nationale Interessen der Bundesrepublik Deutschland und der Integrationsprozess." In R. Hrbek and W. Wessels, eds., *EG-Mitgliedschaft: ein vitales Interesse der Bundesrepublik Deutschland.* Bonn: Europa Union Verlag.

Katzenstein, P. J. (1980). "Problem or Model? West Germany in the 1980s." *World Politics:* 577–98.

Lankowski, C. (1982a). "Modell Deutschland and the International Regionalization of the West German State in the 1970s." In A. S. Markovits, ed., *The Political Economy of West Germany.* New York: Praeger, 90–115.

Lankowski, C. (1982b). "Germany and the European Communities: Anatomy of a Hegemonial Relation. Ph.D. dissertation, Columbia University.

Leicht, R. (1987). *Die Zeit,* Hamburg, 11 September.

Leick, R. (1987). "Germany—The European Egotist." *European Affairs* 1 (1987): 55–61.

Loth, W. (1987). "Vertragsverhandlungen bei abklingender Europabegeisterung—Eine zeitgeschichtliche Einordnung." In *Integration* 3 (July 1987): 107–14.

Milward, A. S. (1987). "Nationale Wirtschaftsinteressen im Vordergrund— Neue Erkenntnisse statt überholter Schulweisheiten." In *Integration* 3 (July 1987): 100–106.

Padoa-Schioppa, T. (1987). *Integration Strategy of the European Community* [A report of a study group, chaired by T. Padoa-Schioppa]. cited in *Europe: Magazine of the European Community* 267 (June 1987).

Time Magazine [The "View from Paris" provided by Jean François-Poncet], 7 September 1987.

Weidenfeld, W. (1986). "Basic Questions of European Integration Seen From a German Point of View." In P. M. Lutzeler, ed., *Western Europe in Transition: West Germany's Role in the European Community.* Baden-Baden: Nomos Verlagsgesellschaft, 9–18.

Wessels, W., and E. Regelsberger, eds. (1988). *The Federal Republic of Germany and the European Community: The Presidency and Beyond.* Bonn: Europa Union Verlag. Published as no. 2 of the series *Analyses of European Policies* by the Institut für Europäische Politik.

21

GERMAN MORALITY AND ISRAEL

Lily Gardner Feldman

On the eve of its fortieth anniversary, the Federal Republic is a vigorous, self-assured, and respected member of the "family of nations." The outcast of World War II has been rehabilitated, and nowhere is the passage from pariah to partner more evident than in the German-Israeli "special relationship." Such a relationship was viewed from the outset by American policymakers like John McCloy as central to Germany's rehabilitation: "The world will carefully watch the new Germany and one of the tests by which it will be judged will be its attitude toward the Jews and how it treats them."[1] Forty years later Germany largely has passed McCloy's test: the special relationship of policy preferences and societal friendships developed in the early 1950s still flourishes.

Yet the partnership between West Germany and Israel may be entering a new phase of diluted commitment because of three factors: the political and societal divisions concerning the role of the past in current efforts to forge a national identity; the priority assigned to other foreign policy goals and other special relationships; and the emergence of new generations devoid of intimate connection to the Holocaust.

This chapter will evaluate the partnership's durability by tracing its origins, examining its present intensity, and identifying the challenges to its centrality for Germans. I will consider motives and actions, government and society, harmony and conflict to demonstrate that during the last four decades ties have been distinctive, warranting the continued appellation "special relationship."

MOTIVES: MORALITY AND PRAGMATISM

From the beginning, one of the German-Israeli relationship's hallmarks was its moral basis, but morality has never been isolated from pragmatism. Chancellor Adenauer indicated in his September 1951 offer of negotiations for restitution and reparations:

The Federal Government and with it the great majority of the German people are aware of the immeasurable suffering that was brought upon the Jews in Germany and the occupied territories during the time of National Socialism . . . unspeakable crimes have been committed in the name of the German people, calling for moral and material indemnity.[2]

Adenauer's supporters in the Christian Democratic Union (CDU) and his opponents in the Social Democratic Party (SPD) confirmed the role of morality, as did Jewish leaders like Nahum Goldmann who wrote of the September 1951 statement:

What happened on that day in the German Federal Parliament was a novel departure in political history . . . the German people . . . freely acknowledged their guilt of past events and assumed responsibility for them.[3]

For Adenauer, then, the burden of history meant the assumption of an ethical obligation toward the Jews and Israel.

For many Germans and Israelis, Helmut Kohl's January 1984 visit to Israel marked the first step in shedding the moral mantle donned in the early 1950s. Kohl appeared to weaken the historical foundation of the relationship when he characterized the visit of "the first chancellor of the postwar generation" as a "symbol of the bridge between our two countries and peoples across the abyss of the past," welcomed the fact that "the young German generation does not regard Germany's history as a burden but as a challenge for the future," and alerted Israelis that West Germany's Middle Eastern policy would be made in Bonn and not in Jerusalem.[4]

Chancellor Kohl's subsequent behavior established a pattern of contradiction and ambivalence concerning his willingness to shoulder the weight of the Third Reich. His initiation and pursuit of the commemoration at the Bitburg cemetery in May 1985 signaled the past's relegation to a mere footnote. Yet Kohl tried to compensate for Bitburg's institutionalization of amnesia by referring to remembrance and historical responsibility on other occasions, for example, to the Central Council of Jews in Germany at Bergen-Belsen on 5 May 1985 and to the Bundestag in the debate over anti-Semitism on 27 February 1986 when he warned:

We strongly contradict all those who refuse to learn from history. . . . To the historically retarded . . . we say that we, and above all the governmental institutions of our republic, will not let them out of our sight. To those who fail to reflect we say that they will have to repeatedly sharpen their awareness of the immeasurable suffering imposed on the Jews.[5]

Nevertheless, the chancellor's strong public defense of Kurt Waldheim soon rendered his words hollow and hardly dispelled concerns about his sense of obligation to the past.

Kohl's confusion about the role of the past seemed confirmed in his spring 1987 speech to the nation. On the one hand, he emphasized the importance of history, its diverse forms, and the role of all Germans in shaping Germany's past. On the other hand, he failed to use the opportunity to insist that the most fateful period of Germany's history, the Third Reich, should be open to only one interpretation, that of the victims:

In Bonn, a Museum of the History of the Federal Republic of Germany is to be built, and in Berlin a German Historical Museum. German history is to be presented there in such a way that people can perceive their part in it— open to interpretations and debates marked by opposing standpoints, open to diverse historical approaches. In a free society there is no single interpretation of history, and certainly not one prescribed by the authorities. Nobody is entitled to impose his standpoint and interpretation of history on others.[6]

During his visit to Israel, as elsewhere, Kohl painted himself as Adenauer's heir, but was that possible after Bitburg and Waldheim? Had he not departed from Adenauer's firm moral commitment? In fact, in the insistence on a pragmatic approach to Israel there are important similarities between Kohl and Adenauer. The morality surrounding Adenauer's 1951 decision to compensate the Jews and Israel was genuine but it was tied to practical considerations that most analysts have overlooked.

To Adenauer the key foreign policy goal was the return of German sovereignty on the basis of equality. The three Western powers insisted that the Occupation Statute would be removed only if Germany showed progress in establishing democracy and a willingness to redress the evils of its past. Israel became instrumental for the revival of German autonomy. Adenauer openly acknowledged this connection:

One of my chief aims as chancellor was to put in order our relationship to Israel and the Jews, both for moral and political reasons. Germany could not become a respected and equal member of the family of nations until it had recognized and proven the will to make amends.[7]

Adenauer's concrete actions revealed the strength of pragmatism: his overtures toward Israel culminating in the 1951 statement appeared to coincide with Allied and domestic pressure for demonstration of a changed Germany; weakening of resolve vis-à-vis Israel during the actual reparations negotiations in May 1952 seemed to parallel the achievement of real gains in sovereignty. Only the threat of Allied sanctions, of resignation by his chief reparations negotiator (the deputy did resign), and of public castigation by Jewish leaders made Adenauer resolve the stalemate in negotiations with Israel.

The pragmatism of German foreign policy dictated a positive attitude toward Israel in 1952 and subsequently. Economic aid to Israel helped give Germany international absolution just as reparations had; arms to Israel furthered the German goal of stemming the tide of communism; financial support for Israeli scientific and technological research produced tangible scientific advantages for the Federal Republic.

From the Israeli perspective, pragmatism also had its negative side. In the 1960s, the Federal Republic's fear of diplomatic recognition of the German Democratic Republic made it reluctant to establish diplomatic relations with Israel and unwilling to remove German rocket scientists working in Egypt. In the 1970s, concern for Arab oil supplies and for political approval by European Community partners rendered West Germany critical of Israeli policies toward the Arabs and Palestinians. In the 1980s, the need for markets led Germany to contemplate the sale to tanks to Saudi Arabia.

The pragmatism of today, then, in its negative and positive manifestations, is not new. Even the efforts of German political leaders to downplay the past are not entirely new. Already in 1966, just a year after he assumed his post as the first West German ambassador to

Israel, Rolf Pauls warned that the past should cease to dominate relations. Like Kohl, Pauls also noted the "special position" Germans occupied vis-à-vis Israel. The relationship remained special because pragmatism was balanced by morality.

Just as morality was authentic in 1951, so it was in the spring of 1965 when Chancellor Erhard observed: "Our relationship to Israel and the whole Jewish world is overshadowed . . . by . . . a tragic and still unforgotten past."[8] And morality has withstood the test of time, such that a minister of state in the Foreign Office could declare in November 1986: "Our insistence on Israel's right to exist in secure borders is not only a political axiom but also a moral obligation."[9] The imprint of the past also has remained indelible for some political leaders, as demonstrated vividly in President von Weizsäcker's speech of 8 May 1985:

All of us, whether guilty or not, whether old or young, must accept the past. We are all . . . liable for it . . . it is vital to keep alive memory. It is not a case of coming to terms with the past. That is not possible. It cannot be subsequently modified or unmade.[10]

What is new is the possibility that the adherents of negative pragmatism are more influential and single-minded than they were in either 1952 or 1966; this brand of pragmatists believes either that Germany has fulfilled its obligation to the past or that the satisfaction of German national interests lies beyond Israel. The old balance between morality and pragmatism may be shifting toward a preponderance of self-interest, aided by the vacillation of some political leaders on the appropriate role of the past. This shift in the balance of motives has not yet been expressed fully in governmental policy toward Israel, which retains its special and preferential quality, but there are signs of a more unfettered attitude toward the past on the part of some policymakers.

POLICIES: PREFERENCE AND PARTNERSHIP

The Federal Republic's desire to make amends, for both moral and pragmatic reasons, led to the September 1952 Luxembourg Reparations Agreement to supply goods and services worth DM 3.45 billion to Israel and the Conference on Material Claims Against Germany (an umbrella for world Jewish organizations). The protocols of the Luxembourg Agreement (together with promises under the Contractual Agreements) provided for financial compensation to individual Jews via the Federal Indemnification Law of 1956 and the Federal Restitution Law of 1957. In both areas, the Federal Republic accorded Israel special treatment.

Although German financial experts wanted to give priority to the London Debt Conference at which Germany settled its prewar and postwar debts, ultimately Adenauer insisted that the Israeli claim take precedence in terms of timing (six moths before the conclusion of the London Debt Conference) and amount (eighteen creditors in London received a total of DM 14.3 billion or about half of their claim; Israel alone received DM 3 billion or almost three-quarters of its original claim).

Aid to Individuals

Approximately 40 percent of all Federal German compensation payments went to individual Israelis (some DM 25 billion by 1985). On two occasions, the Federal Republic set up special funds to cover claimants excluded from federal compensation legislation, many of them residents of Israel. However, when it came in 1986–1987 to discussions concerning a third special fund, some government officials revealed ambivalence toward the past.

Under pressure from the opposition, in November 1986 the government presented a report detailing the legislation, recipients, and amounts involved in past restitution efforts. The opposition had identified groups who remained uncompensated (including homosexuals, mental patients, gypsies, and victims of Mengele's experiments on Jewish twins, one-third of whom live in Israel) and called on the government to create a fund or a foundation to cover all neglected individuals. In the report, the government referred to the "so-called" Mengele twins and denied that Mengele's activities amounted to pseudomedical experiments with attendant long-term health problems. The victims thus were barred from compensation, especially, it was argued, because most of the eighty individuals submitting claims via the Mengele Twins Organization in Tel Aviv either already had received compensation for some other harm or loss occasioned by the Nazis or, the German government reasoned, they were not now financially needy.

Despite these denials of responsibility, the traditional preference toward Israel eventually surfaced and in the summer of 1987 a financial agreement was concluded with the Mengele Twins Organization, without an accompanying resolution of the claims of the non-Jewish victims.

Aid to Israel

The financial compensation to individual Israelis contributed to the survival of the Israeli economy in the state's early years. The implementation of the Reparations Agreement meant contact between various sectors of the two economies and an intimate German knowledge of Israel's economic difficulties, which in turn resulted in development aid and increased trade. Between 1959 and 1978, Israel was among the top four recipients of German development aid; in terms of per capita contributions, Israel was first.

By the beginning of the 1980s, Israel received a smaller percentage of all German capital aid (3.7 percent) than it did at the high point (12.9 percent in 1962), but this amount remained significant for several reasons. By this time, the Federal Republic and the United States were the only two countries to give Israel capital aid. In two important respects—GNP per capita and degree of industrialization —Israel fell outside the guidelines of the Federal Ministry for Economic Cooperation and Development, yet the Federal Republic maintained its aid commitment. Even today, in a period of relative austerity, the Federal Republic provides the same level of aid it has given to Israel for the past twenty years, and in 1987 discussions extended beyond the bilateral relationship to consideration of joint German-Israeli development programs in the third world.

The Federal Republic also has sought to lighten Israel's economic burden by playing the role of advocate in the European Community (EC), initially in Israel's abortive attempt for association status in the 1950s and 1960s, subsequently in the conclusion of two trade and financial agreements in the 1970s, and finally in the 1986 supplemental treaty to accommodate Israel over the accession to the community of Greece, Spain, and Portugal.

In addition to contributing to the Israeli economy through reparations, restitution, aid, and support in the EC, the Federal Republic has helped through arms and funds for science and technology. Despite its restrictive arms export policy in the 1950s and 1960s, the Federal Republic supplied arms to Israel. Quantitatively, Israel received at least 30 percent of all West German aid to non-NATO countries between 1962 and 1972 and perhaps more than 70 percent of all aid to major non-NATO recipients between 1960 and 1965. West Germany sold mainly software to its small number of non-NATO partners but gave Israel hardware gratis. Israel received more than Greece, the Federal Republic's needy NATO ally.

The Egyptian threat to establish formal ties with the German Democratic Republic led to the termination of German arms to Israel in 1965, but the conclusion of diplomatic relations with Israel served as compensation. And the military relationship did not cease; it was simply transformed. Under guidelines prohibiting arms exports to "areas of tension" and related legislation limiting the shipment of arms and defense-related goods, the Federal Republic was severely hampered in supplying hardware to Israel. Yet, West German officials have broadly interpreted the definition of software in Israel's case and have expanded the military relationship in other areas, such as research and development in weapons and technology, the joint training of armed forces, and the exchange of information on strategy and antiterrorist measures. The first official visit to Israel by a German defense minister in April 1986 and the return visit of Israel's defense minister in September 1987 testified to the depth of military ties. There has been press speculation about a new arms deal with Israel in which the United States would act as the financial and physical vehicle for the Israeli placement of orders for submarines from West German firms.

This possibility of renewed military supplies to Israel must be viewed against the background of the earlier debate over German tanks to Saudi Arabia and, therefore, as compensation, a method used frequently in the German-Israeli relationship. Under Chancellor Schmidt, the Federal Republic began to shift the criterion for arms exports from "areas of tension" to "national interest," a process consolidated by the Kohl government. Whereas the government ultimately declined to supply tanks to Saudi Arabia, it did approve the building in Saudi Arabia of a German munitions factory.

The German-Israeli relationship in the security field has developed in two directions: a track of cooperation and joint programs and an impasse over weapons to the Arab world. The evolution of close cooperation with Israel in the area of scientific and technological research has amounted to a revival of the positive symbiosis characterizing relations between Germans and Jews in this field until 1933. In part because of a historical foundation, science and technology has been the one policy area consistently expanding, free of tension. Relations began in the 1960s with an agreement between the Weizmann Institute and the Minerva Foundation (a subsidiary of the Max Planck Gesellschaft) funded by the German government; within a decade the program embraced other Israeli institutions and student exchanges. By the early 1980s, the German government had provided approximately DM 150 million for joint research. The partnership was cemented in 1986 with an agreement to create a German-Israeli foundation for research and development, a first in the Federal Republic's external relations. Chancellor Kohl's personal commitment, complete with a signing ceremony in the chancellery, reflects the importance the German government attaches to the endeavor.

In many ways, this new initiative in science and technology might be considered a renewal of German and Israeli commitment to the overall relationship: it resulted from a 1985 meeting of Helmut Kohl and Shimon Peres in New York's Waldorf Astoria, the same location as the famous 1960 Adenauer–Ben-Gurion encounter that inaugurated a "new era" in German-Israeli cooperation, including economic and military aid to Israel. However, other tendencies in the Federal Republic suggest this agreement merely fulfills pragmatic German interests in Israeli technical know-how.

Special or Normal Relationship?

The Federal Republic's policy relationship with Israel is special because it is preferential. By the mid-1980s the governmental partnership had evolved in such a regular and structured fashion that

German leaders consistently referred to it as a "normal relationship." For the Germans, this "normalization" process began in fact with the formalization of ties through the conclusion of diplomatic relations in 1965.

Whereas the outward appearance of the relationship conformed to the "norm" between firm friends, the historical basis of the relationship continued to be seen as anything but normal. The German government sought to conceptualize these two separate features of policy and foundation, and the articulation came in 1973 when, during the first visit of a German chancellor to Israel, Willy Brandt alluded to "normal relations with a special character." Richard von Weizsäcker repeated the formula during the first visit of a German president to Israel in 1985 and elaborated on it on the occasion of Chaim Herzog's trip to the Federal Republic in 1987:

The fact that you are the first president of the State of Israel to visit our country makes this a most outstanding event in the history of our two peoples. . . . Official, intergovernmental contacts are normal and rest on firm foundations. Practical cooperation is broad-ranging and is borne by a spirit of mutual trust. But beside the intergovernmental relations there are human beings with feelings. We cannot simply put them on the same level. No Israeli can meet a German without recalling the suffering of the Jews under National Socialism. . . . There can be no forgetting the Holocaust. . . . We must be honest with one another and that means first of all being honest in our recollection of the past. Only in this way can a credible and lasting relationship grow between the generations who at that time had not been born and who, today and tomorrow, will have to live and get along with one another in this one world.[11]

For von Weizsäcker and many Germans, governmental relations and societal ties are intimately connected: "There can be no reconciliation without remembrance." Certainly for the Israelis, the strength of societal ties and the imprint of the past are considered the hallmark of the special relationship as President Herzog made clear in April 1987:

I believe at no time in the future will the ties between our two peoples be normal in the usual sense. . . . It is possible, indeed desirable, to have normal diplomatic and economic relations, and thankfully we do have them between the Federal Republic of Germany and Israel. But what happened in the first half of this century cannot be undone. For no people can step out of its own history and disown it. It is a legacy which cannot be denied.[12]

Societal relations continue to be robust today, but the image of the past, the transmission belt between generations, is changing, and may undermine the network of societal connections between Germans and Israelis in the future.

Ties Between Peoples

Public calls for reconciliation by the "Peace with Israel" movement had been an important impulse for Adenauer's 1951 governmental overture toward Israel, but societal relations developed more slowly than governmental ties. Nonetheless, by the early 1970s a dense web of links was in place involving political parties (particularly the SPD and the Labour Party), parliaments, educational institutions (including universities and the Federal Office for Civic Education), trade unions, chambers of commerce, religious groups (such as the Society for Christian-Jewish Cooperation and Sign of the Atonement) and bilateral friendship associations. Second only to the United States, more tourists to Israel hail from the Federal Republic than from any other country. The largest number of twinnings with Israeli towns and cities comes from the Federal Republic. These relations have moved German leaders to point to the fact that Israel is the country with which West Germany has the most intensive exchange of visitors outside the Atlantic alliance.

Cultural relations took even longer to blossom than broader societal contacts and for many years contacts were taboo. A German Cultural Center was opened in Israel in the 1960s, but only in 1981 was it transformed into an official Goethe Institute. In 1974, the Israel Radio Orchestra began to include Wagner in its repertoire but it took until 1981 for the Israel Philharmonic to follow suit and still with major audience protest. Today there is a full range of cultural contact, including opera, theater, ballet and symphony orchestras.

The rallying point for many of the connections between the two societies has been the German-Israeli Society. Its joint conference with the counterpart Israeli-German Society has become an important annual vehicle for maintaining and evaluating the overall relationship. Since 1983, the two organizations have made a particular effort to attract younger members and the youth sections have begun to structure their own bilateral dialogue.

From its inception in 1966 the German-Israeli Society has been one of the primary facilitators of youth exchange, a private initiative supported in significant part by the federal government. For German youth exchanges, Israel stands second only to France in the number of participants, the number of programs, and the amount of funding. Since the early 1960s, some 100,000 young Germans have been sponsored for study trips to Israel. German-Israeli youth exchange now displays a unique feature: in September 1986 the Federal Republic decided to post an attaché for youth exchange to the German embassy in Tel Aviv. Although there has been criticism that youth exchange can amount to state-subsidized tourism, most participants and facilitators believe these programs are important mechanisms for nurturing new mutual images.

LIMITS TO "AUFARBEITUNG DER VERGANGENHEIT"[13]

What German youth seems to lack are accurate and meaningful images of the past. Walter Renn has noted a vast improvement in the content of textbooks dealing with the Third Reich and the Holocaust but still identifies significant gaps, particularly in drawing long-term lessons from the period.[14] The minister for youth, family, and health observed in December 1986 that German youth's confrontation with the past—in the form of enthusiasm for family and local history—is only just beginning. Unfortunately, the curiosity of young Germans is taking hold in the midst of a searing debate among elders over the appropriate role the past should assume in contemporary efforts to shape a practicable national identity. At a time when the post-Holocaust generation needs firm guidance from political leadership about the immutability of the Holocaust's place in history, it is receiving confused and ambivalent messages in the so-called *Historikerstreit* (historians' debate) which erupted in the exchange between Ernst Nolte and Jürgen Habermas in mid-1986 and soon extended beyond the academy into broader segments of society.

Contention among historians over the Third Reich is not entirely new, but the *Historikerstreit* is different for two main reasons: (1) it came on the heels of a series of anti-Semitic episodes in the Federal

Republic; and (2) it constitutes part of a larger process of German self-assertion in the field of foreign policy. Both the internal and the external developments have consequences for German-Israeli relations.

Anti-Semitism and Historical Amnesia

From the beginning of the German-Israeli partnership, there have been diverse forces within the Federal Republic mobilized against the special relationship, ranging from opposition in the FDP and CDU/CSU to the reparations agreement with Israel in the 1950s, to politicians' meetings with Yasir Arafat in the 1970s (when he was still bent on the elimination of Israel), to the Greens' discussions with the Popular Front for the Liberation of Palestine (PFLP) and People's Democratic Front for the Liberation of Palestine (PDFLP) in the 1980s (when these key challengers to Al Fatah are still committed to the destruction of the Jewish state).

Anti-Zionism has been connected on occasion to anti-Semitism, which Alphons Silbermann has concluded is still an important latent or active phenomenon for the majority of the German people.[15] The anti-Semitism and anti-Zionism of the New Left and extraparliamentary opposition quickened in the late 1960s and continued through the 1980s, leading to emigration to Israel of Henryk Broder, a prominent Jewish leftist. Rightist anti-Semitism also proliferated in the late 1950s and 1960s and has thrived through publications like the *Deutsche National-Zeitung.*

Anti-Semitic thoughts have given rise to anti-Semitic actions such as the swastika-daubing of synagogues and cemeteries, physical excesses (right-wing extremists were implicated in the murders of two Jewish public figures in the early 1980s), and the virulent attacks on the Holocaust as a myth (outlawed in the so-called "Auschwitz Lie" legislation which for German Jews and Israelis only trivialized further the Holocaust by embracing all victims of despotism).

The anti-Semitism of the mid-1980s retained many traditional stereotypes. It also possessed the distinctive quality of appearing in open places with clear and proud ownership by respected public figures: the " remedy" of the CDU mayor Graf von Spee, the utterance of CSU Bundestag deputy Hermann Fellner, and the attempted staging of Rainer Fassbinder's *Garbage, the City and Death*. There was considerable public outcry over all three events and the government responded through condemnation or censure. However, the chancellor hardly confronted the problem during the Bundestag debate inspired by these actions when he labeled the racist remarks merely "irresponsible" and viewed anti-Semitism simply as an aberration from which the younger generation is "immune."

Other CDU leaders like von Weizsäcker have not shared the chancellor's conviction and have warned: "Whoever refuses to remember this inhumanity [of the Holocaust] is prone to new risks of infection."[16] And the SPD, FDP, and the Greens have shown more concern than the CDU/CSU, taking the initiative in debates to emphasize the seriousness of anti-Semitism and the reinterpretation of history. For the opposition the government's response in the November 1986 debate on restitution amounted to a dangerous "self-satisfaction" that it had done enough to redress the crimes of the past.

Israelis fear that the historical amnesia and trivialization of the Holocaust expressed in the *Historikerstreit* can translate only too readily into inattention to the plight and priorities of the organized remnant of Hitler's victims, the State of Israel. In 1984, Benjamin Armon referred to two vital alliances: one with life (revived in Israel) and one with death (memorialized at Yad Vashem). Two years later Israel's longest-serving (1974–81) ambassador to Bon, Yohanan Meroz, doubted that either alliance was vital any longer for the Germans. Germans, he suggested, had used the relationship with Israel to forget rather than honor the past. Integrating the past, he warned, might now mean they would forget Israel.[17]

Competing Special Relationships

Bitburg symbolized the integration of the internal and external developments that have changed the environment of German-Israeli relations. Internally, adequate historical consciousness and responsibility[18] would have sensitized German leaders to the total inappropriateness of the Bitburg cemetery for commemorating the fortieth anniversary of 8 May 1945. Bitburg represented to Chancellor Kohl and his advisers (and much of German society) the fitting reward for being a reliable and rehabilitated ally.

For Kohl, this outward stamp of approval from the U.S. president was a logical step after the Verdun handshake of September 1984, the full public demonstration of Franco-German reconciliation. Since the early 1950s, Franco-German relations had progressed, proliferated, and become institutionalized. Even though a structure existed in the form of the 1963 Elysée Treaty, it was only in the 1980s that an intensification of cooperation occurred, especially in the military sphere.

In the past, Germans accepted the appellation "economic giant, political dwarf"; now they seemed to desire political stature, at least on the European continent. The relationship with France, the leadership of the European Community (EC), and the widespread endorsement of the *Europäisierung Europas* (Europeanization of Europe) were key manifestations of this trend toward self-assertion. Kohl now characterized Franco-German relations as a "privileged partnership," emphasizing West Germany's equality as well as the preferential nature of the ties.

Such emphasis on the Federal Republic's European identity had important consequences for the relationship with Israel. Until the early 1980s the Federal Republic's foreign policy had developed through a process of rehabilitation in which Israel was central. Thereafter, it has entered a stage of self-assertion in which the importance of Israel for the Federal Republic's outward image has been downgraded.

During the 1960s, the Federal Republic had championed Israel's cause in the EC, often against France. Franco-German differences over the Arab-Israeli conflict were still visible in the 1970s when the EC began to pursue a common foreign policy. Even in 1980 when the Community issued the Venice Declaration on the Middle East, the Federal Republic prevailed with the term "association" over the French desire for full participation of the PLO in the peace process. But by 1982 and the Israeli invasion of Lebanon, there was little to distinguish the German position from the French.

With regularity, the Community has roundly denounced Israel on Lebanon, settlements, the occupied territories, and Jerusalem. The Federal Republic's presidency of the EC's Council of Ministers essentially coincided with the eruptions in the West Bank and Gaza. The Community has been quick to condemn Israel and both Chancellor Kohl and Foreign Minister Genscher have sought a European role as interpreter to the United States of Arab and Palestinian positions. Israelis who support their government's behavior toward the Palestinians feel Germans, above all, have no right to criticize. Even the Israeli opponents of government policy insist that Germans should avoid *public* expressions of disagreement.

In the past, when the Federal Republic's relations with France and with Israel collided in the EC, the Germans sided with Israel; today they prefer France. For the time being, the Federal Republic is able to balance the two elements of governmental policy toward Israel: the multilateral level of profound criticism in the diplomatic sphere and the bilateral framework of consistent preference in economics, development aid, and science and technology. As the discrepancy between the two increases, it is unclear how durable the coexistence will be.

The collision of Franco-German and German-Israeli relations began after the 1967 Six-Day War when France adopted the Palestinian position. Another competition between special relationships had begun a decade earlier. At the time of the 1952 Reparations Agreement Israel refused the Federal Republic's offer of diplomatic relations, but by 1955 had changed its mind. However, the priority assigned in the Hallstein Doctrine to the delegitimation of the GDR and the attendant fear of Egyptian recognition of East Germany now precluded the Federal Republic from reviving its offer and later prevented it from removing German rocket scientists from Egypt and from continuing arms supplies to Israel. Today, direct competition between the German-Israeli and German-German special relationships no longer exists, but indirectly Israel must compete for attention with Deutschlandpolitik, the centerpiece of the Federal Republic's process of national identity formation and autonomy in foreign policy.

In the pursuit of close relations with France and the German Democratic Republic, the Federal Republic periodically evokes suspicion from the United States. Chancellor Kohl has attempted to allay concerns and prove West Germany's reliability through acceptance of American initiatives such as INF modernization, SDI, and multilateral trade talks. He also has sought to establish extensive connections between the two societies to revive the more automatic friendship of earlier periods; here, too, one can identify potential competition with the priority assigned to German-Israeli relations.

Since Adenauer's 1951 statement, German governments have considered Israel the successor state for the Jewish nation, but after Bitburg a possible change in orientation is perceptible. Speaking before the B'nai B'rith International, Ambassador van Well noted on 21 May 1985 that the process of German-Jewish reconciliation had been slower with American Jewry than with Israel, a situation the West German government wanted to change, particularly since American Jews were now considered the "main torchbearer [of the Ashkenazic heritage]."[19] Van Well implied that alone neither German Jewry, "with altogether 30,000 members," nor Israel, "with a new generation of self-confident citizens who lack the traditional ties with Europe and the U.S.," could perpetuate the German-Jewish dialogue.

The West German government now actively supports American Jewry's role in the dialogue, including visits to the Federal Republic by the leadership of major American Jewish organizations. Now, as in the past, the external process of reconciliation (Versöhnung) with former enemies is emphasized over the internal process of confrontation with the past (Aufarbeitung der Vergangenheit). Even when the German government recognized the discrepancy between the internal and external processes as a result of Bitburg, it still chose to look beyond itself, but this time to the United States and not to Israel.

CONCLUSION

German-Israeli relations remain special forty years after they began, but there are serious challenges within and outside the Federal Republic that will likely intensify in the next decade. Within West Germany, they will involve the younger generations' degree of commitment to the partnership. Outside the Federal Republic, the relationship will be impacted by developments on several continents:

the second détente in East-West relations; the nature of American support for Israel; the role of the EC in the third world; and the outcome of Israel's own identity crisis.

Internal Tests

Youth exchange programs have been integral to German-Israeli reconciliation but can they sustain the relationship and carry it through crises in the future? There are signs of renewed commitment but there are also contradictory forces.

The second post-Holocaust generation of Germans came to political maturity in the late 1960s when the international and German sense of morality concerning the Middle East began to shift toward the Palestinians.[20] This generation is now entering political leadership. As a group, its representatives in the SPD and the Greens, and to a lesser extent in the CDU/CSU and the FDP, have been concerned to honor the past, but they have not yet demonstrated fully how a commitment to the memory of the Holocaust translates into policy toward Israel. Of the three policy options—support; even-handedness; condemnation—they seem to be opting for the last. Nor has this generation yet produced its own equivalent of a von Weizsäcker to remind young Germans that they have a collective responsibility to the past.

The third postwar generation, born in the 1960s and touched most directly by youth exchange programs, is reaching political consciousness as world opinion seems to conclude that Israel has lost its moral fiber. Youth exchange programs and education at home are able to demonstrate that Israel is a multifaceted society whose preoccupation with security is derived from its tragic past, but how will German youth resolve the growing tension between these two images?

Michael Wolffsohn has shown that Germans still side more often with Israel than with the Arabs in public opinion polls, but the number of "undecideds" and "indifferents" has grown significantly.[21] The youngest generations of Germans whose images were shaped by the post-1967 era in the Middle East most likely will be susceptible to indifference or to sympathy with the Arabs and Palestinians. The parallel disenchantment of these generations with the United States can only magnify the trend away from Israel.[22]

Unless young German leaders confront the past and Israel honestly and fairly, working actively to perpetuate nongovernmental networks between the two societies, there may not be a "successor generation" in the German-Israeli relationship. And young Germans must find young Israeli counterparts (or Israelis must find them). These Israelis, whose origins lie largely in the Middle East and not in Europe, may be no more attracted to special relations with Germany than the Germans with Israel.

External Challenges

From the time of the Reparations Agreement, the United States has been a silent partner in German-Israeli relations, either stimulating German initiatives or lubricating the process. Accompanying the West German government's recognition that rehabilitation ultimately rested on American approval was a shared worldview of Israel as the bastion against communism in the Middle East.

The SPD and FDP departed from this perspective in the mid-1960s, but it remained in the CDU/CSU through the early 1980s, albeit in diluted form. Today there is political consensus that détente serves German-German relations, which are the highest priority, and that the Soviet Union is a legitimate world actor, even in the Middle East. The current second American-Soviet détente reinforces the German perspective, which no longer sees Israel serving a singular moral or ideological function in its region. The growing erosion of the American public's commitment to Israel will ease the transformation in German thinking.

As détente progresses and shifts to third world issues, the EC will accelerate its efforts to remove third world conflicts from East-West relations. Encouraged by the Arab World, the Palestinians, and the French, the EC will continue to emphasize the Middle East, but probably with declining sympathy for Israel.

The active German attempts to stimulate a Middle East peace process and the dispatch of German ships to replace American vessels sent to the Persian Gulf are reflections of the EC trend and of the Federal Republic's foreign policy assertiveness. West Germany is moving from the European to the global stage, where the Middle East remains important for the German economy. The Federal Republic has decreased through diversification but by no means eliminated its reliance on Middle Eastern oil. Moreover, the Middle East is growing as a market for German exports, a constant theme in German leaders' visits to the area.

The German-Israeli special relationship will be tested severely in the next decade. It contains the structures and networks to survive the test but it is unclear whether Germans, especially of the next generations, possess the will. The longer Israel takes to regain the values and purpose of humanistic Zionism, the easier it will be for Germans to shed their resolve and to see the Holocaust as a mere "traffic accident in history."[23] Special relationships do not advance when their origins are forgotten, or worse, dismissed as irrelevant. Both international circumstance and domestic change are threatening German memory and with it, the special relationship.

NOTES

1. *New York Times*, 1 August 1949.
2. The text is in Rolf Vogel, ed., *The German Path to Israel. A Documentation* (London: Oswald Wolff, 1969), 33.
3. Quoted in Paul Weymar, *Adenauer. His Authorized Biography* (New York: Dutton, 1957), 406.
4. For the text of Chancellor Kohl's speeches and statements in Israel, see *Deutschland-Berichte*, a newsletter devoted to German-Israeli relations, vol. 20, no. 2 (February 1984).
5. "Statement by Federal Chancellor Helmut Kohl During a Debate on 'Anti-Semitic Tendencies' in the Deutscher Bundestag, Bonn, February 27, 1986," *Statements and Speeches*, vol. 9, no. 3, 7 March 1986 (New York: German Information Center, 1986).
6. "Policy Statement by Chancellor Helmut Kohl to the German Bundes-

tag, Bonn, March 18, 1987," *Statements and Speeches*, vol. 10, no. 4, 23 March 1987 (New York: German Information Center, 1987).

7. Konrad Adenauer, "Bilanz einer Reise: Deutschlands Verhältnis zu Israel," *Die Politische Meinung* 11, no. 115 (1966): 15.

8. Deutscher Bundestag und Bundesrat, *Verhandlungen des Deutschen Bundestages. Stenographische Berichte. 4. Wahlperiode*, vol. 57, 17 February 1965, 8103.

9. The text of Lutz Stavenhagen's statement is in *Deutschland-Berichte* 22, no. 12 (December 1986).

10. For the text of von Weizsäcker's speech, see *Deutschland-Berichte* 21, no. 6 (June 1985).

11. "President Richard von Weizsäcker of the Federal Republic of Germany and President Chaim Herzog of the State of Israel. Exchange of Speeches at a Banquet in Honor of President Herzog at Augustusburg Palace, Brühl, April 6, 1987," *Statements and Speeches*, vol. 10, no. 5, 7 April 1987 (New York: German Information Center, 1987).

12. Ibid.

13. This term is used in preference to the more frequently employed concept of "Bewältigung der Vergangenheit" which assumes that resolution can be achieved and that the past can be mastered.

14. Walter F. Renn, "Federal Republic of Germany: Germans, Jew and Genocide," in Randolph L. Braham, ed., *The Treatment of the Holocaust in Textbooks: The Federal Republic of Germany, Israel, the United States* (New York: Columbia University Press for Social Science Monographs, Boulder, and the Institute for Holocaust Studies of the City University of New York, 1987).

15. Alphons Silbermann, "Antisemitismus in der Bundesrepublik Deutschland," *Bild der Wissenschaft* 13, no. 6 (June 1976); and Silbermann, *Sind wir Antisemiten? Ausmass und Wirkung eines sozialen Vorurteils in der Bundesrepublik Deutschland* (Cologne: Verlag Wissenschaft und Politik, 1982).

16. See note 10 for the 8 May 1985 speech.

17. Yohanan Meroz, *In schwieriger Mission. Als Botschafter Israels in Bonn* (Berlin: Ullstein Verlag, 1986).

18. In their expectations of "late-born" German leaders, both Diaspora and Israeli Jews deliberately prefer these terms to the concept of "collective guilt" whose use is restricted to the German generations of the Holocaust.

19. Embassy of the Federal Republic of Germany, Washington, D.C., 21 May 1985.

20. I am following Stephen Szabo's definition of postwar generations. See "West Germany: Generations and Changing Security Perspectives," in Stephen F. Szabo, ed., *The Successor Generation: International Perspcectives of Postwar Europeans* (London: Butterworth, 1983).

21. Michael Wolffsohn, "Deutsch-israelische Beziehungen im Spiegel der öffentlichen Meinung," *Aus Politik und Zeitgeschichte* 46–47/84 (17 November 1984): 21.
22. On the changing attitudes of young Germans toward the United States, see Andrei Markovits's chapter in this volume.
23. Jitzhak Ben-Ari, "Visions Could Become Reality," in Otto R. Romberg and Georg Schwinghammer, eds., *Twenty Years of Diplomatic Relations between the Federal Republic of Germany and Israel* (Frankfurt am Main: Tribüne-Verlag, 1985), 49.

CONCLUSION: WERE THE ANGRY OLD MEN WRONG?

Peter H. Merkl

In 1979, Axel Eggebrecht, a critical observer of both the Weimar Republic—he was a contributor to *Weltbühne*, among other periodicals—and the Federal Republic, brought together eleven prominent critics of the evolution of Bonn democracy between the covers of a book entitled *The Angry Old Men: Reflections on Germany Since 1945*.[1] Looking backward on three decades of West German missed opportunities and wrong turns, they each explain their line of criticism. Back in 1945, the authors varied in age from twenty-four—Heinrich Böll was twenty-eight—to 46 and all felt they had had plenty of opportunity to experience and hone their judgment on the Third Reich. Ranging from the World War I to the World War II generations, they had all tasted the disfavor of the Nazi regime in jail, in concentration camps, or in exile. Writers, scholars, and politicians (including a Protestant clergyman and former SPD mayor of Berlin), they obviously did not all have the same perspective on the alleged shortcomings of the Federal Republic but their underlying tone was critical, and sometimes rather strident.

CRITICISMS OF THE FRG

What were their complaints about the thirty years of "wrong development" up until 1979, or of opportunities missed at crucial moments? There are important points of agreement: They agree, for example, that West German society never came to grips with the misdeeds of the Third Reich. The lack of such a reckoning, accord-

464

ing to the journalist and political scientist Eugen Kogon, was the "birth defect" of the republic. Denazification also was hopelessly botched. Trials of such major evildoers as the mass murderers of concentration camps were endlessly delayed and ended with ridiculous sentences. Nazi judges and administrators, in particular, were rarely tried and often went right on being senior judges and administrators of the Federal Republic, or retired on princely pensions. Worst of all, there never really occurred a genuine moment of popular recognition of the horrible wrongness of the Nazi regime and its vile deeds. Only the self-chosen new leadership in the political parties at least made some efforts to cleanse the country of the brown pest and to set it on a democratic course. Most people's "inability to mourn" the victims, as the late Alexander Mitscherlich put it, has characterized popular West German attitudes to this day. The criticism seems true enough, if perhaps a little too severe and based on unrealistic expectations of how most people react to their own guilt feelings.

Another widely shared complaint was the lack of cultural and moral values in West Germany today, usually associated with the one-sided pursuit of economic success in the first three decades. West Germany's "wrong turn" was taken the moment the Western occupation zones were set on their path toward a market economy and economic growth, such as with the currency reform and Marshall Plan of 1948, and through the extraordinary economic recovery and expansion of the decades to follow. Many of the angry old men were devout Christians, socialists, or European federalists in the late 1940s whose dreams of a moral renaissance all came to naught. Some also feel that the establishment, or "restoration," of an economic ruling class of the superrich and giant corporations has stifled the unfolding of the democratic spirit in Germany, and, to this day, monopolizes the press and public opinion. This is a theme echoed also by the "postmaterialists" among the second and third postwar generations although the economic recession has muted their antimaterialism.

A third disappointment of the angry old men is the stifling provincial conformism in cultural tastes, and in politics as well. The quiet idylls of the bourgeoisie of this *Pseudo-Biedermeierstaat*, writes Ossip Flechtheim, made every bit of fresh wind, of criticism, seem as if it was a life-threatening hurricane. Any voice of opposition on questions of foreign policy, economics, even culture, he claims, was forever in danger of being branded "subversive," "atheist," or "communist." The political scientist Flechtheim could easily have cited de Tocqueville's essay on *Democracy in America* to underscore his point of conformism but he would probably have hesitated to associate this benumbing tendency with the workings of mass democracy. The late Nobel Prize winner Heinrich Böll, another angry old man, was more forthright in denouncing in his essay the conformist fears during the terrorist phase of the late seventies. The same theme caused him to write the novel, *The Lost Honor of Katharina Blum*, a morality play about hysterical suspicions and public condemnation, and about irresponsible journalism. This criticism has perhaps become less salient in the eighties, although the charge of cultural and political provincialism fits West German politics as much as it does most modern states, West or East.

A final pervasive criticism of the angry old men concerns the survivals of German authoritarianism underneath the veneer of democracy and social modernization. Authoritarianism, they say, has survived especially in the judiciary and in the form of its heavy bias in favor of the authority of the police against the rights of the individual and of the teachers against the students. No other part of the West German establishment has been as shot through with old, "unreconstructed" Nazis as the bench and law enforcement, although there is no lack of authoritarian attitudes among the executives of government, of the army, and of the corporate world. The passage of time and generational change, of course, will eventually remove these old authoritarians, but how can we be sure that German education will not produce new authoritarians to take their place? Moreover, there is a pervasive, popular fear of change, any change in the system, the old men complained. The system-changers, or *Systemveränderer*, are the devils that insecure West German democrats are most afraid of and whom they like to see pursued by judges, police, and by the gumshoed "guardians of the constitution" (*Verfassungsschutz*). What kind of a democracy is this, according to our angry old men, that is afraid of all critics, opposition, and proposals for change, and that relies so heavily on spying on the free thoughts of people, intimidating nonconformists, and engaging in electronic surveillance with the help of every trick in the manual. Is the Federal Republic in danger of becoming a *Verfassungsschutzstaat*, a police state of the "guardians of the constitution"?

By now all these prominent critics are beyond the retirement age of sixty-five, some in their eighties, or dead. There is something very refreshing about the passion with which they put forth their disappointments and complaints from the depths of their patriotic hearts —this is a much nobler, more authentically patriotic concern than the bloody-minded nationalism that led earlier generations of Germans to make war upon their neighbors. The same can be said about the passionate criticism of the angry young men, and emphatically also the angry young women of the most recent West German generations. With all their burning concerns to build a better society, the eventual extirpation of the present flaws of German democracy, if not the realization of all their divergent dreams, cannot be far off. Saying this, however, does not yet signal our agreement with every detail of their analysis. Let us examine, instead, what our experts think of these and other complaints and problems of West German society and politics.

VALUES AND IDENTITY

The logical point to begin a study of political change, as I said above (Introduction, p. 00), is with the values and attitudes in the minds of the people concerned. But these values are neither equally profound nor equally salient among the people concerned. Few are so deeply held as notions of national identity, especially in a nation divided between East and West after a century-long odyssey of misguided nationalism and its disasters. The recent German historians' debate on the German question, which exercised many minds from the pages of the weekly *Die Zeit*, to those of the *New York Times*, may not exactly be the scuttlebutt of everyday conversation in Germany. But Germans of all generations share some of the uneasiness of the historians about all the things that have gone wrong in contemporary German history: the ultimate failures of both Bismarck's Little German nation-state and the Greater German one of the Pan Germans, the collapse of German empire and military might in two world wars, the enormous suffering and loss of German blood, the expulsion of millions of ethnic Germans from the East as a result of the German quest for "a place in the sun," and, last but hardly least, the horrendous crimes committed in this pursuit. Older Germans also are all too aware that the East now begins at the Elbe river and, in fact, that Hitler's Russian campaign brought the Iron Curtain down upon half of Europe and Soviet power into its very heart.

The Historians' Debate

The question for West Germany, however, is not only what to make of this situation but also what to do now. Should West Germans define their identity in the all-German sense of being part of a more inclusive nation, that is, inclusive of East Germany and perhaps even of ethnic Germans still in the East? For years, Germans would fight on the maps of geography over the German division: Calling the GDR East Germany instead of Central Germany was tantamount to recognizing the Oder-Neisse line as the German-Polish border. Also, in 1987 alone, according to official reports, 100,000 Germans from Eastern Europe and the GDR (half of them from Poland) were permitted to immigrate to the Federal Republic, "heim ins Reich." This too was a concrete result of Bonn's Ostpolitik which clearly reestablished the stature of at least West Germany as a bridge, or a middle power between East and West. Or should West Germans only concern themselves with a West German national identity, liberal-democratic, distinctly Western in culture, and penetrated economically by multinational Western (especially American) corporations for the last four decades? Should they try to "normalize German history," and balance the good against the bad, suffering against guilt, as conservative politicians (Strauss, Kohl) and historians (Michael Stürmer, Andreas Hillgruber) have suggested, by reestablishing their historical sense of who they are in reference to a thousand years of German history, and not just to the twelve years of the "thousand years' (Third) Reich"? The Kohl government has been building two big German historical museums in which they hope, by conservative interpretations, to take the symbolic offensive against the malaise of a flawed national identity.[2]

Contrary to appearances, these German controversies are far from new, but have been elevated now to a more intellectual and respectable level. For several decades, already, representatives and periodicals of the German nationalistic right had crudely attacked the prevailing, "breast-beating" historical interpretations in the German media and at the universities, with the help of a handful of "revisionist historians" whom the German historical fraternity preferred to ostracize and ignore. More recently, the writings of the European New Right and passionate German conservative responses to the ill-fated gesture of the Bitburg visit and the American reaction to it[3] have kept the issues alive in Europe, if not in the United States.

On the liberal side where the sociologist Jürgen Habermas and several historians (for example Jürgen Kocka, Hans Mommsen, and Martin Broszat) have defined the ideal German identity as the commitment to a Western-oriented Basic Law, a "patriotism of the constitution," there have also long been efforts to go even beyond the sixties' historical revelations about the Third Reich. Throughout the seventies, books and discussions of "theories of fascism" widened the concept of fascism to include two centuries of feudal oppression and capitalistic exploitation of the German masses, with the misdeeds of the Third Reich as the predictable outcome of the unholy alliance between the *Junkers* and the barons of industry of a hundred years ago. The "long march" of the 1968ers through the media, publishing houses, and some city halls produced further well-crafted television documentaries and newspaper features, and a spate of museum exhibitions of blown-up photographs of historic poverty and oppression. More recently, young volunteer historians have produced workshops of everyday history to discover *and tell about* what exactly happened to average people under the Nazis in a city neighborhood or on a factory floor. The struggle for defining the German identity obviously has been going on all along. The only difference is that, now, the political *Wende* (turnabout) in Bonn has given the upper hand to the conservative interpretations, barring only the more extreme and self-serving ones.

For non-German observers from the *Ausland*, this troubled sea of debates after a while becomes less interesting and, like our contributor Gerald R. Kleinfeld, they head for the *terra firma* of the realities of the German-German situation today. The two German successor states, indeed, have gone the gamut of emotions of a terminally ill patient when he first discovers his illness (of the division) is incurable: denial, despair, accepting resignation—and now the rediscovery of a common fate, the *Schicksalsgemeinschaft* of both Germanies with respect to the maintenance of peace, and the common fear that a major war might ever again originate on German soil. In the meantime, the relative economic strength of West Germany and its integration into the European Community give the West Germans a reasonable substitute for what they seem to have lost in the sands of history.

The Waning Love Affair with America

But there is another angle from which the dilemma of the West German sense of identity can be highlighted in a way that is more likely to affect actual polices on both sides of the Atlantic: anti-Americanism. As Andrei S. Markovits points out above, the significance of German anti-Americanism lies in the special role the United States has played "in the formation and weaning" of the FRG and in the "broken nature of Germany's national identity and historical legacy." Under American political and economic tutelage, there developed an American cultural hegemony in West Germany that was quite contrary to the disdain of the German educated bourgeoisie for American society throughout more than a hundred years. The Nazis and more recent German far right wingers, as on many other subjects, presented a crude version of this bourgeois anti-Americanism and, increasingly, even the Left has scored American capitalism and imperial power. At the same time one can often observe German Greens and socialist visitors feeling very much at home among young Americans however much they may deplore American power or German dependency. Any anti-American stirrings of today—and they often get exaggerated by the American desire for universal popularity—are full of ambiguities and this should hardly surprise us. What really needs to be explained is the long love affair of postwar West Germans (especially the World War II and first postwar generations) with a rose-colored image of America until the generational and rather bourgeois revolt of the sixties reverted to the German bourgeois stereotypes. Perversely, it was the struggle of young Americans for civil rights and against the American involvement in Vietnam that reminded German student militants that we had had unequal race relations and followed imperialistic policies toward the third world all along. As Markovits points out, diverging economic interests between the two countries have further contributed to the present estrangement.

It is worth lingering a moment over the reasons for this love affair because it is so rare in this benighted world that such relationships, however fleeting, lighten the pall of ubiquitous national egotisms and hatreds. The causes of the German romance with Uncle Sam went far beyond the catastrophic defeat, the hunger and devastation, and the shame of German misconduct and mass murder during the war which mercifully stilled for a spell the every-busy tongues of the most Nazified social class, the bourgeoisie. But if it had only been for this enormous existential misery, the Germans could perhaps just as well have idealized one of their European neighbors who might have been more compatible with their own pre-Nazi traditions. All these neighbors, however, were perceived by the vanquished Germans as (understandably) hostile and selfishly interested in taking advantage once more of German weakness. The Americans, on the other hand, were seen as surprisingly well-meaning and unselfish in their approach. During a recent research project on Bavarian local government, for example, this writer and his associates at times were overwhelmed by the vast reservoir of pro-American sentiment still to be found in small towns and villages toward the American occupation of four decades ago. Surprising numbers of older Germans effusively recalled CARE packages received from Americans they had never met, candy and fruit given by unknown GIs to German children, friendly and constructive support by local occupation officers, the Marshall Plan, and so forth. Again and again, villagers in the Bavarian province would ask about a legendary Major Thompson who must have been a veritable local saint, and about legions of other ordinary, decent Americans they did meet. It was obviously love at first sight and whatever may have gone wrong here and there has never really overshadowed the positive attitude of many millions of average Germans toward America, however strident some old or new bourgeois critics may be.

A Very Different Germany

What role does a sense of guilt over the Holocaust play in the German identity today? This is a difficult question and involves treading on psychologically very dangerous ground, given the nature of prejudice. If we recall the scale of prejudicial actions in Gunnar Myrdal's *An American Dilemma*, with racist murder or genocide at the very top, we need to be alert to the dangers of self-reinforcing rationalizations: Once the horrifying deeds have been committed, guilt feelings can lead just as easily to making up *post facto* justifications and continuing the murderous prejudice, as to recoiling in remorse and agreeing to acts of restitution, such as Lily Feldman describes in this volume. Unlike the speeches of President von Weizsäcker and Chancellor Kohl, the relevant attitudes of the neo-Nazi Right and increasing numbers of social conservatives by today clearly show that the rationalizing route is not just an invention of social psychologists. Historians too have often acknowledged that people rarely learn from history and that history tends to repeat itself.

The government and majority of West Germans, on the other hand, as Professor Feldman shows in great detail, have embarked on a determined course of responsibility and restitution and have stuck with it since 1951. Thus the Myrdalian dynamics has worked so far in the positive direction rather than, except for the far Right, in that of self-rationalization and deepening prejudice. The resulting special relationship at first had to compete only with the security interests of the Federal Republic, and with its general reconciliation with France and other European neighbors. More recently, however, the growing Sephardization of Israel and its more exclusive involvement in Middle Eastern dilemmas have combined with generational change in Germany to lessen the popular ties. The Israeli invasion of Lebanon and settlement policies on the West Bank further encouraged a climate of European criticism of Israeli policies. The personal attack of Prime Minister Menachem Begin on Chancellor Schmidt in the early eighties hardly helped reinforce the weakening positive dynamic, while the at first negligible negative trends have increased. In the long run, the passage of generations alone may prove the dominant factor even if Israel "regain[s] the values and purpose of humanistic Zionism" (Feldman). Like the German love affair with the United States, this special relationship too may eventually wither away in a world ruled by national egotisms and indifference.

At this point the findings of Russell J. Dalton's chapter also fit into the picture: German social attitudes have undergone significant and substantial change in the direction of racial and religious tolerance and of democratic dissent. Young Germans differ from their authoritarian, conformist elders. The patterns of social distrust and of the privatizing *Bunkermentalität* (bunker mentality) of the immediate postwar years also have been moderated and this is even true of the once famous work ethic, although the changes in social norms are lagging behind those that have taken place in the political culture. The growth of postmaterialist orientations among the young, in a manner of speaking, amalgamates the concern for social and personal fulfillment with that for greater political liberties. Their new political assertiveness, while it may lead to further confrontations with the establishment, should be considered a boon and not a liability of West German politics.

Mothers and Daughters of Seven Generations

A vital part of the changes that came with the second German postwar generation are the politicized young women of today, inside and out of the women's movements described above by Joyce Mushaben. No other aspect of the social and political evolution exhibits such extraordinary changes as the social role of the mass of German women from the generation of this writer's maternal grandmother—about Adenauer's generational group—and the twenty-year-olds of today. My grandmother was a functional near-illiterate overwhelmed by the social changes taking place in her lifetime, a person with little political insight and immense social superstitions and prejudices. Her daughter, my mother, was at the very end of the World War I generation, received a good elementary and commercial education, and was gainfully employed both before and after the fourteen years of marriage to my father, a man twenty years her senior. She had a lively appreciation for the following generations of women, in particular for that of the women's movement, even

Table C.1

Hypothetical Table of Mother-Daughter Links Between
Generations (by principal child-bearing years)

Mother-daughter influence	Pre-World War I Mothers: were mothers in 1900–1914, believed in Victorian social hierarchy, feminine propriety, religion, and the fatherland. World War I mothers: 1914–1919, were forced by the war and its hardships to take on family responsibility without the men. Between Wars generation of mothers: 1924–1938, returned to religion, conservatism, patriotism; supported Hitler's nationalist revival.
Mother-daughter influence	World War II and Postwar Mothers: 1939–1948, were mothers during war and postwar hardships, had to take on family responsibilities without the men. Economic Miracle Era Mothers: 1950–1965, returned to patriarchal society, religion, patriotism. Generation of Women's Movements: 1968–1979, mobilized for women's interests and rights in politics, economics, family. Today's Young Women: 1980–1990, returned to femininity, "interior values (Innerlichkeit)," romanticism, religion, German identity.

Mother-daughter influence

Mother-daughter influence

Key: Each generation of mothers influences daughters that are twenty to twenty-five years younger during the process of raising them to adulthood.

though her own upbringing condemned her to loneliness and boredom in her old age. She had never learned how an older woman can remain useful and find fulfillment outside the family.

But it is really the changes in women's lives and social environment since 1945 and the generational linkages that make this story so absorbing. Mother-daughter influences link several generations of women: See table C.1. The war imposed enormous demands on mothers of families in the absence of the men. These women, including the *Trümmerfrauen* of 1945–1948 described by Professor Mushaben, may even have learned to be so tough and self-reliant from their own mothers of World War I who also had to shift for themselves and their families under extraordinary deprivations and in the absence of their men. While the feminist attitudes of the young women of the seventies have probably always been present in German society, the assertiveness and political militancy of the second postwar generation need to be explained. Perhaps the mothers of World War II passed on their activist attitude in the process of raising their well-educated and politically aware daughters of the late sixties and seventies. Perhaps the latter's assertiveness was learned from two generations of mothers and grandmothers under conditions of war.

In between these three generations of strong mothers and daughters (of which the next installment is just about to arrive), are their very opposites, pre-World War I Victorian women conforming to a religious sense of social place and feminine propriety, their conservative and religious daughters who came of age during the thirties and were beguiled by Hitler and his propaganda, the women of the quiet, patriarchal fifties, and again those who seek a "return to femininity" and motherliness today. The generational groups, this time defined by prime child-bearing age and socialization of daughters by their mothers, are a little different from the ones used above though the timing of wars is crucial. My assumption of a regular rhythm of mother-daughter political socialization stimulated in one series by the impact of the war experience on mothers and families, and in the other series by the absence of such pressures, may be too schematic and needs to be tested with empirical data to prove it.

Perhaps such constructs even detract from the moral thrust of the emancipatory movement of the seventies and its unique impact on the status of women. Even today's young generation of women in their twenties, for all its rejection of the "harsh feminists" of the seventies, has been determined to retain and utilize all the new rights and freedoms for women conquered by those "abrasive" fighters of yesterday. And although the first phase of the women's movement of the seventies still had to make "the personal into the political," there can be no mistaking the impact of the second and third women's postwar generations on German politics.[4] Women's participation in political leadership positions as well as at the grass roots has mushroomed, as Mushaben documents. No conservative party can ever reconsign German women to the realm of the three Ks (*Kinder, Küche, Kirche*—children, kitchen, and church), nor roll back the legal and institutional changes resulting from the self-assertion of the female majority (53 percent) of the West German electorate.

Community and Social Partnership

The secular values that are embodied in women's claims to their rightful place as individuals have long been in conflict with the religious emphasis on family roles and other prescriptions for German social and even political life. The postwar struggle of the Protestant churches of Germany for the German soul, as Richard Merritt relates, was initially a territorial battle with the communists of East Berlin and East Germany. In the intervening years, however, the growing secularization of West German Society has shifted the focus from anti-communism and resistance to communist dictatorship to the social issues at home. The Protestant churches no longer have much authority to resist changes in the everyday life of the faithful, let alone the vast majority of those that never go to church. The German Catholic church is no more able to withstand the pressure in the long run than are the Protestants, despite the rearguard battles of the present Pope John Paul against communism and the theology of liberation. The social roots of Catholic villages and urban strongholds are eroding with the secular homogenization of German society and the church is slowly losing its authority to tell people how to live. What used to be the broadly based voting power of church-goers behind the CDU/CSU, by the same token, is slowly becoming a vote of secular conservatism today.

The values behind the social partnership between labor and capital, whether at the micro- or meso-level of corporatism, have clearly increased their hold on West German society, over time, as Michael Huelshoff has pointed out. Instead of the socialism favored by many of the founders of the Federal Republic, and by some of the eleven angry old men we cited, there came a consensus on *Mitbestimmung*, social partnership, and governmental restraint, or weakness, in economic intervention. Even after the first postwar recession brought the SPD into the government, the upshot was not socialism but the further development of corporatist arrangements and of the long overdue "humanization of the workplace," The case study of the structural crises of the Ruhr Valley, by Jutta Helm, puts the social partnership to the test. Reeling from coal to steel crises, the Ruhr area is a prime location for the necessary adjustments in its industry and labor market and, despite vast expenditures, the painful restructuring is still far from completed. Still, Professor Helm concludes, the social partnership has not collapsed and the supportive role of government has been far from negligible.

THE RULES OF THE GAME

As we proceed from the changing values of West German society to the more specific, political "rules of the game," our investigation starts, of course, with that odd constitutional document with which the West German politicians—without benefit of popular ratification—intended to govern themselves "for a transitional period," that is, until the Germans of West *and East* could agree on a better one. Called the Basic Law, this provisional constitution has endured beyond all expectations. But, as Donald P. Kommers writes above, the German Parliament had already added thirty-two new articles, repealed five, and amended the Basic Law in countless places a decade ago. While most of the changes may have been minor, there have been a number of conferences on constitutional reform, in particular dealing with such subjects as cooperative federalism, the role of local government in the constitutional system, executive-legislative relations, and the organization of the executive and the two houses of Parliament. In 1969–1970 a major reform rearranged the federal-state relationship and finances in the direction of *Politikverflechtung* (cooperative federalism).[5] And in 1973 the Bundestag convened a Commission (*Enquête-Kommission*) on constitutional reform which had recommendations for change on all the subjects mentioned above when it finally reported in 1976.[6]

Socialist, Liberal Democratic, and Christian

This intensity of constitutional discussion reflects not so much popular dissatisfaction with the provisions of the Basic Law as the big debates among right, center, and left over its particulars. Some of our angry old men, of course, have found fault with it and so have the angry young men and women, attacking it in particular from the left. Right-wing criticisms have fastened upon the "party-and-interest-groups-state" and the new form of cooperative federalism. As the major institutional framework of the Federal Republic, we would expect the Basic Law to constitute something like the ramparts of the founders of the republic against both a return of national socialism, as well as against the "system changers" of the second and third postwar generations. But its flexibility and the relative ease of amendment seem to have spared West Germany the need for any total reform so far. Despite frequent criticisms, the "party state," welfare, and "militant democracy" features have served it well and even the federal system in its own fashion survived the demands of a "centralized society," as Peter Katzenstein put it in his paradoxical fashion.

To be sure, some of the young rebels at times came to sneer at the "free democratic basic order," a phrase often flung at them by establishment judges and politicians in the course of confrontations. While the establishment may prefer a stronger role for authority, some of the left-wing critics, for example during the long campaign against the emergency legislation, seemed inclined to tip the balance between freedom and authority completely in the direction of individual rights and freedoms. But the original amalgam in the constitution of political values derived from liberalism, socialism, and Christian social philosophy has held together well and in a balanced way. Has the Federal Republic become more liberal, more socialist, or more Christian social over the years? Notwithstanding the pronouncements of at least some of the angry old men, one could argue yes to all three: liberal democracy has certainly grown the most, in spite of the vociferous complaints from many quarters. The gradual elimination of traditional authoritarian elements in society and state, given continued prosperity, and their replacement with liberal elements accounts for the overwhelming gains in this respect. It is more difficult to point to advances of socialism unless we carefully define the term first and distinguish social democracy from the communitarian socialist utopias of an earlier age. The working class in Germany certainly made tremendous gains in job satisfaction, rights on the job, economic democracy (*Mitbestim-*

mung), and trade union influence on the government, especially under Helmut Schmidt. The story of the DGB over the last forty years, Donald Hancock shows, is one of successful integration into the social, economic, and political order, no matter what ambivalent feelings may still remain. And the evolution of corporatism, macro or meso, in the West German economy meant also the advance of real trade union influence on economic decisions of great magnitude, such as in the restructuring of Ruhr industries, as Jutta Helm has shown us.

Christian social principles, by comparison, seem to have lost ground with the decline of church attendance, the changes in family law, and the limited legalization of abortion. But even here one can argue that this is only one of several interpretations, and a foolish one at that, defending archaic limitations on the personal dignity and freedom of women, and sanctioning domestic violence against them and the butchery of back-alley abortions, as if they were something intrinsically Christian. Once the dust has settled over these controversies which have driven the majority of German women voters from the Christian Democratic fold, better counsel may prevail and point to the substantial gains rather than the dubious losses: As a result of Christian Democratic stewardship—as compared to, say, SPD rule in the late forties and the fifties—there has been social solidarity and a reconciliation of the social classes (rather than class struggle), cooperation of labor and industry in the achievement of broadly based prosperity, and a limited and decentralized government rather than an interventionist and centralized state.

While it may be difficult to state with conviction what the SPD might have done differently prior to its own great change in the late fifties, CDU/CSU rule then certainly helped to resocialize ex-Nazis and members of the professional military, integrated vast numbers of ethnic refugees, and achieved protection from the East, German reconciliation with Germany's western and southern neighbors, and acceptance into the Western community of nations. It was only *after* these major and frequently forgotten achievements of the first decade of the Federal Republic—and *after* the acceptance of the most important policies of the Adenauer government by the SPD—that subsequent Bonn governments were free to think of internal reforms, improvements on the painfully reconstructed institutions and stop-gap measures of the first decade, and eventually to seek reconciliation with the communist East as well. In comparison with the lasting gains of Christian Democratic policies, the loss of the recent rearguard battles over family law and abortion appears insignificant. The CDU's recent efforts to modernize family law and to achieve equitable solutions for women in all kinds of predicaments, in fact, may even help to win women and youth back to an enlightened church, to wholesome family life, and to a progressive Christian Democratic party in the long run.

The Organized Core of the System

If the Constitution, the nature of the consensus underlying its values —which later generations could modify in an intelligent fashion— and the beginnings of the social partnership now seem inextricably linked with the beginnings of the republic, the same applies to practical politics as Arnold J. Heidenheimer reminds us in his thoughtful chapter on chancellors, their parties, and party finance. The formative years of the Federal Republic were shaped by Adenauer's ability to build up an immense political machine—including the solid support of the voters and of the Western occupying powers and allies—that simply swallowed up the financial resources and autonomy of nearly all other bourgeois parties. As a result, the early fragmented multiparty system was turned into a one-and-a-half party system. In unprecedented fashion, the CDU/CSU under Adenauer even won an absolute majority of the vote in 1957, leaving the SPD far behind.

As Professor Heidenheimer explains, the party system, the method of campaign finance, and whether a chancellor becomes party leader as well as closely related factors. They have patterned West German politics from the early fifties to the Flick scandal of the late seventies and eighties and can be ignored by German leaders only at their peril. The introduction of public party finance by Adenauer was a part of the evolution of his system, but there are also other ways of looking at it, such as from the point of view of making parties less dependent on well-heeled special interests. Some of the angry old men, on the other hand, criticized public financing as a means to make the German party state completely independent of any constituent influence. Arthur Gunlicks has cast his discussion of the ups and downs of party finance in this framework and supplied fulsome details on the legal mechanisms involved. The choice between public and private campaign finance is obviously far more complicated that it may seem to Americans concerned with political action committees buying a venal Congress.

THE WEST GERMAN PARTY STATE

Gordon Smith's chapter on the evolution of the model of the German party system sets the stage for the detailed discussion of the forty-year trajectory of the major parties of today—the Greens are added for completeness. He highlights the emerging bipolarity of the fifties against the shadow of Weimar multipartyism and its reflection in the very first Bundestag of 1949. The long period of CDU/CSU dominance was followed by one of relative SPD dominance that was nearly as long, thanks to the FDP—for the Christian Democrats seem to have a permanent plurality, a near-majority of the popular vote. Being a catch-all party appealing to all classes came easy to the CDU/CSU because its predecessor, the Catholic Center Party, had already cut across the class lines. It was much harder for the SPD and there is still a pre-*Volkspartei* heritage of socialism and trade union solidarity that resists the catch-all course. The small FDP has played the role of promoting alternation in power between the two poles, a functional requisite of a system in which party loyalties among the CDU/CSU and SPD voters are still too strong to allow a substantial enough swing vote for this purpose. Anthony Downs notwithstanding, few party systems actually resemble a market situation.

Centrifugal Forces Return

Professor Smith also describes the centrifugal forces periodically tugging at the centripetal two-and-a-half system we have just sketched: Extremist forces on the right did so already in the early fifties, and again with the NPD in the late sixties, and they have been rising once more in the mid-eighties, for instance with the Republican

Party and others tugging at the Bavarian CSU. The Greens and the SPD wing friendly to them have increased the centrifugal forces of the eighties in the other direction and, in fact, transformed the system into a four-party system at the national level. The minimal hurdle of 5 percent of the electoral system still helps to curb the centrifugal tendencies, but another feature of the electoral law, the ticket-splitting encouraged by the double ballot, is likely to promote the smaller parties in the wings of the party stage. Smith points to the deliberate efforts of both major parties to marginalize ideologically motivated groups in contrast to the "ideological revival" of the Greens, albeit in the latter case without the overwhelming passion for internal consistency and conformity of past ideological movements. The Greens also have derived so much of their strength from being the party of youth, a generational phenomenon rather than a programmatic one, that they may continue to play an important role even if some of their main issues are resolved, as in the case of the INF missiles. But their role may not be the most constructive for the system, for they either counteract the bipolar game or serve merely as a reservoir of young protest and alienation with exchangeable contents.

The Social Democrats

Of the four contemporary parties in the Bundestag, the SPD is perhaps the most interesting because of its 126-year history and its extraordinary adaptability to the changing challenges of German society. When it resurfaced after the Third Reich, as Professor Braunthal points out, it had to adjust again to a rapidly changing society and to challenges both foreign and domestic. West German society not only became very prosperous; there was a substantial shift from its blue-collar worker elements, the mainstay of the prewar SPD, to white-collar employees and the service sector and, at the same time, farmers and independents lost much of the share they once had. Most recently, as some of the old major industries have hit upon hard times, and high technology industries established themselves in the south and elsewhere, the SPD is once more facing a major challenge to its leadership and solidarity.

In foreign policy, too, the party has shown an amazing willingness to rethink its own positions: It switched from opposition to German rearmament and membership in NATO to qualified support, learned to embrace the European Community, and tackled Ostpolitik measures with a determination belying its earlier commitment to reunification and opposition to the Oder-Neisse line. Shut out from governmental responsibility at the federal level, the SPD leadership cleverly engineered first the Grand Coalition, and later its entry into the government as the senior partner of a coalition with the FDP. Together, these two parties were committed to a reformist program at home and abroad that, at least for a while, promised fulfillment also to the rebellious young generation of students and others. Chancellor Willy Brandt proposed to "dare be more democratic," to reconcile East and West Germany, and to construct a "German model" of a modern, enlightened, and prosperous welfare state, in addition to his Ostpolitik initiatives.

The Brandt administration got off to a brilliant start, underlined by its landslide victory of 1972, but gradually became mired in the difficulties of the seventies. The energy crisis took away its financial surplus and threatened a recession. The economic expansion of the earlier decades generated pollution problems that raised an army of environmental citizen initiatives. The resulting curbs on economic growth, and of course the economic downturn itself after such a long period of advance created all kinds of dissatisfaction in the ranks. While Brandt's successor Schmidt, with the help of the FDP, tried to stay the course, the Young Socialists and the SPD left wing had a field day criticizing him for a long list of failures and omissions which, according to them, culminated in his plans for countering the Soviet INF buildup by bringing in new NATO missiles. This missile issue, along with Schmidt's championship of nuclear energy, eventually gave the Greens their opening wedge among the young and some former SPD voters.

The 1982 walkout of the FDP, which had had its own discontents with SPD policies, finally brought the SPD government down for the time being. The party has been declining in its national vote since 1972 but frequently experiences new surges in the public opinion polls which show that it is capable of a comeback. If it can resist the attraction of the Greens[7] and reconcile right and left wings of the party, it may return to power before long, as the leadership within the party passes from the "sons of Willy Brandt" (e.g. Rau, Vogel) to his "grandchildren," such as Oskar Lafontaine, whose plans for moving the party into an eco-socialist position may be a harbinger of the future.

The Ever-Dominant Christian Democrats

The great antagonist of the SPD in the early years of the Federal Republic, as William Chandler explains, was a complex amalgam of conservative and progressive aspects, including Catholic milieu groups spanning the range from Christian socialism to reactionary clericalism, "social gospel" people and conservative Protestants of the Prussian establishment, ex-Nazis converted to religion and the European union in place of German nationalism, and former People's Party (DVP) liberals and entrepreneurs, all united mostly by the desire to stem the tide of the socialist revival. Highly decentralized and pluralist in composition, the CDU/CSU did not really become a national party until the Adenauer machine began to centralize power in Bonn and long after the party had turned conservative (except for its commitment to social welfare). Professor Chandler expertly analyzes the workings of the decentralized federal and group system of the Christian Democrats as it reestablished itself during the years in opposition, 1969–1982, when power within the party gravitated back to the Länder and group fiefs of the organization.

The success and dominant role of Adenauer exacted its price in the form of the never-ending succession crisis. Even the present incumbent, Kohl, who never tires of calling himself Adenauer's heir, is frequently assailed by would-be rivals. At its worst, this succession struggle pitted would-be leaders against each other, such as Kohl and Strauss. But it is also behind the disputes over election strategy that have Kohl hiding behind and supporting the coalition FDP to the point of diverting CDU ballots to that party. Strauss, on the other hand, favored either a straight two-party system which would be achieved by pushing the FDP below the 5-percent threshold and a major effort to win an absolute majority of votes for the CDU/CSU. Or, alternatively, in the seventies he threatened to turn loose his CSU as a "fourth national party" in the other states in order to lure away the most conservative CDU voters and thus to increase his leverage over the sister party. After Kohl's chancellor candidacy of 1976 which yielded a very respectable vote (48.8 percent), Strauss was so angry that, for a fortnight, he pulled his CSU party out of the joint CDU/CSU caucus of a quarter of a century. For the 1980 elections, therefore, he was given the nomination and an opportunity to find out for himself what antagonism his candidacy aroused throughout the country. After this disastrous experiment, the Bavarian minister-president became less obstreperous although Kohl and his associates were careful to keep him out of the post-1982 cabinets and, in particular, to prevent him from becoming foreign minister in place of Genscher of the FDP.

In spite of his bad press and universal underestimation, Helmut Kohl is a "survivor" and, by now, has been CDU chair for more years than the entire Weimar Republic lasted. His campaign for the chancellorship was deliberate and well-planned from beginning to end: His swift career to the top in the Land politics of the Rhineland-Palatinate was no fluke. His insistence that the party must "reconquer the city-halls" from the SPD and his careful attention to the local and Land establishments of the party have brought rich dividends. The programmatic emphasis on a "new social policy" and wooing back the women and white-collar voters have been well-timed for competition with the SPD. His persistent courting of Genscher and the FDP—in contrast with Strauss's confrontational approach — eventually helped to unhinge the SPD-FDP coalition and to topple Helmut Schmidt. In time even the wily Strauss was outmaneuvered as a rival by Kohl's clever strategy. Whatever the acid tongues of his critics may say, Helmut Kohl's political dominance in the eighties has been no accident.

The Balance Wheel of the Republic. The role of the FDP rounds out the account of the West German party system during most of the four decades under consideration, as Christian Søe explains above. The seemingly indispensable coalition partner of nearly all governing parties, the Free Democrats also represent a long and complex tradition that ranges from assertive German nationalism and the conservatism of the imperial National Liberals and Weimar's People's Party (DVP) to the left-wing liberalism of the pre-1918 Progressives and Weimar's Democrats (DDP), the party that practically wrote the Weimar Constitution for the "most democratic democracy" of its time. Unfortunately, the DDP voters also were among those who soon abandoned that republic and followed their nationalism into the Nazi landslide of the last years of Weimar. The same heterogeneity—from FDP defectors to the politics of nationalist mass movements in the fifties to the representatives of conservative business interests, and on to the "social liberalism" of the SPD-FDP coalition —has resurfaced in the postwar union of liberal parties, the FDP of the Federal Republic, but fortunately it became stabilized in the role of a responsible government party. The heterogeneity also explains how the Free Democrats could manage, if not without considerable pains, to switch from a partnership with the CDU/CSU to the SPD and back again.

The liberal core of Free Democratic beliefs, in spite of its heterogeneity, has become linked with the struggle of the party for electoral survival, and with the liberal rationale of the republic itself, as Professor Søe makes clear. While hovering at the edge of extinction from election to election, and in the position of the balancer between two major parties—evidently each incapable of a sustained majority of the popular vote—the FDP has pitched its appeal in such a way as to combine its own survival with an implicitly liberal message: "against the monopoly of any one party" and "Germany needs its liberals." Indeed, the republic would have become far more *staatskonservativ* (statist-conservative), perhaps even clerical-conservative or socialist-corporatist, had the CDU/CSU of the early years or the SPD of the seventies been able to do without the FDP. More recently and under Chancellors Schmidt and Kohl, the chancellors' liberal preferences combined happily with the liberalism of the Free Democrats. For the voters, too, the FDP has always been a welcome refuge from, and a corrective for, excessive Christian or social democracy.

The Green Nemesis. This functional role in the West German party system, from all indications, appears to be beyond the desires and capabilities of West Germany's newest national party, the Greens. It is not that the major parties might not benefit from a Green corrective on their environmental and defense policies, but that the Greens have shown little inclination to play such a role. Divided between the Fundis and Realos, at most the latter might be open to cooperation with one or the other of the major parties. But their basic thrust seems to be in the direction of alternative politics and (several) single-issue concerns, as William E. Paterson points out above. Its "political entrepreneurs" or professionals of "resource mobilization" —shades of the Italian Radical Party—in fact are a more prominent feature of the Greens than its promised "mobilization at the base." While its future survival may not be in doubt, the party appears not to be headed for a functional role such as that of the FDP. Consequently, even SPD politicians and voters today tend to favor future coalitions with the Free Democrats over the pipe dreams of a red-green government. But we cannot be sure that this situation may not change at some point in the future if the Greens should move in new directions.

In sum, then, the West German party system has not changed all that much since the days following the Adenauer era. To be sure, Adenauer did not tolerate the FDP in his government for long and they left it in frustration, only to return in triumph once they had secured promises of his eventual resignation. Since 1961, however, and with only the lapse of three years of Grand Coalition, the Federal Republic has been governed by the two-and-a-half party system in which the FDP plays the role of the king-maker—and king-unmaker. The Greens so far have merely played the role of the court jesters.

THE FRG IN THE WORLD

If we have so far neglected the economic forces that inexorably shape modern polities and their relations with each other—except for the earlier discussion of neocorporatist patterns and of the Ruhr Valley—the subject returns with a vengeance in James Sperling's portrait of German-American relations in the context of a changing international political economy. The rise of West German economic power and the relative decline of American political-economic hegemony against a background of the shared goals of a liberal world economy are only part of the picture, as Professor Sperling points

out. The other side are the emerging differences in domestic economic style and divergent geopolitical and geoeconomic interests.

Economic Emancipation from the United States

Under Presidents Nixon and Ford, a bargain could still be struck
between the gradual American retrenchment and specifically European interests but after that West German, other European, and
Japanese international economic policies more and more went their
own ways. The cycles in American defense and anti-Soviet policies,
in particular, increased the German preoccupation with a sound
currency and German competitiveness on the international market.
The most recent excesses of American trade and budget deficits,
high interest rates, and military adventures under President Reagan
have badly eroded the American claim to leadership even with our
staunchest allies who balked at the continuous and unapologetic
American raids upon their fiscal health.

The linkage between security and economic issues, prior to 1976,
hardly sweetened the pill, although the increasing monetary eman-
cipation of West Germany and the other Europeans from the dollar
offered a way out of the dilemma. As Sperling shows, differing
views of inflation and unemployment have also added to the potential for economic conflict between Bonn and Washington. The future
direction of Atlantic economic relations, he concludes, will depend
largely on what post-Reagan administrations will do at home. If we
are willing to curb our government expenditures and consumption
of foreign goods, the Atlantic partnership may yet get a new lease
on life. If not, the future will see the fragmentation of the alliance
into warring monetary and trade blocs.

West German Dependence on NATO

The larger context of West German security within NATO seems
much clearer and less conflictual by comparison. Even the uneven
German choice between the Americans and the French as nuclear
defense partners is no longer as one-sided as it seemed back in 1964
when this writer interviewed a number of the West German political
and military elite. In 1964, the French option was not seen as an

adequate substitute for the American nuclear umbrella. In 1989, and especially against the background of continuing NATO functions, military cooperation with the French seems a promising step toward survival in the future and a more "decoupled" state of Europe.

The recent establishment of a Franco-German brigade outside the integrated NATO forces also raises other intriguing perspectives because the rearmament of Germany of the fifties has so far been predicated on a strictly nonnational basis—the FRG still has no national army of its own—which also included special limitations on what kinds of arms Germany could manufacture. As Werner Feld points out, of course we should not expect that 2,100 West German brigade members would outweigh the importance of 495,000 West German NATO soldiers. But, under the newly proposed Franco-German Defense Council, the joint brigade may be a harbinger of a decoupled defense policy. Professor Feld also points out the incompatibilities of Franco-German and NATO policies and the continuing German popular preference for NATO. The current era of reductions in NATO nuclear forces, in any case, may open up choices where there have not been any for more than a generation. On the one hand, the reduction of INF forces seems to throw the Germans back upon dependence on the American nuclear umbrella. On the other hand, the European option was never before as available or practicable as it is today. The so-called Strategic Defense Initiative (SDI) is still too nebulous a perspective to permit an assessment of its likely impact on the West German situation.

European Ties and Obligations

The significance of its membership in the European Community is the other side of the coin of West German integration into the West. From the very beginning this was supposed to be at once the "lifeline for gaining equal status among the [European] family of nations for pursuing economic recovery," as specified by the Marshall Plan, and the "rejection of nationalism and a commitment to reconciliation with the neighboring states" (Kirchner). Instead of fueling Imperial Germany's grab for European hegemony and a world role as back in 1910, post-1945 West German economic development was supposed to serve the recovery and prosperity of an economically united Western Europe, a common market that has now grown to 320 million people in 12 nations. On this basis, reconciliation with France and other erstwhile enemies alone constitutes an extraordinary watershed in Europe's conflicted history. Professor Kirchner mentions the fears and sacrifices of this course as well as its gains: The foreclosing of German reunification and the fear of being entrapped in a Catholic, agrarian Europe, or a "West European monopoly capitalist cartel," were among the biggest worries shared, among others, by some of our angry old men. Its greatest gains to the Federal Republic went far beyond its obvious economic successes. The EC did exactly what George C. Marshall had hoped it would do; it created a resurgent Western Europe in which the communist challenge and even the utopian appeal of democratic socialism, at least in its immediate postwar version, had no chance against the vigorous economic forces of recovery. For the Germans, moreover, it provided a nonnationalist identity, a world of Western democratic values in a welfare state context that has outlasted the fading of the love affair with America. It made it possible—far from the overdrawn alternatives of today's "historians' debate"—for the Federal Republic to be a nation of Western Europe without the past shadows of imperial and hegemonic ambitions on the continent.

At the same time, to be sure, the West German commitment to this European role gave the burgeoning German economic forces a legitimate place in the world as long as they were coupled with political self-restraint. As Emil Kirchner describes it, West German supranationalism and the promotion of European unification were problematic at times and yet German leaders on the whole have not given in to the temptation of claiming a role of European political leadership commensurate to the German economic role in the European Community. Even at its most abrasive expression, the German "Lehrmeister and paymaster" posture has usually been gloved in the form of the Franco-German dual hegemony in which the French voice (de Gaulle, Giscard d'Estaing, Mitterand) was generally the more politically significant. Why does the Federal Republic seem less eager to promote European union today, Professor Kirchner asks, and he mentions, among other things, the arrival of a new generation that is more critical of the economic performance of the weaker EC members and of the judgment and effectiveness of the EC Commission in Brussels.

But there are more important orientations that may indeed compete with the European commitment of the FRG, such as its Ostpolitik or a global (rather than regional) trading posture. There are undeniable conflicts between these three and both French and American economic policymakers, if for different reasons,—we Americans in apprehension of the exclusive European trading bloc we ourselves encouraged—have stressed the present and potential conflicts. The possibility of increasing West German participation in Mikhail Gorbachev's *perestroika*, in particular, may make the backdoor economic commitments of the earlier stages of Ostpolitik look like pin money. Contrary to the tenor of the critical voices, however, the Federal Republic is by no means compelled to choose one trading partner over the others. It can continue to work closely with American interests, especially as long as it needs to assure itself of American protection. And the resort to more broadly based European support, for example for credits to Eastern Europe and the Soviet Union, is already a well-established pattern from the days of the natural gas pipeline controversy. The special appeal of German reunification, after all these years, is unlikely to make Bonn leaders suddenly lose their heads and gamble away their security or a large part of their foreign markets.

A more likely result of all these external inducements might be the West German departure from its self-imposed regional role. The global trading interests of the Federal Republic, as Emil Kirchner shows, indeed conflict with some of the regional EC priorities and may point it toward a more demanding role in the world economy. The current debate as to whether West Germany at times "uses" the European Community to achieve non-EC objectives raises intriguing questions. For such manipulative "uses" need not be planned or deliberate; they can simply be implicit in the enhanced leverage that well-advanced integration in the EC gives to one of its major members. In economic negotiations with the Soviet Union or Comecon, for example, the Federal Republic clearly commands such leverage which it might not have if it were on its own. By the same token, Bonn no longer needs to be economically dependent on the

United States—though it still is in defense—because it has its economic involvement with the EC. Professor Kirchner's admonition that the FRG had better not "succumb to the wrong choice between the realities of Western Europe and . . . a mythical Central Europe [*Mitteleuropa*]" is well taken. The reemergence of the German question from the shadows of the past opens up a Pandora's box of ghosts pointing the FRG down dead-end streets.

From Détente to the Second Ostpolitik

It is in this context also, rather than in the more extreme perspectives of the German peace movement, Lafontaine's book, *Afraid of Our Friends*, or the von Bülow paper, that we have to view the "Second Phase" of the SPD's Ostpolitik. The leaders of the peace movement should have sent several dozen roses to the Reagan administration years ago, in the early 1980s, for there might have been no peace movement of any size if it had not been for the incautious words and belligerent cold war posturing of key members, including NATO representatives, of that administration. Verbiage and posing aside, the differences between the present SPD opposition and alliance policies accepted in Washington and Bonn (especially under Foreign Minister Genscher) are not earthshaking but concern more the timing and procedure of East-West negotiations than the substance. After all, the deployment of new NATO missiles in response to the Soviet SS-20s was a policy designed by SPD Chancellor Schmidt together with President Jimmy Carter and other Western leaders, and not Ronald Reagan or Richard Perle. When the Reagan administration, since Reykjavik, came to an agreement with the new Soviet leaders, and the INF weapons on both sides were actually removed and further reductions in nuclear and conventional armament envisaged, the true situation came out.

The SPD position today, as Ann Phillips points out, is far from unilateralism or "the chimera of complete nuclear disarmament," but retains the concept of nuclear deterrence, albeit on a more modest basis of fewer missiles. The pacifist thunder on the left, it turns out, was merely the echo of the cold war thundering on the right. What is even more compelling is the extraordinary influence that SPD initiatives have had, in an era of major party reforms in

Gorbachev's Russia and in Eastern Europe, on the discussion of nuclear disarmament and environmental controls in various Eastern communist parties. While it is obviously still too early to assess the results, they are certainly no worse than the defensiveness and belligerence engendered in the East by the verbal drumfire of the rhetoric of the "evil empire," and could be infinitely better. The Federal Republic and its eastern neighbors obviously have some interests in common, including survival in a nuclear world and relief from industrial pollution—which has become as universal a by-product of communist industrialization as of that of the advanced democracies—and there is much to be gained by all of them by appropriate measures to control both pollution and the nuclear arms race. The SPD-SED initiatives on the elimination of nuclear and chemical weapons from Central Europe deserve serious consideration as part of the overall system of arms control and deterrence in Europe, quite aside from the understandable interest of West and East Germans to eliminate the numerous chemical weapons depots and nuclear explosives in their own small countries.[8] Arms races and arms buildup also take away vast and scarce resources needed by all societies, and especially resources that could be used for development aid for third world countries. This aspect of much of the arms control discussions between SPD representatives and East German and East European communists also deserves emphasis because it is so alien to the public climate that has prevailed in the United States throughout the eighties. Unlike earlier eras, America in the Reagan years was clearly more interested in the satisfactions of its own arms buildup than in the hunger and underdevelopment of third world nations.

As Phillips argues, the SPD's Second Phase of Ostpolitik has much in common with the First or original Phase, and even with SPD foreign policy in the Kurt Schumacher years when Germany's future was seen to be in a "community of peace" of European, including East European, countries. While such a statement may ignore the profound changes in the situation that made Schumacher's policy in the early fifties inappropriate and Willy Brandt's in the seventies eminently successful, it is true that behind both lay the same desire for a modus vivendi of live-and-let-live in Europe that may inspire German eastern policies in the nineties. The envisaged system of peace (*Friedensordnung*) indeed does *not* require, as our cold warriors like to do in the eighties, that the Soviet Union and other communist nations change profoundly *before* the olive branch of economic cooperation and cultural exchange may be extended. But according to the principle of *Wandel durch Annäherung* (change via rapprochement), the objectives still include major changes in communist societies. This policy, moreover, does not expect the other side to be persuaded by threats and confrontation, an approach that has clearly proven to be counterproductive. By reducing the level of armaments and the likelihood of armed conflict, finally, it has indeed earned the name *Friedensordnung*, although it remains to be seen whether it will ever be possible— assuming it is even desirable—for the Europeans to solve their problems without the influence of the great powers, East and West. Without *perestroika*, as Professor Phillips makes clear, Ostpolitik cannot succeed and a similar about-face by post-Reagan administrations in Washington may also be necessary.

The Special Relationship to Israel

Among such goliaths of world politics as the United States, the Soviet bloc, and the European Community, West Germany's relationship to Israel may seem like a *quantité négligeable*, a small symbolic priority easily forgotten in the struggle for security and economic survival in the great world where the big players routinely squash the interests of small and medium-sized states. The 1951 statement of the Bonn authorities committing the Federal Republic to restitution and reparations, in Nahum Goldmann's words, was indeed "a novel departure in political history," never done by any nation before and probably never again in a world replete with foul deeds on a grand scale. Worse yet, the collective moral commitment, as is always likely in cases of great historical guilt, was obviously made exclusively by Germans who bore no individual responsibility for the deeds involved, while those considered individually guilty may have remained recalcitrant and unrepentant to their dying day. What then is the weight of the moral questions raised so eloquently by Professor Feldman in the scales of world politics today, after forty-odd years? What are we to make of what Lily Feldman calls "the [recent] vacillation of some political leaders on the appropriate role of the past" or "signs of a more unfettered attitude" toward it?

The answer, I believe, needs to be based on a far broader and more universal perspective than the ones suggested by the various parties involved, including the historians involved in the great "historians' debate" and the various voices in the American press. It is peculiar to moral obligations that they have to be freely and individually assumed. Their dignity and solemnity suffer greatly when they are cast into the market place of claims and counterclaims as if they were indeed an "insurance claim for damages (*Schadensabwicklung*)," to use Jürgen Habermas's felicitous phrase. This is in fact the story within the story told by Professor Feldman: The "traditional preference for Israel" and the sense of German responsibility for the Holocaust,—not to mention the millions of other victims of their ruthless pursuit of power in World War II, Russians, Poles, Yugoslavs, and many other nationalities including the ethnic Germans who perished during the flight caused by the collapse of Germany's aggression in the East—have indeed surfaced again and again against denials of responsibility, foot-dragging, deliberate obstruction, and other lapses.[9] It is in the nature of moral choices that they should occur freely and in the midst of contending forces. If they were mandatory or compelled, they would lose their moral character. The moral choice for German responsibility has asserted itself freely, again and again (and obviously not by all Germans, or even less by all responsible, as we can learn from every concentration camp trial), and so it shall ever be; free also from damage claims and strident insurance agents.

Finally, there is also the major impact of the Holocaust on West German foreign policy that stems from the great historical German crimes of World War II. As the German historian Ludwig Dehio pointed out more than thirty years ago, the ruthless hegemonic appetite of Germany in the twentieth century was the result of what in the nineteenth century was still the understandable desire of Germans to have their own nation-state like many of their neighbors. The economic buildup of the Empire turned this seemingly harmless nationalism into an all-out bid for world power. Frustrated dramatically by a grand counteralliance in World War I, this mission then fell into the depraved hands of Nazi leaders who succeeded in gathering the support of the German masses behind an even more ruthless renewal of the bid for world power. While the genocide on the Jews and mass murder on the millions of Russians, Poles, and others were hardly the original target, their horrible deaths clearly were a measure of the ruthlessness of the pursuit and of the depravity of the German leadership of the Third Reich, down to the cruelty of minor officialdom in the infliction of harm on innocent human beings. To have supported such an immoral regime in its ruthless quest for world power, even if the popular knowledge of the Holocaust and other mass murders was most imperfect, is the moral responsibility of the prewar and World War II generations. And this is also the legacy that has chastened German nationalism and the foreign policy of the Federal Republic to the core. West Germany, even though it is far more prosperous and economically strong than any previous German state, has adopted a self-restraint of extraordinary proportions, deliberately acting as a modest, regional power and foregoing major power plays as a matter of routine. This has been a crucial result of the historical German guilt and the Holocaust, and it has shown no signs of diminishing over the generations. After Auschwitz, no German government will ever again launch an all-out effort for world power.

NOTES

1. *Die zornigen alten Männer: Gedanken über Deutschland seit 1945* (Reinbek: Rowohlt, 1979).
2. See also Charles S. Maier, *The Unmasterable Past: History, Holocaust, and German National Identity* (Cambridge, Mass.: Harvard University Press, 1988).
3. Many German conservatives and even middle-of-the-road people felt that American public opinion reacted irrationally to finding the dreaded SS runes on twenty-seven of some 2,000 soldiers' graves. None of the American journalists bothered to find out how many of those twenty-

seven really were Nazi criminals and not post-1943 draftees to the Waffen-SS and hence exonerated by postwar denazification standards. None addressed the qustion of personal responsibility or of its expunction by death, or by being buried for 40 years.

4. See also Merkl, "West German Women: A Long Way from Kinder, Küche. Kirche," in Lynne B. Iglitzin and Ruth Ross, eds., Women in the World: 1975–1985, The Women's Decade (Santa Barbara: Clio Press, 1986), 27–52.

5. Cooperative federalism is not the best translation of the politically integrated planning and financing agreed upon because the phrase describes more properly the modification in the American type of federalism. One could even say that the Federal Republic already had cooperative federalism before the Great Reform because of the unequal distribution of legislative and administrative powers and the character of the upper house.

6. See Beratungen und Empfehlungen zur Verfassungsreform. Schlussbericht der Enquête-Kommission Verfassungsreform des Deutschen Bundestages Parts I and, II (Bonn, 1976). Other subjects under consideration were the role of parliament, the administrative and planning processes, executive ordinances, elections, advisory councils, and the direct election of the federal president.

7. See also Merkl, "The SPD After Brandt: Problems of Integration in a Changing Urban Society," West European Politics, 11 (January 1988): 40–53

8. In the 1983 elections at the height of the antimissile campaign, the Greens put out a poster with a map of the Federal Republic showing all the locations of chemical weapons, nuclear, and other harmful sites choking up that Oregon-sized country. The poster required no further explanation for public consumption.

9. The most recent example of the West German sensitivity toward the subject of the Holocaust occurred on the occasion of a commemoration speech by Bundestag President Phillip Jenninger for the fiftieth anniversary of Kristallnacht, the 1938 national pogrom that was a major harbinger of the Holocaust to come a few years later. The West German audience and observers appeared far more mortified by Jenninger's awkward formulations than were representatives of German Jewish organizations and of the Israeli government who in fact found excuses for the Bundestag President. Jenninger nevertheless resigned in disgrace and was replaced by Rita Süssmuth.

INDEX